Off-Campus Library Services

Off-Campus Library Services has been co-published simultaneously as *Journal of Library Administration,* Volume 31, Numbers 3/4 2001 and Volume 32, Numbers 1/2 2001.

The *Journal of Library Administration* Monographic "Separates"

Below is a list of "separates," which in serials librarianship means a special issue simultaneously published as a special journal issue or double-issue *and* as a "separate" hardbound monograph. (This is a format which we also call a "DocuSerial.")

"Separates" are published because specialized libraries or professionals may wish to purchase a specific thematic issue by itself in a format which can be separately cataloged and shelved, as opposed to purchasing the journal on an on-going basis. Faculty members may also more easily consider a "separate" for classroom adoption.

"Separates" are carefully classified separately with the major book jobbers so that the journal tie-in can be noted on new book order slips to avoid duplicate purchasing.

You may wish to visit Haworth's website at . . .

http://www.HaworthPress.com

. . . to search our online catalog for complete tables of contents of these separates and related publications.

You may also call 1-800-HAWORTH (outside US/Canada: 607-722-5857), or Fax 1-800-895-0582 (outside US/Canada: 607-771-0012), or e-mail at:

getinfo@haworthpressinc.com

---

meeting the needs of scholars at universities, budgeting issues, user education, staffing in the electronic age, collaborating libraries and resources, and how vendors meet the needs of different customers.

The Age Demographics of Academic Librarians: A Profession Apart, by Stanley J. Wilder (Vol. 28, No. 3, 1999). *The average age of librarians has been increasing dramatically since 1990. This unique book will provide insights on how this demographic issue can impact a library and what can be done to make the effects positive.*

Collection Development in a Digital Environment, edited by Sul H. Lee (Vol. 28, No. 1, 1999). *Explores ethical and technological dilemmas of collection development and gives several suggestions on how a library can successfully deal with these challenges and provide patrons with the information they need.*

Scholarship, Research Libraries, and Global Publishing, by Jutta Reed-Scott (Vol. 27, No. 3/4, 1999). *This book documents a research project in conjunction with the Association of Research Libraries (ARL) that explores the issue of foreign acquisition and how it affects collection in international studies, area studies, collection development, and practices of international research libraries.*

Managing Multicultural Diversity in the Library: Principles and Issues for Administrators, edited by Mark Winston (Vol. 27, No. 1/2, 1999). *Defines diversity, clarifies why it is important to address issues of diversity, and identifies goals related to diversity and how to go about achieving those goals.*

Information Technology Planning, edited by Lori A. Goetsch (Vol. 26, No. 3/4, 1999). *Offers innovative approaches and strategies useful in your library and provides some food for thought about information technology as we approach the millennium.*

The Economics of Information in the Networked Environment, edited by Meredith A. Butler, MLS, and Bruce R. Kingma, PhD (Vol. 26, No. 1/2, 1998). *"A book that should be read both by information professionals and by administrators, faculty and others who share a collective concern to provide the most information to the greatest number at the lowest cost in the networked environment." (Thomas J. Galvin, PhD, Professor of Information Science and Policy, University at Albany, State University of New York)*

OCLC 1967-1997: Thirty Years of Furthering Access to the World's Information, edited by K. Wayne Smith (Vol. 25, No. 2/3/4, 1998). *"A rich–and poignantly personal, at times–historical account of what is surely one of this century's most important developments in librarianship." (Deanna B. Marcum, PhD, President, Council on Library and Information Resources, Washington, DC)*

Management of Library and Archival Security: From the Outside Looking In, edited by Robert K. O'Neill, PhD (Vol. 25, No. 1, 1998). *"Provides useful advice and on-target insights for professionals caring for valuable documents and artifacts." (Menzi L. Behrnd-Klodt, JD, Attorney/Archivist, Klodt and Associates, Madison, WI)*

Economics of Digital Information: Collection, Storage, and Delivery, edited by Sul H. Lee (Vol. 24, No. 4, 1997). *Highlights key concepts and issues vital to a library's successful venture into the digital environment and helps you understand why the transition from the printed page to the digital packet has been problematic for both creators of proprietary materials and users of those materials.*

The Academic Library Director: Reflections on a Position in Transition, edited by Frank D'Andraia, MLS (Vol. 24, No. 3, 1997). *"A useful collection to have whether you are seeking a position as director or conducting a search for one." (College & Research Libraries News)*

Emerging Patterns of Collection Development in Expanding Resource Sharing, Electronic Information, and Network Environment, edited by Sul H. Lee (Vol. 24, No. 1/2, 1997). *"The issues it deals with are common to us all. We all need to make our funds go further and our resources work harder, and there are ideas here which we can all develop." (The Library Association Record)*

Interlibrary Loan/Document Delivery and Customer Satisfaction: Strategies for Redesigning Services, edited by Pat L. Weaver-Meyers, Wilbur A. Stolt, and Yem S. Fong (Vol. 23, No. 1/2, 1997). *"No interlibrary loan department supervisor at any mid-sized to large college or university library can afford not to read this book." (Gregg Sapp, MLS, MEd, Head of Access Services, University of Miami, Richter Library, Coral Gables, Florida)*

Access, Resource Sharing and Collection Development, edited by Sul H. Lee (Vol. 22, No. 4, 1996). *Features continuing investigation and discussion of important library issues, specifically the role of libraries in acquiring, storing, and disseminating information in different formats.*

Managing Change in Academic Libraries, edited by Joseph J. Branin (Vol. 22, No. 2/3, 1996). *"Touches on several aspects of academic library management, emphasizing the changes that are occurring at the present time. . . . Recommended this title for individuals or libraries interested in management aspects of academic libraries." (RQ American Library Association)*

Libraries and Student Assistants: Critical Links, edited by William K. Black, MLS (Vol. 21, No. 3/4, 1995). *"A handy reference work on many important aspects of managing student assistants. . . . Solid, useful information on basic management issues in this work and several chapters are useful for experienced managers." (The Journal of Academic Librarianship)*

The Future of Resource Sharing, edited by Shirley K. Baker and Mary E. Jackson, MLS (Vol. 21, No. 1/2, 1995). *"Recommended for library and information science schools because of its balanced presentation of the ILL/document delivery issues." (Library Acquisitions: Practice and Theory)*

The Future of Information Services, edited by Virginia Steel, MA, and C. Brigid Welch, MLS (Vol. 20, No. 3/4, 1995). *"The leadership discussions will be useful for library managers as will the discussions of how library structures and services might work in the next century." (Australian Special Libraries)*

The Dynamic Library Organizations in a Changing Environment, edited by Joan Giesecke, MLS, DPA (Vol. 20, No. 2, 1995). *"Provides a significant look at potential changes in the library world and presents its readers with possible ways to address the negative results of such changes. . . . Covers the key issues facing today's libraries . . . Two thumbs up!" (Marketing Library Resources)*

Access, Ownership, and Resource Sharing, edited by Sul H. Lee (Vol. 20, No. 1, 1995). *The contributing authors present a useful and informative look at the current status of information provision and some of the challenges the subject presents.*

Libraries as User-Centered Organizations: Imperatives for Organizational Change, edited by Meredith A. Butler (Vol. 19, No. 3/4, 1994). *"Presents a very timely and well-organized discussion of major trends and influences causing organizational changes." (Science Books & Films)*

Declining Acquisitions Budgets: Allocation, Collection Development and Impact Communication, edited by Sul H. Lee (Vol. 19, No. 2, 1994). *"Expert and provocative. . . . Presents many ways of looking at library budget deterioration and responses to it . . . There is much food for thought here." (Library Resources & Technical Services)*

The Role and Future of Special Collections in Research Libraries: British and American Perspectives, edited by Sul H. Lee (Vol. 19, No. 1, 1993). *"A provocative but informative read for library users, academic administrators, and private sponsors." (International Journal of Information and Library Research)*

Catalysts for Change: Managing Libraries in the 1990s, edited by Gisela M. von Dran, DPA, MLS, and Jennifer Cargill, MSLS, MSed (Vol. 18, No. 3/4, 1994). *"A useful collection of articles which focuses on the need for librarians to employ enlightened management practices in order to adapt to and thrive in the rapidly changing information environment." (Australian Library Review)*

Monographic/"Separates" list continued at the back

Z
675
.U5
O452
2001

Off-Campus
Library Services

Anne Marie Casey
Editor

Off-Campus Library Services has been co-published simultaneously as *Journal of Library Administration,* Volume 31, Numbers 3/4 2001 and Volume 32, Numbers 1/2 2001.

The Haworth Information Press
An Imprint of
The Haworth Press, Inc.
New York • London • Oxford

KVCC KALAMAZOO VALLEY
COMMUNITY COLLEGE
LIBRARY

Published by

The Haworth Information Press®, 10 Alice Street, Binghamton, NY 13904-1580 USA

The Haworth Information Press® is an imprint of the The Haworth Press, Inc., 10 Alice Street, Binghamton, NY 13904-1580 USA.

Off-Campus Library Services has been co-published simultaneously as *Journal of Library Administration,* Volume 31, Numbers 3/4 2001 and Volume 32, Numbers 1/2 2001.

Articles in this collection are © Central Michigan University Libraries and the CMU College of Extended Learning, and are reprinted here by permission, except "Foreword," by Sul H. Lee, © 2001 by The Haworth Press, Inc.

The development, preparation, and publication of this work has been undertaken with great care. However, the publisher, employees, editors, and agents of The Haworth Press and all imprints of The Haworth Press, Inc., including The Haworth Medical Press® and Pharmaceutical Products Press®, are not responsible for any errors contained herein or for consequences that may ensue from use of materials or information contained in this work. Opinions expressed by the author(s) are not necessarily those of The Haworth Press, Inc.

Cover design by Thomas J. Mayshock Jr.

Library of Congress Cataloging-in-Publication Data

Off-campus library services / Anne Marie Casey, editor.
      p. cm.
      Proceedings of the 9th Off-Campus Library Services Conference sponsored by Central Michigan University Libraries and Central Michigan University's College of Extended Learning, held in Portland, Oregon, April 26-28, 2000.
      Co-published simultaneously as Journal of library administration, v. 31, nos. 3/4 and v. 32, nos. 1/2, 2001.
      Includes bibliographical references and index.
      ISBN 0-7890-1339-8 (alk. paper) – ISBN 0-7890-1340-1 (pbk.: alk. paper)
      1. Academic libraries–Off-campus services–Congresses. 2. Libraries and distance education–Congresses. 3. University extension–Congresses. I. Casey, Anne Marie. II. Off-Campus Library Services Conference (9th : 2000 : Portland, Or.) III. Journal of library administration.
Z675.U5 O452 2001
025.5–dc21
                                       2001024503

Indexing, Abstracting & Website/Internet Coverage

This section provides you with a list of major indexing & abstracting services. That is to say, each service began covering this periodical during the year noted in the right column. Most Websites which are listed below have indicated that they will either post, disseminate, compile, archive, cite or alert their own Website users with research-based content from this work. (This list is as current as the copyright date of this publication.)

Abstracting, Website/Indexing Coverage ...... Year When Coverage Began

- *Academic Abstracts/CD-ROM* **1993**

- *Academic Search: data base of 2,000 selected academic serials, updated monthly* **1995**

- *Academic Search Elite (EBSCO)* **1993**

- *AGRICOLA Database* **1991**

- *BUBL Information Service: An Internet-based Information Service for the UK higher education community*
  <URL: http://bubl.ac.uk/> **1999**

- *Business ASAP* **1993**

- *CNPIEC Reference Guide: Chinese National Directory of Foreign Periodicals* **1995**

- *Current Articles on Library Literature and Services (CALLS)* ... **1992**

- *Current Awareness Abstracts of Library & Information Management Literature, ASLIB (UK)* **1998**

(continued)

(continued)

Special Bibliographic Notes related to special journal issues
(separates) and indexing/abstracting:

- indexing/abstracting services in this list will also cover material in any "separate" that is co-published simultaneously with Haworth's special thematic journal issue or DocuSerial. Indexing/abstracting usually covers material at the article/chapter level.
- monographic co-editions are intended for either non-subscribers or libraries which intend to purchase a second copy for their circulating collections.
- monographic co-editions are reported to all jobbers/wholesalers/approval plans. The source journal is listed as the "series" to assist the prevention of duplicate purchasing in the same manner utilized for books-in-series.
- to facilitate user/access services all indexing/abstracting services are encouraged to utilize the co-indexing entry note indicated at the bottom of the first page of each article/chapter/contribution.
- this is intended to assist a library user of any reference tool (whether print, electronic, online, or CD-ROM) to locate the monographic version if the library has purchased this version but not a subscription to the source journal.
- individual articles/chapters in any Haworth publication are also available through the Haworth Document Delivery Service (HDDS).

Off-Campus Library Services

CONTENTS

ALL HAWORTH INFORMATION PRESS
BOOKS AND JOURNALS ARE PRINTED
ON CERTIFIED ACID-FREE PAPER

ABOUT THE EDITOR

Anne Marie Casey, MA, AMLS, has been Director of Off-Campus Library Services at Central Michigan University (CMU) since 1999. While serving as Off-Campus Librarian from 1991-1999, her responsibilities included coordinating the Off-Campus Library Services Conferences. Prior to working at CMU, Ms. Casey provided library services for off-campus and nontraditional students at National University in San Diego (1987-1991). Ms. Casey has an AMLS degree from the University of Michigan, an MA in Medieval Studies from the Catholic University of America, and a BA in Classics from the University of Massachusetts.

Foreword

We are pleased to offer readers of this volume the proceedings of the 9th Off-Campus Library Services Conference sponsored by Central Michigan University Libraries and Central Michigan University's College of Extended Learning, held in Portland, Oregon, April 26-28, 2000.

The conference addressed a wide range of off-campus programs relating to distance education and providing library services in support of these programs. The articles discussed administration of library distance programs; providing traditional library services such as bibliographic instruction and reference to distance learners; surveying the effectiveness of distance library service; providing document delivery options; working with distance faculty; and providing distance learners with the same library technology that on-campus users enjoy.

In recent years distance library programs have emerged from intrastate programs to being international in scope and interest. The papers included are well researched and make an important contribution to this newly emerging field of library service. Consequently, we believe these papers will appeal to a broad spectrum of librarians and deserve the wider dissemination that the *Journal of Library Administration* provides.

Sul H. Lee
Editor
Journal of Library Administration

[Haworth co-indexing entry note]: "Foreword." Lee, Sul H. Co-published simultaneously in *Journal of Library Administration* (The Haworth Information Press, an imprint of The Haworth Press, Inc.) Vol. 31, No. 3/4, 2001, p. xix; and: *Off-Campus Library Services* (ed: Anne Marie Casey) The Haworth Information Press, an imprint of The Haworth Press, Inc., 2001, p. xix. Single or multiple copies of this article are available for a fee from The Haworth Document Delivery Service [1-800-342-9678, 9:00 a.m. - 5:00 p.m. (EST). E-mail address: getinfo@haworthpressinc.com].

© 2001 by The Haworth Press, Inc. All rights reserved.

Preface

Welcome to the Ninth Off-Campus Library Services Conference Proceedings. Once again, the Central Michigan University Libraries and the Central Michigan University College of Extended Learning have provided generous support of both this conference and these Proceedings.

The papers included here were selected by a twenty-three member Program Advisory Board using a juried abstracts process. Because emerging terminology is always problematic for publications of this type, the spelling of terms and phrases such as "Web," "e-mail," "Web page," and "Web-based" has been standardized throughout. All of the contributed papers have been formatted consistent with the conference *Guidelines for Preparing Manuscripts* distributed to contributors. Typographical errors have been corrected and cited references have been formatted consistent with guidelines published in the *Publication Manual of the American Psychological Association* (4th ed.), Frequently Asked Questions About the *Publication Manual of the American Psychological Association* (4th ed.) http://www.apa.org/journals/faq.html, and other reputable sources.

P. Steven Thomas

[Haworth co-indexing entry note]: "Preface." Thomas, P. Steven. Co-published simultaneously in *Journal of Library Administration* (The Haworth Information Press, an imprint of The Haworth Press, Inc.) Vol. 31, No. 3/4, 2001, p. xxi; and: *Off-Campus Library Services* (ed: Anne Marie Casey) The Haworth Information Press, an imprint of The Haworth Press, Inc., 2001, p. xxi.

Acknowledgments

I am once again indebted to the support and commitment of this year's contributors and presenters. The thirty-four papers presented here typify the strong professional service ethic evidenced at all OCLS Conferences since 1982.

Special thanks go to Connie Hildebrand, who again has served as the Conference Coordinator ("guiding light") for this year's conference. She was ably assisted by Anne Marie Casey, Monica Hines Craig, Marissa Cachero, and P. Steven Thomas. Special thanks and appreciation also go deservedly to the Program Advisory Board who thoughtfully reviewed dozens of submitted Conference paper proposals.

I would be remiss, indeed, not to recognize the unflagging encouragement and support of Thomas J. Moore, CMU Dean of Libraries and Delbert J. Ringquist, CMU Dean of the College of Extended Learning.

Program Advisory Board
and Executive Planning Committee*

Chris Adams
U-Study Coordinator
University of Saskatchewan
  Libraries

Paula Arnold
Library Personnel Officer
Boston College

Rita Barsun
Walden University Library
  Liaison
Walden University/Indiana
  University

Shirley J. Behrens
University of South Africa
Department of Information
  Science

Ann Taylor Blauer
Head of Informational Services
University of South Alabama

Jonathan R. Buckstead
Reference Librarian for
  Extension Services
Austin Community College

Nancy Burich
Coordinator for Distance
  Learning
University of Kansas

Marissa Cachero*
Off-Campus Library Services
Central Michigan University

Debbie Cardinal
Program Manager
WILS

Anne Marie Casey*
Off-Campus Library Services
Central Michigan University

Jean Caspers
Distance Education Librarian
Oregon State University

Monica Hines Craig*
Off-Campus Library Services
Central Michigan University

Jack Fritts
Consortium Director
SWITCH

Kay Harvey
Head Librarian
Penn State McKeesport

Connie Hildebrand*
Off-Campus Library Services
Central Michigan University

Pam Horan
Coordinator of Off-Campus
  Library Services
University of Portland Library

Michael Hutton
Associate Vice President
Learning Resource Centers
Brevard Community College

Maryhelen Jones
Director, Fogelson Library
College of Santa Fe

Thomas J. Moore*
Dean of Libraries
Central Michigan University

Srivalli Rao
Assistant Professor/Branch
  Librarian
Mercy College Libraries

P. Steven Thomas*
Off-Campus Library Services
Central Michigan University

Johanna Tuñón
Head of Distance Library
  Services
Nova Southeastern University

Susan Barnes Whyte
Reference & Extended Service
  Librarian
Linfield College

9th Off-Campus Library Services Conference Proceedings: Introduction

The Proceedings of the 9th Off-Campus Library Services Conference were compiled and edited by P. Steven Thomas, formerly an Off-Campus Librarian at Central Michigan University. The 9th Conference Proceedings includes papers that cover topics such as the administration of off-campus library programs, bibliographic instruction and information literacy, cooperation and partnering, professional issues and research, programs outside of the U.S., technology based services and virtual applications.

The 9th Off-Campus Library Services Conference, held in Portland, OR from April 26-28, 2000 was the latest in a series of conferences that have successfully provided a forum for the sharing of ideas on current topics of interest in the field of off-campus or distance learning librarianship. Previous conferences were held in Providence (1998), San Diego (1995), Kansas City (1993), Albuquerque (1991), Charleston (1988), Reno (1986), Knoxville (1985), and St. Louis (1982). The next conference is planned for April 2002.

The Off-Campus Library Services Conferences are sponsored by the Central Michigan University Libraries and CMU's College of Extended Learning. International in scope and participation, the conferences have attracted academic, corporate, medical and military librarians from the United States, Canada, the West Indies, Europe, Asia, Africa, Australia, and New Zealand as well as college and university faculty, administrators and government officials. All attendees

[Haworth co-indexing entry note]: "9th Off-Campus Library Services Conference Proceedings: Introduction." Casey, Anne Marie. Co-published simultaneously in *Journal of Library Administration* (The Haworth Information Press, an imprint of The Haworth Press, Inc.) Vol. 31, No. 3/4, 2001, pp. 1-2; and: *Off-Campus Library Services* (ed: Anne Marie Casey) The Haworth Information Press, an imprint of The Haworth Press, Inc., 2001, pp. 1-2.

have been involved in one of the fastest growing and most innovative sectors in higher education–the provision of library services and instructional support to adult learners located at a distance from their main campuses.

Anne Marie Casey
Editor

Conference Introduction

This year's contributed papers reflect many of the same concerns that have surfaced at previous Off-Campus Library Services Conferences (e.g., program accreditation and library services for distance learners). But clearly, these papers also reflect an overwhelming awareness of the challenges facing off-campus librarians who are trying to adapt electronic resources to effectively meet the information access and delivery needs of distance learners (particularly vis-à-vis the World Wide Web). As forward reaching as many of these attempts have been, however, many contributors have sought out the wisdom of previous contributors to these Proceedings, surprisingly, as far back as the 5th Off-Campus Library Services Conference held in Albuquerque, New Mexico in 1991. *An International Comparison of Library Services for Distance Learning,* a paper presented by Alexander Slade and Marie Kascus at the Eighth Off-Campus Library Services Conference (Providence, Rhode Island, 1998) was among the most frequently cited papers from preceding OCLS Conferences. Important revisions to the *ACRL Guidelines for Distance Learning Library Services,* adopted in 1998, have also figured centrally into many of the papers presented this year. It is clear that library services to distance learners are taking on an increasingly global focus.

One can hardly pick up a copy of an education- or information-related periodical these days without seeing the phrase "off-campus" or "distance learning" figuring prominently in the title of an article or in the editorial pages. A sign of the times and future to be sure.

[Haworth co-indexing entry note]: "Conference Introduction." Co-published simultaneously in *Journal of Library Administration* (The Haworth Information Press, an imprint of The Haworth Press, Inc.) Vol. 31, No. 3/4, 2001, p. 3; and: *Off-Campus Library Services* (ed: Anne Marie Casey) The Haworth Information Press, an imprint of The Haworth Press, Inc., 2001, p. 3.

Marketing Library Resources and Services to Distance Faculty

Kate E. Adams
Mary Cassner

University of Nebraska-Lincoln

SUMMARY. As academic libraries and librarians experience an increasingly complex higher education environment, it is essential to market library resources and services effectively. One component of a library's marketing plan for distance learners can be an assessment of the needs of distance faculty. Teaching faculty are influential in affecting student perceptions and their use of the library. This paper reports on an assessment of the needs of faculty who teach classes in distance graduate degree programs. Results from the survey provide strategic direction for delivering and marketing services to distance learners and distance faculty.

KEYWORDS. Marketing, faculty, distance learning, distance education, library services

In the past, academic libraries may have enjoyed a monopoly in providing information resources and services to students and faculty. However, the same cannot be said today. Users have a variety of options available to meet their research needs. Networked access and remote authentication allow users to access online databases from homes and work sites. With the click of a mouse, users can retrieve hundreds of hits from the World Wide Web, and e-mail or download full-text articles and documents. Users expect to have their research needs met instantaneously via the computer. A resulting impact for

[Haworth co-indexing entry note]: "Marketing Library Resources and Services to Distance Faculty." Adams, Kate E., and Mary Cassner. Co-published simultaneously in *Journal of Library Administration* (The Haworth Information Press, an imprint of The Haworth Press, Inc.) Vol. 31, No. 3/4, 2001, pp. 5-22; and: *Off-Campus Library Services* (ed: Anne Marie Casey) The Haworth Information Press, an imprint of The Haworth Press, Inc., 2001, pp. 5-22.

academic libraries is the potential loss of what Wolpert (1998, p. 32) terms as "brand identity." Teaching faculty are using electronic technology to deliver courses to distance learners. Many higher education institutions offer full degree programs over the Internet and World Wide Web. Not infrequently, students and even faculty believe that the Web can effectively take the place of the academic library. With changing user expectations, academic libraries must move beyond the traditional service model to remain viable.

As academic libraries and librarians redefine their roles in the increasingly complex higher education environment, it is essential to effectively market library resources and services. Marketing "embraces an entire suite of management activities which include determining market niches, defining products and services, setting prices, promoting services, and building good public relations" (Olson & Moseman, 1997, p. 20). The term "marketing" is defined as:

> The organized process of planning and executing the conception, pricing, promotion and distribution of ideas, goods and services to create exchanges that will (if applicable) satisfy individual and organizations' objectives. Marketing collects and uses demographic, geographic, behavioral and psychological information. Marketing also fulfills the organization's mission and, like public relations, inspires public awareness and educates. (*Marketing and public relations . . .* , 1999, p. 3)

Olson and Moseman (1997) believe that a critical component of any marketing activity is knowledge of customers as well as what they deem valuable and important. Cooper, Dempsey, Menon, and Millson-Martula (1998, p. 42) refer to library customers as "groupings of library constituents." In higher education, teaching faculty are an essential customer group. Instructors are influential in affecting student perceptions of, and their use of, the library. Faculty can require students to utilize scholarly journals, books, and reference materials from the libraries' print or electronic collections. They can refer students to reference librarians for assistance in search strategies and selecting databases. Instructors can also invite librarians to provide library instruction on a formal or informal basis.

One component of an academic library's marketing plan can be an assessment of the needs of distance faculty. In fall 1997, the authors had administered a brief survey to teaching faculty in conjunction with a survey of distance learners enrolled in the extended education master's degree program offered through the College of Human Resources and Family Sciences. Seven of the thirteen faculty responded to the five-question survey. Faculty required the same use of the library by extended students as by on-campus students. Respondents expected students to use books, journals, and the World Wide Web for their coursework. However, faculty reported limited contact with the library staff and services (Cassner & Adams, 1998).

Like many other post-secondary education institutions, the University of Nebraska-Lincoln (known as UNL) has recently expanded its distance education curricula. As of fall 1999, UNL offers twelve master's degree programs and a doctoral program in administration, curriculum and instruction. Distance learner enrollment numbers around 650 graduate students. During the current semester, thirty faculty from seven colleges are teaching distance graduate courses. While the majority of distance courses are now delivered via the Internet and the World Wide Web, courses are also delivered via videotape, interactive television, videoconferencing, and e-mail.

The University Libraries' program for distance learners, established in 1990, includes remote access to 150 databases and 400 electronic journals, liaison librarian provision of reference assistance and instruction, as well as delivery of materials to distance students. In 1995, the Distance Education Coordinator position was increased to a .5 FTE assignment. The Distance Education Services page is located on the Libraries' main page at http://iris.unl.edu. It provides links to electronic reference, departmental liaison librarians, request forms via the Web or e-mail, electronic renewal, and circulation policies. Books are mailed directly to the distance learner, while journal articles may be mailed, faxed, or sent via the Internet. The Distance Education Coordinator works with distance administrative units to distribute subject-specific handouts to distance students every semester. One library support staff member fills distance requests from the Libraries' collections or through interlibrary loan. New distance students are also sent a personalized welcome message via e-mail. Liaison librarians frequently provide individualized reference assistance for distance students. Several liaison librarians are members of class listservs and are aware of class assignments.

The Distance Education Coordinator mails subject-specific handouts to distance faculty and contacts faculty individually via e-mail prior to start of the semester. The Coordinator also sends generic messages during the semester, for example, to remind faculty of the distance education page or alert them to new databases. Liaison librarians also contact the teaching faculty near the beginning of the semester about specific course assignments.

Given the expanded number of distance graduate programs at UNL, the authors chose to conduct another survey of distance teaching faculty. It was hoped that a more extensive survey of distance teaching faculty with a broader population could provide feedback as the Libraries assess the needs of faculty who teach distance courses. Specific research questions formulated prior to writing the survey included:

To what degree are faculty satisfied with library resources and services offered to distance students?

To what degree are faculty aware of the scope of library resources and services available to distance students?

To what degree are faculty satisfied with the services of the Libraries' Distance Education Coordinator and the Subject Specialist/Liaison Librarian for their department?

Have faculty invited the Subject Specialist Librarian or the Distance Education Coordinator to give instruction to extended education students? If so, what delivery method was used?

What is the level of usage of selected resources for course-related research?

To what degree do faculty require the use of library resources for extended education students in comparison to the classes they teach on campus (not through extended education)?

What services and resources would faculty suggest the Libraries offer to distance students?

What services and resources would faculty suggest the Libraries offer to instructors of extended education courses?

What factors might impede faculty use of UNL services and/or resources?

However, the survey was also aimed with a broader purpose: to market library resources and services to distance faculty. The survey was conducted not only to solicit faculty input but also to increase awareness of library resources and services offered to distance instructors and extended education students. The wording of the survey questions served as an educational tool by enumerating library resources and services available to distance faculty and students. The URL for the Libraries' home page was provided.

REVIEW OF THE LITERATURE

The review of the literature showed some surveys of distance faculty. Often the surveys have been conducted in tandem with surveys of distance students, and have focused on instruction and library skills. Behrens (1993, p. 11) characterized faculty attitude towards the need for students to have library skills as "a less obvious but very real obstacle." She concluded from her study of the University of South Africa that lecturers were unaware of the scope and role of library skills in the learning process. Ruddy (1993) asked faculty about their requirements for student use of the library. She reported contradictory results between professed need for extensive library use and the class assignments.

Lebowitz (1993) surveyed faculty who taught off-campus students to determine faculty expectations of student library use as well as future needs. Respondents gave low rankings for the necessity of providing off-campus students with instruction on library resources and reference. Craig and DuFord (1995) reported that while over 80% of the graduate faculty required the use of library services and materials to complete course assignments, only 35% responded that they offered library instruction.

The theme of the 1998 summer issue of *Library Trends* was service to remote users. Cooper et al. (1998) conducted informal e-mail surveys and phone interviews with six distance faculty. They concluded that while the teaching faculty expectation is for distance learners to use an academic library, faculty "make no distinction between the skills needed by a student on campus and one at a remote site" (p. 57). Landrum (1987) noted a decade earlier that "faculty attitudes are the most significant factor in affecting students' use of the library" (p. 15). She urged librarians to survey faculty for their current use of libraries as well as future needs, as part of analysis prior to designing a market plan.

METHOD

Data for the study were collected by a self-administered survey distributed in fall 1999. Surveys were sent to eighty faculty, the entire population, who had taught one or more graduate distance courses at the University of Nebraska-Lincoln during each fall semester and summer session between fall 1997 and fall 1999. Courses taught are master's graduate degree programs offered at a distance: Business Administration, Education, Engineering (beginning fall 1999), Entomology, Human Resources and Family Sciences, Industrial and Management Systems Engineering, Journalism and Mass Communications, Manufacturing Systems Engineering, and Textiles, Clothing and Design. Faculty from Computer Sciences and Engineering were included, although the master's degree is no longer offered via distance. Faculty who teach in a distance doctoral program in Administration, Curriculum and Instruction were included. Also in the study were faculty who teach "solo" distance graduate courses that are not part of a graduate curriculum offered entirely at a distance.

Faculty members were given the opportunity to respond to the survey via e-mail or surface. A three-step procedure was employed with an introductory letter and survey sent via e-mail in October 1999 to the population of eighty instructors. Faculty were given the option of returning the completed survey via e-mail or printing the survey and returning it via campus mail. Two weeks after the e-mail survey was sent, the investigators mailed print cover letters and surveys as well as self-addressed envelopes to faculty members who had not yet responded. After ten days, faculty who had not responded were sent another letter and survey via e-mail. Thirty-nine faculty, or 50%, returned the surveys via e-mail (27) or surface mail (12). Three surveys were not usable.

The instrument used in the study was a self-administered survey designed by the investigators. [See Appendix for sample survey.] The format included a combination of open- and close-ended questions. Participants had the opportunity to add comments in each of the eight major questions. Close-ended questions included Likert rating scales and categorical (yes/no) scales. The first question focused on the degree of satisfaction with library resources and services offered to distance students. Services and resources were grouped into categories, such as electronic resources, obtaining materials, and document delivery. Following this were questions related to satisfaction with assistance from the Libraries' Distance Education Coordinator and the subject specialist/liaison librarian assigned to the faculty member's academic department. Another set of questions focused on library instruction for extended education students. Faculty were also asked to specify whether they required distance learners to use library resources and services more extensively, the same, or less than on-campus students. Questions sought suggestions for additional library resources and services for both distant students and faculty. As a final question, faculty were asked what might impede their use of library services or resources.

Survey data were analyzed by the investigators and summary sheets prepared. For close-ended questions, percentages of each response were determined. "No response" to questions (lack of any response) was also noted. All comments by faculty, whether solicited or not solicited, were recorded.

RESULTS

Overall, faculty were satisfied with library resources and services offered to their distance students. They indicated a high degree of satisfaction with the Libraries' Distance Education Coordinator as well as the subject specialist/liaison librarian assigned to their particular academic department. At the same time, very few faculty had invited librarians to provide instructional presentations for their extended education students. Many faculty often require distant students to use books, journal articles, and/or the World Wide Web for class assignments. A slight majority of faculty require approximately the same use of library resources for distance students as they do for on-campus courses they teach. Some faculty provided responses to questions regarding suggestions for additional services or resources that might be offered to them or to their distant students. Likewise, some faculty noted impediments to their use of library services and resources. Many instructors also included additional comments at the end of the survey.

The first group of questions involved faculty satisfaction with library resources and services offered to their distance students. [Note: All percentages given in these results refer to respondents who indicated their degree of satisfaction. Percentages do not take into account those who marked "not observed" or who did not respond to the question.] Seventy-five percent of faculty were very satisfied with the University Libraries' home page, while 23% were somewhat satisfied. Sixty percent of survey respondents were very satisfied with the Libraries' online catalog, while 36% were somewhat satisfied. Similarly, 71% of faculty were very satisfied with the Libraries' Distance Education Services' Web page and 29% were somewhat satisfied.

Faculty satisfaction with electronic indexes was lower. Twenty-three percent of respondents were very satisfied with general procedures for remote access to use restricted databases (proxy server). Fifty-three percent were somewhat satisfied, 18% were somewhat dissatisfied, and 6% were very dissatisfied with procedures for using the proxy server. In rating degree of satisfaction with journal article database selection, 26% were very satisfied, 63% somewhat satisfied, and 10% somewhat dissatisfied. Seventeen percent of respondents were very satisfied with the Libraries' electronic journals with 59% somewhat satisfied, 19% somewhat dissatisfied, and 5% very dissatisfied. Thirty-six percent of faculty were very satisfied with the Libraries' Internet Resources Collection, which is a collection of selected Web sites arranged by subject, while 64% were somewhat satisfied. There was a high level of satisfaction with the Libraries' electronic reference service. Eighty-two percent of survey respondents were very satisfied with the electronic reference service and 18% were somewhat satisfied. Nine faculty members included narrative comments about electronic resources. Most of the narrative responses expressed pleasure with the Libraries' electronic resources or noted that they were not aware of these resources.

A section of the survey involved convenience and ease of use in obtaining print materials from the University Libraries. An equal number of respondents (44%) were very satisfied or somewhat satisfied in using the Web to request photocopied articles and book loans. Twelve percent, however, indicated they were very dissatisfied with this service. Seventy-three percent of faculty were very satisfied with requesting materials via e-mail, 18% somewhat satisfied, and 9% somewhat dissatisfied. Seventy-five percent were very satisfied with use of fax to request materials and 25% were somewhat satisfied. Sixty-one percent were very satisfied and 23% were somewhat satisfied in using the mail to request materials. However, 16% expressed some dissatisfaction with this service.

Three survey questions related to degree of satisfaction regarding timeliness of delivery of library materials to students. Sixty-seven percent of faculty were very satisfied with mail delivery of photocopied articles to students. Twenty-five percent were somewhat satisfied with this service while 8% were very dissatisfied. An identical number (67%) of faculty were very satisfied with fax delivery of photocopied articles to their students. However, 33% were somewhat satisfied. Fifty-eight percent of faculty respondents stated they were very satisfied with the timeliness of delivery of books to their students via mail. However, 17% indicated they were somewhat satisfied, 8% were somewhat dissatisfied, and 17% were very dissatisfied.

Students enrolled in classes through the University of Nebraska-Lincoln have borrowing privileges at other academic libraries in Nebraska. Faculty were asked to assess their level of satisfaction with this service. Responses indicated that 33% were very satisfied with this service, 50% were somewhat satisfied, and 17% were very dissatisfied with this service.

Only five faculty members provided optional comments regarding obtaining print materials. Four indicated that they did not have information pertinent to rating this service. One faculty member stated that although the library staff had been accommodating, he/she had a problem related to the policy of recalling books that distance students may have checked out.

The second broad area of survey questions related to faculty satisfaction with the assistance they have received from librarians whose assignments included serving extended education students. The survey indicated that faculty were very satisfied with the Libraries' Distance Education Coordinator: responsive to students' requests for assistance (94%); available during appropriate service hours (93%); willingness to provide instructional presentations such as library instruction (79%); and willingness to provide descriptive handouts in print format (87%). Eight optional comments related to the Distance Education Coordinator were made. Several were highly complimentary while other faculty indicated they do not use this service.

Faculty indicated that they were satisfied with the services provided by the Subject Specialist Librarian assigned to their specific academic department. Respondents rated as "very satisfied": responsive to students' requests for assistance (88%); available during appropriate service hours (94%); and, willingness to provide library instruction (93%). Eight respondents made comments regarding Subject Specialist Librarians. Most expressed pleasure with the level of service provided by their specific departmental librarian. One indicated that he was unaware of this individual's name.

The third area of questions asked faculty whether librarians had provided presentations (library instruction) for their extended education students. Only 15% of faculty stated that they had invited the Subject Specialist/Liaison Librarian to give instruction to their distance students. Of those that marked "yes," instruction was provided by a variety of means: satellite television, e-mail or class listserv, videotape, and live appearance at class. Seventeen percent of faculty indicated they had invited the Distance Education Coordinator to provide instruction for their extended education students. The instruction was provided through satellite television, in-class presentations, U.S. mail, and written materials that were scanned into programs. Two faculty comments indicated that the presentations were "good" or "helpful" while another stated that she was unaware that librarians could provide this service.

The fourth question related to the frequency that faculty require their students to use resources for course-related research for their extended education classes. Books were used: very often (31%), often (13%), sometimes (22%), not often (6%), or not at all (28%). The frequency of journal article usage was: very often (33%), often (15%), sometimes (21%), not often (6%), or not at all (24%). Survey respondents stated that their usage of the World Wide Web for student course-related research was: very often (43%), often (24%), sometimes (12%), not often (9%), or not at all (12%). The required usage of electronic journals was: very often (12%), often (12%), sometimes (30%), not often (12%), not at all (33%). There was very little usage of electronic reserves: very often (9%), often (6%), sometimes (6%), not often (9%), or not at all (70%). Eight faculty provided additional comments. These included a wide spectrum of replies including comments that students are not required to use the library, as well as that students are always expected to make use of library resources and services.

Instructors were also asked whether the extended education classes they taught required more or less use of library resources in comparison to courses they taught on campus. The results were more extensive use of library resources [by extended education courses] (13%), less extensive use of library resources (32%), and approximately the same use of library resources (55%). Seven faculty included optional comments. These ranged from a comment that students are not asked to use the library to a comment that students are always expected to make use of library resources and services.

The sixth question asked faculty to suggest additional services or resources they would like the Libraries to offer to extended education students. Several of the fifteen respondents indicated they had no suggestions at this time, that their courses did not require the use of the library, or that they were unaware of the services offered by the Libraries. One comment stated, "You are doing a fine job with our students at the present time–they rave about the service!!!" Another faculty member stated, "Just try to stay up with the ever changing technology and make the systems as simple as possible."

The next question asked respondents to suggest additional resources or services they would like the Libraries to offer to them as faculty members teaching extended classes. Faculty provided twelve comments. Many had no further suggestions. Examples of other comments include "more awareness regarding what is available" and the addition of more electronic journals.

Faculty were also asked what might impede their use of UNL Libraries' services and/or resources. The fifteen responses varied from "nothing" to "lack of knowledge of what services are available" to lack of time or knowledge of the latest technology. One faculty member indicated a problem accessing the Libraries' catalog using a particular browser. Another respondent mentioned a difficulty in accessing a particular index, which uses an ICA client that must be installed.

At the end of the survey, faculty were given the opportunity to add comments. Fourteen comments were provided. Some respondents remarked that their courses did not require the use of library resources. One faculty member stated, "just responding to this survey made me mad that I did not think of using your services before now." Others were complimentary, such as "I think that you've done a great job–the cooperation of the library staff has certainly made our distance education programs more successful than they would have been without your help and innovations."

Input was also solicited from several administrators whose responsibilities include distance education. Administrators were asked to specify what might impede faculty use of the UNL Libraries' services and/or resources. One administrator noted that faculty are not fully aware of what is available to them. Faculty usually learn of the Libraries' distance services by word of mouth, from other faculty. Experienced distance faculty may refer new distance faculty to the Distance Education Coordinator. Administrators noted the challenge of keeping up with the rapid changes in technology. Timeliness of materials delivery was deemed important.

DISCUSSION

The percentage rate of returned surveys (50%) was disappointing although not unexpected. Of the thirty-nine faculty who returned the survey, six or seven typically did not answer the majority of questions. Of surprise was the large number of respondents who indicated "not observed" in response to questions related to basic resources. For example, almost 20% of distance faculty marked "not observed" when asked to rate their degree of satisfaction with the Libraries' home page as well as the online catalog.

Of prime importance to customers in the business world are two basic expectations, namely promises of service that are kept and a solid performance by the product and the company. However, customers may not consider that some problems are beyond the company's control. In academic libraries, technology represents one such example. Survey findings showed lower levels of satisfaction with the proxy server technology. In many cases, the proxy server/authentication process is administered outside the library. Librarians need to communicate clearly to distance faculty and distance learners the extent of library responsibility for proxy server and other system problems. Communication should clarify expectations (Cooper, 1998). Survey dissatisfaction with databases may similarly reflect dissonant expectations regarding content and scope of databases. Another explanation for some dissatisfaction could be the limited number of full-text databases currently available. As some respondents stated, distance learners are dependent on full-text databases due to their physical distance from the library. Distance faculty expect the library to keep up with changing technology and make it user friendly.

While technology has expanded and enhanced information access, it has also caused depersonalization (Cooper, 1998). Librarians can offset depersonalization by putting a human face on the virtual library for faculty as well as students. Distance librarians can bring their knowledge of information resources and organization, and expertise in information technology, to the forefront in collaboration with teaching faculty. Librarians, instructional designers, and teaching faculty can form a powerful partnership in delivery of distance courses. Yang and Frank (1999) suggest strategies that distance librarians can adapt in partnering with distance faculty.

CONCLUSION

The authors' earlier survey had been conducted in conjunction with a detailed survey of distance students in one academic college (Cassner & Adams, 1997). The current survey, meanwhile, was larger in population and covered all colleges currently offering distance graduate programs at the University of Nebraska-Lincoln. The survey instrument covered the range of distance library services and resources. It was designed to assess the needs of faculty who teach courses in distance graduate degree programs. The authors defined needs as degree of satisfaction with library resources and services offered to distance faculty and learners. Faculty input for additional services was sought. The instrument also served as a feedback mechanism for degree of usage of library resources that support distance courses. An additional purpose of the survey was instructional in nature. The survey provided an overview of available services and resources. Thus, it was also developed as a marketing strategy.

Survey results indicated, overall, a high degree of faculty satisfaction with library services and resources. Faculty offered some comments on services and resources as well as suggestions for future direction. Generally, comments were centered on keeping up with technological developments as well as increasing the availability of full-text databases. The instrument also served to market the multiple library resources and services.

As academic libraries continue to move from the ownership model to an access environment, assessment measures such as faculty user satisfaction must be explored (Saunders, 1999). In addition to survey instruments, focus groups and other interview techniques can elicit user input for shaping the library's future direction, while fostering communication and offering an element of personalization.

Librarians, as active participants in the higher education community, can offer their expertise in instruction and electronic technology to enhance institutional success.

REFERENCES

Behrens, S. J. (1993). Obstacles to user education for off-campus students: Lecturers' attitudes to library skills. In C. Jacob (Comp.), *The Sixth Off-Campus Library Services Conference Proceedings: Kansas City, Missouri, October 6-8, 1993* (pp. 11-23). Mount Pleasant, MI: Central Michigan University.

Cassner, M., & Adams, K. (1998). Instructional support to a rural graduate population: An assessment of library services. In P. S. Thomas & M. Jones (Comps.), *The Eighth Off-Campus Library Services Conference Proceedings: Providence, Rhode Island, April 22-24, 1998* (pp. 117-130). Mount Pleasant, MI: Central Michigan University.

Cooper, R., Dempsey, P. R., Menon, V., & Millson-Martula, C. (1998). Remote library users–Needs and expectations. *Library Trends, 47*(1), 42-64.

Craig, M. H., & DuFord, S. (1995). Off-campus faculty perception of the value of library user education. In C. J. Jacobs (Comp.), *The Seventh Off-Campus Library Services Conference Proceedings: San Diego, California, October 25-27, 1995* (pp. 69-73). Mount Pleasant, MI: Central Michigan University.

Landrum, M. C. (1987). Marketing library services to faculty. *Colorado Libraries, 13,* 15-16.

Lebowitz, G. (1993). Faculty perceptions of off-campus student library needs. In C. J. Jacob (Comp.), *The Sixth Off-Campus Library Services Conference Proceedings: Kansas City, Missouri, October 6-8, 1993* (pp. 143-154). Mount Pleasant, MI: Central Michigan University.

Marketing and public relations activities in ARL libraries: A SPEC kit. (1999). Washington, DC: Association of Research Libraries, Office of Leadership and Management Services.

Olson, C. A., & Moseman, S. S. (1997). Overlooked? Understaffed? Don't stop marketing! *Information Outlook, 1,* 20-23.

Ruddy, Sr. M. (1993). Off-campus faculty and student's perceptions of the library: Are they the same? In C. J. Jacob (Comp.), *The Sixth Off-Campus Library Services Conference Proceedings: Kansas City, Missouri, October 6-8, 1993* (pp. 227-240). Mount Pleasant, MI: Central Michigan University.

Saunders, L. M. (1999). Human element in the virtual library. *Library Trends, 47*(4), 771-787.

Wolpert, A. (1998). Services to remote users: Marketing the library's role. *Library Trends, 47*(1), 21-41.

Yang, J. & Frank, D. (1999). Working effectively with scholars: A key to academic library success. *Georgia Library Quarterly, 36*(2), 9-12.

APPENDIX

Survey of UNL Faculty Who Have Taught Extended Education Classes

1. *How satisfied are you with the following library resources and services offered to your distance students?*

	Very Satisfied	Somewhat Satisfied	Somewhat Dissatisfied	Very Dissatisfied	Not Observed
ELECTRONIC RESOURCES					
UNL Libraries' Home Page [http://iris.unl.edu]	____	____	____	____	____
UNL Libraries' [online] Catalog [to search for books, journal titles]	____	____	____	____	____
UNL Distance Education Services	____	____	____	____	____
Indexes/Full-Text Materials	____	____	____	____	____
General procedures for remote access to use restricted databases [proxy server]					
Database selection [journal article databases that support your curriculum]	____	____	____	____	____
Electronic Journals [e-journals available via Web]	____	____	____	____	____
Internet Resources Collection [collection of selected Web sites arranged by subject]	____	____	____	____	____
Electronic reference service [to ask a reference question via IRIS]	____	____	____	____	____

Optional comments regarding *Electronic Resources*:

OBTAINING PRINT MATERIALS

Requesting Photocopied Articles and/or Book Loans [convenience and ease of use]

Via Web	____	____	____	____	____
Via e-mail	____	____	____	____	____
Via fax	____	____	____	____	____
Via mail	____	____	____	____	____

Delivery of Photocopied Articles to Students [timeliness]

Via mail	____	____	____	____	____
Via fax	____	____	____	____	____

APPENDIX (continued)

Delivery of Books to Students [timeliness]
Via mail   _____   _____   _____   _____   _____

Reciprocal borrowing from other
Nebraska libraries [students have   _____   _____   _____   _____   _____
borrowing privileges at other academic libraries in Nebraska]

Optional comments regarding _Obtaining Print Materials_:

2. _How satisfied are you with assistance from librarians whose duties include serving your extended education students?_

	Very Satisfied	Somewhat Satisfied	Somewhat Dissatisfied	Very Dissatisfied	Not Observed

LIBRARIES' DISTANCE EDUCATION COORDINATOR
[Coordinates Library services to extended education students and faculty]

–Responsive to students'   _____   _____   _____   _____   _____
requests for assistance

–Available during appropriate   _____   _____   _____   _____   _____
service hours

–Willingness to provide   _____   _____   _____   _____   _____
instructional presentations
[library instruction]

–Provides descriptive handouts   _____   _____   _____   _____   _____
in print format

Optional comments regarding _Libraries' Distance Education Coordinator_:

SUBJECT SPECIALIST/LIAISON LIBRARIAN FOR YOUR DEPARTMENT
[Librarian assigned to your academic department]

–Responsive to students'   _____   _____   _____   _____   _____
requests for assistance

–Available during appropriate   _____   _____   _____   _____   _____
service hours

–Willingness to provide   _____   _____   _____   _____   _____
instructional presentations
[library instruction]

Optional comments regarding *Subject Specialist/Liaison Librarian for Your Department*:

3. *Have librarians provided instructional presentations for your extended education students?*

Have you invited the **Subject Specialist/Liaison Librarian** to give instruction to your extended education students?

_____ Yes   _____ No

If you answered "yes," was the instruction provided by the **Subject Specialist/Liaison Librarian** via:

_____ E-mail/listserv
_____ Satellite television
_____ Other (please specify delivery mode)_____

Have you invited the **Distance Education Coordinator** to give instruction to your extended education students?

_____ Yes   _____ No

If you answered "yes," was the instruction provided by the **Distance Education Coordinator** via:

_____ E-mail/listserv
_____ Satellite television
_____ Other (please specify delivery mode)_____

Optional comments regarding *instructional presentations for your extended education students:*

4. *How frequently have you required your students to use the following resources for course-related research for your extended education classes?*

	very often	often	sometimes	not often	not at all
Books	_____	_____	_____	_____	_____
Journal Articles	_____	_____	_____	_____	_____
World Wide Web	_____	_____	_____	_____	_____
Electronic Journals [e-journals available via Web]	_____	_____	_____	_____	_____
Electronic Reserves	_____	_____	_____	_____	_____
Other (please specify resource)	_____	_____	_____	_____	_____

APPENDIX (continued)

Optional comments regarding *student use of resources for course-related research:*

5. *In comparison to the courses you teach on campus (not through extended education), do your extended education courses usually require:*

_____ More extensive use of library resources
_____ Less extensive use of library resources
_____ Approximately the same use of library resources

Optional comments regarding *use of library resources for your extended education courses:*

6. *What additional services and/or resources would you suggest the Libraries offer to extended education students?*

7. *What additional services and/or resources would you suggest the Libraries offer to you as a faculty member teaching extended education classes?*

8. *What might impede your use of UNL Libraries' services and/or resources?*

9. *Please add additional comments, if you choose.*

Using a "Summit Meeting"
to Negotiate Library Agreements

Gary L. Austin

Morehead State University (Kentucky)

SUMMARY. This paper discusses agreements among academic libraries in Kentucky to assist off-campus students with their library needs. In May 1999 a summit was held to formalize the agreements and to extend them to support courses being offered through the newly formed Kentucky Commonwealth Virtual University.

KEYWORDS. Distance education, library services, cooperative agreements

INTRODUCTION

Morehead State University is one of six regional public universities in Kentucky. Its mission is to serve the higher education needs of twenty-two counties in the eastern part of the state, and has been offering distance education courses since 1995.

The University offers courses using several methods, including traditional (face-to-face), compressed video, correspondence courses, and–most recently–Internet courses. Morehead State has three Extended Campus Centers, which provide full student services, classes, compressed video labs, and computer labs. There are also sixteen other sites in eastern Kentucky where students can take compressed video classes. Internet classes are offered from both from the main

[Haworth co-indexing entry note]: "Using a 'Summit Meeting' to Negotiate Library Agreements." Austin, Gary L. Co-published simultaneously in *Journal of Library Administration* (The Haworth Information Press, an imprint of The Haworth Press, Inc.) Vol. 31, No. 3/4, 2001, pp. 23-29; and: *Off-Campus Library Services* (ed: Anne Marie Casey) The Haworth Information Press, an imprint of The Haworth Press, Inc., 2001, pp. 23-29.

campus and in cooperation with other Kentucky Universities through the recently opened Kentucky Commonwealth Virtual University. Students can earn a Bachelor's degree as well as Master's degrees in Education and Business Administration. In Fall 1998, off-campus enrollment was 590 students (FTE).

One major change in distance education in Kentucky occurred this year with the formation of the Kentucky Commonwealth Virtual University and the Kentucky Commonwealth Virtual Library. The KCVU is a non-degree granting institution that offers Web-based courses to citizens of Kentucky and around the world. The programs are offered by the various colleges and universities, with the KCVU acting as a central clearinghouse and information center. The KCVL provides indexes and full-text databases to all citizens of Kentucky through the Universities, Community and Technical Colleges, Public Libraries, and School Libraries. Private colleges can also join if they wish. Along with the databases, the KCVL has provided a common library automation package (Endeavor) for all Universities and Colleges.

There are still questions about how library services will be offered to students through the KCVU. The KCVL provides a help desk staffed by librarians to help people with their questions. However, since the programs are actually offered by individual institutions, those institutions must also take responsibility for providing library services to KCVU students in their programs. There has been talk about allowing KCVU students to designate a nearby "home library" which will provide them with library services, even if they are taking classes from a University on the other side of the state.

Camden-Carroll Library is the only library for the University. The responsibility for administering the Extended Campus Library Services program lies with the ILL/Extended Campus Librarian. Among the services provided are document delivery services, library instruction, course reserve readings, and reference services. The Extended Campus Librarian is assisted by one full-time assistant and by student help as needed.

All formal library instruction and document delivery functions for off-campus students and classes are handled through the Extended Campus Library Services Office. Students can request materials using the Office's toll-free number, by fax, or by Web form. The Library's online catalog and most of its 45+ indexes are accessible through the World Wide Web. Certain databases, such as those that require IP authentication, can be accessed from the Extended Campus Centers' computer labs.

As part of its goal of providing adequate services, the Library also maintains agreements with five community college libraries and one private college library in Eastern and Southeastern Kentucky. The library has also established temporary agreements with other area libraries to provide services for a short period of time, such as a single semester. Southern Association of Colleges and Schools (SACS) accreditation criteria require that these agreements be formal and reviewed yearly.

The agreements allow students to use libraries in their local area to do their initial research. The major services covered by the agreements include circulation privileges, course reserve services, and access to Internet workstations so students can access the databases provided by Morehead State University. This last point is especially important, since in a recent report published by the U.S. Department of Congress, Kentucky ranked 43rd in the "Percent of Households with Computers," and ranked 44th in the "Percent of Households with Internet Access" (Falling through the net . . . , 1999). Other services, such as ILL/Document Delivery, are provided through the main campus.

Many changes have taken place in the agreements over the years. For example, Camden-Carroll Library once provided a workstation and a subscription to ERIC on CD-ROM for the associated libraries. When the library began offering online access to the FirstSearch selection of databases in 1997, ERIC subscriptions were canceled and the libraries were provided with search cards instead. Still later, the First-Search databases were made available through Camden-Carroll Library's Web page and the search cards were phased out in favor of password access for each student. As these changes occurred, the agreements were modified in a piecemeal fashion until gradually it seemed we were using the facilities of these libraries but providing little in return. Although we haven't heard any complaints, the Extended Campus Librarian and the Head of Reference felt that we should look closely at the agreements before any problems might occur. It was decided to invite librarians from the six libraries to a "summit meeting" on the Morehead State University campus. A similar meeting had been held in 1995. By bringing as many of the libraries as possible together at the same time, it was hoped that good ideas and suggestions for improved services would result.

In 1995, the Extended Campus Librarian's predecessor had held a meeting with the librarians from these libraries. The meeting was held on the Morehead State University Campus and allowed the participants to discuss areas of concern with each other. The Extended Campus Librarian felt that such a meeting would be a good way for everyone to review the agreements at the same time. After receiving permission and support from the Library Director, the Head of Graduate and Extended Campus Programs, and the Vice President for Academic Affairs, the meeting was held in May 1999.

Representatives from three of the six libraries attended the meeting. Also attending the meeting were representatives from two of the three technical schools in eastern Kentucky. They were invited since the technical schools are part of the KCVU and KCVL, and we are considering pursuing agreements with them in the future. Two of the Extended Campus Centers were also represented.

The morning sessions consisted of opening remarks by the Library Director and the Extended Campus Librarian, followed by a discussion of the KCVL and how it might have an impact on distance education in Kentucky. The history of the agreements was reviewed.

After a lunch provided by the library, the participants began discussing possible changes to make them more accurately reflect current practices. Some suggestions involved adding services that were already being provided by the libraries, but which had never been specified in the agreements. For example, Morehead State University students could obtain circulation privileges from the libraries as a community user. Since this service was offered to any member of the community, the agreements had never provided for it.

A long discussion of copyright and reserve readings occurred. The libraries asked that the agreement specifically state that any materials placed on reserve in their libraries must follow their own copyright policies. We agreed to that request but asked that the libraries provide us with a copy of their copyright policy so we could inform our faculty members. Since Camden-Carroll Library recently instituted an electronic reserve service, we see the number of photocopies placed at remote locations becoming fewer. We will still place monographs as needed.

Other ideas and issues discussed during the meeting included the following:

Provide the Libraries with Copies of Syllabi for Courses in Their Area

We are still pursuing this idea with the Office of Distance Learning and the Office of Extended Campus programs. There is currently no central repository of these syllabi so obtaining them may be difficult. We hope in the future to be able to obtain copies which can be scanned and placed on a Web server so the Librarians can access them when they need to find out about student assignments.

Provide the Libraries with a Login to our Databases

One major surprise for us was that these libraries did not have access to many of the databases we offer. (Since the databases were purchased through a consortial arrangement, we assumed all libraries had the same access.) They wanted to be able to log in students who didn't have their own password, and to be able to practice searches so they could train our students when they came to the library. We are working with our university Information Technology department to find a way to provide them access.

Provide the Library with Some Journal Subscriptions

Even though the students have access to full-text databases through our Web page, the libraries asked that we provide subscriptions to some of the more popular journals requested by our students. We have agreed to provide them with five journal titles.

FORMAL SIGNING CEREMONY

A final request of these libraries, which we were only too happy to grant, was to have a formal signing ceremony for the agreements, since the libraries wished to use the agreements as part of their public relations effort. In previous years the agreements were passed back and forth by fax or mail for signatures.

The "summit meeting" proved to be a useful tool for negotiating library agreements. Morehead State University is aided by the fact that we are working within a limited geographic area, which allows us to easily meet with our cooperating libraries. Still, with the advent of video and/or Web conferencing, even libraries that maintain agreements with far away institutions may find it possible to use the summit meeting approach. With the Kentucky Commonwealth Virtual University, there may be more opportunities in the future for cooperative arrangements.

REFERENCES

Falling through the net; defining the digital divide. Washington, DC: U.S. Dept. of Commerce, National Telecommunications and Information Administration, 1999. Internet: http://www.ntia.doc.gov/ntiahome/fttn99/contents.html.

The Kentucky Commonwealth Virtual Library Web page is located at http://www.kcvl.org.

The Kentucky Commonwealth Virtual University Web page is located at http://www.kcvu.org.

APPENDIX

EXTENDED CAMPUS LIBRARY SERVICES AGREEMENT

Morehead State University and _____ Library, _____ College enter into the following agreement on this date, October 18, 1999.

Morehead State University (MSU) agrees to:

1. Provide _____ Library with reserve materials for the use of MSU students.
   1. Provide an inventory of materials sent to the library.
   2. Prepare all materials for checkout.
   3. Deposit and retrieve all materials through the Extended Campus Library Services office; materials will be retrieved by the beginning of the next semester.
   4. Accept responsibility for materials damaged from normal usage.
   5. Accept responsibility for collecting reserve materials that are not returned to the site by the end of the semester, and for collecting the fines and fees accrued for these materials after the end of the semester.
   6. Inform Morehead State University faculty of the copyright policy for reserve materials at _____ Library.

2. Provide brochures and other information concerning the Morehead State University Extended Campus Library Services programs.

3. Provide extended campus sites with a toll-free telephone number for student referral to the Extended Campus Library Services office on campus.

4. Respond to suggestions from _____ Library concerning the perceived informational needs of the extended campus community.

5. Block the transcripts of MSU students owing $25 or more to _____ Library.

6. Upon request, provide librarians at _____ Library with necessary training on databases offered by MSU to its students.

7. The Camden-Carroll Library Extended Campus Librarian will travel to each site which maintains an agreement at least once a semester to discuss problems, concerns, and issues with the librarians at Library.

   _____ College agrees to:

8. Provide a library card and circulation privileges to MSU students. MSU students are responsible for following the circulation policies and procedures of the College.

9. Provide reserve services to MSU students.
   A. Provide space for deposited materials in either a public access or reserve area, as deemed appropriate by the professor and librarians.
   B. Provide circulation control; obtain the student's name and social security number or MSU ID number on the check-out card.
   C. Retain overdue check-out cards for the MSU Extended Campus Library Service.
   D. _____ College Library reserves the right to refuse any materials it feels violate copyright law or _____ College Library's copyright policy.

10. Provide local reference service and assisted searches on databases provided by Morehead State University for the use of its students.

11. Assist MSU students in making document requests to the Extended Campus Library Services office.

12. Make readily available to the public brochures and other information provided by MSU concerning the MSU Extended Campus Library Services program.

Annual evaluations of the above procedures will be conducted by the MSU Extended Campus Librarian and the Director of _____ College Library. These annual evaluations will be subject to review by the director of the MSU library, the dean of the MSU Graduate and Extended Campus Program, and the presidents of MSU and _____ College Library.

Either party may revoke this agreement in writing up to 30 days before the beginning of the subsequent semester.

Signed:

_____   _____

Director   Director
_____ Library   Camden-Carroll Library
_____ College   Morehead State University

Computer Mediated Conferencing, E-Mail, Telephone: A Holistic Approach to Meeting Students' Needs

Rita Barsun

Walden University Library Liaison
at Indiana University-Bloomington

SUMMARY. Following an introduction to computer mediated conferencing (CMC), the use of CMC in an online orientation for Ph.D. candidates in a dispersed residency institution is described. Although psychology faculty moderate the forum, the librarian plays an active role, by invitation of the chair and faculty of the psychology program. The librarian's interaction with students begins with the CMC forum but e-mail messages, telephone calls, and face-to-face consultation become part of the communication network. Both instructional and social objectives are detailed.

KEYWORDS. Computer mediated conferencing, library instruction, distance learning

COMPUTER MEDIATED CONFERENCING (CMC)

A prediction five years ago that Computer Mediated Conferencing (CMC) would become a way of life (Everett & Ahern, 1994) may soon be realized. Woolley (1996) notes an increase from two CMC

[Haworth co-indexing entry note]: "Computer Mediated Conferencing, E-Mail, Telephone: A Holistic Approach to Meeting Students' Needs." Barsun, Rita. Co-published simultaneously in *Journal of Library Administration* (The Haworth Information Press, an imprint of The Haworth Press, Inc.) Vol. 31, No. 3/4, 2001, pp. 31-44; and: *Off-Campus Library Services* (ed: Anne Marie Casey) The Haworth Information Press, an imprint of The Haworth Press, Inc., 2001, pp. 31-44.

products in 1994 to more than 60 commercial and freeware products in 1996 and later (1998) states that CMC software is proliferating rapidly. The growing popularity of computer conferencing is also evidenced elsewhere in the literature (Bichelmeyer & Kiggins, 1998; Murphy, Drabier, & Epps, 1998; Schwan, 1997; Smith, 1997).

Woolley (1996) describes CMC as a form of group discussion that uses text messages on a computer as a communication medium. (CMC) can be synchronous, with all parties on line at the same time, or asynchronous, done at times convenient for each person with no need for all to be online simultaneously. The CMC discussed in this paper is an asynchronous system delivered via a Web browser. Eastmond (1995) offers an interesting metaphor for asynchronous CMC:

> Computer conferencing is like having a room full of typewriters, perhaps set on different desks, clustered by subject area. During the week, day and night, men and women enter the room from different doors, rarely at the same time. They spend anywhere from a half hour to two hours at a time reading what others have typed at the keyboard on each topic and adding their own ideas. Some of them will make photocopies of what they and others have said so that they can refer to it later. Then they leave, only to return in a couple of days to see who has responded to them, what they have said, and how the various topical discussions have progressed. (p. 68)

Schwan (1997) lists five communication technology characteristics specific to asynchronous CMC:

- The underlying symbol system: Communication proceeds in a solely text-based manner, totally lacking visual or vocal cues.
- The spatial relations of the participants: hundreds or thousands of miles may separate them.
- The temporal relations between communications: The asynchronous manner in which it proceeds may result in delays between the production of messages and their reception.
- The permanence of exchanged utterances: The storage of the text-based exchanges permits participants to review, revise, and further process the postings.
- The number of addresses involved in the communication process: CMC permits large groups of students to participate.

Smith (1997) uses the term "aspatial" to describe the physical separation, "acorporal" to describe the lack of visual or vocal cues. Closely tied to the acorporal aspect of CMC is its "astigmatic" nature, whereby participants are judged by the content of their communication rather than by age, appearance, body shape, gender, or race (Smith, 1997).

SELECTED STRENGTHS AND WEAKNESSES OF CMC

An essential component of CMC is its ability to lessen students' feelings of isolation and to create a learning community. Community is important for creating and achieving the goals that could not be achieved by an isolated individual (Kok & Brown, 1998). Distance learners do not have the opportunities for community building that are prevalent on a college campus, such as informal talks with instructors after class, face-to-face consultations with them in their offices, and opportunities to meet with fellow students outside the classroom to go over homework and discuss ideas (Chung, Rodes, & Knapczyk, 1998).

Because students removed from their instructors and fellow students must work more independently than those in traditional settings, a strong sense of ownership is especially critical for distance learners. Attributes of ownership include a sense of personal goals and products, self-monitoring skills, self-regulation, critical thinking skills, intrinsic and extrinsic motivation, communication skills, and personal autonomy (Chung et al., 1998). Similar qualities essential to success in online learning are described in the *What Makes a Successful Online Student?* (Web site: http://128.174.149.91/model/StudentProfile.htm).

However, many who enroll in distance education courses do not do so because their learning styles or motivation make them good candidates but because of convenience. By fostering a cooperative learning-centered environment where students can share concerns and develop their ideas in a low-stress environment, CMC can increase ownership and self-sufficiency (Chung et al., 1998).

Interviews with students and faculty in a distance education program in Canada identify two benefits in particular: peer interaction and "operations." Operational strengths include the way in which CMC matches preferred learning styles, the availability of choices for and independence of action, having a written record of the discussions readily available, and the opportunity to choose the location of the computer (Burge, 1994).

Perhaps one of the greatest strengths of CMC is that it promotes not just active learning but also interactive learning (Burge, 1994; Donnelly, 1995; Murphy et al., 1998; Everett & Ahern, 1994). The instructor is no longer the center of the "classroom." Rather, the role of the instructor changes from that of expert presenter to discussion facilitator (Berge, 1995).

Another benefit of text-only communication noted by students is that they pay more attention to what is being said and are able to remember the information longer than if it were just spoken (Eastmond, 1995). They have time to look at the screen and reflect on what they really want to say (Murphy et al., 1998). Thus, shy or contemplative students have more of an opportunity to participate (Bichelmeyer & Kiggins, 1998).

Because messages are unhampered by irrelevant physical characteristics, some students feel that they more truly convey their fellows' personalities (Eastmond, 1995; Murphy et al., 1998). In contrast, other students interviewed by Eastmond (1995) consider the lack of aural and visual cues a weakness, as do some of the students interviewed by Burge (1994).

"Asynchronous anxiety" is a term used to describe the feeling of not being connected (Crouch & Montecino, 1997). The lack of feedback or a delay in feedback from fellow students and from the instructor is a definite cause of frustration (Burge, 1994; Eastmond, 1995). Asynchronicity is a drawback also in that it often results in disjointed transactions and poorly referenced communiqués (Eastmond, 1995). Some students experience difficulty in following multiple concurrent discussions (Burge, 1994; Eastmond, 1995; Winiecke & Chyung, 1998) and threads of discussion can become confusing if not actively managed (Anderson & Kanuka, 1997).

A further weakness of CMC is that the quantity of information can be overwhelming, especially if one does not log in every day (Burge, 1994; Eastmond, 1995). Murphy et al. (1998), however, note that students share intellectual, practical, and emotional strategies for dealing with information overload.

The technology itself can be a barrier, a problem not unique to CMC and an issue that can be partly addressed by giving students an opportunity to become familiar with the hardware and software before the class begins (Brown, 1998; Crouch & Montecino, 1997; Donnelly, 1995; McDonald, 1998; Whyte, 1995). Providing timely and easily accessible technical support is essential, a point stressed by Donnelly (1995).

CMC AS PART OF AN INTEGRATED DELIVERY SYSTEM

To be effective in delivering instruction, building community, and fostering ownership CMC must be used in concert with other communication media (Berge, 1995; Eastmond, 1995; Schwan, 1997). In addition, the role the moderator or facilitator plays can greatly influence the success of CMC (Berge, 1995; Hillesheim, 1998; Woolley, 1998). Psyc8000, the online orientation course which is the focus of this paper, takes into consideration the need for additional channels of communication and the importance of the type of support and guidance the facilitator contributes.

The primary method for delivery of content and discussion for Psyc8000 is the Psychology Forum, which uses Web Crossing (or WebX), one of the commercial CMC programs. As is common to CMC, the discussions are threaded around specific topics. Each message added to a discussion item is posted to the bottom of the discussion item. Subsequent replies are added in chronological order, resulting in a long document containing the initial question or topic and the associated responses (Kok & Brown, 1998).

Psyc8000 is required for students entering the Ph.D. in Psychology Program. It resembles the orientation courses for Master's students in both psychology and education in length (12 weeks) and in its goal of assisting students in surmounting barriers faced by adult students in an online program.

As is the case with the other online orientation courses, a Web-based Orientation Syllabus provides the framework for the course. The tone of the Syllabus is carefully crafted to be one of encouragement and camaraderie. Each week has a list of Specific Objectives & Activities. The brief paragraphs, which describe each activity, contain hyperlinks to additional information, usually contained in a Module specifically designed to supplement the Syllabus. The Modules include information about how to contact Walden personnel for support or answers to questions and include links to Web pages related to the Module topic. As such, the Syllabus can be described as a "gateway

Web site," periodically evaluated and revised to ensure that the information is current and that it continues to meet the needs of students (Kok & Brown, 1998). Students have high regard for the Syllabus, as shown by their questions regarding continuing access to it, sharp contrast to a tendency by some students to dispose of hyperlinked syllabi once a course is completed (Doty, 1999).

A faculty mentor, the First Year Advisor (FYA), guides each group of 10-12 students through the course. There are usually four such groups each quarter. The FYAs make an effort to contact students before the quarter begins, either by phone or by e-mail, to welcome them and to offer reassurance to those who may be experiencing trepidation and feelings of inadequacy. Once the quarter starts, FYAs carry out three of the four roles for moderators described by Berge (1995).

Pedagogical [andragogical (Reio, no date)]
As educational facilitators, they guide the students through a series of benchmarks. Most FYAs begin each week of the course with a posting to the Forum explaining the goals for that week.

Social
They create a friendly environment in which learning is promoted by lauding those who are staying on schedule and by offering encouragement, advice, and assistance to those encountering difficulties. E-mail messages and/or phone calls to individuals with special needs supplement the public postings. FYAs also reply to each student's posting, even if it is only to acknowledge that the posting was noticed and read.

Managerial
FYAs set the objectives, procedural rules, and decision-making norms. They keep a record of each student's progress and, when necessary, move misplaced postings to the correct folders.

Technical
With the ultimate goal of making the technology transparent, information technology staff and the librarians of the Walden University Library Liaison program at Indiana University-Bloomington implement this role.

Psyc8000 and the other Walden online orientation courses introduce students to the electronic environment, to specific requirements of the

Walden program, and to the bewildering array of acronyms which define tasks and policies. In addition, since many Ph.D. candidates completed their Master's programs 5-20 years earlier, Psyc8000 eases their return to academia. Most students are at the same time enrolled in one or more credit courses. Psyc8000 is intended to complement the credit courses and to assist students in overcoming obstacles they may encounter there.

Unlike the other orientation courses, Psyc8000 requires students to interact with the Liaison Librarian in determining their information needs so the student and librarian can work together to address them. Although the responsibility for, and the majority of correspondence and interaction with, Psyc8000 students is the purview of the Liaison Librarian, the Assistant Liaison Librarian (Jay Wilkerson) usually works with four or five of the students each quarter.

The librarian's involvement in Psyc8000 begins the second week and continues until, and sometimes beyond, Week Twelve. The first formal contact with students is a letter, which introduces the Liaison Librarian and the Assistant Liaison Librarian, and explains the Library Assignment. There is also a brief description of the library services offered by the Walden University Library Liaison program (WULL), a recommendation to visit the WULL Web site, and an invitation to e-mail the librarian or to call on the toll-free line. The URL, e-mail address, and 800 number are provided in the letter as well as on the librarian's business card, which is enclosed with the letter. Also included with the letter is a synopsis of *Six Stages for Learning to Use Technology* (Russell, 1996). To make the letter more personal, each student's address is typed on the envelope instead of on a mailing label and colorful postage stamps are used rather than the University's metered mail labels.

During Week One each student is to post a brief biography to the Forum, although slow starters may not post until several weeks into the course. As soon as a biography appears, the librarian sends an e-mail message welcoming the student to the program and reminding him or her of the Library Assignment. The message usually contains a comment on something mentioned in the biography; e.g., research interests, hobbies, pets, family, geographic area. Thus, from the beginning the Forum can serve as a springboard for more personal contact via another medium.

Daily monitoring of the Forum is necessary in order to be alert to the "teachable moment" and provide timely responses to questions or comments about library services, resources, or research. Depending on the nature and content of the student's posting, the response is made publicly to the Forum or privately through e-mail–and occasionally by a telephone call. Because most Walden students are employed full time, the Forum must also be monitored weekends, evenings, and holidays as that is when students are most likely to post.

Postings by the librarian are carefully calculated to relate to the Weekly Objectives & Activities listed in the Syllabus. The postings often contain citations for print materials or hyperlinks to relevant Web sites. The first posting occurs during Week Two. One of the Activities for that week is to access the American Psychological Association (APA) Web site to explore the benefits of student membership, among them a relatively inexpensive subscription to the APA PsycINFO full-text database. Here is an excellent opportunity to alert students to the shortcomings of many full-text databases, as the APA PsycINFO indexes only APA publications (about 35 journals among the more than 1400 in the PsycINFO or PsycLIT available from vendors).

The Week Two posting and subsequent Syllabus-related postings often serve as impetus for questions and further discussion, with contributions by both students and faculty. Unfortunately, early and sometimes continuing battles with technology or the press of their credit courses may keep some students from following up on or even reading the information. Thus, during Week Twelve the librarian posts the URL for a Web site, which summarizes the content of her postings and links to any sites which had been included.

The objectives of the Library Assignment closely resemble those of the Personalized Research Consultation Service (PERCS) program for graduate students at Bowling Green State University (Gratch & York, 1991). The order has been changed to indicate the sequence of priorities for Psyc8000.

- To make graduate students aware of the full range of services and resources available to them for their research.
- To assist graduate students in devising ways to save time in searching for and locating materials.
- To equip graduate students with information-seeking strategies for finding sources to assist with topic formation.
- To prepare graduate students to conduct effective literature reviews for the proposals and theses/dissertations (p. 5).

The long-term goal is that students develop the skills and tools necessary to become independent researchers. By interacting with them and instructing them early in their Walden experience, the librarian lays a foundation upon which the students can continue to build, with or without the assistance of the librarians.

The first conversation between the librarian and students focuses on where and how they will obtain materials. With papers due on the 15th of the third (last) month of the quarter, students must be sure that they plan for the time it may take to locate and obtain books and journal articles. Although Walden's contract with the Indiana University-Bloomington (IUB) Libraries enables students to request materials directly from IUB Libraries, the cost may appear a barrier to some. Thus, students express interest in exploring local libraries' interlibrary loan services and the policies of academic libraries toward unaffiliated users. Another tactic is to compare commercial providers in terms of content, cost, and speed. Students especially appreciate being introduced to the library's Web page, which links to the few cost-free full-text scholarly journals on the Web. Basically, all alternatives are considered until both librarian and student are satisfied that the student has an adequate information network.

Once the student's research topic for that quarter is approved, it is time to move to identifying the materials. The first step is to ascertain where the student may have already looked–library catalog, database, World Wide Web–the strategies used, and the results. Seldom is all of the preceding satisfactory. Building on what the student has already done, the librarian conducts an exploratory search and sends an explanation of the search strategy to the student, usually within less than 24 hours. If the student has a phone line dedicated to Internet access, student and librarian can both log on to the database and see the same screen as the librarian talks him or her through the search. Besides being a time saver, the phone contact enables the student to help the librarian refine the strategy as together they evaluate the results.

If the student does not have a dedicated phone line, it is necessary to send step-by-step instructions via e-mail. In such cases the student is asked to work through the interactive tutorial for PsycLIT (developed for Walden by an IU library school student) before attempting to follow the instructions. An alternate approach is to invite the student to "play" in the database using keywords, then to let the librarian know which records appeared relevant. If feasible, the Thesaurus terms or MeSH from the relevant records are used to plan a strategy, which is then relayed to the student, with an explanation of how the indexing terms were used as a guide. Whenever possible the student is introduced to the building block technique and shown how the Thesaurus can assist in selecting search terms. Telephone and e-mail follow-up messages continue until the student can assure the librarian that he or she was able to conduct the search(es) and is satisfied with the results.

The amount of assistance and time required for students to complete the Library Assignment varies greatly, depending on their access to resources, their understanding of or experience with good search techniques, and their computer literacy. In a few cases, it is merely a matter of confirming that a student has the skills and access to resources needed for doctoral work.

The Syllabus, the librarian's introductory letter and initial e-mail greeting to each student, a formal posting by the FYAs, and the Library Assignment posting all explain that every student is required to make contact to initiate discussion regarding his or her research needs. Despite the many channels through which the assignment is explained, at least half the students still do not understand it or are hesitant or unwilling to make that contact. Thus, a further combination of e-mail messages, phone calls, and face-to-face contact come into play.

Although most interaction and instruction take place in the virtual environment, Walden offers a variety of opportunities for face-to-face contact, important for fostering relationships. Such an opportunity is provided twice each quarter, four-day intensive academic residencies (C-4s) held at hotel conference centers in various geographic areas to facilitate travel for those living in different parts of the country. Psyc8000 students must attend a residency within 30-60 days of enrolling. Each C-4 begins on a Wednesday afternoon and concludes at noon on Sunday. The agenda includes lectures, seminars, individual advising with faculty and other Walden personnel, information technology and library workshops, and a well-orchestrated orientation for those attending their first C-4. The librarians take turns attending the C-4s. In addition to the individual advising sessions and library workshops, they present a two-hour Library Orientation.

During the week preceding the C-4 and the week of the C-4 the librarian uses Forum postings and e-mail messages to urge students attending the C-4 to sign up for an individual advising session with whichever librarian will be at the C-4, an excellent opportunity for individualized consultation and hands-on instruction. The face-to-face sessions often enable students to meet the formal criteria for the Library Assignment, but more often than not they serve as incentive for continuing interaction. Students who do not or cannot, because of the tight schedule, meet with one of the librarians individually usually learn enough from the Library Orientation to realize how much help they can receive and are less reluctant to make that initial contact or accept offers of assistance.

Whyte (1995) emphasizes that communication by telephone is an integral part of CMC. As explained above, it is especially beneficial for instruction in searching online databases when a student has a second phone line. At times the phone enables either of the librarians to resolve students' technical problems. Sometimes it is used for personal reasons, as students call to vent their frustration, to share their triumphs, or simply to hear a human voice. If a student's postings or e-mail messages hint at negative feelings, the librarian initiates the call. Having a corporate phone credit card makes it possible to call when not in the office, especially helpful with students who live in different time zones.

The objectives listed earlier (Gratch & York, 1991) undergird everything done in Psyc8000. The first was to make students aware of the full range of services and resources available to them for their research. By the time they complete the Library Assignment, students understand how the librarians can assist them. More importantly, they have a foundation on which they can now build, with or without assistance from the librarians. Together they and the librarians have explored ways to save time in searching for and locating materials and information-seeking strategies for finding sources to assist with topic formation. The ultimate success of the instructional effort in Psyc8000 will be whether the students conduct effective literature reviews for their dissertations.

Although the instructional objectives are the primary focus of the Library Assignment, the social objectives of building community and fostering ownership are an essential aspect. The librarian is constantly alert to cues concerning a student's personal situation in Forum postings or in e-mail discussions about the research process. Brief inquiries often provide openings for students to share details about their families, their health, their aspirations, or their concerns. Personal communication and words of encouragement are interspersed with discussions of the information seeking process. The librarian also looks for ways to help students feel part of the group. Interacting with students in all four sections of Psyc8000 enables her to facilitate contact between those who have like interests or who live in the same geographic area. Sometimes the librarian invites a student from an earlier Psyc8000 class to mentor someone in the current Psyc8000 group who lives nearby. The relationship with students in Psyc8000 is intense, as reflected in the more than 1,000 e-mail messages each quarter in addition to the Forum postings, telephone calls (some lasting more than an hour), and group or individual sessions at the C-4s.

The Library Assignment officially ends when students post to the Forum a summary of their interaction with the librarians, scheduled for Week Eight, and the librarian notifies the faculty moderators that students have met the criteria. Interaction with the students usually continues beyond Week Eight and even past the deadline for submitting papers, as they privately share their successes and sometimes their disappointments. Once the quarter ends and they "graduate" from Psyc8000, many continue to contact the librarians for assistance and/ or to send personal greetings.

CONCLUSION

Brunt (1996) asked, "Can you put your arm around a student on the Internet?" Those willing to expend the time and effort can come close to answering "Yes!" Walden University administration, faculty, and staff are keenly aware of the barriers to success for adult students in a distance education program, especially during the initial months or even the first year. In addition to the 12-week online orientation courses for Ph.D. students in psychology and for Master's students in psychology and education, there are similar but less compressed CMC online orientation courses for Ph.D. students in administration/management, education, health services, and human services. The courses are but part of a university-wide effort to help students surmount barriers to success.

Hillesheim (1998) explains that the effort begins with the application process, where students' personal characteristics–maturity level, motivation, and self-discipline–are as carefully assessed as their academic credentials. Mention has already been made of the four-day orientation program at residencies. The First Year Advisors (FYAs) who participate in Psyc8000 are part of a corps of FYAs carefully selected for the qualities that best meet the needs of new students. All FYAs guide students through the first year by a combination of postings to Forums created for their particular group, phone calls, e-mail messages, and face-to-face meetings if at all possible. Academic advisors employ the postal system, telephone conferences with small groups of new students, phone calls to individual students, e-mail messages, and presentations at residencies to instruct and encourage them. Through the Alumni Network Connection new students can contact Walden graduates to serve as coaches (Kok & Brown, 1998). There is also a peer support listserv for first-year students, appropriately titled "newbies."

REFERENCES

Anderson, T., & Kanuka, H. (1997). *On-line forums: New platforms for professional development and group collaboration.* Edmonton, Alberta: University of Alberta. (ERIC Document Reproduction Service No. ED 418 693).

Berge, Z. L. (1995). Facilitating computer conferencing: Recommendations from the field. *Educational Technology, 35*(1), 22-30.

Bichelmeyer, B. A., & Kiggins, E. A. (1998) *Using Web-based conferencing in post-secondary instruction.* Madison, WI: Distance Learning '98. Proceedings of the Annual Conference on Distance Teaching and Learning. (ERIC Document Reproduction Service No. ED 422 845).

Brown, B. M. 1998. *Digital classrooms: Some myths about developing new educational programs using the Internet.* Retrieved from the Web on November 19, 1999 <http://www.thejournal.com/magazine/98/dec/feat04.html>.

Brunt, J. M. (1996). Can you put your arm around a student on the Internet? *Adults Learning, 7*(5), 115-116.

Burge, E. J. (1994). Learning in computer conferenced contexts: The learners' perspective. *Journal of Distance Education, 9*(1), 19-43.

Chung, H., Rodes, p. , & Knapczyk, D. (1998). Using Web conferencing to promote ownership in distance education coursework. *Orlando, FL: WebNet 98 World Conference of the WWW, Internet, and Intranet Proceedings.* (ERIC Document Reproduction Service No. ED 427 691).

Crouch, M. L., & Montecino, V. (1997). *Cyberstress: Asynchronous anxiety or worried in cyberspace.* Orlando, FL: WebNet 98 World Conference of the WWW, Internet, and Intranet Proceedings. (ERIC Document Reproduction Service No. ED 412 938).

Donnelly, D. (1995). The digital log. *Telematics and Informatics, 12*(2), 131-138.

Doty, P. (1999). Stepping stones or serving spoons: An essay on student use of hypertext syllabus. *Internet Reference Services Quarterly, 4*(1), 1-5.

Eastmond, D. V. (1995). *Alone but together: Adult distance study through computer conferencing.* Cresskill, NJ: Hampton Press, Inc.

Everett, D. R., & Ahern, T. C. (1994). Computer-mediated communication as a teaching tool: A case study. *Journal of Research on Computing in Education, 26*(3), 336-357.

Gratch, B. G., & York, C. C. (1991). Personalized research consultation service for graduate students: Building a program based on research findings. *Research Strategies, 9*(1), 4-15.

Hillesheim, G. (1998). Distance learning: Barriers and strategies for students and faculty. *The Internet and Higher Education, 1*(1), 31-44.

Kok, K., & Brown, R. (1998). *Isolation and belonging in a distance community.* Retrieved from the Web on November 23, 1999: http://www.waldenu.edu/publ/richardb/1998/alliance/paper.html.

McDonald, J. (1998). Interpersonal group dynamics and development in computer conferencing: The rest of the story. In *Distance Learning '98. Proceedings of the Annual Conference in Distance Teaching & Learning,* Madison, WI.

Murphy, K. L., Drabier, R., & Epps, M. L. (1998). Interaction and collaboration via computer conferencing. In *Proceedings of Selected Research and Development Presentations at the National Convention of the Association for Education Communications and Technology,* St. Louis, MO.

Reio, T. G., Jr. (No date). Curiosity and the Andragogical Model. *Journal of Excellence in Higher Education* (No volume, issue number, or date). Retrieved February 24, 2000 from the World Wide Web: http://www.uophx.edu.Joehe/Past/curiosity.htm.

Russell, A. L. (1996). *Six stages for learning to use technology.* Indianapolis, IN: Proceedings of Selected Research and Development Presentations at the 1996 Convention of the Association for Educational Communications and Technology. (ERIC Document Reproduction Service No. ED 397 832).

Schwan, S. (1997). Media characteristics and knowledge acquisition in computer conferencing. *European Psychologist, 2*(3), 277-285.

Smith, M. A. (1997). *Voices from the WELL: The logic of the virtual commons.* Retrieved from the Web on November 20, 1999: http://www.sscnet.ucla.edu/soc/csoc/papers/voices/Voices.htm.

Walther, J. B. (1993). Impression development in computer-mediated interaction. *Western Journal of Communication, 57,* 381-398.

Whyte, S. B. (1995). Spanning the distance: Using computer conferencing as part of a team-taught research/writing class. *The Reference Librarian, 51/52,* 267-279.

Winiecke, D. J., & Chyung, Y. (1998). Keeping the thread: Helping distance students and instructors keep track of asynchronous discussions. In *Distance Learning '98. Proceedings of the Annual Conference on Distance Teaching and Learning,* Madison, WI.

Woolley, D. R. (1996). *Choosing Web conferencing software.* Retrieved from the Web on November 27, 1999: http://thinkofit.com/webconf/wcchoice.htm.

Woolley, D. R. (1998). *The future of Web conferencing.* Retrieved from the Web on November 27, 1999: http://thinkofit.com/webconf/wcfuture.htm.

Emerging Technologies:
Tools for Distance Education
and Library Services

Nancy E. Black

University of Northern British Columbia

SUMMARY. This article discusses the effective use of various technologies in delivery and library support of distance education at the University of Northern British Columbia. It examines how technology has helped transform the traditional to the virtual, has provided better options for the learner and has successfully overcome the barrier of distance and isolation.

KEYWORDS. Library services, distance education, library technology, Canadian libraries

INTRODUCTION

Situated in the geographical centre of the province of British Columbia Canada, Prince George has a population of approximately 80,000. Although it is considered to be in the centre of the province, it is isolated from the major communities such as Vancouver (about a 10-11 hour drive), Edmonton and Calgary in Alberta (about a 10-11 hour drive), as well as some of the smaller centres, such as Prince Rupert to the west (about a 10 hour drive). (See Appendix A, Map of British Columbia.) The main industries in Prince George are its saw-mills and pulpmills. In addition to industry, the city has a public

[Haworth co-indexing entry note]: "Emerging Technologies: Tools for Distance Education and Library Services." Black, Nancy E. Co-published simultaneously in *Journal of Library Administration* (The Haworth Information Press, an imprint of The Haworth Press, Inc.) Vol. 31, No. 3/4, 2001, pp. 45-59; and: *Off-Campus Library Services* (ed: Anne Marie Casey) The Haworth Information Press, an imprint of The Haworth Press, Inc., 2001, pp. 45-59.

library, university, college, art gallery, regional museum, symphony, and amateur and professional theatre. University of Northern British Columbia serves the northern region of BC that is the equivalent to the size of Germany. The sheer size of this province presents certain challenges that we have been able, for the most part, to overcome with the use of various technologies in the provision of library support for distance education.

BACKGROUND

Established in 1990, the main campus of the University of Northern British Columbia was officially opened August 1994, with the first full day of classes taking place on September 8, 1994. In the first year there were approximately 1,400 students and nearly 300 faculty and staff. As of the fall of 1999, there are approximately 3,300 students and over 300 faculty and staff. UNBC capitalizes on its northern setting and this is reflected in some of our key programs: Northern Studies, First Nations Studies, Environmental Studies, International Studies, and the Collaborative Nursing Program.

At UNBC, we have set high standards for ourselves, particularly when it comes to using the new technologies. The expectations are high, because our standards are high. As a new university, there are external and internal pressures to achieve a high standing and reputation in the academic community. It goes without saying that a strong reputation will attract and retain students, faculty, and funding; this in turn will help the university achieve its goal of excellence. In the annual *Maclean's* rating of Canadian universities, in the category of *Primarily Undergraduate,* UNBC ranked ninth out of 21 universities in 1998. In the 1999 rating in the same category, UNBC ranked eighth (Universities, 1999). Within five years of its official opening, we have become one of the top ten primarily undergraduate universities in Canada.

Since its inception, UNBC recognized the economic potential of forming partnerships with regional colleges to provide a more physical presence in northern BC and to foster distance learning–our mandate, after all, is "a university in the north, for the north." To this end, UNBC has established regional offices in colleges of these communities: Prince Rupert, Terrace, Quesnel, and Fort St. John. A fifth office is set up in New Aiyansh in partnership with the Wilp Wil*x* O'oskwhl

Nisga'a. These offices, with faculty and staff, are instrumental in terms of course delivery, library connections, as well as the promotion and outreach to registered students and potential students. A full time Regional Services Librarian and support staff are based on campus to provide library services. Appendix B, (Regional Sites Served by the University of Northern British Columbia), indicates the communities where most of our distance students live across the northern region of British Columbia. Interestingly enough, some colleges seem to be experiencing higher enrollment rates than previous years. While this may be due to a variety of factors, one possibility is the attraction of transferring to UNBC as a distance student.

At UNBC, the enrollment of distance learners has doubled since 1994, from 119 to approximately 235. The majority of these students are part time, female and between 35-49 years of age, many of whom have full time jobs and families; in other words, the typical distance learner profile.

Thirty to fifty courses per term are offered as distance courses. Some courses are offered out of the UNBC regional offices and made available to the other regions, including on campus students. Some courses are offered from the main campus and are available to on campus and off campus students. Course delivery is through four avenues: face to face, audio conference, videoconference, or over the Web. The majority of courses are delivered via audio conference, however, some courses have been designed as Web courses, and a few have been delivered using the LearnLinc software (interactive and synchronistic, with audio), or through Web CT (asynchronistic, not as interactive, no audio, unless the phone is used). Library instruction, however, has been primarily conducted on the telephone from campus with groups or individuals in front of computers at their sites. All distance courses place demands and expectations on the library from the students as well as the faculty. The technologies we use help meet those demands.

ONLINE LEARNING IN CANADA

Just how much and how quickly are institutions and students moving towards online learning? According to a brief comment made in our local newspaper the prediction, if correct, is that 2.5 million North Americans will be using online learning by 2002. The profile of this type of learner has a college degree, good income, and is ready to spend money to study online. In Ontario, 3,000 students are taking online courses. The TeleCampus Online Course Directory out of New Brunswick (http://database.telecampus.com) lists thousands of available online courses (Online Learning, 1999). Courses listed in this directory are offered by 650 institutions in 22 countries. It is estimated that 16% of these are offered by Canadian institutions, although Canada only represents 5% of the world population. It is further estimated that Web-based learning will grow from $197 million (US) in 1997 to $5.5 billion (US) a year by 2002 (Crone, 1999).

Federal Minister for Industry Canada, John Manley, is striving to make Canada the most wired nation in the world. His goal is to install 250,000 computers in Canadian schools by 2000 (Canada aiming, 1998). There is no doubt that Canada is gearing up and preparing itself for full participation in Web based research and learning.

QUALITY OF DISTANCE EDUCATION

Much of the literature discusses the quality of distance education in terms of academic value and recognition, quality of course content, long term stability and availability of the courses, credibility of the source, recommendations for consumer awareness, and available support for the student from faculty and librarians. Some of the literature questions whether library services to distance learners are seamless (Wolpert, 1998). Because UNBC is young, we have a competitive edge that has allowed and demanded innovation both from the human resources as well as the technical resources we employ. Hence, while some literature is critical of quality, delivery, and access of distance services, we are in an excellent position of being able to offer distance services that are very close to being seamless.

In her article "Companies go the distance with on-line education program," Michelle Naval quotes Rick Buckingham, president of NB-based Mosaic Technologies: "There's a lot of correspondence courses being offered by everybody. Quite frankly, there's a lot of smoke and mirrors in the industry, with everyone saying they offer an on-line course when it's really just a correspondence course. There's a big difference between a correspondence course and a highly interactive course" (Naval, 1998).

Stephen Barley cautions that while there is considerable social and economic promise for computer-based training, much of this promise rests on "a fledgling set of technologies . . . the realities of implementing Web-based education are likely to be different from what its proponents' rhetoric implies" (Barley, 1999). Although technology has brought changes, the distant student is still, according to the literature, very isolated and alone, especially when it comes to library support.

How does a distance education program in a university avoid some of the pitfalls of providing more than just "smoke and mirrors?" Again, the literature argues that an effective approach must be user-centered (Niemi et al, 1998; Luther, 1998; Cooper & Dempsey, 1998), highly interactive (Dewald, 1999), and include collaboration within the university (Luther, 1998) and market analysis (Wolpert, 1998). Failure to take the "institutional, demographic, and cultural issues into account may thwart the larger objective" of providing access to knowledge through distance learning (Barley, 1999). Equally important is to be familiar with and a commitment to follow the professional standards and guidelines for library services for distance education as outlined in the ACRL guidelines (Association of . . . , 1998), and CLA guidelines (Library Services, 1993).

These are lessons we have learned well and applied at UNBC in the provision of Regional Services to distance learners. Because we are committed to building stability and fulfilling the mandate of the university, our niche market is very clearly the northern British Columbia region. We provide courses which meet the needs of the learner, with a specific focus on professional programs, (teaching, nursing, social work, for example), and courses with a northern, rural, and remote component (First Nations, Natural Resources, Environmental Studies, Northern Studies). While some students outside the northern region are enrolled in our courses, we have moved away from the desire to offer distance courses worldwide. We have accepted that this is not possible to do and still maintain the high standard and quality of course delivery, access and professional support. In recognizing and responding to the needs of our northern region users, we are creating and building a niche market. As mentioned above, we have set high standards for ourselves in the delivery of quality, user centered distance education. This commitment, we believe, attracts and retains students, engenders loyalty, and will have many long-term benefits for the institution.

USING TECHNOLOGY FOR LIBRARY SUPPORT
OF DISTANCE LEARNING

Ann Wolpert notes that "Librarians have yet to understand how the work itself might change" as a result of technological innovations (Wolpert, 1998). Because we have effectively integrated the technical tools with our delivery, without losing sight of the quality of the courses and customer service values, the work has in fact changed for librarians and the faculty. We rely heavily on the technology to streamline the work, deliver the service in a more convenient, timely fashion, provide access to the library catalogue and databases, and enhance the quality of all course instruction, including library instruction.

In terms of library support for UNBC distance learners, as much emphasis as possible is placed on instruction and being able to offer access, coaching, and direction to information in traditional and non-traditional formats. It is also important to consider the learning needs and characteristics of the distance learner (Niemi et al., 1998). Typically, they will bring a level of maturity and experience to their courses, and will be more focused in their goals and motivation. Often there are anxieties and stress related to time, returning to school, meeting the demands of the course, and adjusting to the various technologies they must be able to use. In other words, the regional services librarian will spend more time anticipating users' needs, and helping them be prepared to do their own research.

This is accomplished through face to face library instruction, print guides, an online tutorial (with plans to add more online tutorials), and online instructions for our databases. Visits to regional sites for face to face library instruction generally occur in the fall, and sometimes in winter or spring terms. The majority of library instruction and assistance is conducted from campus in front of computers over the telephone. This has proven to be extremely effective, cost efficient, and convenient for both the user and the librarian. This approach can be tailored more specifically to the users' needs and also allows considerable "hands on" for the student or faculty member at the other end.

The UNBC Library home page (www.library.unbc.ca) provides links to the Catalogue, Databases, Tutorial, Services, Information, and Useful Links. Both the catalogue and databases are Web-based, however, users can also telnet into our text-based catalogue, which at this point actually provides a few better options than the Web-based cata-

change we have informally noted is distance students are recognizing the necessity of and are more willing to make an investment in the technology. As a result, they are prepared to meet the expectations and demands of the courses, and can therefore take more responsibility and control of their research.

DISADVANTAGES

When it comes to the electronic technologies, there are disadvantages that cannot be ignored, and must be taken into consideration when evaluating how a new tool may or may not enhance the service. There is tremendous pressure to jump on the bandwagon, to be on the "cutting edge," to be seen as forward thinking, and to have the advantage over the competitors. This pressure often encourages institutions to jump too soon without consideration to the market it serves. Sometimes, it may be all right not to be on the "cutting edge."

Something that is easy to overlook, goes unnoticed until it isn't working, is time consuming, but is very important, is the maintenance, upkeep, upgrades and regular testing of all the various tools we employ. The more technical options we provide, the more we have to change, fix, correct, improve, check, update, and so on. It is critical to have an organized maintenance program. User frustration and impatience with poorly maintained tools can be very detrimental to distance education and ultimately the organization.

With so many rapid changes in technology and with products quickly becoming obsolete, it is very challenging to keep up. It is a balancing act to determine when, how or why it is necessary to change, and the ripple effect of a change in on campus technology to the end users of that technology. Choosing the "right" technology for the needs of delivery of distance education should involve careful evaluation, collaboration and feedback from users, and constructive criticism to the creators and vendors of the products.

CONCLUSION

The downside of providing a seamless, highly efficient service is that sometimes it can be rendered invisible and taken for granted. We have to remember that we are often not the only ones who are invisible; our users are also not a highly visible group. To overcome this barrier, technology can be used effectively to make distance education and library support more visible to users and potential users. Creative use of Web pages, online tutorials, finding aids, electronic forms for requests and feedback, and clear links to and from other Web pages can all be beneficial in raising the profile. What should not be overlooked or underestimated is the librarian who is easily accessible to the user and who is directing the technology.

The advantages of the new technological tools in delivering distance service are obvious. We are able to offer our distance learners far more options and avenues. This, in turn, provides convenience, eliminates barriers of distance and isolation, saves the learner time, streamlines procedures and document delivery, makes communication easier, and can be used to provide library instruction in a way that was not previously possible.

There is also something to be said for the sheer convenience the technology gives distance learners in terms of distance learning, library support and library access, and communication. What it really means is that distance is no longer an insurmountable factor in preventing students from getting the education they want and require.

REFERENCES

Association of College and Research Libraries. (1998). ACRL guidelines for distance learning library services. *College & Research Libraries News, 59,* 689-694.

Barley, S. R. (1999, October). Computer-based distance education: Why and why not? *The Education Digest 65*(2), 55-59.

Canada aiming to be world's most wired nation. (1998 June 29). *Computing Canada,* 27.

Cooper, R. & Dempsey, P. R. (1998). Remote library users–Needs and expectations. *Library Trends 47*(1), 42-65.

Crone, G. (1999, July 7). Logging on to Online U. *Financial Post,* p. C6.

Dewald, N. H. (1999). Web-based library instruction: What is good pedagogy? *Information Technology and Libraries 18,* 1, 26-31.

Library Services for Distance Learning Interest Group Canadian Library Association. (1993). Guidelines for library support of distance learning in Canada. *CACUL Occasional Paper Series,* no. 8.

Kirk, E. E. & Bartelstein, A. M. (1999). Libraries close in on distance education. *Library Journal 124*(6), 40-43.

Luther, J. (1998). Distance learning and the digital library. *Educom Review 33*(4), 22-27.

Martin, C. (1998, January/February). Telelearning in Canada. *Teaching Magazine*, 25-28.

Naval, M. (1998, June 8). Companies go the distance with on-line education program. *Computer Dealer News, 14,* 9-10.

Niemi, J. A., Ehrhard, B. J. & Neeley, L. (1998). Off-campus library support for distance adult learners. *Library Trends 47*(1), 65-74.

Online learning takes off. (1999, November 13). *Prince George Citizen,* p. 43.

Sheppard, R. (1998, November 23). Reinventing the classroom: riding the tide of change. *Maclean's 111*(47), 64.

Universities 1999: Primarily Undergraduate. (1999, November 15). *Maclean's 112*(46), 68.

White, H. S. (1999). The changes in off-campus education. *Library Journal 124*(3), 128-130.

Wolpert, A. (1998). Services to remote users: Marketing the library's role. *Library Trends 47*(1), 21-41.

APPENDIX A. Map of British Columbia

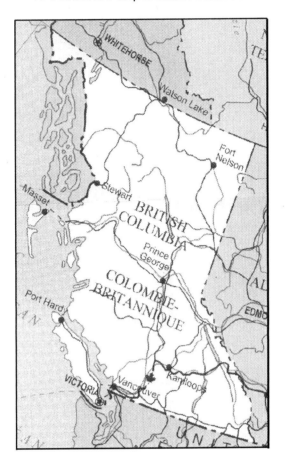

APPENDIX B. Regional Sites Served by the University of Northern British Columbia

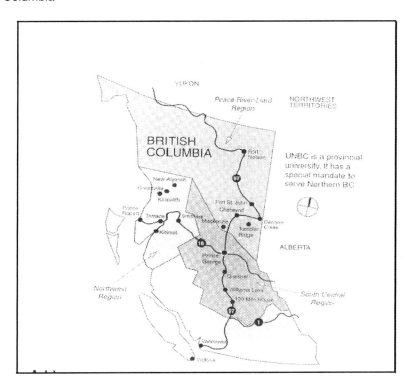

. . . And a Free 800 Line! Managing Technical and Information Support for Distance Education

Amy Blair

Michigan State University

SUMMARY. Library Distance Learning Services (LDLS) at Michigan State University was developed in 1993 as a result of the campus-wide adoption of a decentralized model for services to our off-campus population. With its "high-tech, high-touch" philosophy, LDLS has taken on increasing responsibilities in information delivery and triage through increased use of its 800 line, e-mail and Web technologies.

KEYWORDS. Library services, distance education, technical support

THE PAST

Back in the day, we put the books in the trunk of the car, drove them to the nearest reasonable location to that particular off-campus program, and left them there for periods of time that often stretched to years because we simply forgot about them. We relied on the phone for requesting, the U.S. Mail for delivery, or faxing, but only if we felt

[Haworth co-indexing entry note]: ". . . And a Free 800 Line! Managing Technical and Information Support for Distance Education." Blair, Amy. Co-published simultaneously in *Journal of Library Administration* (The Haworth Information Press, an imprint of The Haworth Press, Inc.) Vol. 31, No. 3/4, 2001, pp. 61-65; and: *Off-Campus Library Services* (ed: Anne Marie Casey) The Haworth Information Press, an imprint of The Haworth Press, Inc., 2001, pp. 61-65.

daring and desperate. The campus-wide decentralization of services to off-campus programs and units in the early nineties paved the way for the reconstitution and renaissance of Library Distance Learning Services (LDLS) at Michigan State University (MSU).

The impetus for rebirth arrived in 1993 in the form of a need for library and information services to support the 82 county MSU Extension offices. This was followed almost immediately by a request from the College of Nursing to provide services to off-campus students located in the four off-campus MSN programs in Michigan. Services included research assistance and information delivery via fax, U.S. Mail, or UPS. The technology of the time included a telnet version of the library catalog and a few basic telnet accessible indexes, such as Medline, PsycINFO, and ACAD (Expanded Academic Index).

Following the installment of our 800 number, courtesy of an internal grant from University Outreach at Michigan State University, the period from 1994-1996 found us establishing partnerships for library services with other selected Michigan libraries, establishing a reputation as being solid, reliable, and rapid, and marketing our services campus-wide to those colleges and departments developing off-campus courses and programs. We are designed to use the increasing amount of technology available to make information delivery faster and more efficient.

In the mid-nineties, the rise of Web technology allowed us to increase the number and usefulness of online indexes, most notably the Electronic Reference Library, as well as provide our first "full-text" database in the form of ACAD. Although in reality only 20% full-text, ACAD's availability marked the turning point in providing a heightened form of access for remote users.

The development of MSU's Virtual University in 1997 increased our clientele dramatically and expanded the scope of the 800 line from a relatively straightforward request line to an information triage line that provides technical support, information/referral, general course information, and information delivery/research assistance for students/faculty/staff in off-campus programs, units, and the Virtual University. We provide assistance to virtually everyone!

1999 finds the 800 number prominently displayed on the new MSU home page as the number to call for questions about the MSU pages. The 800 number is now printed on the back of every student and faculty ID card, as well as the Classroom Help Card provided to all teaching faculty. As a result of the most recent library reorganization (1999), the main information lines of the library are now located in Library Distance Learning Services, allowing us to build upon the information triage skills developed with the 800 lines.

THE PRESENT

The unit is currently staffed with 3.5 FTES and 75 student hours/ week to provide 90 hours of coverage and service within the library. In order to provide 800 line coverage 24 × 7, the 800 lines are transferred to Computer Operations at 10 p.m. nightly until 8 a.m. the following morning. LDLS receives over 2000 calls per month. Calls can be divided into the following topics:

The 800 Line

- Distance Learning/Extension Requests
- Virtual University Questions
  - Course Information
  - Enrollment Support
  - Technical Support
- Technical Assistance
  - Pilot Accounts
  - Dial-Up Assistance (MichNet)
  - Troubleshooting
  - Transfer to Computer Consulting
- General MSU Information
- "Gateway" to MSU

- CBT (Computer Based Training)
  - Software Support
  - Enrollment
  - Course Access
- MSU Marketing
  - InfoRetriever
  - Easing Cancer Pain CD
- Math
  - Math Placement Exam
  - Fundamentals of Math
- Various University Projects
  - Early Reservation System
  - Academic Orientation Program
- And, oh, so much more...

Statistics for articles/books/research requests have remained fairly constant for the past five years, even with the increase in off-campus and VU programs and the subsequent increase in students. This can most likely be attributed to the increased availability of full-text databases and full-text journals online that are provided through the library Web site at http://www.lib.msu.edu. Statistics are as follows:

- Total Number of Students in Off-Campus/VU Programs (FS99)
  - **4419/year**
- Average number of articles sent (94/95 - 98/99)
  - **2800/year**
- Average number of books sent (94/95 - 98/99)
  - **235/year**
- Average number of research requests (94/95 - 98/99)
  - **178/year**
- Average number of fiche titles copied (94/95 - 98/99)
  - **94/year**

LDLS serves a wide variety of MSU programs:

Current Distance
Learning Programs:

- Nursing:
  - Kalamazoo
  - Okemos
  - Lansing
  - Muskegon
- Social Work:
  - Saginaw
  - Marquette
- Regionals: - Non-cohort group courses
  - North Regional
  - South-East Regional
  - Upper Peninsula Regional
  - West Regional
- Virtual University
- K-12 in Philanthropy

- Agriculture and Extension Education (AEE)
- Applied Plant Science (APS)
- Battle Creek Food Science
- Community University Healthcare Partnership (CUHP)
- Criminal Justice
- Ecology Administration
- Education Administration (EAD)
- Epidemiology
- FCE – Masters in Child Development
- H A L E Program
- Human Environment and Design (HED)
- Independent Study (Doctoral)
- Kalamazoo Center for Medical Studies
- Master of Arts in Curriculum and Teaching (M.A.C.T.)
- Outreach Adjunct - Nursing
- Outreach Adjunct - Veterinary
- Teacher Education

We can be contacted in any of the following ways–800 line, fax, e-mail, or via request forms on our Web site at: http://www.lib.msu.edu/outreach.

At present, here's exactly what we do:

Here's exactly what we do...

- Information Delivery
  - Articles - Faxed, Mailed, UPSed
  - Books - UPSed
  - Quick Reference
  - E-mail Reference
  - Interlibrary Loans
- Research Assistance
  - Database Searching (including the Web)
  - Search Formulation for the "do-it-yourselfer."
- Technical Assistance
  - Authorization/Activation
  - Troubleshooting/Triage
  - 800 Line Assistance
  - Training - Information Literacy and more!

THE FUTURE

Although normally unpredictable at best, there are a few trends and events that should occur in 2000. Our beta testing of a proxy server to provide access for all to our IP accessible databases such as Lexis-Nexis should be available in Spring 2000. This will further increase the amount of full-text available and provide greater access for the MSU population. Greater access to more databases and online journals will increase the need for training while maintaining, or perhaps decreasing, the need for article delivery.

Calls to the 800 line and the library information lines will continue to increase as a result of new programs, new students, and new technologies. LDLS will also begin to handle reference triage in the Spring of 2000, with all calls to the Main Library Reference Desk funneled through the LDLS main information lines. The reference calls will be immediately answered in LDLS using basic reference tools or directed to the appropriate reference area.

We will continue to provide a level of service that is "high-tech and high-touch" as we promote the concept of "The MSU Libraries–Information at your fingertips."

Extending Library Boundaries
Without Losing the Personal Touch

Dianne Brownlee
Frances Ebbers

St. Edward's University

SUMMARY. Providing library services to a distance education site removed from a main campus poses problems for libraries, especially for St. Edward's University, a small academic library that wishes to retain the personal, nurturing relationships it fosters with library patrons. Problems we were committed to solving included providing an environment conducive to lifelong learning and remaining true to the library's teaching mission. Because no increase in library staff was budgeted, current library staff members had to be amenable to adding new duties to provide an infrastructure of services to distance education students that were similar to services offered to our on-campus community.

KEYWORDS. Library services, distance education, librarians

St. Edward's University, a small, private Catholic-affiliated liberal arts university in Austin, Texas, is recognized within the community for its values-based curriculum, small classes, low teacher/student ratio, and caring faculty and staff. The university has a growing program of off-campus courses, not unlike many other institutions across the United States. The ever-increasing commitment of resources to these programs challenges the Scarborough-Phillips Library to provide personalized service to a new population of students enrolled in

[Haworth co-indexing entry note]: "Extending Library Boundaries Without Losing the Personal Touch." Brownlee, Dianne, and Frances Ebbers. Co-published simultaneously in *Journal of Library Administration* (The Haworth Information Press, an imprint of The Haworth Press, Inc.) Vol. 31, No. 3/4, 2001, pp. 67-73; and: *Off-Campus Library Services* (ed: Anne Marie Casey) The Haworth Information Press, an imprint of The Haworth Press, Inc., 2001, pp. 67-73.

distance education courses, as well as to the many students and other patrons who simply wish to access the library from a remote location.

Within the university community, the Scarborough-Phillips Library enjoys a well-deserved reputation among faculty, staff, and students for providing a high-level of customer service to library patrons. These services include a library that is open 103 hours a week, a reference desk that is staffed by professional librarians 64 hours a week, individual student appointments with librarians, librarian visits to faculty offices, individualized library instruction seminars offered several times a month, and a bibliographic instruction program of approximately 250 classes a year taught in library instruction class-rooms, as well as off-campus locations. At the core of this service philosophy is the library mission statement which affirms the provision of "equal access to library service."

With an enrollment of approximately 3600 students, St. Edward's offers traditional four-year bachelor's degrees in the Arts and Sciences, as well as two graduate degrees, a Master of Business Administration and a Master of Arts in Human Services. In addition, St. Edward's has a twenty-seven year long experience with a highly successful New College program; an undergraduate degree-seeking program aimed at adults returning to college. Two years ago a fast-track Bachelor of Business Administration completion program called PACE (Program for an Accelerated College Education) was added to New College's offerings. Recently, the University's graduate and New College programs have been further expanded and a conscious commitment made to double the number of non-traditional students in five years.

While the library has always had a commitment to provide library services that meet the needs of adult students, with growing New College, MBA, and MAHS programs comprised primarily of adults living an average of 10-50 miles away from campus and a number of students enrolled from other Texas cities and even other states, library staff anticipated the need to further expand library services beyond its physical boundaries. In July 1992 the library's online catalog made its debut, with remote access available through dial-up modem. The following year, UMI's ABI/Inform and Periodical Abstracts were made available through the Information Gateway of the online catalog through data tape loading. As the technological capabilities of the World Wide Web advanced, the library discontinued loading tapes of database abstracts, and contracted to offer a then fledgling group of online databases, accessible from the library's Web page.

Ever mindful of the need to serve a diverse and increasingly remote student population, the library has subsequently entered into a number of consortia agreements which resulted in access to Web-based library resources, including InfoTrac, OVID, Ebscohost, Lexis-Nexis, IDEAL full-text journals, OCLC (60 databases), CQ Researcher, Austin American-Statesman, Ethnic Newswatch, Zack's Investment Research, Electric Library, ACM Digital Library, Encyclopedia Britannica, The Handbook of Texas, College Catalogs Online, Federal Register Online, CCH-Capital Changes, and CCH-Standard Federal Tax Reports (current as of September 1999).

The mission statement written specifically for distance services emphasizes that the library is committed to "providing distant students with ready access to materials, services, and professional instruction that are pertinent to the programs offered by the university and sufficient to support the educational needs of off-campus students." The Scarborough-Phillips Library endorses the *ACRL Guidelines for Distance Learning Library Services* and its clearly stated mandate to provide "access to adequate library services and resources."

Realizing the need to offer classes and degree programs to a growing population of students located in Williamson County, 25 miles northwest of the campus, the University joined a cooperative consortium of area institutions called a MITC or Multi-Institutional Teaching Center located at suburban Westwood High School. To coordinate the various services needed to support this distance education program, the duties of a Distance Services Librarian were assumed by Fran Ebbers, currently Circulation/Reference Librarian and System Administrator. Several meetings between circulation, reference, interlibrary loan, and instruction personnel were held to anticipate the types of services that would need to be coordinated among these various departments. Each of these staff members and librarians agreed to assume additional responsibilities to extend personalized service to off-campus students.

Although it is impossible to clone the friendly, service-oriented circulation staff at a remote site, efforts are made to maintain a close liaison with students at program orientations and during library instruction sessions. Claudia Kweder, Circulation Supervisor, who determines whether the request can be filled through our collection, handles all requests for books by distance students. If so, Claudia retrieves the books, checks them out to the user on the library system, and packages materials for courier delivery. Requests for books not in our collection are routed to Interlibrary Loan. In addition, Claudia makes a point of personally contacting the patron with an anticipated delivery date as well as due date information and options for returning materials to the library through the courier service. The Interlibrary Loan Department handles all requests for journal articles. ILL also coordinates the courier delivery and pickup as well as maintaining a supply of packaging materials at the off campus location. E-mail reference service is offered to distance students and a reference librarian volunteers to respond to all e-mail requests within 24 hours. Dianne Brownlee, Instructional Services Librarian, travels to the off-campus site each semester to deliver personalized library instruction for classes as well as orientation sessions for students new to the programs.

When the off-campus program began in earnest in fall 1998, a full complement of classes was held at Westwood High School, 25 miles northwest of the campus. Fortuitously, the summer prior to the beginning of the MITC consortial agreement, Tex-Share membership was offered to private universities and colleges in Texas. This meant that St. Edward's University could participate in a statewide program, which offers courier service to all Tex-Share libraries throughout the state at a greatly reduced price compared to private courier service. Another part of the Tex-Share program is a reciprocal borrowing agreement and a commitment to interlibrary loan sharing of resources.

A strong working relationship was established with the librarians at the Westwood High School Library site. The MITC contracted with the school district to keep the Westwood library open additional hours from Monday through Thursday when classes were conducted. In addition, daily courier service was begun from the St. Edward's campus to the Westwood site. The Westwood librarians agreed to receive both interlibrary loan and books loaned from our regular collection, check identification of patrons, and package the books for return by courier to the Scarborough-Phillips Library. In return, St. Edward's library staff demonstrated the online Web catalog to the Westwood librarians and agreed to lend some of our collection to Westwood high school students in the International Baccalaureate program. Dianne

Brownlee, Instructional Services librarian, traveled to Westwood each semester for on-site bibliographic instruction. Westwood is technologically well equipped, but IP authentication to online databases was a problem from that site. On several occasions, a circulation staff member assisted at the library orientation sessions to explain circulation services. The library established a visible link on its Web page, which gives information about services to off-campus students and contact information, including direct telephone numbers and e-mail addresses. Courier service from the Westwood site to St. Edward's was also offered to students who attend classes on campus, but who found it more convenient to return materials to Westwood for courier delivery to the library.

After the program had been in place for a year at the Westwood High School location, St. Edward's University was offered the chance to partner with Motorola University and offer its MBA, PACE and New College classes from their site. This necessitated an evaluation of services and the need to revise policies. Because of security concerns, negotiations with the site coordinator at Motorola University became necessary. Since students no longer have access to a library facility, albeit a high school library, contact is now made through a St. Edward's University site administrator located at Motorola. Negotiations are currently under way to provide courier service to the new site. Once the program has been in place for several months, a re-assessment will be conducted to determine the need for a mobile reference collection on-site. Although the Motorola University site offers the latest technology for student and instructor use, IP authentication for licensed database access remained a problem. In fall 1999, the university's computer services department launched a proxy server for students using ISPs other than that of St. Edward's University.

The staff of Scarborough-Phillips Library is very sensitive to the possibility that expansion of services to off-campus students is sometimes done at the expense of depersonalizing the process. Because our remote users are often distance learners, we found it useful to benchmark what we consider to be basic needs and expectations with regard to services currently offered by the library.

Users expect constant, around-the-clock access to online databases mounted on user-friendly systems. We meet this goal, despite the fact that vendor's platforms are beyond our control. Our online catalog is intuitive and contains numerous help screens. Our catalog is down for maintenance during publicized hours from 10 p.m. Saturday night to 10 a.m. Sunday morning, while access to online databases is still available. The computer itself is taken down only for repair or upgrade.

Users may expect twenty-four hour help desk or technical support. Realistically, we will not meet this goal. Neither the computer help desk nor the library's technical support staff are available all the hours the library is open. However, we do offer instructions for solving technical problems through information posted both to the library's Web page and that of Instructional Technology. Our Web page also contains instructions for connecting to the proxy server and contacts for assistance.

What we can offer is a concerted effort to establish a personal relationship between library staff and off-campus students. We meet this goal with a public services staff that is more than willing to assist patrons in their information needs. We provide e-mail reference, online reference help, and book and journal request forms on our Web page. We make an attempt to personally contact remote patrons who request materials to clarify delivery options. In fact, our circulation staff is so service oriented that one staff member agreed to deliver materials to a patron in a parking lot near her home after she left work at 11 p.m.

We are working to provide extensive information describing specific resources and the full range of services available at the "home" library. This is a goal in progress as we provide more handouts on line and other self-help information. We are working to boost the amount of information available through our Web page.

Many libraries provide a greater range of services such as conducting online database searches for their students with less emphasis on creating lifelong learners. Our library mission statement differs slightly from this goal because of our commitment to teaching. We instruct our patrons in online database searching in bibliographic instruction classes and one-on-one at the reference desk. We also provide our students with handouts that explain our catalog, online databases and search strategies. At this time, we are working to provide all of our handouts online on our Web page.

As more students become "distant" from their home institution, they will need to use a variety of libraries in addition to the "home" library to complete their academic assignments. We meet this goal with our participation in the Tex-Share program that allows patrons to request a Tex-Share card for courtesy borrower privileges at any academic library throughout the state of Texas.

On a campus with a twenty-seven year tradition of providing a nontraditional program of study, our library staff is experienced in identifying discrete groups of users: off campus, nontraditional, New College, Motorola University, and traditional undergraduates. The challenge has been to anticipate the needs of each group. To this end, we conduct an annual survey of library services. In the future, we plan an online survey on our Web page. We provide a personalized program of library instruction for all off-campus courses. Our Web page has a special section specifically for off-campus programs at Motorola University. In addition, we provide courier service to the off-campus site at no charge to our patrons.

As the university anticipates the growth of its off-campus programs, the library is maintaining a proactive position rather than reactive. Faculty and students may expect that their distance learning experiences will be the same as their experiences in traditional educational settings, which may lead to service expectations that can be unrealistic. It is important, therefore, for any library providing service to distant users to anticipate user expectations.

We have found open communication between faculty, students, library staff, and managers at the remote location to be an important part of a successful distance education program. However, for the Scarborough-Phillips Library, the vital ingredients necessary to provide personalized service to remote library users have been a more creative use of resources and a committed staff willing to change roles and take on additional responsibilities.

REFERENCES

Cooper, R., & Dempsey, P. R. (1998). Remote library users-needs and expectations. *Library Trends, 47*, 42-65.

Kirk, E. E, & Bartelstein, A. M. (1999, April 1). Libraries close in on distance education. *Library Journal, 124*(6), 40-43.

Luther, J. (1998). Distance learning and the digital library. *Educom Review, 33*(4), 22-27.

Niemi, J. A., Ehrhard, B. J., & Neely, L. (1998). Off campus library support for distance adult learners. *Library Trends, 47*, 66-76.

Consortium Solutions
to Distance Education Problems:
Utah Academic Libraries
Answer the Challenges

Amy Brunvand
Daniel R. Lee
Kathleen M. McCloskey

University of Utah

Carol Hansen

Weber State University

Carol A. Kochan
Rob Morrison

Utah State University

SUMMARY. The Utah Academic Library Consortium (UALC) is continuing to develop cooperative projects to serve both on campus and distance learners. By cooperating rather than competing, UALC libraries are developing a package of services available to all academic students in Utah to support new and existing distance education programs. This paper describes collaborative efforts to increase information resource access statewide to meet the needs of distance learners and take advantage of changing technologies.

KEYWORDS. Library consortia, library services, distance education

[Haworth co-indexing entry note]: "Consortium Solutions to Distance Education Problems: Utah Academic Libraries Answer the Challenges." Brunvand et al. Co-published simultaneously in *Journal of Library Administration* (The Haworth Information Press, an imprint of The Haworth Press, Inc.) Vol. 31, No. 3/4, 2001, pp. 75-92; and: *Off-Campus Library Services* (ed: Anne Marie Casey) The Haworth Information Press, an imprint of The Haworth Press, Inc., 2001, pp. 75-92.

INTRODUCTION

There are two categories of problems facing distance education students–technological problems and bureaucratic problems. Solving most technological problems is a simple matter of programming.[1] Bureaucratic problems, in comparison, can be really difficult to solve. On-campus students face minimal bureaucratic problems when they tackle standard library research tasks such as getting a library card, signing up for a computer account, browsing books on library shelves to select the ones they need, requesting interlibrary loans, attending library instruction short courses, or identifying interesting publications using computer databases. For distance education students, bureaucratic barriers to the same services can be insurmountable. A single barrier can mean the student is cut off from library resources. In addition to students' information access problems, Utah academic libraries face other critical issues, including journal pricing, competition for students and state funds, historic lack of support for library collections, and few librarians with experience serving distance learners.

The Utah Academic Library Consortium (UALC) is a group of 14 academic, medical and law libraries at nine public and two private higher education institutions plus the Utah State Library. Utah has been able to cut through some of the bureaucratic red tape by developing cooperative projects to serve both distance education and on-campus students. UALC member libraries have developed cooperative borrowing agreements, statewide licensing of databases, shared information literacy courses, document delivery options and cooperative collection development. The success of cooperation led Utah libraries to seek and receive a statewide pool of academic library funding from the Utah Legislature. These statewide programs give all Utah students access to a standardized set of library and information services regardless of what resources their own institution's library can offer. By cooperating rather than competing, UALC libraries are developing a package of services available to all academic students in Utah to support new and existing distance education programs.

OVERVIEW OF DISTANCE EDUCATION IN UTAH

Nine public schools comprise the Utah System of Higher Education (USHE). There are four universities: the University of Utah (Salt Lake

City), Utah State University (Logan), Weber State University (Ogden), and Southern Utah University (Cedar City). The four community colleges are: Salt Lake Community College, College of Eastern Utah (Price), Dixie College (St. George), and Snow College (Ephraim). Utah Valley State College (Orem) is the sole state college. Along with private school UALC members, Westminster College (Salt Lake City) and Brigham Young University (Provo), UALC libraries serve over 151,000 students. Statistics on distance learners are not uniformly reported and obtaining precise statistics is difficult. According to an article in *The Salt Lake Tribune* (Egan, 1999), 25,000 students enrolled in distance learning classes in Utah in 1998, and of these, 8,200 were enrolled in Utah State University programs. Full time equivalent distance education students in Utah numbered 2,150.

The Utah State Board of Regents is the governing body of USHE in conjunction with each institution's Board of Trustees. Appointed by the governor, this board oversees policies, procedures, and planning for higher education. The Commissioner of Higher Education also serves as the Chief Executive Officer for the Board of Regents.

The USHE Technology and Distance Education Initiative is administered by the Board of Regents' Telecommunications Advisory Committee. This initiative is a long-range plan to "enhance education through new and advanced technologies" (USHE, 1999c, 1999d) and to address rising higher education enrollments through technology rather than through building traditional campuses. Goals include using technology to remove "time and place barriers," providing quality access to technology-delivered education, supporting a knowledge-based economy, and changing the focus from a teacher-centered to a learner-centered education. Funding is based on one-time legislative appropriations plus ongoing funds. Grants are available to public institutions for developing technology-delivered courses.

The Higher Education Technology Initiative (HETI) provided grants for curriculum development. For example, HETI helped Utah State University develop a master's program in Instructional Technology, now delivered on the EDNET system, and also provided start-up funds for the creation of online courses at many institutions.

The Utah Education Network (UEN) is a partnership between public and higher education which coordinates the electronic delivery of courses, degrees and educational resources to Utah citizens. UEN delivers telecourses through two channels, KUED (Channel 7) and

KULC (Channel 9). UtahLINK is an online service providing educational resources for students and teachers (Smith, 1995). Many public institutions deliver courses and degree programs through EDNET and the Utah Education Network Satellite System (UENSS). EDNET is a two-way video and audio microwave network, with nearly two hundred sites at academic institutions, state offices, and public schools. UENSS is an interactive digital satellite broadcast system providing one-way video and two-way audio courses. UENSS was funded in 1997 by the Utah Legislature to replace Utah State University's old telephone-based distance delivery network. As of Autumn 1999, eighty-five UENSS sites have been established, including several in Colorado, Nevada, and Wyoming. Eventually, this system is expected to link with satellite networks in other states to enhance the Western Governors University.

A Council of Chief Academic Officers (CAO) acts as a review board for all statewide technology-delivered courses and programs. This group is responsible for reviewing all aspects of distance delivery for the Board of Regents and coordinating activities with UEN. Specific activities include making funding recommendations and developing, planning and formulating needs assessment criteria for distance delivery of higher education. A separate Telecommunications Advisory Committee, also established by the Board of Regents, coordinates UEN, KUED, Channel 9, and EDNET. A centralized operations center is located at the University of Utah.

The Utah Electronic Community College is a new consortium of the state's five community colleges. Courses are available through a single online catalog with the goal of providing all Utah residents with access to two-year degrees. Degrees are granted from one school but courses can be taken from any of the participating schools. Courses are delivered by EDNET, CD-ROM, videotape, and television.

University Centers were established to deliver upper-division, mainly baccalaureate courses to two-year schools. There are five centers around the state that offer degree-granting programs to students who are unable to attend four-year schools. Policies established by the Board of Regents assign main library service responsibility to the host college, though the delivering institution augments library resources. These are the only policies specifically addressing library services for distance learners.

The Board of Regents created policies to coordinate and plan all courses and degree programs delivered by statewide networks. *Policy R355: Planning, Funding, and Delivery of Courses and Programs by Statewide Telecommunications Networks* (USHE, 1999b) provides the framework for this process. Policy *R315: Service Areas for Off-Campus Courses and Programs* (USHE, 1999a) designates specific geographic "service areas" where lower division, upper division, graduate, and applied technology programs are assigned to specific institutions. Institutions must seek approval by the Board of Regents before delivering programs outside their "designated service area."

These policies provide guidelines for addressing "turf wars" between institutions. For years, Utah State University, the state's land grant institution, delivered lower and upper division classes and degree programs into the "backyards" of other schools but is now limited in many locations to providing only graduate-level programs. Tuition dollars are collected into a central fund by the Regents and doled out to the public institutions on a formula basis. Public institutions receive funding based on FTE's and not actual students, which results in fewer resources for support services. The Regents' policies do allow institutions to receive full tuition and funding for distance learners. This makes enrolling distance learners attractive from a financial perspective and spurs competition for these students.

UTAH HIGHER EDUCATION CHANGES AND CHALLENGES

The Utah State Board of Regents (1999) compiled a list by county of degree programs offered by all USHE institutions. This report lists associate, bachelor's and master's level degree programs offered by specific colleges and universities in each county. A total of 1,108 degrees are offered in 29 Utah counties. A county by county examination reveals that 419 programs are available outside of the "home" county where a public institution is located. This report does not include online courses.

Higher education enrollments increased more than 40% at USHE institutions in the 1990's–from 86,177 students in 1990 to 122,417 students in 1999. USHE and Governor Michael Leavitt are focusing on technological means of delivering courses to accommodate the increase in student population rather than on "bricks and mortar."

Politics has played a powerful role as local legislators lobby for upgrades to schools in their own districts, bypassing the Board of

Regents. When a school is allowed to expand the scope and academic level of its degree programs, libraries have not received a corresponding upgrade in resources to support the new programs.

Technology is rapidly increasing the viability of distance information delivery. Projects that were impossible using CD jukeboxes or tape loads function smoothly on the Internet, and all USHE institutions utilize distance delivery technology or offer online courses. Five schools received legislative funding to establish branch campuses this decade, despite the emphasis on using technology. Continual outreach efforts are needed to keep faculty at remote sites aware of what library services are offered (Rozum & Brewer, 1997). The number of distance learners is increasing and distance education providers will be major players in Utah's higher education future.

UALC AND LIBRARIES 2000

Morrison et al. (1995) note that while there is stiff competition between schools for students and state funding, Utah academic libraries have had a strong history of cooperation. In 1997, this spirit of cooperation led UALC to approach the Utah Legislature with a proposal called *Libraries 2000* which was a request for shared statewide funding for library information resources and services. *Libraries 2000* proposed a combined effort to fight the ongoing battle of journal price inflation and to provide more resources for every library than could be purchased by any library acting on its own. The request to the Legislature stated:

> The libraries seek funding for projected inflation in library materials for the next three years. By pooling inflationary funding in a line item appropriated to the Regents for distribution, this initiative will offer each institution more value for dollars invested than would be received if each library received an individual allocation. Part of the funding will be used for cooperative projects to enlarge the pool of information resources available in the state by encouraging the purchase of new titles (print or electronic) not yet held in the state, by discouraging duplicate holdings, and by utilizing state-wide purchases of print and digital books and journals. (Utah Academic Library Consortium Council, 1997)

The 1997 Utah Legislature appropriated $3.1 million to fund *Libraries 2000,* and in March, 1997 UALC librarians met at the University of Utah to answer the following questions and decide how best to accomplish the goals of *Libraries 2000*:

- Can we build a true statewide collection, rewarding the cancellation of duplicate subscriptions and encouraging subscriptions to journals not held in state?
- Can we move journal articles from UALC libraries to patron desktops? How fast?
- How can we better serve Distance Learning Students?

Libraries 2000 statewide collection development initiatives along with pre-existing UALC cooperative projects have built a package of standardized services for all academic students in Utah. These services support new and existing distance education programs and guarantee that Utah distance education students will have access to a certain level of library resources. UALC services include: Academic Pioneer, cooperative collection development, reciprocal borrowing, Utah Article Delivery, online library instruction, and promoting services to faculty and students.

ACADEMIC PIONEER: ACCESS TO ELECTRONIC DATABASES AND FULL-TEXT

The *Academic Pioneer Vision Statement* states that Pioneer will "offer digital library collections and electronic services selected to serve the needs of students, faculty, and staff of the member libraries of UALC, regardless of their location–on campus, at home, across the state, or around the world" (Utah Academic Library Consortium Council, 1999). When *PC Week* magazine selected its 1999 "Fast-Track 100" list for educational and government institutions "that are most innovative in their use of cutting-edge technologies and applications," the Utah information-technology networks were ranked first and fifth, respectively. One of the projects cited was the Pioneer online library project (Moad, 1999).

Pioneer: Utah's Online Library is a set of statewide licensed databases divided into Academic Pioneer (the full selection for UALC member libraries) and Pioneer (a subset of Academic Pioneer databases which are licensed for access from all public, school and academic libraries). Partners in the Pioneer project include public libraries, higher education, public education, UEN, and the State of Utah.

The Pioneer Committee and UALC statewide collection development subject initiatives guide the choice of resources. The Pioneer homepage includes links to local information such as Utah government information, and genealogical resources, as well as "premium Pioneer databases" purchased for all Utah citizens through statewide or UALC consortium licensing agreements. The premium databases include periodical indexes and reference sources, as well as access to the archives of the two major local newspapers, *The Salt Lake Tribune* and *The Desert News*. As part of Academic Pioneer, the UALC Science Initiative has been able to offer full-text scientific journals from the Association of Computing Machinery, American Chemical Society, Canada Institute for Scientific and Technical Information, and the Institute of Physics. The UALC Education Initiative selected Exceptional Child Education Resources and Education Abstracts Full Text, and Criminal Justice Abstracts was acquired to support a criminal justice distance learning degree.

The library systems department at the University of Utah's Marriott Library provides technical support for the Academic Pioneer. All UALC libraries can link from the Web to resources offered by both Pioneer and Academic Pioneer. The relative technological simplicity of the Web has made statewide distribution more practical than previous resource sharing attempts using CD-ROM jukeboxes or tape loads. Statewide availability of Pioneer databases and resources has made it possible for Utah libraries to collaborate on help sheets and library instruction. Pioneer gives students at small schools access to specialized databases and full text journals that would otherwise be out of the price range or collection development focus of smaller collections.

Authorization is still a problem. UALC has voted money to purchase proxy servers for all smaller schools, but getting them to work is the proverbial "simple matter of programming." In theory all students should have access to Pioneer, in practice off-campus access depends on local technological expertise.

RECIPROCAL BORROWING PROGRAM

The UALC reciprocal borrowing program was established in 1982 in order to extend library services to students, faculty, and staff throughout the Utah academic community. The cooperative borrowing agreement lets a patron from any UALC library borrow circulating materials directly from any other UALC library. Patrons may return the materials to the interlibrary loan office of their own library. One problem that remains to be solved for cooperative borrowing is the problem of valid borrowers having proper identification, since many distance education students are not issued official identification cards. To address this problem, the agreement was recently revised to allow patrons to checkout materials with a picture ID and proof of current registration. This program is a cornerstone of a true statewide collection, and UALC committees are planning to promote it more heavily.

UTAH ARTICLE DELIVERY (UTAD)

Utah Article Delivery (UTAD) is a patron initiated, fax-based document delivery service developed to speed the delivery of journal articles between UALC member libraries. The goals of the program are to:

- Provide article delivery in a time frame defined by patron expectations.
- Promote the notion of a single Utah academic library collection as opposed to individual institutional collections.
- Serve as a collection development tool by identifying journals that should be part of a statewide collection.
- Provide interlibrary services and/or document delivery services to distance education students.

At the time UTAD was developed, many distance education students in Utah had little or no access to interlibrary services. For example, Utah State University, whose students form the largest contingent of distance learners, did an excellent job of providing library materials from their own collection through the Distance Education Library Services office, but did not provide interlibrary services to these students. Remote students usually relied on local public libraries, drove to the nearest academic library, or did without important library materials.

The UTAD planning process and the goals of the project are discussed by Kochan & Lee (1998). A model of patron initiated document delivery had already been tested at Utah State University (Kochan & Elsweiler, 1998). Eventually a plan was developed that allows users to e-mail requests for journal articles from a Web-based form and receive the requested articles on their personal or office fax machine. Requests come to the Marriott Library at the University of Utah where staff look up UALC journal holdings on OCLC and process requests as follows:

1. Requests for articles available at the requestor's home library are cancelled.
2. If the requested article is available at the Marriott Library a copy is faxed directly to the requestor.
3. If the article is unavailable at the Marriott Library but available in another UALC library, the request is forwarded to that library and filled from there.
4. If the article is not available at UALC libraries, the request is forwarded to Infotrieve, a commercial document supplier, and faxed directly to the requestor at no charge. In all cases, the published expectation is that the requestor will receive his or her article within two working days. In many cases requestors receive articles the same day they placed the request.

UTAD went live in its current form in January, 1999. For a discussion of the process that took the service from planning to implementation, see Kochan, Lee and Murdoch (1999). UTAD was an instant hit and usage quickly reached the current average of over 100 requests per day. In the first nine months of the project 11,949 requests were processed through UTAD. Of those requests, 32% were supplied by Infotrieve, 26% were supplied by the Marriott Library, and 18% were cancelled. Most of the cancellations occurred because the patron was requesting materials available at their home library. More staff was added to meet the increased demand. The service now employs 1.75 FTE.

Although there is no mechanism to distinguish distance education students from other requestors, the service is heavily promoted to remote users and the service clearly benefits them. To gauge the success of the service, a survey of UTAD users was conducted early on. Eighty percent of the survey respondents said that the service met their needs, and 62.5% described the timeliness as either fast or faster than expected. Users liked the speed of delivery and the option to have materials faxed directly to them. UALC is able to achieve faster turn-around times chiefly by taking the borrowing library out of the work-flow. Borrowing libraries are no longer verifying citations, so staff time is saved. Staff time is also saved at the receiving end as articles go directly from the lending source to requestors. In both cases the sav-ings in staff time is felt in improved service to users. In addition, UTAD is generating a database of statewide requests providing data for future statewide collection development decisions. UTAD data currently indicate a need for better statewide access to nursing and psychology journal literature.

As helpful as UTAD is, relying solely on fax delivery for distance education students limits the service to those who have access to a fax machine or are located near a distance education center. To eliminate this restriction, UALC plans to move towards Web delivery of articles in the near future. This way a user can read or print their requested article from the same computer used to make the request. Another limiting factor of the UTAD service is that the access to the UTAD request form is limited by IP address. Only three institutions in the state have proxy servers available for their students. The remainder of distance education students must either go to a UALC campus or an extension site to access the Web form. UALC is investigating other means of authenticating users directly from student rosters or the patron databases in member libraries' integrated library systems. The other improvement that is needed is a global search of UALC catalogs, since OCLC records do not always show accurate volume holdings.

ONLINE LIBRARY INSTRUCTION

In the early 1990's there was a dramatic need statewide, across all types of libraries and educational institutions, to teach distance learn-ers, and others, about the Internet. The Internet was quickly becoming a part of everyday life for many people, but few people understood how it evolved, what it was, or how important it would soon become. UALC librarians saw this as a universal problem best solved by a cooperative statewide instruction initiative.

A task force developed Utah's first online statewide course, the "Internet Navigator" (Hansen & Lombardo, 1997; Lombardo, 1998). The course was offered for credit beginning in January 1996 at most of Utah's public and private academic institutions. In addition the course was freely accessible for non-credit self-instruction to anyone with access to the Web. It was used extensively by academic instruction librarians, and public library trainers statewide and beyond.

The Internet Navigator course consists of six modules, each with its own assignments, quiz and glossary. The design was meant to be flexible so that modules or lessons could be used independent of the larger course as needed. This course has been used successfully by thousands of distance learners since 1995. One serious problem with the course was the lack of a definite plan for ongoing maintenance and support. Maintenance and updates were completed sporadically by a few individuals. Although the course continued to flourish, it became increasingly difficult to make significant revisions due to lack of state-wide planning.

By early 1999 a whole new set of information and instruction needs critical for distance learners developed that were not adequately ad-dressed in the existing Internet Navigator. The Web had grown dra-matically, and within an eighteen-month period many important li-brary indexes, catalogs and reference tools were made available on the Web. Most distance learning students and even members of the gener-al public now have a basic understanding of what the Internet is, and how it works. The problem had shifted from the need to teach "what is the Internet?" to how to best teach students to use the Web effectively for research and how to enable patrons to access the many traditional library resources now on the Web. For example, since the advent of the Internet Navigator in 1996, Weber State University's WSU Online student population had grown from under 200 to over 2,000 students in 1998. By working to meet the needs of the distance learner, UALC sees the added benefit of better meeting the needs of many students who increasingly prefer to access library resources off campus.

Beginning in late 1998, the UALC Distance Learning Committee and the UALC Reference Instruction Committee worked together to address these new problems. Their efforts were aided by the recent and fortunate influx of new instruction librarians at several institutions and increased dialogue among distance learning/outreach librarians and instruction librarians. Discussions in UALC committees emphasized developing curriculum to meet standardized information literacy competencies. By March of 1999 a new task force, the Information for Life Task Force, was created. This task force includes at least one member from each UALC library. In May 1999 the UALC Directors funded the Information for Life Task Force's $25,000 grant proposal. The proposal includes a plan for rotating management of the course among institutions and provides for ongoing financial support by UALC. The abstract of this proposal reads as follows:

> UALC Librarians will work together to create online instructional units covering shared information resources using the Internet Navigator course as an online instruction model. A team of librarians and Web development professionals will collaborate to redesign course modules to focus on information literacy competencies and will add units designed to provide instruction on Pioneer databases and other shared resources. This team will use the latest Web technologies and newest models for delivery of information skills instruction to the academic community and the citizens of Utah. (Utah Academic Library Consortium Information for Life Task Force, 1999)

As of November 1999, drafts of significant content additions have been written by task force members and posted on the task force Web site. A freelance Web designer, programmer and graphic artist have been hired to assist with improving the look of the content. By June of 2000 the Information for Life Task Force members will have completely rewritten significant portions of the Internet Navigator, addressing specific information literacy competencies and the current and future needs of students in Utah. Online and distance learning students will have access to an entire course, independent modules or tutorials. Modules or segments of modules may be customized to meet the needs of university faculty and reference and instruction librarians statewide. Tutorials for Pioneer resources can also be used statewide.

PROMOTING UALC SERVICES TO FACULTY AND STUDENTS

The *ACRL Guidelines for Distance Learning Library Services* (Association of . . . , 1998) identify promoting library services to the distance learning community as a management and administrative responsibility. The World Wide Web offers an excellent opportunity to address the problem of promoting library services to distance learners.

The UALC home page, created in 1996, offers access to the working documents and services of the organization. Four major headings provide links to member libraries and their institutions, consortium services, council and committee documents, and documents of interest. The service component includes Internet access to electronic library resources especially useful to students in distance learning programs and complies with a number of ACRL guidelines. While the pages provide an important resource to members, missing from the UALC site was a page designed specifically for distance learning students and faculty.

To address this need, the UALC Distance Learning Committee created a Web page in lieu of a printed brochure. One of the UALC Distance Learning Committee's ongoing charges is to promote and integrate the ACRL guidelines into academic library policies statewide. An ad hoc sub-committee of the larger Distance Learning Committee took these into consideration as they met to define the components of the page. The site brings together information pertinent to the needs of distance learning students and faculty, identifies distance learning issues related to librarianship, and offers basic information about distance learning classes and library services statewide.

Of primary importance was a chart identifying academic librarians at each university or college charged with serving distance learning students. The chart serves as an expansion of the larger committee membership listing. In addition to the librarians' addresses, email and phone numbers, the library's URLs and URLs for sites designed specifically for distance learning students are given and hot linked.

The committee agreed that the resources page, designed for students and faculty, should be focused and not lengthy. The student page is identified as a Student Help page. A Resources Available section provides links to online library catalogs, periodical indexes and databases, Ebsco Alert Service current table-of-contents awareness, and a link to "Citing Print and Electronic Research Sources" that gives examples from several citation manuals. A second section links to Services Available. Interlibrary Loan, UTAD, remote reference service, electronic reserve and remote access to databases unique to their institution comprise the listings in this category. Since the intent is to identify library services statewide, each service is described and drop down boxes provide links to library services available at each of the UALC institutions.

Resources for faculty focus on the basics of faculty/librarian collaboration. The page reminds faculty to contact their librarian and offers a list of types of services potentially available to faculty through their library. The list contains suggestions such as: access to library catalogs and databases, reference assistance, reciprocal borrowing, document delivery, and help designing course assignments. The list may seem simplistic to librarians, but in fact, many faculty don't always know what services libraries are currently offering. Following the list, three admonitions are stated: "Get to know your librarian," "Familiarize yourself with library resources," "Familiarize yourself with the technology." After each statement a paragraph explains how each relates to their responsibilities as faculty teaching distance education classes.

The fourth segment of the Web page fulfills the "Selected Resources for Distance Education and Instruction" component of the site. This page is divided into three segments: publications, guidelines, and Web sites. Again, the intention was not to attempt to provide a comprehensive list, but to highlight good sources with quality links.

Determining exactly which department or entity within an institution offers distance learning programs is often confusing. One wonders how often this is a deterrent to students trying to decide whether to pursue advanced education or not. The final segment of the page provides links to local distance learning programs and Utah higher education distance learning Web sites. This page not only identifies the departments at each institution, but provides links as well. The ability to update and enhance the site as changes and new issues appear accommodates the UALC Distance Learning Committee's needs for serving the distance learning population of Utah. Likewise, the site draws attention to the needs of distance learning students and faculty and our commitment to them, thereby enhancing the value of the UALC Web site to the Utah academic library community.

CONCLUSION

Cooperative consortial programs have helped overcome bureaucratic barriers so that UALC supported resources and services are equally accessible to on and off campus students. UALC has been successful in promoting the idea of a statewide library collection that expands the information resources available to all students in the state. Cooperation has also been a successful political strategy to gain support for libraries. Technical problems authenticating valid users still prevent some students from getting access to UALC resources, and other technological problems still exist locally, but in theory every student has access to a wide range of collections and services.

NOTE

1. The New Hacker's Dictionary (Raymond, 1991) points out that this phrase is "used ironically to imply that a difficult problem can be easily solved because a program can be written to do it; the irony is that it is very clear that writing such a program will be a great deal of work."

REFERENCES

Association of College and Research Libraries. (1998). ACRL guidelines for distance learning library services. *College & Research Libraries News, 59*, 689-694.

Egan, D. (1999, April 18). Virtual U. Struggles to Get Real. *The Salt Lake Tribune*, pp. C1, C8.

Hansen, C. & Lombardo, N. (1997). Toward the virtual university: collaborative development of a Web-based course. *Research Strategies, 15*, 68-79.

Kochan, C. A. & Elsweiler, J. A. (1998). Testing the feasibility of unmediated document delivery services with EBSCOdoc: the Utah State University experience. *Journal of Interlibrary Loan, Document Delivery and Information Supply, 9*(1), 67-77.

Kochan, C. A. & Lee, D. R. (1998). Utah article delivery: A new model for consortial resource sharing. *Computers in Libraries, 18*(4), 24-28.

Kochan, C. A., Lee, D. R., & Murdoch, R. G. (1999). Partnering for the future: integrating traditional interlibrary lending and commercial document delivery into a seamless service. *Racing Toward Tomorrow: Proceedings of the Ninth National Conference of the Association of College and Research Libraries, April 8-11, 1999*. Chicago: Association of College and Research Libraries, 115-119.

Lombardo, N. (1998). The Internet navigator: Collaborative development and delivery of an electronic college course. *PNLA Quarterly, 63*(1), 12-14.

Moad, J. & Neil, S. (1999, March 15). 100 Innovators in government and education. *PC Week*. [Online] Available: http://www.zdnet.com/pcweek.

Morrison, R.; McCloskey, K. M.; Hinz, J. P.; Zandi, M.; Pierce, P. G., Benedict, K. C. & Brunvand, A. (1995). Developing off-campus services in Utah: A cooperative experience. In C. J. Jacob (Comp.), *The Seventh Off-Campus Library Services Conference Proceedings, San Diego, California, October 25-27* (pp. 261-268). Mount Pleasant, MI: Central Michigan University, pp. 261-268.

Raymond, E. S. (Ed.) (1991). *The new hacker's dictionary.* Cambridge, MA: MIT Press.

Rozum, B., & Brewer, K. (1997, Winter). Identifying, developing, and marketing library services to cooperative extension personnel. *Reference and User Services Quarterly, 37*(2),161-9.

Smith, S. G. (1995). UtahLINK: a model for statewide educational use of the Internet. In: *The Internet Initiative.* Chicago: American Library Association, 153-63.

Stackpole, B. (1999, March 14). Online learning spans the vast lands of Utah. *PC Week 16*, no. 11: 72.

Utah Academic Library Consortium Council. (1997). *Libraries 2000: Statewide Information Resources and Services, A Funding and Accountability Proposal.* Unpublished proposal.

Utah Academic Library Consortium Council. (1999). *Academic Pioneer: Vision Statement August 1, 1999.* [On-line] Available: http://www.ualc.net/internal/directors/vision2.html.

Utah Academic Library Consortium Information for Life Task Force. (1999) *Information For Life: Utah Information Literacy Initiative.* [On-line] Available: http://library.weber.edu/carol/ualc/nav.

Utah State Board of Regents. (1999). *Program Offerings of USHE Institutions by County: FY 1998–FY 1999.* Unpublished report.

Utah System of Higher Education (1999a, October 26). *R315, Service Areas for Off-Campus Courses and Programs.* [On-line]. Available: http://www.utahsbr.edu/policy/r315.htm.

Utah System of Higher Education (1999b, October 26). *R355, Planning, Funding, and Delivery of Courses and Programs via Statewide Telecommunications Networks* [On-line]. Available: http://www.utahsbr.edu/policy/r355.htm.

Utah System of Higher Education. (1999c, October 26). *Technology and Distance Education Initiative. Long-Range Plan. DRAFT. Background.* [On-line]. Available: http://www.utahsbr.edu/tech/plan.htm#Background.

Utah System of Higher Education. (1999d, October 26). *Technology and Distance Education Initiative. Long-Range Plan. DRAFT. Goals.* [On-line]. Available: http://www.utahsbr.edu/tech/plan.htm#Goals.

APPENDIX

Utah Library and Higher Education Web Sites

Pioneer Utah's Online Library
http://pioneer-library.org/

Internet Navigator
http://www-navigator.utah.edu

State of Utah Education Page
http://www.state.ut.us/html/education.htm

Utah Academic Library Consortium
http://WWW.ualc.net/

Utah Education Network
http://www.uen.org/

Utah Electronic Community College
http://WWW.utah-ecc.org/

Utah System of Higher Education (USHE)
http://www.utahsbr.edu/

USHE Technology and Distance Education Initiative
http://www.utahsbr.edu/tech/intro.htm

UALC Distance Learning Resources home page
http://medlib.med.utah.edu/ualcdl/

Developing an Effective Off-Campus Library Services Web Page: Don't Worry, Be Happy!

Jonathan R. Buckstead

Austin Community College

SUMMARY. Developing an effective off-campus library service Web page does not have to be a grueling task. This paper explores the methodologies and general rules of thumb in creating a Web page that will get and hold the attention of your distance learners.

KEYWORDS. Library services, distance education, Web page development, library Web sites

INTRODUCTION

Among the first tasks that are often assigned to a new or (used) distance learning librarian these days is the development of a unique Web site that caters to the needs of the distance learning community, whether that community merely consists of on-campus students who also access resources from off-campus or does in fact, consist of dedicated distance learners who are strictly enrolled in official distance learning courses.

In this paper, I will outline the methodologies that are frequently utilized in developing Web pages in general and will then focus upon the specific design and content issues that face distance learning

[Haworth co-indexing entry note]: "Developing an Effective Off-Campus Library Services Web Page: Don't Worry, Be Happy!" Buckstead, Jonathan R. Co-published simultaneously in *Journal of Library Administration* (The Haworth Information Press, an imprint of The Haworth Press, Inc.) Vol. 31, No. 3/4, 2001, pp. 93-107; and: *Off-Campus Library Services* (ed: Anne Marie Casey) The Haworth Information Press, an imprint of The Haworth Press, Inc., 2001, pp. 93-107.

librarians as they go to task in developing effective Web pages for their distance learning clientele. The terms "Web page" and "Web site" will be used interchangeably throughout the paper.

My initial work with Web page design in support of distance learning began at Austin Community College in 1995, shortly after I was hired as the Reference Librarian for Extension Services. At that time, the College had not yet developed a Web-based library support system for its Open Campus (distance learning) students. However, there was indeed a strong, traditional support system in place, which consisted of a book/document delivery service (via US mail or fax) as well as a toll-free "reference" hotline, which was accessible during normal hours of operation. At that time, eligibility to access the OPAC via telnet dial-up and to utilize all other off-campus services was limited to students who were *only* enrolled in distance learning courses. Thus, any promotion and marketing of off-campus resources and services was strictly aimed at this group, although anyone could access the OPAC if they could get a hold of the instructions on how to do so. Instructions on how to access the OPAC were provided along with other informational flyers in a packet that would be sent out to all distance learning students each semester. Because of the vast number of Open Campus students that were enrolled at that time, coordination with the Open Campus department was crucial in terms of gathering a list of names and addresses of all the Open Campus students and generating mailing labels to be adhered to manila envelopes.

As time went on, it became apparent that the cost and workload involved in compiling numerous information packets each semester far exceeded the return that we were yielding on our distance learning student interaction statistics. Thus, I was compelled to search for an alternative mechanism by which information regarding our services and resources could be disseminated to distance learning students.

PAGE EVOLUTION

The process depicted in the previous section continued for several years until which time the Library's OPAC was replaced with a Web-based catalog. It was at this point that I realized the potential of developing a Web page that would be able to provide information on the various resources and services that were available not only to distance learning students but to on-campus students who needed access to these resources and services from off-campus as well. It no longer seemed necessary to restrict access to resources and services to just Open Campus students. Since there was no longer any concern for postage and duplication costs in terms of producing hundreds of informational packets, providing across-the-board access seemed feasible. It is important to note, however, that although the page that was ultimately developed and placed into service provided unrestricted access to resources and services to all students from off-campus, there were and still are, a unique set of services that are restricted to only Open Campus students in addition to a common core of resources and services.

SEARCHING FOR A MODEL/LITERATURE REVIEW

In reviewing the literature currently available in the area of Web page design, I encountered a plethora of information from many sources within academe and outside of it. However, very little material seemed to be available on Web page design within the context of distance learning library support programs. Thus, as I proceeded to search for a model for my new Web page, I realized that due to the lack of literature on the subject, perhaps searching the WWW for pages that already exist might be the best approach to locating a model. In searching the Web for pages, I encountered many models from institutions representing all levels of higher education. The next step, then, was to determine the common elements among them while at the same time, create some new elements that would make my site not only unique, but also more tailored toward the needs of my clientele at Austin Community College.

Thus, my concern here was not so much on designing a "for-profit" Web page, but designing one that "does the trick" as far as catching and holding the attention of distance learners. Developing an effective Web page involves first and foremost, the devising of a *plan*.

TARGET AUDIENCE

Even in the not-for-profit world of academic libraries, there is a need to adhere to certain basic principles of marketing and promotion when developing a Web page for a specific audience; not unlike the modus operandi that one encounters in the business world. Success in developing an effective Web page often hinges on how well conceived, developed and planned the idea or concept is behind the entire project (Niederst, 1999). As you begin thinking about why you are developing a Web page, you need to also think about *who* your target audience is and *what* their specific needs are at the present time and what they might be down the road. One useful technique is to put yourself in the place of the distance learner and then ask yourself why a distance learner might want to come back to visit your site and what they might expect to find in it. It is important when doing this initial brainstorming that you don't lose track of why you are developing this page and for whom it is being designed.

SURVEY INSTRUMENT

As I began to plan out the Austin Community College Off-Campus Library Services Web Site, it dawned on me that perhaps one of the best ways to gauge what the target audience might want to see in a specialized Web site would be to create a survey and use the feedback to facilitate the development of the initial Web site content. Although I would subsequently decide to pursue the creation of a survey instrument to serve this purpose, I did not create and use it initially to solicit feedback from the target audience. Rather, I went ahead and simply created a basic Web site that included the essential elements that I believed would "do the trick" in terms of engaging my target audience. The reason for my creating the Web site first and then subsequently creating the survey instrument was because I did not feel that I would receive a sufficient sample from my target audience had I mailed out surveys to each distance learning student. Rather, I counted on publishing the initial Web site and then subsequently creating an online form-style survey instrument (Figure 1) which would be included on the primary page of the Web site, close to the top. The survey instrument would include a few questions regarding the patron's experience and frequency in using the Internet and of course, several questions relating to the content of the Web site.

I can report to you today and say that I have received a lot of feedback from many users of the Web site, including both distance learning students as well as on-campus students accessing the site from off-campus. Much of the feedback has either been very positive and/or constructive.

(ORIGINAL) CONTENT/COMPONENTS

It is very important that the content or elements of your Web site be as original as possible. Unfortunately, there are all too many Web sites out there that merely contain links to other Web sites and are essentially nothing more than meta-lists (Black, 1997). Thus, if you strive to place as much original content on your Web site as possible, the chances are much greater that a viewer will not only find what they are searching for, but also be more apt to return to your site in the future.

As I began to develop original content for my off-campus Web site, I must admit that I was greatly influenced by the content of many other excellent Web sites that already existed in cyberspace. However, I was intent on creating as much of an original product as possible, given the extent of my own personal knowledge of providing services to distance learners.

After thorough examination of many existing off-campus Web sites, I was able to combine my original elements with those gleaned from other sites and come up with a list of components that I regarded as essential or "backbone" components to any off-campus Web site:

Essential Components (Figure 2):

- Header (including school logo)
- Title
- Introductory section
- Hot links to services
- Hot links to resources
- Hours of operation information
- Point/s of contact
- Snail mail address/phone number/email address of DL librarian
- Page author information
- Last update section

Including only the components listed above in an off-campus library services Web page would be sufficient. However, in order to have an even more "effective" Web page, I would highly recommend some or all of the following additional components:

FIGURE 1

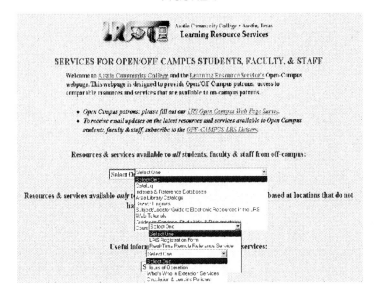

Recommended Components:

- Survey (cgi or mailto) (Figure 1)
- Online library registration form (cgi or mailto) (Figure 3)
- BI tutorials (PowerPoint/html format) (Figure 4)
- Video conferencing link (including synchronous audio/video) (Figure 5)
- Toll-free hotline number (Figure 5)
- Email reference link (Figure 6)
- Listserv (Figure 6)
- Technical support link (only if video conferencing link is available) (Figure 6)
- Material request form (cgi or mailto) (Figure 7)
- Links to library catalog (Figure 2)
- Links to electronic resources available from off-campus (including access instructions)
- Links to other library catalogs (Figure 2)
- Links to search engines (Figure 2)
- Links to documentation style pages (Figure 2)
- Links to library policies (circulation, etc.) (Figure 2)

FIGURE 2

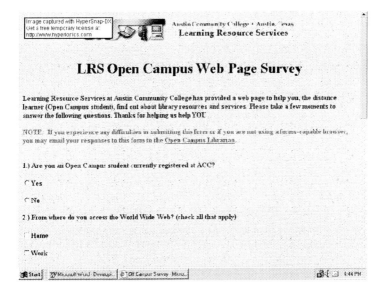

FIGURE 3

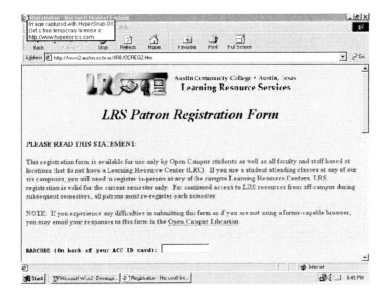

FIGURE 4

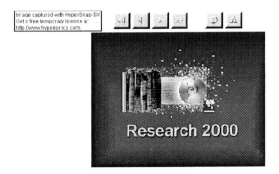

Slide 1 of 58

FIGURE 5

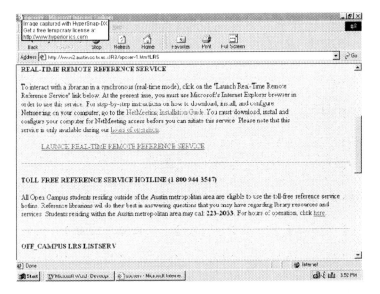

FIGURE 6

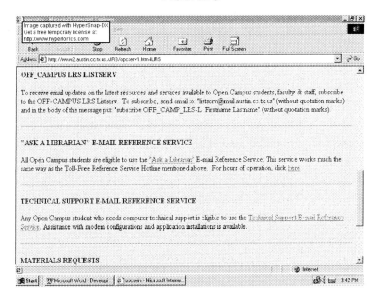

FIGURE 7

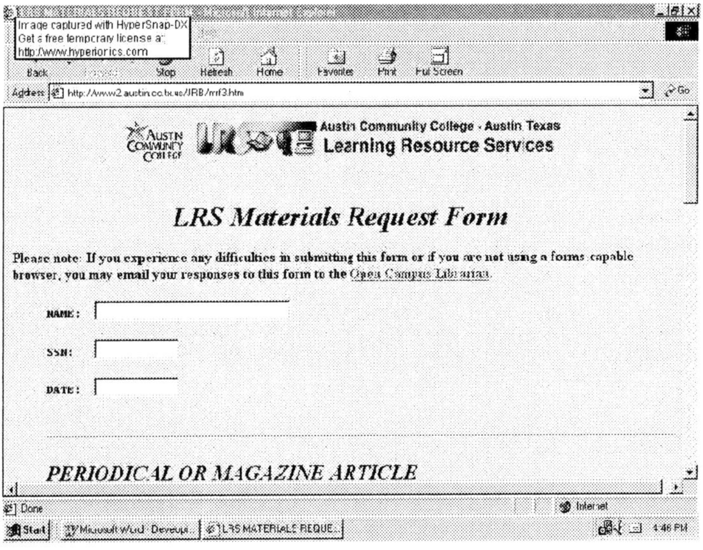

PRIORITIZATION OF CONTENT

Another aspect of Web page design that needs to be considered during this step is the *prioritization* of the newest and most important content of your Web site. In other words, the "opening page" of your Web site should contain the most critical information pertaining to your distance learning resources and services; this may include primary links to second-level pages and/or actual paragraphs detailing specific resources and services that are available to your distance learning communities. Be sure that any links that you may have on your primary page are well annotated and edited. Concise descriptions of links "up-front" make for a much better impression.

UPDATING/EDITING OF CONTENT

An effective off-campus library services Web site is one that is updated on a regular basis. Although you may not have any new resources and/or services that require promotion on a regular basis, merely changing the date on the page to reflect the current date is a way to suggest to viewers that you are paying attention to the Web site and not neglecting it. Editing of the content of your Web page involves not only ensuring that words are spelled correctly, but also that there are no blatant grammatical errors as well. Many "WYSIWYG" (what you see is what you get) html-editors, such as Netscape's Composer, include built-in spell/grammatical checkers.

WEB SITE DESIGN

The overall design of your Web site is perhaps the most crucial of all aspects in developing an effective off-campus library services Web page. Maintaining a simple, consistent page layout throughout your Web page is very important. First of all, it makes it much easier for the viewer to navigate through your Web page and find the information that you want to provide to them. If your Web page consists of secondary and even tertiary pages, common graphics, navigational buttons, etc. should all appear on each subsequent page of your Web site (Planey & Donc, 1996). This makes for a much more user-friendly

Web site and one that will also be more useful for those viewers who have learning disabilities.

EQUIPMENT

Server

When thinking about the end result, the hardware/software that is needed to create your Web page is really quite minimal. Starting with the larger hardware and moving down to software, of course, some kind of server will be required, whether this server resides within the walls of the library where it is maintained by library staff, or if it resides outside of the library and is maintained by your institution's computing center. In the case of Austin Community College, the original page that was published resided on the College's Web server until the library was able to acquire its own server. The page and its associated files were then transferred to the library server where they now reside.

Html Editor

When considering the hardware and software applications that are required at the point of page development and storage, there are numerous options available to the page author, thanks to the endless technological innovations that continue to flood the computing market. As is required with any type of page development, a good, yet easy-to-use html editor is essential. An html editor is really nothing more than a word processor that converts ASCII-text into html coding so that what you create is visible as a Web page via a Web browser. There are many types of html editors now available on the market, ranging from those that require complete command of the html language, to those that require no html language proficiency whatsoever. Although I have a fairly good command of html coding, I still tend to prefer those editors that do not require any knowledge of html. Plain and simple, they're just darn easier to use! Some of the more popular "easy-to-use" html editors on the market today would include Microsoft FrontPage and Netscape Composer, both of which are considered WYSIWYG editors and are included as free components tied to the respective browser packages. The WYSIWYG idea, as associated with html editors, suggests that whatever data is entered into the editor at the time of page development will also appear the same way when the data is ultimately published. Other editors which are available either as freeware or shareware and worth mentioning, include RCEdit, CutePage, HTML Writer, YAHE (Yet Another HTML Editor), and HyperTab. As with any shareware or freeware application, don't be surprised if you encounter deficiencies with these editors. Many of them are not fully operational; however, for a fee, the vendor will send you the full application. In most cases, though, the shareware/freeware application will work sufficiently in order for you to create some basic pages.

FTP Client

Once you have created your preliminary page and are ready to publish it on a server, you will need to use an FTP client in order to transfer your saved Web page to the server. FTP stands for "file transfer protocol" and is an application that allows saved pages or documents to be transferred from a floppy, hard, or zip drive to a Web server. A great FTP client for Windows that I personally recommend is called WS_FTP LE, which is available as a freeware program for education purposes from Ipswitch.com. Once installed, WS_FTP LE will allow you to easily transfer your pages to and from the Web server as you create them and/or update them. One of the easiest ways to work with pages that you have already created is to save all pages in a separate folder on your hard drive and pull them up in your html editor as needed to update or modify them. Once this is done, you can then transfer the updated pages to your Web server via the WS_FTP LE program. Any previous versions of your pages that are residing on the Web server will be overwritten with the new ones automatically.

MARKETING/PROMOTION

The marketing and promotion of your new off-campus Web site is perhaps the single most critical factor for ensuring that your target audience, the distance learner, will not only discover your Web site, but will also return to it time and time again. As with the promotion of any off-campus library services, promoting a Web site can be done in similar ways.

One way which I find to be quite effective in "getting the word out" about my Web site is to include in a welcome letter each semester to all distance learning faculty, the URL to the Web site. By including the URL of your Web site along with a brief summary of the resources and services (in bullet format) available in it, you are effectively promoting your Web site. Of course, despite all of the marketing and promotion that is done with your Web site each new semester, the greatest ongoing challenge facing the developer of an off-campus Web site is to actually persuade the distance learning faculty not only to include the URL of your Web site in their syllabi, but to mention it in class during the first several weeks of each semester.

STATISTICS

Once you have your off-campus library services Web site up and running, you need to have some mechanism in place to be able to gather usage statistics as patrons hit your site. One of the easiest ways to do this is to place a counter on your Web site. There are many commercially available counters waiting to be downloaded from various sites on the Internet. In fact, many of them are free. One of the most comprehensive utility sites currently available on the WWW is called ZDNet.com. Upon running a simple query in the search engine provided at this Web site, I encountered the following freeware page counters: CGIMachine-Counter v2.2; ASP.counter v1.0; MyTimer; to name but a few. Of course, one can simply type in "page counter" into any of the popular search engine dialog boxes and the resulting list of hits will astound you. Again, many of the sites will offer free counters or at least the cgi scripting needed to create the counter, for free.

Once you have a counter in place on your Web site, you will then be able to easily track the number of visitors to your site on a daily, weekly, monthly basis or whatever schedule is most convenient for you. Although page counters can provide a simple measure of the number of visitors to your Web site, one of their limitations is that they do not provide feedback on which components of your Web site were utilized and which ones weren't. Feedback on the usage of different components of your Web site should come from the various "cgi" or "mailto" forms that are included in your site. As patrons take advantage of your email reference option or your library registration form, you will receive email from them which can then be stored in a special folder on your computer and/or printed out and placed in a file for statistical purposes.

MAINTENANCE

Another extremely important task that is associated with the development of any Web site is site maintenance. By maintenance, I am referring to the periodic checking of each and every "hot link" that is included in the Web site and ensuring that they are in fact taking the patron to their pre-determined destination. For any number of reasons, these links may change; your local server address might change or an external Web site URL can change. Keeping these links up-to-date is critical to maintaining an effective Web site that a distance learner will want to return to time and time again.

CONCLUSION

Developing an effective off-campus library services Web site does not have to be an unbearable task. In fact, it can be downright enjoyable as long as you do your homework. This paper hopefully provided you with some insights into the steps involved in the creation of an effective Web site for distance learners. Whatever components you should decide to include in your Web site, you should bear in mind that the end user, the distance learner, will benefit most from those components that provide the most content, up-front.

REFERENCES

Black, R. (1997). *Web sites that work*. San Jose, CA: Adobe Press.
Do-It. (1998). *World wide access: Accessible web design* [On-line]. Available: http://weber.u.washington.edu/~doit/Brochures/Technology/universal.design.html (1999, August 5).
Flanders, V. & Michael W. (1996). *Web pages that suck*. San Francisco: Sybex.
Internet.Com. (1999). *What makes a great Web site?* [On-line]. Available: http://webreference.com/greatsite.html (1999, September 9).

Kent, p. (1998). *Poor Richard's Web site: Geek-free, commonsense advice on building a low-cost Web site.* Lakewood, CO: Top Floor Publishing.

Niederst, J. (1999). *Web design in a nutshell.* Sebastopol, CA: O'Reilly.

Planey, B., & Doric E. (1996). Hung up in Web page design? Take time to think about it. *Dallas Business Journal, 19*(28), p. B6.

Still, J. M. (Ed.) (1997). *The Library Web: Case studies in Web site creation and implementation.* Medford, NJ: Information Today, Inc.

Sweet, C. E. (1997, June/July). The Novice's guide to basic Web page design. *Database Magazine,* 66-74.

Wanliss-Orlebar, A. (1996). Five keys to home page design. *Public Relations Tactics, 3*(3), 8.

Weiss, A., Tapley, R., & Daniels, K. (1997). *Web authoring desk reference.* Indianapolis, IN: Hayden Books.

Document Delivery Options
for Distance Education Students
and Electronic Reserve Service
at Ball State University Libraries

Hildegund M. Calvert

Ball State University

SUMMARY. During recent years Ball State University has added a number of new courses as well as new delivery methods to its distance education program. Currently, there are plans to expand further, especially the Nursing program. In an effort to comply with the *ACRL Guidelines for Distance Learning Library Services,* University Libraries initiated a number of new services. In this paper the author reviews the literature, discusses Interlibrary Loan initiatives to facilitate research for and document delivery to distance education students and describes the development of the electronic reserve program.

KEYWORDS. Library services, distance education, electronic reserves, Interlibrary Loan

INTRODUCTION

Brophy and Craven stated in 1998 that lifelong learning is becoming an important issue worldwide as countries attempt to adjust to rapid economic, social and political changes. They examined how lifelong learning might affect libraries and investigated how UK libraries are supporting non-traditional learning, including distance learning.

[Haworth co-indexing entry note]: "Document Delivery Options for Distance Education Students and Electronic Reserve Service at Ball State University Libraries." Calvert, Hildegund M. Co-published simultaneously in *Journal of Library Administration* (The Haworth Information Press, an imprint of The Haworth Press, Inc.) Vol. 31, No. 3/4, 2001, pp. 109-125; and: *Off-Campus Library Services* (ed: Anne Marie Casey) The Haworth Information Press, an imprint of The Haworth Press, Inc., 2001, pp. 109-125.

These researchers believe that the essence of lifelong learning is that individuals remain engaged in learning throughout their lives, providing opportunities for universities to develop new relationships with their students. The authors remind us that it is important to realize that lifelong learners will want to receive their education at the place and time of their choice, convenient to them. He points out that academic libraries have an opportunity to provide services as long as they are willing to meet the students' demands for flexibility and convenience (Brophy, 1998).

American universities are responding to these developments and are employing new technologies in the delivery of distance education classes. In order for academic libraries to succeed and meet these challenges, librarians will need to be prepared to be lifelong learners as well. They must stay abreast of developments in technology and aim towards offering new electronic services and resources as soon as possible after they become available (Slade & Kascus, 1998).

REVIEW OF THE LITERATURE

Document delivery has long been seen as one way to fill the research needs of distance learners. In the past, requested materials have generally been delivered by regular mail or perhaps by courier service. More recently, document delivery is defined as using new information storage and retrieval, copying, and communications technology to locate the original document and transmit a copy of it quickly to the requestor.

The conflict between the continuous increase in journal prices and the decline or slow growth of library budgets has contributed to an increasing number of document delivery services outside libraries (Khalil, 1993). A 1996 study appears to contradict Khalil's findings somewhat in that it contends that customers' satisfaction is only minimally dependent on actual delivery speed. Instead it is suggested that the value of personal contact in the form of staff availability and telephone interaction with staff appears to increase customer satisfaction (Weaver-Meyers & Stolt, 1996). This study concentrated on researching traditional interlibrary loan services without giving special consideration to distance learners. Calvert's experience with providing assistance to distance education students does not support that viewpoint. In most instances, speed has been very important to distance learners who order material from Ball State University Libraries. These students often reside in remote parts of the State of Indiana and more recently also in other states. When they request material, there is usually a very short turn-around time, and they are less interested in personal contact than they are in getting their requests filled within the time they specify. It is the rate of success in meeting these demands that will decide how distance learners rate their satisfaction with inter-library loan/document delivery services. Saunders supports the belief that speed is an important factor and sees the Internet as a catalyst in the evolution of document delivery (Saunders, 1997).

Ward discusses the possibility of outsourcing as a way to fill re-search needs for materials the library does not own and of offering end users the option to submit requests directly to a document supplier without the library mediating (Ward, 1997). The availability of elec-tronic indexes has lead to an increase in the demand for delivery of documents, which are often available in electronic format. Nicholls found that CD-ROMs appear to have outlived their attraction. Howev-er, he also notes that many librarians report that their users still prefer photocopies to electronic copies (Nicholls, 1997). He gives no infor-mation or detail on how he arrived at this finding nor does he give specifics as to who the users are and where they are located in relation to the library that serves them. Further research is needed to determine whether Nicholls' statement is true as well when distance learners are involved or whether their preferred mode of delivery might be elec-tronic copies. Most distance education students and faculty served by University Libraries prefer electronic copies. They usually do not have the time needed to wait for printed copies to be mailed to them. Until University Libraries implement the email document delivery option discussed later in this paper, the only option for obtaining electronic copies are aggregate full-text databases. Unfortunately, these can cur-rently be accessed only from within the Ball State domain and there-fore exclude distance education students. University Libraries Au-tomation is working on a password protection solution and hopes to make access to aggregate databases available to all Ball State Univer-sity students by the beginning of Spring semester.

Saunders portrays document delivery as a subset of interlibrary loan, especially in those cases where library staff mediate the transac-tion and purchase the requested material from an outside supplier instead of ordering it from another library. Some interesting questions are raised with regard to libraries ordering materials and giving them to users to keep without charging them. Saunders acknowledges that it would cost libraries more to have these materials returned to them but at the same time wonders how libraries can justify giving away materials that were obtained with public or institutional funds. She questions what percentage of the staff and materials budget can legitimately be diverted for document delivery services and whether the availability of personal or departmental accounts for ordering material will make end users more self-sufficient and less dependent upon a full-service library (Saunders, 1997).

An additional factor that might contribute to such a development is the fact that libraries, responding to user demands, provide access to an ever-increasing number of full-text databases. If declining statistics in circulation, attendance and interlibrary loan requests at Ball State University Libraries can be seen as an indicator, it could be argued that to some extent end users are already more independent. Ward points out that while the charge per item is higher than with traditional ILL, it should be possible to reduce staff cost considerably. She sees full-text databases as a self-service document delivery option offered to eligible patrons and cites OVID and the Institute of Scientific Information as examples. In these non-traditional interlibrary loan/document delivery options, certain parameters, such as a maximum dollar amount per item or blocks against ordering locally owned material, can be set by the library (Ward, 1997).

Cain investigates how libraries are changing and redirecting their energies toward access rather than ownership. He also examines the transformation that is taking place in the way information is delivered, especially with regard to periodical indexes, abstracts and articles. He contends that the business is competitive and technologically dynamic but believes that it will be years before a true access environment is achieved. He provides a model for a successful periodical access system libraries may consult when facing decisions about which sources and services to offer (Cain, 1995). Even though this article is somewhat dated, the model still has merit and the same factors still need to be considered when making such decisions today.

Prentice sees issues relating to copyright and control of access to information in the digital age as important factors that will define what academic libraries can and cannot do to support research and the teaching/learning requirements of the institution. She wonders if libraries will be able to afford charges copyright holders may levy for digitizing material and points out that the question of who will pay for access will become more critical as content owners press to place charges on access to information (Prentice, 1997). Ball State University Libraries are currently facing this very dilemma and must make difficult decisions each time new databases are purchased. They must review the pricing structure and choose between giving access to a set number of simultaneous users or allowing unlimited access, and may have to select an option for financial reasons even though it may be less beneficial to users.

Jackson discusses the proposed redesigning of access and delivery services in research libraries. She states that the goal is to utilize technology to provide the best possible access to instructional and research materials and keep the costs for such services at a minimum. Jackson hopes that the North American Document Delivery Project developed by ARL in 1993 (NAILDD Project) will further the development of standards, software and system design capabilities, will lead to improved interlibrary loan and document delivery services for users and make them more cost-effective for libraries (Jackson, 1994).

One possibility for providing the services described by Jackson is to give users unmediated access to document delivery services. However, currently there are not many libraries that are willing to grant such far reaching privileges because they would not be able to absorb the potentially exorbitant cost this service might incur. At Ball State University Libraries unmediated access is only available if users are willing to use their personal credit card to pay for what they order. Otherwise, Interlibrary Loan staff mediate requests, making sure that the Libraries do not own the material. They also look for traditional, preferably free, interlibrary loan sources before going to document delivery services. In order to speed up the process, Interlibrary Loan facilitates the electronic transmission of requests where possible, making use of the OCLC interlibrary loan link, the Clio request software and is planning to take advantage of OCLC ILL direct request as well. Other services developed for the benefit of distance learners include on-line tutorials for assignments students are required to complete for English classes as well as televised instruction sessions.

Gloria Lebowitz reviewed library services available to distance students in 1997 and found that the basic models are the same as those described in a 1991 study. She found that a major addition in 1997 was access to Web sites and home pages that allow distance students to search other libraries' resources, request information, and contact a librarian. Lebowitz advises librarians responsible for handling research needs of distance learners to be proactive and convince faculty and administrators to include plans for library services in the early planning stages. Librarians should learn about all degrees and programs offered off campus, be aware of different delivery formats used for teaching off-campus classes, know the number of students enrolled and be cognizant of future projections. Ongoing input from teaching faculty and course administrators regarding this information will permit librarians to plan and design library services for future users (Lebowitz, 1997). Ball State University Libraries have been able to follow this advice because they have a representative on a committee that includes faculty from different disciplines as well as administrators and is responsible for monitoring developments in distance learning and for taking corrective action when needed. The library liaison has the opportunity to make sure that library services are given proper consideration.

Statistics in an April 1999 article indicate that the number of higher education institutions in the United States that offer courses via distance education jumped from about one-third in 1995 to an estimated eighty-five percent in 1998 (Kirk, 1999). Students enrolled in distance education classes are generally older, working adults with limited time. They generally do not want to devote significant time to library research and are not willing to travel to the library. Document delivery in the traditional sense is therefore no longer sufficient to satisfy the needs of these students and should no longer be considered only as an adjunct to traditional interlibrary loan services.

The scope of services libraries offer to distance education students varies greatly from institution to institution. Libraries that receive sufficient funding cater to students and make use of the latest technologies. Those with more limited budgets rely on public or academic libraries close to the students' home or have off-campus centers with small library collections. Often services and collections in these public libraries and centers are not tailored to the off-campus program needs (Coder, 1998). In Florida legislators, educational administrators and the public believed that technology would easily and inexpensively solve problems of providing library service to increasing numbers of distance education students. The library community was able to supply documentation that disproves such beliefs and to show that digital information does not fully replace print information. Manus explains the creation of the Florida Distance Learning Library Initiative and discusses the five components developed by that organization and recommended for inclusion in distance learning programs (Madaus & Webster, 1998).

Ball State University has staffed learning centers throughout the state that assist students with their research needs, offer a place to study and also act as receive sites for televised courses. University Libraries are taking a proactive role to offer support and ensure that resources are available to students off-campus as well as to those on campus. In February of 1998, the State of Indiana began offering all its residents access to INSPITE (Indiana Spectrum of Information Resources). INSPIRE is a collection of full-text databases in the arts and humanities, social sciences, business, science and technology. In order to make access to INSPIRE transparent to the Ball State community, University Libraries added a link on the Libraries' Web site. Unfortunately, Ball State students enrolled in distance education classes who are not Indiana residents do not have access to the resources of IN-SPIRE.

The revised *ACRL Guidelines for Distance Learning Library Services* approved in July 1998 follow national accreditation standards and instruct universities to ensure that resources and services offered to distance education students are equal to those that support on-campus programs. Kirk believes that as a result of these recommendations, librarians have started to take a more active role in promoting their services and are more likely to demand that they are included in the development of distance education programs from the beginning. Library professionals are encouraging their institutions to follow the ACRL guidelines and offer the services stipulated for distance education students (Kirk, 1999).

The main focus of Blakely's 1992 article is geared towards faculty who teach distance education classes and to the students enrolled in such programs. It discusses different delivery modes for teaching and addresses problems students in off-campus locations might face. There is a reference to a 1988 recommendation concerning library services, which suggests the use of a WATS line and collect call requests as well as first class mailing of materials. The article points out that many universities have already established computer access to library holdings and have arranged to have materials delivered to off-campus locations (Blakely, 1992). Since that article was written, technology has paved the way for further improvements in service to off-campus students. Ball State University makes a toll free number available to off-campus students and also uses Web technology and the Web-based catalog to provide on-line services.

In a 1997 article, emerging distance education is seen as a change in paradigm and as the beginning of a new learning environment. Examples of how different institutions are coping with this development are given for both distance education and innovations in the learning environment. There are no specifics regarding library services. The only mention is a vague statement to the effect that besides delivering courses, institutions must also provide all of the support services learners will need in the new environment (Miller, 1997). Carolen Ruschoff, on the other hand, states that important issues confronting academic librarianship include the obligations libraries have to distance education such as full text delivery, copyright and pricing concerns (Ruschoff, 1997). Walling describes the University of South Carolina's support for a distance education program in the College of Library and Information Sciences. She points out that students use interlibrary loan, FAX and the Internet; however, they often have to travel to major libraries to complete assignments. According to Walling, the program is successful because the University spends considerable time obtaining support from those libraries where they expect their students to seek assistance (Walling, 1996).

DISTANCE EDUCATION AT BALL STATE UNIVERSITY

Ball State University has a long history of offering distance education classes through the School of Continuing Education, and defines distance education as offering formal instruction by non-traditional modes of delivery including by computer or satellite. The commitment to make higher education accessible to Indiana residents who are unable to reach a traditional campus because of time and distance began in the early 1970s. The first course was a television class on the history of city planning, and in the late 1970s the MBA program was initiated.

Today, one way to deliver distance education courses is by a closed-circuit television network, the Indiana Higher Education Telecommunications System (IHETS). This is an interactive televised delivery system that brings the classroom to the student. Students on campus attend classes in distance education studio classrooms while off-campus students attend class at designated reception sites throughout Indiana. A digital tele-responder, an instrument similar to a telephone, enables students to participate in class discussions. Students who register for a televised class are assigned to a Learning Center or a Receive Site that is most convenient to their home or workplace. Sites are located at hospitals, elementary and secondary schools, libraries, vocational schools, and other public facilities. Other delivery methods include cable, correspondence, on-site instruction with Ball State faculty traveling to sites convenient to students, and most recently as a result of improved technology, internet-based courses. Classes offered lead to Associate's Degrees in General Arts and Business Administration, the Baccalaureate Completion track in Nursing, Master's Degrees in Business Administration and Computer Science. A Master of Arts in Social Psychology and a Master in Nursing-Nurse Practitioners Track are additional programs scheduled to become available by distance education.

DOCUMENT DELIVERY
AT BALL STATE UNIVERSITY LIBRARIES

Ball State University Librarians first studied the possibility of offering electronic document delivery (EDD) services to students in the early 1990s, when periodical subscription prices experienced exponential price increases. EDD was seen as a means to fill gaps caused by reduced subscriptions. They studied the availability of commercial EDD systems and their compatibility with Ball State University Libraries' automated system and considered EDD as an adjunct to interlibrary loan and collection development. Interlibrary Loan (ILL) was expected to continue to try to obtain the requested material from the most inexpensive source, using commercial document suppliers as a last resort only. Recommendations at that time were to subscribe to CARL Uncover with access from dedicated PCs in the Reference area. This meant that patrons had to come to the Library to search CARL and complete an Interlibrary Loan form if they needed to order material. There was to be no circumstance where patrons would be allowed to automatically charge their document orders to the library. Interlibrary Loan staff were to mediate all requests, unless users were willing to charge materials to their own credit card. The Library was going to absorb the charges incurred when material was ordered from a journal title that was cancelled as a result of budget constraints. Once the material arrived in the Interlibrary Loan Office, it still needed to be delivered to the patron who ordered it. Traditional methods of document delivery such as campus mail, patron pick up, U.S. mail and a statewide courier service were employed to deliver to the end-user.

The Interlibrary Loan Librarian has for a number of years been the Library Liaison for distance education students at Ball State University Libraries. This author first assumed these responsibilities in 1995 and soon realized the need to make speedier services available to distance education students. The possibility of using Web technologies for enhancing services to interlibrary loan customers, including those enrolled in distance education classes, was studied. The result of these investigations was an Interlibrary Loan Web page that included online forms for requesting material. It soon became apparent that distance education students require different types of information than do on-campus students. A separate Web page tailored specifically to the needs of distance education students was designed. The page included links to the Interlibrary Loan Web page and on-line request forms, an email button for contacting the Library Liaison, as well as other useful information and services. Students enrolled in distance education classes who have access to the Internet are encouraged to submit their ILL requests electronically. They are instructed to indicate that they are distance students and to specify the preferred mode for receiving their material. In most cases speed is of the essence and the turn-around time between ordering material and the date it is needed is quite brief.

The issue of speed became even more pressing in 1999 when the Nursing Department informed the Library that they would be offering several graduate nursing classes exclusively via distance education. It was anticipated that students would come from all parts of Indiana as well as from other states. As a result, demands for on-line databases that include full-text documents and a commitment to provide distance students with library resources that are equal to those available on campus are increasing. The decision was made to expand document delivery for distance students to include material owned by University Libraries. Books requested from the Libraries' collection are charged to the distance education student's account and mailed via U.S mail. Articles from journals available in University Libraries are copied and mailed via U.S. mail or faxed if students have access to a fax machine.

Interlibrary Loan utilizes Ariel for the majority of their borrowing and lending activities of non-returnable items. Ariel is a software package developed by the Research Library Group (RLG) which makes it possible to scan articles, photos and other documents and transmit the electronic images to other Ariel workstations anywhere in the world and print them out on a Windows-compatible printer. In February 1999, RLG released version 2.2 of the Ariel software. An exciting enhancement of this release was the capability to send and receive documents via email. According to Ariel documentation received with release 2.2, all the recipient needs is an email program capable of handling MIME attachments. Further research revealed that the National Library of Medicine is offering free of charge DocView, an Ariel-compatible software program that makes it possible to receive document images sent over the Internet from remote Ariel workstations. This meant that Interlibrary Loan would be able to forward documents to end users' email accounts once they install the DocView software on their computer. DocView also has a built-in document ordering function that could be used to fill requests for material owned by University Libraries. The user orders a document and the order is sent directly to an Ariel system and is automatically printed by the Ariel system. The library then scans the article using an Ariel station and sends it to the user's computer that is running Doc-View. A dialog box alerts the user of the arrival of the new document. Hardware and software requirements are specified on the National Library of Medicine's Web site along with instructions for installing the program. The directions are very intuitive and most users should have no problems with the installation. In addition to DocView, there are several other software programs available.

The Library Liaison for Distance Education realized the potential this software had for document delivery services. It could be used to quickly transmit documents to distance education students at remote sites even if they had no access to a fax machine, a Learning Center or a Receive Site. At the beginning of Fall Semester 1999, this author submitted a proposal to the Library Administration to test the software and to offer it in form of a pilot project to the Science Faculty who reside in a different building some distance from the Library. Many faculty consider it an inconvenience to walk to the Library to pick up their materials. The proposal was approved and testing of the Ariel email function was set up. A number of librarians downloaded the DocView software and installed it on their PC. Interlibrary Loan staff scanned an article and transmitted it to the participants' email accounts. The transmission worked exactly as described in the DocView documentation and the end-users were able to open, read and print the article.

One obstacle Interlibrary Loan encountered after testing was completed was that somehow the Interlibrary Loan email account to which patrons submit their requests electronically was corrupted, and quite a few requests were lost. An investigation by Library Automation revealed that a separate email account needed to be set up for the use of Ariel to forward documents to users' email addresses. Additional testing and implementation was delayed until after the second email account could be set up. At the same time, the Science Librarian was discussing the possible purchase of OVID with the Nursing Department. It was expected that Interlibrary Loan staff would mediate all requests, and the possibility of using DocView and Ariel for that service seemed logical. The Library Administration decided to postpone implementation of the proposed pilot project until negotiations for OVID had been completed and to offer the two services concurrently.

ELECTRONIC RESERVES
AT BALL STATE UNIVERSITY LIBRARIES

Ball State University Libraries first studied the possibility of offering an electronic reserve service in spring of 1997. In March 1997, the Electronic Reserves Working Group submitted a formal proposal for such a project to the Dean's Advisory Council. The concept for such a program was encouraged by the growth of distance education. The University's membership in the Indiana Partnership for Statewide Education (IPSE) provided additional momentum and support for developing an electronic reserve service. Further inspiration came from the IPSE library committee which stipulated that a model library system should include reserve materials in electronic form whenever possible. A pilot project for an electronic reserve service was proposed and was implemented during Spring Semester 1998. The purpose of the electronic reserve service was seen as a means to provide improved access to material on reserve for Ball State University students both on campus and at remote locations. It was further seen as a way to improve library services for increasing numbers of distance learners and as an addition to a growing list of electronic services offered by University Libraries in support of distance education.

Besides hardware and software needs, workflow concerns and potential problems with printing on the available dot matrix printers were considered. The Working Group also spent considerable time discussing copyright issues and developed extensive guidelines for handling requests for copyrighted materials and for obtaining copyright clearance. The issue of how to deal with faculty's own sites and how to avoid copyright violations was also extensively discussed. Access was to be made available via a Periodical/Reserve Web page linked to the University Libraries' Web site. Course reserve materials offered on the Web page in electronic format were to be available to Ball State University students on campus and to distance education students from their computers wherever they might be. To satisfy copyright requirements and licensing agreements, access was to be password controlled. A further issue that needed to be resolved was whether library staff would scan materials or whether the process should be out-sourced to other offices at the University. The question of who would be responsible for maintaining files and disk space on the Library Web server and develop password protection required by the IPSE guidelines also resulted in some lively discussions.

Eventually seven instructors participated in the pilot project and placed a total of sixty-nine articles on electronic reserve. At the completion of the pilot project, a questionnaire was distributed to the seven project participants asking them to have their students complete the questionnaire and return it to University Libraries for evaluation. Overall the project was received favorably. Students liked the fact that electronic reserves were available 24 hours a day, 7 days a week and that they did not need to come to the library to view the material. A major complaint was the poor print quality and poor legibility on screen. This deficiency needed attention if the service was to benefit distance education and students enrolled in those classes.

In summer of 1998 University Libraries began migration to a new automation system, and full implementation of the electronic reserve service was postponed until after the new system was installed. It was expected that a number of enhancements would be possible with the new system. For example, documentation for the reserve module indicated that it would permit the addition of HTML links to catalog records for users to locate and access electronic reserve material in WebCat, the new library catalog. Discussions with University Computing Services (UCS) led to the use of Web File Manager (WFM) for maintenance and password control. The WFM software was developed by UCS for Web publishing and is capable to authenticate users based on their current enrollment or employment status at Ball State University. WMF also facilitates the transfer of files to and from a UCS computer account. This meant that Periodical/Reserve staff would be able to handle file maintenance and configure password protection without having to rely on Library Automation. In addition, this procedure ensured that University Libraries would remain in control of the copyright clearance process and alleviated fears of potential contributory infringement if an instructor should fail to comply with a publisher's denial of copyright.

Remaining workflow issues were resolved and details for processing were worked out. As a result, Adobe Acrobat Capture is now used for the scanning process. It produces PDF image files of acceptable size and readable resolution as well as high quality onscreen legibility. Print quality is almost as good as a photocopy even with the available dot matrix printers. Next, Acrobat Exchange is used to crop scanned documents which includes the removal of dark edges or blank spaces. This process reduces file size and makes scanned articles look more professional. Unfortunately, so far no solution has been found to increase the loading speed for off-campus users by much, and printing remains rather slow unless laser printers are available.

In order to make the reserve service convenient and hassle free for both faculty and their students, Reserve staff prepare reserve material, provide access and handle copyright permission requests. The new library automation system makes it possible to use the MARC 856 to add hot links from a record in the Web-based catalog to outside documents. Doing this gives users direct access to the document from the bibliographic record in the catalog. Students can search for needed material by instructor name, course number or name, and author and title of the article they want. The full record in the catalog includes the URL with a hot link to the PDF file that contains their reading.

In an effort to satisfy IPSE guidelines for password protection, the decision was made to have patrons use their VAX login and password to view electronic reserve documents. This process also minimizes maintenance time for the Library. If students fail to login correctly, a help screen explains the process to them. Faculty are invited to participate in the electronic reserve service in a memo they receive each semester for traditional reserves. Currently, the electronic reserve service is only available for textual materials, such as photocopied articles. In the future, it may be expanded to include a variety of digitized audio-visual materials, and service in the branch libraries. Plans to link to files faculty produce for their own Web pages from WebCat are also considered.

In Spring 1999 twenty-one instructors participated in the service and placed 457 items on electronic reserve, a 553% increase compared to summer 1998. The number of instructors grew to twenty-five in Fall 1999. They taught a total of thirty classes and placed 467 items on electronic reserve. Out of these twenty-five instructors, one was also teaching a distance education class. No instructors from the Nursing program had placed materials on electronic reserve as of Fall 1999. It is anticipated that this will change as they gear up to expand their offerings to include significantly more distance education courses. University Libraries is in close contact with the coordinators for the Nursing Department and have encouraged them to consider placing materials on electronic reserve for their students' convenience.

CONCLUSION

Ball State University Libraries' interest in distance education is demonstrated by the strong commitment to provide service to distance learners. Significant progress has been made using technological advances for improving document ordering and delivery and for providing access to library resources, including electronic reserve. All public service areas have added email functions to their Web page to improve communication with users. Reference Service uses Web technology to answer reference questions, and Instructional Services has developed an online tutorial to be completed by students in library instruction classes. Currently discussions are taking place to add additional online services to further improve assistance to users both on campus and off. Among the possibilities considered are allowing users to perform renewals and recalls on line. It is expected that distance education is here to stay and that it likely will continue to grow in scope and the geographical areas it covers. Students enrolled in distance education classes expect to receive their instruction at the time and place of their choice. University Libraries must stay vigilant and proactive in their quest to provide service to these students or risk being replaced by service providers willing to do so.

REFERENCES

Association of College and Research Libraries. (1998). ACRL guidelines for distance learning library services. *College & Research Libraries News, 59*, 689-694.

Blakely, T. J. (1992). A model for distance education delivery. *Journal of Social Work Education, 28*, 214(8).

Brophy, P., & Craven, J. (1998). Lifelong learning and higher education libraries: Models for the 21st century. In P. S. Thomas & M. Jones (Comps.), *The Off-Campus Library Services Conference Proceedings: Providence, RI, April 22-24, 1998* (pp. 47-61). Mount Pleasant, MI: Central Michigan University.

Cain, M. (1995). Periodical access in an era of change: Characteristics and a model. *Journal of Academic Librarianship, 21*, 365-370.

Coder, A. (1998). Services challenges of a virtual library clientele. In P. S. Thomas & M. Jones (Comps.), *The Off-Campus Library Services Conference Proceedings: Providence, RI, April 22-24, 1998* (pp. 133-137). Mount Pleasant, MI: Central Michigan University.

Dugan, R. E., & Hernon, P. (1997). Information Policy. *Journal of Academic Librarianship, 23*, 315.

Jackson, M. E. (1994). Library to library: Interlibrary loan, document delivery, and resource sharing. *Wilson Library Bulletin, 69*(3), 73-74.

Khalil, M. (1993). Document delivery: A better option? *Library Journal, 118*(2), 43-47.

Kirk, E. E., & Bartelstein, A. M. (1999). Libraries close in on distance education. *Library Journal, 124*(6), 440-442.

Lebowitz, G. (1997). Library services to distant students: An equity issue. *Journal of Academic Librarianship, 23*, 303-308.

Madaus, J. R., & Webster, L. (1998). Opening the door to distance learning. *Computers in Libraries, 18*(5), 51(5).

Miller, G. E. (1997). Distance education and the emerging learning environment. *Journal of Academic Librarianship, 23*, 319-321.

Nicholls, P. (1997). Changing times: CD-ROM and document delivery. *Computers in Libraries, 17*(9), 59-63.

Prentice, A. E. (1997). Copyright, WIPO and user interests: Achieving balance among the shareholders. *Journal of Academic Librarianship, 23*, 309-311.

Ruschoff, C. (1997). What are the most important issues confronting academic librarianship as we approach the 21st century? *Journal of Academic Librarianship, 23*, 319-322.

Saunders, L. (1997). Documents on demand: How the net fits in. *Computers in Libraries, 17*(9), 45.

Saunders, L. (1998). Distance learning challenges us to adapt our services. *Computers in Libraries, 18*(5), 45.

Slade, A., & Kascus, M. (1998). An international comparison of library services for distance learning. In P. S. Thomas & M. Jones (Comps.), *The Off-Campus Library Services Conference Proceedings: Providence, RI, April 22-24, 1998* (pp. 259-297). Mount Pleasant, MI: Central Michigan University.

Walling, L. L. (1996). Going the distance: Equal education, off campus or on. *Library Journal, 121*(20), 59-62.

Ward, S. M. (1997). Document delivery: Evaluating the options. *Computers in Libraries, 17*(9), 26(4).

Weaver-Meyers, P., & Stolt, W. A. (1996). Delivery speed, timeliness and satisfaction: Patrons' perceptions about ILL service. *Journal of Library Administration, 23*(1/2), 23-41.

Beyond the Rhetoric:
A Study of the Impact
of the ACRL Guidelines
for Distance Learning Library Services
on Selected Distance Learning Programs
in Higher Education

Jean Caspers

Oregon State University

Jack Fritts

SWITCH, Inc.

Harvey Gover

Washington State University

SUMMARY. Several methods currently under way to track the usefulness of the *ACRL Guidelines for Distance Learning Library Services* are described and the results gathered thus far are reported upon. Included are a detailed review of recent literature on closely related issues; the history and development of the guidelines as they have evolved from their inception in 1963 to the most recent revision completed in 1998; a report on the guidelines dissemination efforts both during and after revision, including articles and papers or presentations at library and other professional conferences; and research methodology, including phone, postal, and e-mail surveys.

KEYWORDS. Library services, distance education, guidelines, Association of College and Research Libraries

[Haworth co-indexing entry note]: "Beyond the Rhetoric: A Study of the Impact of the ACRL Guidelines for Distance Learning Library Services on Selected Distance Learning Programs in Higher Education." Caspers, Jean, Jack Fritts, and Harvey Gover. Co-published simultaneously in *Journal of Library Administration* (The Haworth Information Press, an imprint of The Haworth Press, Inc.) Vol. 31, No. 3/4 2001, pp. 127-148; and: *Off-Campus Library Services* (ed: Anne Marie Casey) The Haworth Information Press, an imprint of The Haworth Press, Inc., 2001, pp. 127-148.

INTRODUCTION

Covered in this study are the methodology and preliminary results of a multi-tiered survey on the usefulness of the *ACRL Guidelines for Distance Learning Library Services* to the national regional accreditation associations and at selected post secondary institutions which offer distance learning programs. The authors surveyed these institutions to determine whether the guidelines were utilized in program planning and delivery. The interest was to learn whether the guidelines had an impact on institutional funding and support of library services to distance learning students. In providing an overview of some of the most fundamental issues involved, Williams (1994) stated:

> Times have changed and are continuing to change as both the clients served by the library and the structure of delivery systems for information change . . . . Many commute to and from campus, often at night or on weekends, and many are enrolled in programs offered at some distance from the campus, and even, at times, some distance from the instructor. It is one thing to talk of opening the library a sufficient number of hours to serve dormitory students; it is perhaps a bit more difficult to make sure that this kind of captive population learns to use library resources, especially if the population comes from a variety of ethnic and cultural backgrounds. But it is quite another thing to talk about providing library resources for a student taking courses from the University of South Carolina that are broadcast via satellite to a site in West Virginia or that is delivered via videotape to a student in Ohio. (p. 25)

These are some of the issues the guidelines are designed to address. The authors hoped to discover indicators of the extent to which the guidelines are being utilized at selected individual institutions. The authors were also interested in learning whether accrediting agencies and professional organizations considered the guidelines as part of their institutional or programmatic analyses. In addition to the survey of academic institutions, representatives of selected regional accrediting agencies and professional accrediting organizations were interviewed about their view of the usefulness and applicability of the guidelines in their work with institutions.

One of the purposes of the guidelines was to provide direction for library support for those involved in distance learning activities and program or service support at any level within an institution of higher education. As the introduction to the 1998 revision states:

> Library resources and services in institutions of higher education must meet the needs of all their faculty, students, and academic support staff, wherever these individuals are located, whether on a main campus, off-campus, in distance education or extended campus programs, or in the absence of a campus at all; in courses taken for credit or non-credit; in continuing education programs; in courses attended in person or by means of electronic transmission; or any other means of distance education. (Association of College and Research Libraries, 1998, p. 689)

Distance education is a rapidly growing segment within higher education. As technological change continues, more and more institutions are adding distance learning options to their menu. There are many reasons for this shift to occur. According to Burge (1996), "Institutions that offer distance mode courses are doing so mainly because they want to maintain or increase student numbers and/or research funding in times of reduced resources and increased competition" (p. 846). Other institutions may have different goals in mind. In a 1996 article on linkages between libraries and administrations, Rosenquist-Buhler (1996) said:

> Some universities see the potential for distance education as a growth market and are willing to invest in the admittedly expensive technologies necessary for resource development. They hope to recover costs over time by increasing the volume of students reached without constructing new buildings or hiring additional faculty. The opportunity to educate students throughout their life span also promises greater financial reward than the traditional four- or five-year program. (p. 223)

Whether an institution moves into distance learning programs for monetary or altruistic reasons, there is still a need for library and research support of the distant programs. Rosenquist-Buhler (1996) also stated that:

> The university of choice in the future will be the one that brings the greatest number of services to the student. Access to schol-

arly research materials has been a vital missing element in distance education. The evolution of the virtual library builds the research foundation necessary for the virtual university of tomorrow. (p. 220)

Distance learning programs are enjoying a tremendous period of growth at this time. Such programs address the needs of students who do not have ready access to a traditional institution or traditional on-campus programs. Such students do have need of continuing education or advanced coursework for promotion or job success. Students constrained by distance, time, family or work responsibilities need the opportunities offered by distance learning programs. In defining distance education and its users Roberts (1996) said:

> In practical terms, distance education is designed to serve learners who are unable, for reasons of geography or schedule, to attend courses on-campus. Principles of access and equity of opportunity have been important values driving the field. . . . Finally, learners need strong learner support systems outside of "classroom" time, and so methods of providing two-way communication such as counseling, coaching, and library services have been developed. (p. 812)

Our focus in this paper is on the inclusion of library services and support in the distance learning process within higher education as evidenced by the use of the ACRL Distance Learning Section's *ACRL Guidelines for Distance Learning Library Services*. Most researchers into distance learning are in agreement that library support is a key element. The overriding question is how to meld that element into the overall process.

REVIEW OF RELATED LITERATURE

The literature on distance learning or distance education addresses many issues, but to date little specific attention has been paid to the question of the impact of guidelines on off-campus library services. However, there is a growing body of literature that considers the need for strong library support as part of the delivery of distance learning programs and covers the same issues delineated in the guidelines. In a discussion of his experience with distance teaching, Faulhaber (1996) speaks not only of the need for library involvement, but also of the level of support needed for successful preparation and delivery. He said:

> Distance education without a digital library is not possible. However, there is still a long way to go before digitally supported distance education is feasible for most faculty members. Few institutions can afford to provide the level of staff support that I received in teaching my Old Catalan class. Instead of providing such services directly, libraries, in collaboration with other partners like computer centers and instructional technology programs, must begin to provide the tools that faculty members and students need in order to create these resources themselves. (p. 855-856)

Macauley and McKnight (1998) of Deakin University published a paper on the University's Web site proposing a model for library cooperation in the delivery of post-graduate courses to distant students. In this document they stated that:

> Libraries are an integral part of the academic mission of a university. Libraries can enhance a university's reputation by providing access to world-class information resources and services and can help to stimulate research by promoting collections and services widely. Libraries are already a part of the research culture of a university. (p. 8)

There is the possibility that as such cooperation grows, institutions will begin to redefine themselves and their organizational processes. Rosenquist-Buhler (1996) spoke about the idea of partnerships when she said:

> Powerful partnerships between libraries and distance education units, for example, are now developing. These partnerships are changing the way research libraries provide services to users and are enhancing the potential for expanding distance learning programs. In addition, these alliances may well reshape university instruction in the future. Factors influencing these closer-working relationships include not only technological developments both in distance education and in libraries, but also a changing student population with an increased need for lifelong learning . . . . (p. 220)

Rosenquist-Buhler (1996) went on to say, "Library and distance education administrators need to work closely together to ensure that the needs of distance learners are identified and resources are funded" (p. 224).

Macauley and McKnight's position paper (199?) sounded a similar note when they said:

> The goal is for a three way partnership to be formed–the candidate, the supervisor(s) and the librarian. Each partner can focus on their tasks whilst still working together, thus creating a whole which is greater than the sum of the parts. The purpose of the model is to provide complementary expertise to assist the candidate and the supervisors. (p. 5)

Another case for partnership is made by McManus (1998) in his discussion of other reasons for early library involvement in distance learning planning:

> For at least two reasons, librarians must be involved early in the development of distance education programs. The first can be illustrated by a problem that arises every day at any reference, circulation, or reserve desk: the instructor has assigned materials that 'the library is bound to have.' While this presents difficulties on campus, the simple inconvenience and frustration (and concomitant ill will) are not easily resolved for distance students. Secondly, librarians remain the experts in information/knowledge packaging. It has been, and continues to be, our jobs to know what students need and can use and what is available. (p. 433)

As he pointed out, faulty expectations can much more easily be dealt with onsite than remotely. Advance involvement can mean the difference between a successful and an unsuccessful program. It is also important to remember and to help institutions remember that the librarians are experts in the acquisition and dissemination of information. McManus (1998) further stated that:

> If librarians and libraries don't become pedagogical players in the information and education enterprise, then turning to the Internet as the first source for information will make sense to more and more students *and* university administrators. I think

that distance learning, information technology, and libraries have too much to offer for that scenario to become true. Yet, libraries must be active, political, effective builders of learning *knowledge structures* if the money that legislators and administrators save is not at their expense. (p. 435)

This partnership process also works in both directions. Service enhancements designed to meet the needs of distant students will improve local access and services as well. The guidelines speak of the need for distant students to receive equal or better services and support to that offered on-campus. McManus (1998) noted, "But what we've found, in addition to satisfying external mandates, is that programs designed for one group or another (on campus or off) invariably lead us to integrate those services into better library services to all students and faculty" (p. 434).

In a 1996 article on the role of the library, Rodrigues pointed out that, "The library needs of distant learners are not unique. They are similar to those of on-campus students. Apart from the manner in which they are accessed, requested and delivered, the same resources are required, the same questions are asked, and the same quality of service is expected" (p. 23).

McManus also pointed out that "The Southern Association of Colleges and Schools requires that planned adequate library services *must* be offered to students at distance sites, equal to the services on-campus students receive" (p. 434).

A final comment on partnering between libraries and distance learning units comes from a 1994 article in which Abbott observes:

> . . . but when librarians are the last to hear about a new initiative 100 miles away and no one has considered the need to provide library support, adequate staff, access to the cataloger, or money for phone calls or mailing, there is a serious problem. Here is another reason for librarians to seek out involvement on campus planning, budget, or other committees where there might be a chance to influence the planning process for off-campus education. (p. 83)

As librarians, we cannot serve the students if we are unaware of the programs or offerings available. The needs of distance learners and the role of the library in addressing those needs should also be considered.

Some of the literature speaks about the sense of isolation expressed by some distance learning students. In many instances, the library or an individual librarian is the only point of contact between the distant student and the main campus.

Johnstone and Krauth (1996) identified some questions that should be considered in the delivery of distance education:

> Will students in *virtual* learning situations be isolated, with no semblance of human contact with their instructors? How can effective advising and academic support services be provided to distance-learning students? Will students in distance-learning degree programs have some guarantee that an electronically delivered program will continue to be supported long enough to enable them to complete the degree? (p. 39)

They also point out that distance is not necessarily the primary area of concern since, "research and evaluation studies have consistently demonstrated that the achievement and satisfaction of students who learn via technology can equal those of students in regular classrooms" (p. 39).

Rosenquist-Buhler (1996) offered some thoughts about the interaction between the librarian and the distant student:

> The librarian is still the major library contact person for the user, and that contact now becomes even more important, especially while the student is developing skills and confidence in the system. While the contact between librarian and user now occurs via some artificial communication format rather than in person, the link is still vitally important. (p. 224)

Riggs (1997) also addressed this issue in an editorial when he said:

> Students taking classes at a remote location should expect the same level of library service as that provided to their peers on campus. . . . The distance learner has to be perceived in the same value structure as the on-campus learner. If this is not the case, then distance education could be viewed as a stepchild. Distance education requires a strategy for change–essentially, to conjure with values different than those that have implicitly conditioned the library's organizational past. (p. 209)

Miller (1997) discussed distance learning in the context of changes in learning and the learning environment. He began by saying:

> . . . we are faced with changes in the dynamics of society. For educators, these changes contribute to a radical change in, first, the context of our work and, second, a reconsideration of the basic assumptions and operating principles upon which we conduct our work. This new environment for teaching and learning is both caused by changes in technology and made possible by technology. (p. 319)

Miller continues his discussion of these changes and points out that lifelong learning has become a necessity. In his description of these societal changes he listed some common characteristics of the new learning environment, saying it will:

- Be lifelong, supporting learners through their individual lives as well as their career changes;
- Be learner-centered, giving lifelong learners greater control over the time, place, and pace of study;
- Emphasize both formal and informal collaboration, providing a communications-rich environment for students to work together in teams and to form informal study groups at great distances;
- Emphasize individual inquiry and use of original data and resources rather than lecture and use of prepared texts; and
- Be structured to ensure that learners gain direct experience in solving problems, making decisions, and exploring values, both as individuals and as members of teams (p. 320).

On a related note, Roberts (1996) identifies four trends in distance learning: "(1) The projected growth of distance education activity; (2) a trend to digital and networked technologies; (3) the increased use of the home as a learning site and of computers, not print, as the most common methods; and (4) the economic impact and costs of distance education" (p. 814).

These trends have important implications for library service and support. The way in which libraries operate is changing to accommodate these types of changes in the approach to education and learning. As institutions move more aggressively into distance learning programming, questions about institutional and programmatic accreditation have begun to arise. This brings us back to our starting point. The Guidelines are designed to provide guidance for institutions involved in distance learning activities. As we stated above, libraries need to be active partners in the development and delivery of distance learning programs. By improving access to information, libraries enrich the learning experience for all users, regardless of location. Providing new levels of access changes the whole idea of the library from storehouse to facilitator. Rosenquist-Buhler (1996) said:

> Not only do these developments reconfigure the idea of library service by including remote users as members of the libraries' primary clientele, but they also expand the potential for distance education by allowing students to access vital research materials regardless of the students' location. The more information libraries are able to provide electronically, the more equality of access distance learners have and, therefore, the more academically rigorous and competitive distance education programs can become. (p. 221)

The *ACRL Guidelines for Distance Learning Library Services* should provide a linkage between libraries and curriculum planning. The guidelines give libraries an opportunity to engage their institutions in dialogue about the implications and realities of involvement in distance learning. As has been stated above, the library must be a full and active partner in the planning, implementation, and delivery of distance learning programs. The library is a key support structure in such programming by virtue of its role as a contact and guide for the student in seeking information and resources beyond the provided fundamental course materials.

Such considerations lead directly into the question of accreditation. Too frequently, library issues are only addressed as part of an institutional self-study and then allowed to slip back below the threshold of awareness. As technology brings change to higher education, the role of the library needs to assume a higher profile. Abbott (1994) described the role of accreditation thusly:

> Accreditation, especially by the regional associations, can and should play the all-important role of keeping all of us focused on the future needs of our students and community constituents. The associations as well as the evaluation strategies are created and

managed by our peers. It is, in my view, one of the few opportunities for interested colleagues to work together in a supportive atmosphere on the tough questions of who we are and where we are going. (p. 78)

There is new activity in the area of evaluation and review. Johnstone and Krauth speak about groups, such as the Task Force on Distant Learning and the Western Cooperative for Educational Telecommunications, which are working to develop a common framework for quality by developing standards. Mugridge (1997) sounded a warning note about the development of guidelines for students:

> ... there are legitimate areas of concern to which we have not felt able to respond in a set of general guidelines. These include the need for courses delivered at a distance from their point of origin to be culturally sensitive and to be adapted in ways that take account of local differences; the need for adequate support systems for remote students; and the provision of additional indicators of course quality to students. (p. 60)

Currently, accrediting bodies review institutional operations within a defined framework. The rigor with which library services, collections, and support are considered varies from organization to organization. Williams (1994) stated it this way:

> As we move into an age in which there is no *best* source for all information, accreditors are faced with determining whether institutions are getting information to users in the best possible way while at the same time outfitting students to function in a world that is information rich. (p. 27)

Wolff and Steadman (1994) spoke of elements derived from interviews with librarians at institutions offering off-campus programs. The two identified the following:

> Our interviews with librarians suggest four key elements in the provision of library services for off-campus programs. First, institutions should take responsibility for developing library support for off-campus students, rather than transferring such responsibility, often unknowingly, to other institutions' libraries.

Second, all institutions should develop a basic collection at each site where degree programs are offered or provide immediate access to such collections through on-line services under the institution's control. Third, institutions should provide research support to students directly, rather than assigning this to the staffs of other libraries. Fourth, institutions need to engage in periodic reviews not only of library collections and services but also of the expectations of library usage for each discipline and course and how those expectations are being realized. (pp. 17-18)

There seems to be agreement among authors that the agencies themselves are not going to be the final arbiters of the linkage between libraries and distance learning programs. Some of the regional accrediting agencies have indicated a willingness to incorporate more stringent expectations into their review process, while others leave the task of making their case to the institutions themselves. Williams (1994) said:

While most of the accrediting associations have backed off from developing true performance measures for libraries, opting instead for the broader concept of outcomes assessment, libraries must face up to the fact that they must be able to say what they contribute to the university. The challenge is to move beyond the sort of "home, mother, and apple pie" statements that so often find their way into library literature and into on-campus justifications for the library without trying to quantify what they do to the point that they tease out consideration of everything that is important to the operation. (p. 30)

One view holds that the question of standards and/or guidelines is going to be primarily the venue of the institutions themselves. As Perrin (1994) said:

Most institutions and programs are already inundated with some form of externally mandated assessment; therefore, the "value-added" aspect of accreditation must be seen as truly relevant, especially in times of severe economic downturn. As institutions operate with continuously shrinking budgets, it is time for accreditors at both institutional and programmatic levels to cooperate maximally with each other to ease the economic burden that multiple accrediting visits and processes may place on a campus. (p. 5)

The library must be proactive in this process and clearly demonstrate to the institution the value added components to be found with full library support and involvement.

GUIDELINES HISTORY AND DEVELOPMENT

Since their inception more than three decades ago, the Association of College and Research Libraries' *ACRL Guidelines for Distance Learning Library Services* have been the product of the pooled efforts of top leaders in all aspects of distance teaching and learning in higher education. Reflecting the phenomenally rapid growth and development of this area of specialization within librarianship, the Guidelines themselves have evolved into an increasingly complex document over the decades. The guidelines as we know them today are the culmination of the following series of documents, the first of which originated in processes initially undertaken in 1963:

ACRL Guidelines for Library Services to Extension Students, 1967
ACRL Guidelines for Extended Campus Library Services, 1981
ACRL Guidelines for Extended Campus Library Services, 1990
ACRL Guidelines for Distance Learning Library Services, 1998

Although we think of the guidelines today as being a product of the Distance Learning Section, as are the latest guidelines, the original 1967 *ACRL Guidelines for Library Services to Extension Students* predate the 1989 founding of the Section by twenty-two years. A subcommittee of the ACRL Committee on Standards prepared the original guidelines, as it was then known (Tanis, 1967). Thirteen years later, the committee, which by then had assumed its now familiar name as the ACRL Standards and Accreditation Committee, or SAC, undertook a review of the original Guidelines in January, 1980. After a year of work, the newly revised and retitled *ACRL Guidelines for Extended Campus Library Services* were published (*ACRL guidelines for extended . . .* , 1981).

Within seven years, the need to update the guidelines was again felt, and a task force was appointed for this purpose at ALA Midwinter

1988. In addition to reviewing the literature, the task force held two hearings on the 1981 guidelines, one at ALA Annual in July 1988, and the other at the October 1988 Off-Campus Library Services Conference. Additional input came from previous users, from the Extended Campus Library Services Discussion Group, and from regional and professional accrediting agencies. The resulting proposed draft revision was published in the May 1989 *College & Research Libraries News,* and hearings were held a few weeks later at ALA Annual 1989. A final draft was prepared for publication in response to this latter hearing testimony (Association of . . . , 1990).

From the beginning, those undertaking preparation or revision of the guidelines have sought the widest possible input from everyone involved in all aspects and on all levels of distance teaching and learning in higher education. Because writing the initial guidelines was a pioneering effort, close to four years were required for conceptualizing, drafting, and finalizing them. The process was initiated in 1963 with a review of the meager literature on library services to college and university extension students conducted by a subcommittee of the ACRL Committee on Standards (CoS). E. Walfred Erickson, librarian at Eastern Michigan University and member of CoS, chaired the subcommittee. Following the literature review, Erickson prepared, as an initial starting point, a position paper on problems affecting the instructional role of library services in extension programs (Tanis, 1967).

A milestone in the preparation efforts occurred in July 1965, with the convening of a CoS sponsored national conference, Library Services for College Extension Centers. This august assemblage included representatives of the following: accreditation associations, the Association of University Evening Colleges, the U.S. Office of Education, the National University Extension Association, the Association for Field Services in Teacher Education, and several divisions of ALA (Tanis, 1967).

Sometime after the 1965 Library Services for College Extension Centers conference, a second draft of what was to become the Extension Guidelines was prepared. The draft was submitted to leaders in the library profession and college extension work. The advice of numerous public and state librarians was solicited and received. The many comments of the experts consulted were incorporated into the final draft guidelines. Field directors of college extension programs were identified as having been particularly generous with their contributions to the efforts of the committee (Tanis, 1967, p. 55).

Establishing a philosophical base still valid and in use today, the 1967 guidelines were designed as a set of principles, which college and university libraries, extension librarians, and directors of extension programs could draw upon in the establishment of sound library service to extension students. Emphasis was placed on the instructional role of books and related materials in the education of the extension student. The CoS made a deliberate and conscious choice to draw up broad guidelines in lieu of the traditional standards, because extension programs by their very nature were marked by great diversity and . . . a long history of innovation and experimentation (Tanis, 1967, p. 55).

Revision processes very similar to those of the past were followed in the revision of our current 1998 guidelines. By 1996 the need for revision of the 1990 guidelines had become evident. Appointment of a special entity such as a task force was no longer necessary due to the existence by that time of the Guidelines Committee of the Extended Campus Library Services Section (ECLSS). ECLSS had been brought into existence while the 1990 guidelines were in preparation and had evolved from the Extended Campus Library Services Discussion Group, which had contributed to the preparation of the 1990 guidelines.

Harvey Gover prepared the revision of the 1990 guidelines, then chair of the guidelines Committee, whose contribution in this most recent cycle of revision was very similar to that made by E. Walfred Erickson in the preparation of the original guidelines. For more than two years Gover brought the guidelines through multiple subsequent drafts. These drafts were based upon input from two open hearings, one at ALA Midwinter, 1997, and the other at Annual, 1997. Further input came from members of the Guidelines Committee, the ECLSS Executive Board, the ECLSS general membership, and "other librarians and administrators involved in post-secondary distance learning programs from across the nation and around the world (Gover, 1998, p. 690).

In addition, Gover received input from requests for suggestions for revision which appeared in widely-read national academic and library publications, distance education listservs, and through ECLSS Web site and print publications. Further, numerous other individuals, consortia, and representatives of professional and accrediting associations provided information on their own efforts to ensure excellence of library services for . . . distance learning programs (Gover, 1998, p. 690).

Toward the end of the revision process, in the ALA elections of April 1998, ECLSS members voted to change the section name to Distance Learning Section. Consequently, "Distance Learning" was likewise adapted into the title and text of the then near complete, new guidelines.

The guidelines as we have them today are a living document, with processes of continuous, ongoing revision. The Guidelines Committee is under mandate from SAC to incorporate further outcomes into the present approved draft. Further adoption of an outcomes orientation for the current guidelines will not be viewed as a major revision and will require only the approval of SAC. A more extensive revision is anticipated within the next five to seven years, reflecting the still rapidly accelerating pace of development for distance learning programs and their complementary library services.

DISSEMINATION OF THE 1998 GUIDELINES

As noted above, the revision process included the distribution of various drafts of the guidelines for comment by many individuals and groups. By the time the guidelines were officially reissued by ACRL in October of 1998, the draft had become well known within the international community of distance education librarians.

Since the October 1998 publication of the newly approved guidelines in *College & Research Libraries News,* followed shortly by their placement at the ACRL Web site, the DLS Guidelines Committee embarked on further dissemination efforts. A plan to distribute copies of the guidelines directly to accrediting agencies, state librarians and library school directors was approved by the ACRL leadership. By September 30, 1999, a direct mailing including specially printed booklet copies of the guidelines and cover letters, signed by DLS Section Chair Harvey Gover and either ACRL President Larry Hardesty or ACRL Executive Director, Althea Jenkins, was sent out to eight accrediting bodies, fifty state librarians, and fifty-seven library school directors.

In addition, the Guidelines Committee solicited from members of the Off-Campus Library Services List citations of publications referencing the guidelines by DLS members and other librarians, including papers or presentations at professional conferences, both library and other higher education conferences. Besides the official ACRL publications, a total of five publications and twenty presentations (fifteen at library conferences and five at non-library academic conferences) between October 1998 and November 1999, featuring or referring to the guidelines, were identified by this process.

An additional method for assessing the distribution of the guidelines was the use of three search engines offering *link* searches on the Web. Forty-four separate sites with links to the official ACRL version of the guidelines were identified on November 23, 1999.

The list below catalogs the dissemination efforts noted during this period.

OFFICIAL ACRL PUBLICATIONS

Association of College and Research Libraries. (2 Oct. 1998). ACRL guidelines for distance learning library services [On-Line]. Available <http://www.ala.org/guides/distlrng.html>.

Revised ACRL Guidelines for Distance Learning Library Services [On-Line]. (1999, June). ALA News Release. Available <http://www.ala.org/news/v4n19/revisedguidelines.html>.

Association of College and Research Libraries. (1998). ACRL guidelines for distance learning library services. *College & Research Libraries News, 59,* 689-694.

Copies of Guidelines distributed by ACRL: September 30, 1999

- 50 state librarians
- 57 library science degree program directors
- 8 to the following higher education accrediting bodies:

Middle States Association of Colleges and Schools (Commission on Institutions of Higher Education)

New England Association of Schools & Colleges (Commission on Institutions of Higher Education)

New England Association of Schools and Colleges (Commission on Vocational, Technical and Career)

North Central Association of Colleges and Schools (Commission on Institutions of Higher Education)

Northwest Association of Schools and Colleges (Commission on Colleges)

Southern Association of Colleges and Schools (Commission on Colleges)

Western Association of Schools and Colleges (Commission for Community and Junior Colleges)

Western Association of Schools and Colleges (Senior Colleges and Universities)

ARTICLES FEATURING THE GUIDELINES

ACRL Guidelines call for virtual libraries equivalent to campus. (1999). *Virtual University News, 1,* 1-2, 4.

Baker, N., & Marquardt, S. (1999). Library support for distance education. *Library Issues, 20,* 1-4.

Kirk, E. E., & Bartelstein, A. M. (1999). Libraries close in on distance education. *Library Journal, 124*(6), 40-42.

Morrison, R. (1999). Academic resources available to help public libraries serve distance learners. *Directions for Utah Libraries, 10,* 4-5.

New ACRL guidelines for distance learning library services. (1999). *JLSDE, The Journal of Library Services for Distance Education, 2,* 1. Available <http://www.westga.edu/library/jlsde/jlsde2.1.html>. Reprint of the text of the Guidelines.

PAPERS OR PRESENTATIONS AT LIBRARY CONFERENCES

Abbott, T. E. (1999, April 10). Discussion on distance education library issues. Association of College and Research Libraries (ACRL) Conference.

Abbott, T. E. (1999, June 27). *How knowledge of user studies has changed instruction in DE, how digital libraries have effected instruction, and how library instruction is changing.* American Library Association (ALA) Annual Meeting, New Orleans.

Abbott, T. E. (1999, March). *The library's role in distance education and associated costs.* Louisiana Library Association–Academic Section Spring Conference.

Abbott, T. E. (1999, May). *The librarian as leader in electronic information literacy* (Internet discussion participant and featured speaker). Illinois Association of College and Research Libraries (IACRL) Dive In Conference, Wheaton, Illinois.

Cardinal, D. (1999, June). Presentation. WILSWorld99.

Caspers, J. S., & Ragan, L. (1999, June). *The Evolution of distance learning environments.* North American Serials Interest Group (NASIG) Annual Conference, Pittsburgh.

Caspers, J. S., & Finney, C. (1999, January). *Visions for library distance education services. Visions on the frontier.* Northwest Off Campus Library Services First Annual Meeting, Bend, OR.

Gover, H., & Caspers, J. S. (1999, January). Presentation and discussion of the *ACRL guidelines for distance learning library services.* LITA Section Discussion Group meeting. American Library Association (ALA) Midwinter Meeting, Philadelphia.

Gover, H., Caspers, J.S., & Lee, C-C, Parton, W. (1999, June). *Presenting the ACRL DLS guidelines: The future is now.* American Library Association (ALA) Annual Meeting, New Orleans.

Jones, M. (1999, July). *The ACRL guidelines for distance learning library services: Context, content, and connections.* New Mexico Consortium of Academic Libraries (NMCAL), Santa Fe.

Kearley, J. (1999, June). *Going the distance: Interlibrary loan in the virtual information environment.* ALA Annual Meeting, New Orleans.

Ronayne, B. (1999, June) ACRL/IS/DSL Poster Session. ALA Annual Meeting, New Orleans.

Sloan, Bernie. (1999, June). Presentation. WILSWorld99.

Sloan, Bernie: (1999?) Presentation. Illinois Association of College and Research Libraries (IACRL) Dive In Conference, Wheaton, Illinois.

Thornton, G., Meloy, W., & Caspers, Jean. (1999, April). *Going the distance: Library services to a global community.* Association of College and Research Libraries Ninth Annual Conference, Detroit.

PAPERS OR PRESENTATIONS
AT ACADEMIC CONFERENCES BEYOND
THE LIBRARY COMMUNITY

Abbott, T. E. (1999, May). Presentation. New England Board of Higher Education Conference. Boston.

Hinchliffe, L. (1999, February). *Distance learning library services, teaching and learning using the Internet: Enhancing distance learning*. 1999 Illinois Higher Education Distance Learning Conference.

Hinchliffe, L. & Naylor, S. (1999, August). *But we don't have a million dollars! Distance learning library services with limited budget and personnel*. Distance Learning '99: 15th Annual Conference on Distance Teaching and Learning, Madison, Wisconsin.

Marquardt, S. (moderator), Caspers, J.S., Finney, C., & Race, S., (1999, November*). Providing library services at a distance*. Western Cooperative for Educational Telecommunications (WCET) Annual Meeting, Portland, OR.

Sykes-Berry, S., & Mullaly-Quijas, P. (1999, August). *So you want to provide library support for distance education programs: A blueprint for getting started*. 15th Annual Conference on Distance Teaching and Learning, Madison, Wisconsin

METHOLOGY

During the summer of 1999, Bernie Sloan, a researcher at the University of Illinois, asked members of the Off–Campus Library Services List about institutional use of the DLS guidelines. As part of the message, Sloan noted that the IACRL/IBHE Liaison Committee (Illinois Association of College and Research Libraries/Illinois Board of Higher Education) had endorsed the Guidelines and was recommending that the IBHE consider the guidelines when reviewing distance learning programs. Sixteen subscribers responded to the list in answer to his request.

The results were mixed. Some institutions clearly have not considered the guidelines or given much thought at all to library support for distance learning. Others felt that the guidelines serve as a useful template for internal library planning. Three respondents stated that they had incorporated or were in the process of incorporating many items from the guidelines into their standard practices, and several others felt that they were moving in that direction as well. None of the respondents felt that the entire document was in use or incorporated into planning for services, however. Some respondents spoke more to the nature of guidelines and their perceptions of library activities than to actual consideration or use of the guidelines themselves.

The authors of this paper intend to expand on this information by conducting a larger, more focused survey. Those who responded to

Bernie Sloan's question will be included in this study and be given the opportunity to expand on their responses and perceptions.

The authors of this study further intend to contact representatives of each of the eight regional accreditation agencies asking about the importance of library services in accrediting of higher education distance education programs. Copies of the standards currently in use for academic library services by each regional agency will also be requested in order to update the 1994 study by Gilmer (1995), in which the standards used by each agency in 1989 were compared with those in use by 1994.

Selected academic library directors will also be surveyed, perhaps in conjunction with a survey planned by ACRL, to learn whether their libraries have adopted the guidelines, whether the guidelines have been integrated into any campus documents, and whether the guidelines are to be used in preparation for an accreditation review. Directors will also be asked whether the guidelines have been used in whole or in part, and if in part, what sections have been used. Institutional structures for distance learning programs will also be checked to determine whether there is a correlation between program structures and willingness to use the guidelines.

Since the surveys and other data gathering methods described in this study are ongoing, any results gained since the preparation of this paper will be reported upon in the authors' presentation at the Portland Conference.

REFERENCES

Abbott, T. E. (1994). Distance education and off-campus library services: challenges for the accreditation process and librarians. In Garten, E. D. (Ed.), *The Challenge and practice of academic accreditation* (pp. 77-86). Westport, CT: Greenwood Press.

ACRL guidelines for extended campus library services. (1981). In *ACRL Guidelines and Standards, 1974-1988* (pp. 85-86). Chicago, IL: ALA Publishing Services, 1988. (ERIC Document Reproduction Service No. ED 296 724).

Association of College and Research Libraries. (1967). Guidelines for library services to extension students. *ALA Bulletin, 61*(1), 50-53.

Association of College and Research Libraries. (1990). ACRL guidelines for extended campus library services. *College & Research Libraries News, 50*, 353-355.

Association of College and Research Libraries. (1998). ACRL guidelines for distance learning library services. *College & Research Libraries News, 59*, 689-694.

Burge, E. J. (1996). Inside-out thinking about distance teaching: making sense of reflective practice. *Journal of the American Society for Information Science, 47,* 843-848.

Faulhaber, C. B. (1996). Distance learning and digital libraries: two sides of a single coin. *Journal of the American Society for Information Science, 47,* 854-856.

Gilmer, L. C. (1995). Accreditation of off-campus library services: Comparative study of the regional accreditation agencies. In C. J. Jacob (Comp.), *The Seventh Off-Campus Library Services Conference Proceedings, San Diego, CA, October 25-27, 1995* (pp. 101-110). Mount Pleasant, Michigan: Central Michigan University, 1995.

Gover, H. (1998). Revising the "Guidelines." *College & Research Libraries News, 59*(9), 690.

Guidelines for library services to extension students. (1967). *ALA Bulletin, 61*(1), 50-53.

Johnstone, S. M., & Krauth, B. (1996). Balancing quality and access: some principles of good practice for the virtual university. *Change, 28*(2), 38-41.

Macauley, P., & McKnight, S. (1998). *A new model of library support for off-campus postgraduate research students.* A position paper posted on the Deakin University Web site: http://www.deakin.edu.au/library/newmodelliboc.html.

McManus, M. G. R. (1998). Neither Pandora nor Cassandra: library services and distance education in the next decade. *College & Research Library News, 59,* 432-435.

Miller, G. E. (1997). Distance education and the emerging learning environment. *Journal of Academic Librarianship, 23,* 319-321.

Mugridge, I. (1997). Remote delivery of courses: guidelines for students and institutions. *Open Learning, 12*(2), 59-62.

Perrin, K. L. (1994). Challenges for accreditation in a rapidly changing environment. In Garten, E. D. (Ed.), *The Challenge and Practice of Academic Accreditation* (pp. 3-5). Westport, CT: Greenwood Press.

Riggs, D. (1997). Distance education: rethinking practices, implementing new approaches. *College & Research Libraries, 58,* 208-209.

Roberts, J. M. (1996). The story of distance education: A practitioner's perspective. *Journal of the American Society for Information Science, 47,* 811-816.

Rodrigues, H. F. (1996). The role of the library in distance education. *Microcomputers for Information Management, 13*(1), 21-30.

Rosenquist-Buhler, C. (1996). New partners in distance education: linking up to libraries. *Library Administration & Management, 10,* 220-225.

Tanis, N. E. (1967). The preparation of the guidelines. *ALA Bulletin, 61*(1), 54-55.

Williams, D. E. (1994). Challenges to accreditation from the new academic library environment. In Garten, E. D. (Ed.), *The Challenge and Practice of Academic Accreditation* (pp. 23-31). Westport, CT: Greenwood Press.

Wolff, R. A., & Steadman, M. H. (1994). Accreditation expectations in the age of new technology. In Garten, E. D. (Ed.), *The Challenge and Practice of Academic Accreditation* (pp. 7-21). Westport, CT: Greenwood Press.

Providing Services and Information to the Dispersed Off-Campus Student: An Integrated Approach

Anthony K. Cavanagh

Deakin University, Australia

SUMMARY. Deakin University in Victoria, Australia has provided a full library service to its off-campus students since its formation in 1977. Electronic access to the catalogue has been available since 1992 and over 150 networked databases including several with full-text are currently in use. Yet despite ready availability and high use of electronic resources, our students are still heavy users of document delivery of books and journal articles, indicating that the so-called virtual library by itself is unlikely to meet the library needs of off-campus users adequately. The paper considers the difficulties facing off-campus students and concludes that access to electronic services and facilities, despite its limitations, offers the best solution to many of the needs of these students. A particular difficulty for many distance students is obtaining the necessary software and setting themselves up to use electronic services. The Deakin Learning Toolkit was developed to meet these needs. Supplied as a free CD-ROM to all students and staff of the University, it provides software, information and tutorials on an easy to install and use disk. Library-related features of the Toolkit are described in detail.

KEYWORDS. Library services, distance education, Australia, electronic library services

INTRODUCTION

The last five years have seen a revolution in the electronic resources available to off campus students. Advances in information technology

---

[Haworth co-indexing entry note]: "Providing Services and Information to the Dispersed Off-Campus Student: An Integrated Approach." Cavanagh, Anthony K. Co-published simultaneously in *Journal of Library Administration* (The Haworth Information Press, an imprint of The Haworth Press, Inc.) Vol. 31, No. 3/4, 2001, pp. 149-166; and: *Off-Campus Library Services* (ed: Anne Marie Casey) The Haworth Information Press, an imprint of The Haworth Press, Inc., 2001, pp. 149-166.

have allowed libraries to extend the range of services provided to students and thus reduce their isolation. Yet our experience is that the majority of our students still want to read books and articles in paper format and contact the library by phone, mail and fax. The number who use electronic resources and services is steadily increasing (around 35% of requests to the library delivery service are received electronically) so that the library has become what is sometimes known as a "hybrid library"–one that provides integrated access to a full range of both electronic and print resources.

This paper will briefly describe the library services provided by Deakin University, a leading Australian distance education university, to its 12,400 off-campus students who are dispersed throughout Australia with some 700 resident overseas. It considers the problems facing dispersed and isolated students and concludes that access to electronic services and facilities, even with their limitations, offers the best solutions to many of the needs of these students. Major difficulties for many distance students are obtaining the necessary software to use electronic services and learning how to use such software, as well as learning how to search library catalogues and databases. The remainder of the paper discusses the development and implementation of the Deakin Learning Toolkit, a CD-ROM supplied by mail to all off campus students (and available to on-campus students and academic staff) of Deakin University. While its original purpose was to deliver a suite of software to off-campus students to facilitate their study at Deakin, it has grown to include library tutorials and search software, bibliographic software, commercial computer-based training modules, faculty and course information including course handbooks and student services information. It is indeed a "one-stop-shop," as its creators intended, and is, I believe, one of the most significant developments in providing services and access to the distance student.

DEAKIN UNIVERSITY–A DEMOGRAPHIC AND LIBRARY SERVICE OVERVIEW

Australia has a long tradition of providing distance education programs to its scattered population, commencing with the correspondence courses offered by the University of Queensland from 1909 (Store, 1982). Store was unable to trace the development of library services to external students in many institutions but it is probably fair to say that such services were minimal, at least before World War II, although some universities, such as Macquarie and Deakin, have provided library services from their earliest years. A number of institutions, including Deakin University, have in the past sought to assist off-campus students through "study centers" located in public libraries and other tertiary institutions in major towns within their state, or even interstate. These contained course study materials and the library also provided a collection of books and audio-visual items that could be borrowed. As off-campus study became truly national and then international, and the number of study programs expanded, it proved impossible to maintain these centers and most institutions now provide a library delivery service to their off-campus students. Crocker (1991) surveyed library services in Australia in the early nineties while Slade and Kascus (1998) bring the information up to date as part of their international survey of library services for off-campus and distance education students in 1998. Cavanagh (1997), Cavanagh and Tucker (1998) and McKnight (1998) have described the library delivery service of Deakin University in detail and only selected issues will be discussed in this paper.

Deakin University has six campuses in the state of Victoria, Australia. Three are located in Melbourne, two in the regional city of Geelong and the sixth is in Warrnambool. There is 250 miles between its furthest campuses, posing administrative and library difficulties for the availability of courses and programs. It has provided a library delivery service to off-campus students since its inception in 1977 (Cavanagh, 1997). Appendix A shows the distribution of its off-campus students while Appendix B gives statistical information on the library delivery service and costs in 1998.

It can be seen that relatively few of our students are geographically isolated, a typical situation with most off-campus programs. Nevertheless, they have chosen to study in the off-campus mode for very good reasons–they are working and do not have the time to attend classes, they may be housebound or have a young family, or they simply do not wish to be tied to the restrictions of face-to-face classes. For these and other reasons, it is critical that all off-campus students be provided with a full library service, irrespective of their location. The figures in Appendix B indicate that students can and do make heavy use of a library delivery service but they also wish to use libraries in person. Schemes such as the recent UK Libraries Plus initiative enable "part-time, distance, and placement students to borrow from libraries in close proximity to where they live or work" (Adam Edwards, 1999). Information can be obtained on the Web site: http://www.lisa.sbu. ac.uk/uklibrariesplus.

A similar program has operated in Australia for many years with academic libraries throughout the country publishing their borrowing conditions through a Web site maintained by Deakin University at: http://www.deakin.edu.au/library/otherlibs.html.

Each year, more than 500 Deakin University distance students apply to the Off Campus Library Service for letters of introduction to use other convenient libraries. This may be particularly relevant where a student is resident overseas (Anon, 1999a). However, providing letters of introduction to other libraries in no way diminishes the responsibility of the home library to support its students–it merely allows them further choices in their search for information.

A distance library service stands or falls on the quality of the information resources available to its users. As will be discussed below, serving distance learners requires proactive intervention by library staff to ensure that paper resources are available in adequate numbers to meet the needs of both on and off-campus students–a single copy on counter reserve is not sufficient. It also requires that priority be given to finding ways to allow external users access to the entire electronic resources of the library (Esterhazy, 1999; Krieb, 1999). After all, as more on-campus students and faculty dial in to the library from home or their offices, they are in an almost identical position to an off-campus student. The Library promotes the advantages to students of their making available electronic services; in fact it is part of the library's strategic plan that all services are available to all its students (and staff), irrespective of mode of study or location. At Deakin University, there is no separate "distance education" collection; rather the entire resources of the six campuses, something over one million volumes, 14,000 journal titles and over 150 networked databases, are available for all users. Library staff participate in school and faculty board meetings and report back on new and remade course programs as well as actively soliciting reading lists from academic staff so that library staff can order material in advance. Galley sheets of new course units are checked by Acquisitions staff and multiple copies of recommended books are ordered using a formula that relates numbers of students anticipated, whether the course is taught on or off or both, and the number of recommended items on the reading list. Many of the library's electronic databases are supplied through SilverPlatter and are available to remote users via a password server accessible from the Library Home Page. Others such as Expanded Academic ASAP require IP recognition. As all undergraduates must use a commercial ISP to access the University, this meant that for several years they did not have access to this important full text resource. The library has recently installed proxy server technology to authenticate patron's library ID numbers to use this database. All told, external users have access to approximately 150 networked databases. The only major database set still not available to external users is Project Muse but making it available to off-site users is under current investigation.

WHAT ARE THE NEEDS OF AND PROBLEMS FACING THE DISPERSED STUDENT?

Dispersed students in this context are students who do not attend classes at either the home or a satellite campus and may not ever visit a campus. They study on an independent basis, receiving all their instruction through a combination of print-based materials, video and audiotapes, some material in electronic format and some contact through phone or teleconferencing or weekend schools with tutors. They provide the library with its greatest challenge–how to fund and provide library and information support for what many administrators see as an additional, costly and, in their eyes, unnecessary service. Some of the challenges may be summarized as follows:

- the students may never come on campus so that they rarely receive information literacy training and are unable to use in-person assistance from librarians
- if they live in a small isolated or rural community, they frequently do not have access to a library and even if they receive training, they soon forget most of what they have learned
- they face isolation and lack of peer support and miss the networking so useful to on-campus students
- they frequently do not know or don't find out what services are available or how to access them–their library expectations are often very low
- they may face delays and expense in contacting the library and obtaining materials and in returning them

- their institution may not offer a library service or there are so many barriers that students give up trying to use it
- even if they have access to the Internet, the pace of change is so great that it is very difficult for them to keep up with the number of new electronic services from the library
- due to IP filtering and similar limitations, they may be able to access only a fraction of the resources their on-campus colleagues may use
- services are not adequately publicized so that students are not aware of them.

Several of the above are recognizable as "standard" difficulties facing distance learners but others can be reduced by efficient and well publicized library support. Yet because of their isolation and lack of contact with the library, we cannot easily teach many of these students what we believe they need to know to use the library effectively, and we struggle to alert them to the many resources available. Despite the availability of several guidelines for library support, for example Australia (Crocker, 1982), Canada (Canadian Library Association, 1999) and the United States (Association of College and Research Libraries, 1998), discussion on the off-campus list server (OFFCAMP@cwis-20.wayne.edu) during 1999 indicated major concern among many librarians about the cost of providing library services, just what services and materials should be supplied and simply, how to go about setting up a library service. It is in meeting some of these needs that I see information technology playing its greatest role.

IS ELECTRONIC THE ANSWER?

The proliferation of so-called "virtual" universities has sharply focused (and in some cases polarized) the views of librarians and distance educators on the role of libraries in distance education. There is the danger in the future that too much will be expected of students to find their information needs on "the net" while the institution is unwilling to provide more than token document delivery. Experience has shown us that even prolific users of electronic resources still require the additional back up of paper-based materials on occasions and will submit information requests when they are unable to locate suitable references themselves. Thus while 35% of requests for library materials to Deakin University are sent electronically and over 200 email queries are fielded each month in busy periods by off-campus library staff, we still supply 53,000 books and 22,000 photocopies yearly. This is ample proof that far from removing the need to provide a document delivery service, electronic access does not reduce demand and may even raise it.

A nagging concern is the so-called full-text database. While vendors will generally list the titles and date spans of full-text serials in their databases, they usually do not spell out what is not included, e.g., editorials, book reviews, missing issues, graphics and sometimes tables of data (Franck and Chambers, 1998; Brennan and Brukhardt, 1999). Rarely is the electronic version a faithful reproduction of its paper counterpart. Some full-text databases also have long delays with entry of data so that a full-text database can be months behind available paper copy. Both these deficiencies can seriously reduce the usefulness of a full-text database and students need to be made aware of it. The trend for users to restrict their searches to only full-text items may have implications for libraries' hard copy collections but it is a sign of the times–many students will only put in the minimum effort to find what they need. To them, "the print materials are the new microforms, the things (they) will try to avoid at all costs" (Lester, 1999). We still provide printouts of searches of non-full-text databases for the students to select articles for the library to copy. These are almost always specialized, such as CINAHL, ERIC, and Biological Abstracts, and provide a much greater in-depth coverage than the general purpose full-text variety.

Another serious restriction is the limited access to electronic resources for many external users because of license restrictions or lack of IP recognition. Licensing agreements may allow access only from on campus or require that each user be issued with a separate password or, in extreme cases, require that only a librarian has access to the password–a librarian is required to physically log a user in (Krieb, 1999). Multiple user access may be so prohibitively expensive that an institution can only afford one or two simultaneous connections, thus severely restricting availability of the resource. Some database vendors will not allow their product to be networked, thus again limiting its availability, while others refuse access to their journals via a proxy server (Krieb, 1999). It is obvious from the examples given here that the off-campus student still faces many restrictions in accessing electronic resources and we, as librarians, need to continue to look for ways to ensure that these barriers are broken down. There are currently too many different access methods, which cause frustration to both users and libraries. Vendors need to devise simpler, standardized access methods if they wish to continue selling their products to libraries.

Copyright restrictions appear to be an almost universal barrier to creative use of the new technology. The Australian Parliament is currently debating a new Copyright Amendment (Digital Agenda) Bill which it is hoped will confirm that the exemptions which allow libraries or users to make a copy of an item for the purposes of study or research free from copyright payments will also apply to digital copying and communications equipment and material in digital form. This then will probably allow a library to send an electronic version of an article (from an electronic journal) to an off-campus student as a PDF file or e-mail attachment. But the new Bill seemingly excludes another service we would like to offer, sending scanned images from a hardcopy journal to the desktop of the user.

Thus while the new information technology undoubtedly has enormous potential to make available a range of information resources unheard of just a few years ago, it is something of a two-edged sword. It can deliver to anyone anywhere in the world, providing they have Internet access. Yet a number of its claims must be treated with caution; much of the available information is only available at a price and practitioners such as Feenberg (1999) and Green (1999) are openly questioning the educational values of many of the programs being "taught" through "packaged courses" where there is no interaction with staff or other students. It is good to recognize the limitations of the technology because one is then aware of some potential pitfalls. However, rather than concentrate on these perceived (and real) problems of information technology, I would rather see what it can offer the library and off-campus students, especially when used in conjunction with a library delivery service for traditional paper-based materials. Some of the advantages include:

- an ability to offer self-paced, Web-based tutorials on using the library catalogue, searching databases and searching the Internet to all students, irrespective of their location and access to a traditional library

- an ability to provide services such as "frequently asked questions," an electronic suggestion box, an electronic information desk, electronic conferencing and chat facilities, and email access to library staff, again irrespective of the student's location
- once IP filtering problems have been overcome, an ability for all students, including those on campus, to search databases, both bibliographic and full-text, at their convenience from their home or office
- an ability to allow students to access the library catalogue electronically and request their material (books and journal articles) while on line, again at their own convenience and irrespective of location
- an ability for off-campus students to place their own holds and renew their own loans, just as many on-campus students can do
- an ability to access reserve material (from an electronic reserve) and items such as examination papers (also stored electronically), both of which are usually only available to on-campus students

All of the above is currently available to students but there is little literature evidence of high use of such services. Indeed, Krieb (1999) reported "dismay at the lack of use" of their electronic journals, despite extensive publicity and the ability to access them directly from the library Web page and the online catalogue. He attributed the low use to unavailability of access for external patrons. This is just one of several barriers to an extension of electronic services to off-campus students. I will now consider the strategy adopted by Deakin University to promote and encourage students to use electronic access to University and Library services and facilities.

THE DEAKIN LEARNING TOOLKIT

Historical Background

It is well recognised that many off-campus students are not confident about using electronic technology. Until recently they have often had little exposure to computers, and while many may use a computer for limited applications such as word processing, relatively few (perhaps 30-40%) have taken the next step of buying a modem and configuring their system to connect to the internet. Geographical isolation only adds to the problem, as there are often no Internet service providers in the area and few people to consult. Deakin University has been actively promoting computer services to off-campus students and to staff and students wishing to dial in from home since the early 1990s. The early menu driven program TEAS was developed for specific subjects, and was only available to postgraduate students in those subjects although it did include an email form for students to request items from the library. It was replaced by a program Interchange which allowed the downloading of a suite of software that was the Deakin standard. This included Netscape, Eudora, the library catalogue via telnet and the SilverPlatter ERL databases via WinSPIRS and MacSPIRS and a direct link to the library homepage. The main problems with Interchange were its comparative user unfriendliness, especially for people with only basic computing skills who often could not install the software themselves, and the fact that Interchange would automatically update the software each time it was used. This slowed down access and often lead to disk space problems for patrons. Even more frustrating was modem pool saturation with users unable to connect until late at night on nearly every night of the week. At the time, all staff and students were entitled to free dial-in access to the Deakin network but the network was not really capable of supporting all the staff and students who wanted to make use of it. This, coupled with skyrocketing calls to the Information Technology Services (ITS) Help Desk, prompted ITS to make three radical decisions in 1997 to enable it to meet its strategic objectives:

- the ITS Help Desk would be outsourced to a commercial provider
- all undergraduate students would be required from 1998 to arrange their own Internet Service Provider (ISP) although access via the modem banks would still be available to staff and postgraduate students
- ITS would produce and distribute a CD-ROM containing the software and accompanying information that students would need to undertake their study at Deakin. It would require minimal computer knowledge to load, would run on both Windows and Macintosh platforms, and would provide advice on selecting an ISP and include an installation kit for the University's preferred ISP.

In early 1998, 25,000 CD-ROMs were produced and distributed by direct mailing to off-campus students and from various on-campus sites such as the Library, ITS offices and student union offices. The feedback has been so overwhelmingly positive that the University recently nominated its use of information and communications technology to flexibly deliver support services to its students for an Institutional Award under the Australian Awards for University Teaching Program. The lynchpin in provision of these services is the Deakin Learning Toolkit (Anon, 1999b).

Development of the Toolkit

Development of the Toolkit was not the responsibility of any one group although its production was coordinated by ITS staff (Addie and Hellyer, 1999). The Library welcomed the opportunity to include a wealth of information on library services and resources. ITS, the Library, Student Services and Flexible Learning Divisions cooperated to develop the Toolkit, thus ensuring that all students, whether on or off-campus, had access to the widest range of resources and services. The Teaching Award application further noted, "Today's learner needs to be a competent user of electronic services and to have developed good research skills by the time they complete their degree. The Deakin Learning Toolkit, with its suite of interactive software and information on University services and facilities, encourages all students to develop that competence and at the same time, ensures equity of access for everyone" (Anon, 1999b, p 4).

For the Library, the timing of the Toolkit was fortuitous because material being developed for the Toolkit could be incorporated into the Library's Web pages and vice versa. Three special tutorials, on Internet Searching, Using EndNote (bibliographic software), and Using Web/Mac/WinSpirs (database search software), were created by Library staff for the 1999 version of the Toolkit (Hopkins, 1998; McKnight, 1999). These are also available by links from the Library home page. One of the beauties of the Toolkit is that users can read much of the information and work through the tutorials off line, only connecting via the browser software when necessary, such as to search the catalogue or a database. Once online, live links in the Toolkit enable the user to move around within the Toolkit or to go directly to other Web resources. The live links also enable the user to download the latest versions of software from a Software Library maintained by ITS. An electronic forms section allows them to link to the Library home page and electronically request material or make subject requests; or the forms can be printed and manually completed and faxed or mailed.

The concept of providing software and information to students on a self-loading CD-ROM was unique at the time in Australia although a similar solution to the same type of problem had been proposed at the University of California, Berkeley in 1995-1996. However, the suite of software was provided on diskettes, not a CD-ROM, and the project has apparently been less successful because of a marked reluctance of users to pay for an ISP account, thus not relieving the load on modem banks (Shelton, 1997). Several other Australian universities have sought permission to use the Toolkit concept and it is likely to be followed by others with their own version of a CD-ROM. Furthermore, calls to the help desk for Toolkit-related inquiries are about 8% of those recorded in the Interchange period, so it appears that students are able to handle the loading and operation of the Toolkit satisfactorily and presumably are more easily able to access the University network.

CONCLUSION

The World Wide Web and associated technology have the potential to break down many of the barriers that prevent off-campus students from participating fully in the information and resources available to on-campus students. Yet it has inadequacies that need to be recognized and there is still a strong requirement for libraries and institutions to support students through a traditional library service. Major barriers to the successful use of services for many off-campus students are lack of knowledge of what is available, and uncertainty in setting themselves up and configuring equipment to access their institution's electronic resources. The Deakin Learning Toolkit was developed to provide both software and information on the University's resources and services in the compact form of a CD-ROM that required minimum computer knowledge on the part of the user to install. While a key objective was to extend the range of services to off-campus users, this important development has directly benefited the whole student population and staff, as it can be used by anyone wishing to access the Library and the University from home. By actively supporting and promoting new communications technologies, while continuing to provide a full service by traditional methods, the Library allows maximum flexibility to its students in seeking and obtaining resources.

THE DEAKIN LEARNING TOOLKIT SUITE OF SOFTWARE

The Deakin Learning Toolkit (DLT) provides all the software for a student to access Deakin's online support services. Some of the applications are freely available for download on the Web; others the University has licensed for staff and student use. Included are:

- Netscape Communicator for Web browsing and net access;
- Eudora for email;
- anti-viral programs for both PCs and Mac;
- Adobe Acrobat Reader to view PDF documents;
- a number of commercially produced computer-based training modules on IT skills development;
- an installation kit for establishing Internet access through a commercial ISP;
- FirstClass for computer conferencing;
- Web/Win/MacSpirs for providing library database access;
- an "electronic forms" section enabling the submission of library requests via the Web or by email through Eudora; and
- EndNote for the construction and maintenance of academic bibliographies.

In total, 24 software programs for Windows and 20 for Macintosh are packaged on the DLT for student installation and use. Manuals and guides are provided in PDF format.

THE DLT PROVIDES INFORMATION AND TRAINING

Information and training on the DLT assists students in determining University policies and in effectively using University academic services and facilities. Included are:

- Web browser-accessible Undergraduate and Postgraduate Handbooks;
- a tutorial on using the Internet for academic research purposes;

- a tutorial on using EndNote to construct and maintain academic bibliographies;
- a tutorial on accessing SilverPlatter ERL databases; and
- a number of discipline subject guides developed by the University library.

THE DLT PROVIDES ACCESS TO SERVICES

The DLT acts as a portal to Deakin and off-campus Web sites, providing student access to:

- *Library services* including an online Helpdesk, indexing and abstracting services, and access to an increasing number of electronic full-text journals;
- online *health services* information and access;
- online study guides and *study skills development services;*
- Jobs Ready and other Web-accessible *career development services;* and
- computer conferencing to support a wide range of student, chaplain and University initiated *virtual learning community development services.*

(Source: Anonymous. (1999b). *Application for Institutional Award.* Support Services for Australian Students. Australian Awards for University Teaching. (Unpublished). Geelong: Deakin University).

REFERENCES

Adam Edwards, J. (1999, September 29). *A big plus for lifelong learners.* UK libs plus-press release. [Online]. Available E-mail: sconul@mailbox.ulcc.ac.uk [1999, September 29].

Addie, J., & Hellyer, M. (1999). *Taking IT to the streets: the Deakin Learning Toolkit.* In EduCAUSE in Australasia Conference Proceedings, Sydney, April 18-21, 1999.

Anonymous. (1999a). Posting from an overseas student to the Remote/Overseas Students conference site on the University's FirstClass conferencing facility. Used with permission.

Anonymous. (1999b). *Application for an institutional award.* Support Services for Australian Students. Australian Awards for University Teaching. (Unpublished). Geelong: Deakin University.

Association of College and Research Libraries. *ACRL Guidelines for Distance Learning Library Services,* final version, approved July 1998 [Online]. Available: http://www.ala.org/acrl/guides/distlrng.html [1999, November].

Brennan, P. M., & Brukhardt, J. (1999). What does electronic full-text really mean? A comparison of database vendors and what they deliver. *Reference Services Review, 27,* 113-127.

Canadian Library Association. Library Services for Distance Learning Interest Group. *Guidelines for library support of distance and distributed learning in Canada.* Draft Revision, November, 1999. [Online]. Available: http://uviclib. uvic.ca/staff/sslade/guidelines.html [1999, November].

Cavanagh, A. K., & Tucker, J. (1998). A library service to distance learners: what should the library provide? In E.F. Watson & N. Jagannathan (Eds*.), Library Services for Distance Learners in the Commonwealth: a Reader* (pp. 109-122). Vancouver, BC: Commonwealth of Learning.

Cavanagh, T. (1997). Flexible learning–where does the library fit in? In R. Hudson, S. Maslin-Prothero & L. Oates (Eds.), *Flexible Learning in Action Case Studies in Higher Education* (pp. 153-159). London: Kogan Page.

Crocker, C. (Ed.) (1982). *Guidelines for library services to external students.* Ultimo, NSW: Library Association of Australia.

Crocker, C. (1991). Off-campus library services in Australia. *Library Trends, 39,* 495-513.

Esterhazy, J. (1999). Providing authenticated access to Web resources. *College and Research Libraries News, 60*(8), 617-618.

Feenberg, A. (1999). *Distance learning: promise or threat?* [Online]. Available: http://www-rohan.sdsu.edu/faculty/feenberg/TELE3.HTM [1999, November].

Franck, C., & Chambers, H. (1998). *How full is the full in full-text?* [Online]. Available: http://www2.potsdam.edu./LIBR/franckcr/ALA.html [1998, November].

Green, M. (1999). Educational progress without people? A theoretical perspective on delivery technology in higher education. *AARL: Australian Academic and Research Libraries, 30*(2), 95-106.

Hopkins, S. (1998). *Designing tutorials for the Deakin Learning Toolkit.* Unpublished paper presented at CRIG Annual User Education Seminar, Melbourne, November 25, 1998.

Krieb, D. (1999). *You can't get there from here: issues in remote access to electronic journals for a health sciences library.* [Online], spring 1999, 6 pages. Available: http://www.library.ucsb.edu/istl/99~spring/article3.htm [1999, September].

Lester, D. (1999, October 1). Response to question about full-text databases. [Online]. Available E-mail: OFFCAMP@cwis-20.wayne.edu [1999, October 1].

McKnight, S. (1998). Library services to off-campus students: an Australian perspective. In P. Brophy, S. Fisher & Z. Clarke (Eds.) *Libraries without walls 2: the delivery of library services to distant users, proceedings of a conference held on 17-20 September 1997 at Lesvos, Greece* (pp. 52-62). London: Library Association Publishing.

McKnight, S. (1999). Delivering library services to remote users: the Deakin Learning Toolkit. In Z. Clarke, P. Brophy, & S. Fisher (Eds.), *Libraries without walls 3:*

the delivery of library services to distance users, Lesvos, Greece, September 10-14, 1999. London: Library Association Publishing.

Shelton, A. (1997). A service approach to providing off-campus Internet access. *Cause/Effect,* Spring, 57-59.

Slade, A., & Kascus, M. (1998). An international comparison of library services for distance learning. In P. S. Thomas & M. Jones (Comps.), *The eighth off-campus library services conference proceedings: Providence, Rhode Island, April 22-24, 1998* (pp. 259-297). Mount Pleasant, MI: Central Michigan University.

Store, R. (1982). Looking out from "Down Under": Are Australian problems so different? In C. Crocker (Ed.), *Library Services in Distance Learning* (pp. 11-27). Sydney: Library Association of Australia Special Interest Group in Distance Education.

APPENDIX A

Student Enrolments at Deakin University (1998 Data)

Total Student Population–29000
Total Off-Campus Students–12400 (43%)
Female: Male Ratio–60:40
Undergraduates (incl. Hons.)–61.2%
Postgraduate by Coursework–35.4%
Research–3.5%

Remoteness of Students

Approximately 83% of off-campus students live in or near a town with a university campus
Approximately 5.3% of those eligible to use the Library Delivery service live overseas

APPENDIX A (continued)

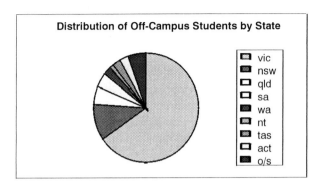

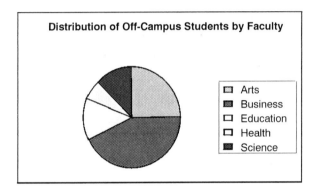

APPENDIX B

The Collection and the Library Service

Collection (as of December 31, 1998):

- Books (volumes held)–1409306
- Book titles held (including duplicates)–960234
- Books (volumes acquired) in 1998–60563
- Periodical titles held–14151
  (includes approximately 2600 full-text electronic journals and over 150 databases accessible remotely)

Off-Campus Library Service (1998):

- Total requests received–78948
- Total books and audio-visual items supplied–52594
- Total journal articles (incl. from electronic full-text databases)–21542
- Total items supplied–74136
- Subject (reference) requests–1387
- Total time for subject requests–818 hours

Borrowing in Person (1998):

- Total items borrowed in person by off-campus students–32933 (38.6% of total)

Staffing of the Off-Campus Library Service (1998):

Approximately 10.5 persons across all campuses, including 1 librarian, 4 library technicians (paraprofessionals), 5.5 clerical staff.

Costing of Service (1998, in Aust$):

	With freight* costs	Without freight* costs
Cost per request	$11.55	$6.46
Cost per item supplied	$12.76	$7.15
Cost per student enrolled	$75.80	$42.50
Cost per student using service (est. 40%)	$189.60#	$106.25#

*NOTE: Freight costs are met by a Library Delivery Fee which all off-campus students pay as part of their general service fee to the University.

#NOTE: This estimate is based on earlier work at Deakin University which showed that between 40% and 45% of off-campus students used the delivery services at least once per year.

CatchTheWeb–Personal:
A Versatile Web-Based Demonstration
and Tutorial Creation Tool

Douglas Cook

Shippensburg University

SUMMARY. CatchTheWeb–Personal is a versatile Web research management tool, which can enable the librarian to capture content from the Web and package it into a presentation. Working in conjunction with Microsoft Internet Explorer, CatchTheWeb makes it easy to create a presentation based on pages currently existing on the Web. The presentation can then be saved onto a disk and viewed with any Web browser. Presentations can also be placed on the Web as tutorials.

KEYWORDS. Library instruction, distance education, online tutorials, Web tools

INTRODUCTION

CatchTheWeb–Personal (CTW) was created as a Web research management tool. And indeed it does very nicely at its originally intended function. Smith (1999, July/August), in reviewing tools that could be used by researchers to manage information found on the Web, said about CTW, "It was the next best thing to having colleagues there to look over my shoulder." Smith went on to say that CTW allowed her to demonstrate the exact path that she followed on her

[Haworth co-indexing entry note]: "CatchTheWeb–Personal: A Versatile Web-Based Demonstration and Tutorial Creation Tool." Cook, Douglas. Co-published simultaneously in *Journal of Library Administration* (The Haworth Information Press, an imprint of The Haworth Press, Inc.) Vol. 31, No. 3/4, 2001, pp. 167-176; and: *Off-Campus Library Services* (ed: Anne Marie Casey) The Haworth Information Press, an imprint of The Haworth Press, Inc., 2001, pp. 167-176.

search and also permitted her to record notes that occurred to her when searching. CTW has the added bonus of enabling pages garnered from the Web to be packaged as a presentation. The final presentation, including notes, can be emailed and viewed in any Web browser.

Because of its versatility CTW has a great application to library instruction, particularly for off-campus patrons. In view of the fact that we are increasingly reliant upon the Web as a gateway to our resources, even librarians at universities that do not offer distance education courses are finding themselves engaged in trying to serve patrons who do not regularly come into the library building. Orientation formerly imparted in face-to-face instructional encounters needs to be placed on the Web where it can be used as point-of-use assistance. CTW can be used to package tutorial programs of this type.

Our first use of CatchTheWeb–Personal was to create an instructional back-up demonstration of our Web-based OPAC. At least once a year when we are doing a library instruction class either our OPAC or the Web will go down. I'm sure that you have experienced the horrid feeling that creeps into your stomach when your well-prepared presentation becomes useless because of your over-reliance on the Web as a live instructional tool. In the past we used a set of overhead transparencies to cover these emergencies. With CTW, creating a backup presentation is an uncomplicated process. CTW has a short learning curve and an excellent Help file. If you have already done the difficult task of mentally organizing the presentation, it is very easy to recreate a Web session and pull it into CTW. We kept the resulting presentation on a disk ready for an emergency.

Also, we have done tutorials with CTW for several Web-based products to which we own access–PsycINFO and Sociological Abstracts. We have a "Tutorials" button on our home page, as well as "Help" buttons near both databases. These CTW tutorials are, in fact, presentations of these products along with explanatory notes. They provide excellent introductory instruction for off-campus patrons. Although CTW was created to be a research management tool it does quite well as a simple tutorial program.

Creating a presentation or a tutorial is a simple matter of dragging and dropping a taskbar icon–a Pushpin–on top of the Web page that you would like to pull into CTW. If you are the type of person who prefers to go searching serendipitously and then organize later (as I must admit that I am), this is an excellent program to use. You can pull all of your potential pages into CTW and then rearrange them to your heart's content. CTW has a note field that allows you to add written narration for the final presentation. CTW also allows you to pull in pages that you have created. If you are using Microsoft FrontPage, you can create a page, for example an introductory or a concluding screen, and drag CTW's Pushpin icon and drop it on your FrontPage creation to pull it into CTW.

LITERATURE REVIEW

A number of articles can be found which review CatchTheWeb. Many of them were published or placed on the Web in the spring of 1998 when CTW was first made available. These articles are typically short news announcements touting the highlights of the program. (Ward, 1998; Math Strategies announces, 1998; Math Strategies releases, 1998; CatchTheWeb 2.0, 1998; Georgia, 1999). One article published in October of 1999 announces the availability of CTW–Enterprise, an Intranet version of CTW (CatchTheWeb Enterprise, 1999).

Several more enlightening articles actually review CTW-Personal (Moskowitz, 1998; Weiss, 1998; Thompson, 1999). Weiss says that numerous products have tried to help Web users record their browsing sessions, usually for off-line browsing, but CatchTheWeb delivers a novel and useful variation: Capture any number of selected Web pages, categorize them into topics and chapters, add annotations, and package the entire portfolio into a navigable presentation that can be sent to and viewed by others.

These three authors spoke highly of CTW's ease of use and extreme versatility. Other than lamenting the fact that CTW cannot use Netscape Navigator to gather pages (although Netscape can play back CTW presentations), these reviews were highly favorable. CTW seems to fill a need in the Web research field.

A third group of articles compared CTW with other similar products (Kramer, 1999; Smith, 1999; Dreyfuss, 1998; Ozer, 1998). Some of the programs that are comparable to CTW are Hot Off the Web, Surf Saver, Organizer, and Web Buddy. These reviewers highlight strong and weak points for each of these products including CTW. The strength of CatchTheWeb, in comparison to these other programs, is its ability to put together a presentation. Its main weakness is its incompatibility with Netscape. Although Hot Off the Web works with a variety of browsers, it does not do a good job in capturing frames. Hot Off the Web also has minimal organizational capacities. Organizer's main feature is its ability to organize content in a variety of ways, including organizing content by client. Surf Saver is a browser add-on that gives you the option to capture text without graphics. Surf Saver is a basic program without the added options of the others. Web Buddy uses the familiar file folder tab format to organize data. Although Web Buddy has most of the features of these other programs, it does lack a workspace search function. Ozer reported that after reviewing each of these programs and putting them to the test, CTW was the best of this group. In fact, CTW was awarded *PC Magazine*'s "Editor's Choice" as being the best Web capture and presentation tool on the market in 1998 (Ozer).

The final type of article found in the literature that reviews CTW applies the program to specific uses. Canale (1998), in *Realty Times,* describes how CTW can be used in the real estate business. He suggests that realtors use CTW to capture their Web sites to show offline with a laptop to prospective clients. Smith (1999, March), a Web researcher, explains how she uses CTW to capture the content of Web searches that she does for clients. When finished she uses CTW to create presentations to present her findings.

CTW is generally described as an easy-to-use and a versatile Web research management tool. It is regarded highly in the computer literature. It has been applied to several professional fields. And as I will demonstrate, CTW also has a tremendous potential use for library instruction.

CATCHTHEWEB–SESSION DESCRIPTION

To illustrate CTW's use, remember the last time you put together a tutorial. Let us talk about creating a tutorial for the PsycINFO database as accessed by SilverPlatter. I begin by starting both CTW and Microsoft Explorer. (There is an option that will start Explorer when CTW is started.) Initiating CTW adds a "Pushpin" icon to the Windows Desktop taskbar. I then go out onto the Web with MS Explorer and gather all the pages that I think that I might need. If I am doing a tutorial, I imagine myself explaining the program to someone else. I pull screens into CTW's "Archive" by dragging and dropping the Pushpin onto the page I want. For our PsycINFO tutorial I gathered startup screens, search screens, software-provided help screens, etc. I ran several sample searches and gathered each page into the Archive. CTW will also capture a specific frame or all frames if that option is being used in the original pages. When you bring a page into the program, CTW gives you the opportunity to add information to a notes field. I usually save this task for later. When I feel that I have been through my mental explanation thoroughly, I then move to CTW's workspace, where everything is now ready for me to shape into a presentation.

CTW's workspace has four windows that are opened simultaneously as the default. [See Figure 1.] Each can be toggled off, and the size of each can be controlled. The "Archive" window is a listing of all the Web pages that have been pulled into the program and saved with the workspace. Pages in the Archives are organized by URL. The second window is the "Topic" frame. This window allows you to arrange and rearrange pages from your Archives files. It is possible to put "Chap-

FIGURE 1. CTW Workspace Screen

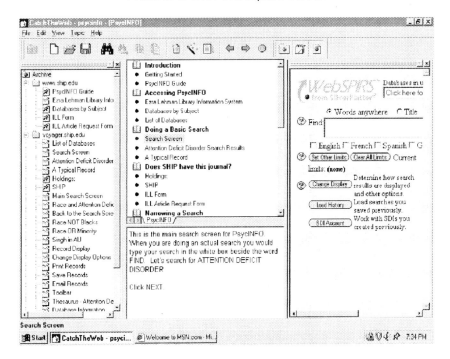

ter" headings at the section breaks of your "Presentation" into this window to make it easier to see your outline. The third window is a "Notes" window. A note can be attached to each page that will display with the presentation. This is particularly helpful when creating tutorials, as it allows you to include the narration that you would have given if you had been present. The fourth window in CTW's work area is a viewing window. The "Browser" window shows you the particular page on which you are working in the Topic screen.

I think of the Topic workspace as a kind of slide light box–a place to look at all the pages that I have gathered and to put them in their best presentation order. The pages can easily be arranged and rearranged by dragging and dropping them. I add Chapter headings that divide and organize my presentation. When I get all my pages into their best arrangement, I usually find that I need to go back to the Web to pick up things that I missed on the first round.

At this point I often want to create an introductory or an explanatory page. It is possible to use an HTML editor such as MS FrontPage to do so. Math Strategies offers a free downloadable HTML editor–Slider–which will allow you to create simple title or explanation pages using templates. With Slider or FrontPage open you can drag and drop the taskbar Pushpin onto your new page, so that your created page goes directly into CTW's Archive. If you use Netscape Composer or some other editor, it is necessary to view the final creation in MS Internet Explorer before bringing your page into the Archive. Essentially any graphic that can be put onto the WWW can be included in a CTW presentation. Using Slider with CTW allows you to create custom designed presentations.

When I have my presentation organized into its fairly final form, I usually work with the Notes screen. If the presentation will end up as a tutorial, I put an explanation of the page that will show with that screen during the presentation. If I am working on a presentation, then I usually put shorter explanations or reminders to myself of what I would like to say. It is possible to preview your presentation from within CTW. If you need to make changes at this time, it is simple to do so.

When you are pleased with your presentation, you run the "Publish Wizard." The Wizard gives you a number of options. The Published Presentation can be viewed with any WWW browser. [See Figure 2.] Your Presentation is very portable and can be emailed. The final

FIGURE 2. CTW Presentation Screen

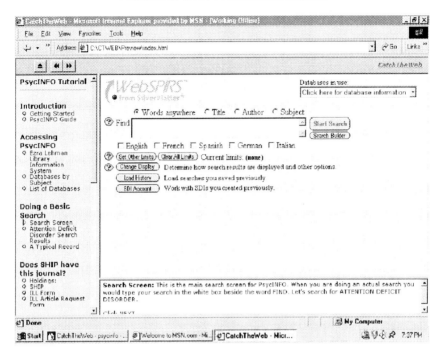

Presentation can be saved as an EXE file. The presentation can be saved on a disk, a hard drive or FTP'd to a Web site. The presentation can also show itself continuously, which would be helpful in a display setting. It is possible to customize your Presentation in a number of ways. Your library's logo can be shown on the start screen. Table of Contents, Notes, and Navigation Controls can be toggled on or off. Navigation Controls can be displayed in English, French, German or Spanish.

Two types of final presentations are possible. Choosing "Bookmarks Only" creates a presentation that includes only the URLs of the Web pages included in the presentation. The advantage of a Bookmark presentation is that it takes up very little file space. However, a Bookmark Presentation must be viewed on the Web so that the pages can be refreshed each time. A "Content Only" presentation bundles all the pages and the necessary information to play the Presentation back offline. There are enough options included in CTW's Publish Wizard to meet almost any instructional presentation need.

CONCLUSION

One of the things that I really like about CTW is its ease-of-use. It is such a simple and intuitive program that it is possible to have a short presentation finished within a few hours. Other tutorial programs are more complex than CTW and also take a much longer time to learn. If most of your presentations are Web-based, CatchTheWeb–Personal is an excellent tool for you to learn.

At Shippensburg University, we have used CatchTheWeb to create basic demonstrations incorporating Web pages. We have used this software to create a backup presentation that describes, and in part emulates, the functions of our Web-based OPAC. CatchTheWeb has allowed us to easily create point-of-use Web tutorials for such programs as PsycINFO, which are available to our off-campus students. CatchTheWeb is an excellent Web research management and presentation tool and would be of great value to any librarian who creates Web-based presentations or simple online tutorials.

REFERENCES

Canale, S. (1998, September 28). How to show your website to customers–Offline. *Realty Times*. [Online]. Available: http://www.realtimes.com/rtnews/rtapages/19980928_offline.htm [November 14, 1999].

CatchTheWeb 2.0 answers 'What's next?' for Web users. (1998, December 14). *PR Newswire*. [Online]. Available: ProQuest Direct. [November 14, 1999].

CatchTheWeb Enterprise bows at Online World–99. (1999, October 25). [Online]. Available: http://www.catchtheweb.com/pr1099.htm [November 20, 1999].

Dreyfuss, J. (1998, October 26). Two ways to better manage the Net. *Fortune*. [Online], *138,8*. Available: ProQuest Direct. [November 14, 1999].

Georgia, B. L. (1999, July). CatchTheWeb 2.0.3. *Home Office Computing*. [Online], *17,7*. Available: ProQuest Direct. [November 14, 1999].

Kramer, M. (1999, February 1). *Putting Web findings to work*. [Online]. Available: http://www.zdnet.com/pcweek/stories/news/0,4153,387426,00.html [November 14, 1999].

Math Strategies announces CatchTheWeb. (1998, January 28). *PR Newswire*. [Online]. Available: ProQuest Direct. [November 14, 1999].

Math Strategies releases CatchTheWeb to capture dynamic Net content. (1998, April 14). [Online]. Available: http://techmall.com/techdocs/TS980415-1.html [November 14, 1999].

Moskowitz, L. (1998, April 6). *Capture, organize and present Web pages*. [Online]. Available: http://www.pcworld.com/pcwtoday/article/0,1510,7673,00.html [November 17, 1999].

Ozer, J. (1998, July 1). Capture the Web. *PC Magazine, 17*(13), 45-46.

Smith, P. (1999, March 29). *Getting more from your Internet research.* [Online]. http://www.sla.org/chapter/ctor/courier/v36/v36n3a5.htm [November 14, 1999].

Smith, P. (1999, July/August). Making Web research pay off: A research manager roundup. *Online.* [Online], *23*(4). Available: ProQuest Direct. [November 14, 1999].

Thompson, D. (1999, March 19). Software 'captures' and compares Web pages. *Sacramento Business Journal.* [Online], *16*,1. Available: ProQuest Direct. [November 14, 1999].

Ward, E. (1998, April 14). *New Win 95 app collects Web pages, email, and newsgroups for presentations.* [Online]. Available: http://www.urlwire.com/newsarchive/041498.htm [November 17, 1999].

Weiss, A. (1998). *Catch the Web.* [Online]. Available: http://www.iw.com/daily/reviews/1998/04/2401-catchtheweb.html [November 14, 1999].

APPENDIX

Technical Details

CatchTheWeb–Personal is a Windows based product that installs in a few minutes. Current cost is $39.95 per copy. Minimum requirements to run the program are Internet Explorer 4.0, Windows 95, 98 and NT, 16 MB RAM and 4 MB Disk Space. Technical support is very good. I have called them a number of times with various questions and in each case have gotten the answer to my difficulty quickly and in a friendly fashion.

Contact Information

CTW is marketed primarily over the WWW. Math Strategies can be contacted at:

Math Strategies
600 Green Valley Road
Greensboro, NC 27408
Sales, info@catchtheweb.com
Technical Support, support@catchtheweb.com
Phone: 336-855-7065

CatchTheWeb–Enterprise

In October 1999, Math Strategies announced the release of a larger version of CatchTheWeb. This version, entitled CatchTheWeb–Enterprise, is billed as "a product for Web research collaboration" (CatchTheWeb Enterprise, 1999). It enables members of a group to work on the same project to capture and store Web information. The software is placed on an Intranet server which stores the images and other components of captured Web pages in an SQL database. This database can be accessed by client software from the desks of a number of researchers within an organization. An advanced search engine for the SQL database is also included with the server software.

APPENDIX (continued)

My Web Site

I have attempted to gather resources about the educational and training uses of CTW on my Web page–http://www.ship.edu/~dlcook/ctw/). Please check out this site and let me know if you are using CTW in any fashion.

Shippensburg University Library's Web Site

Lehman Library has several instances of CTW in use as point-of-need tutorials at http://www.ship.edu/~library.

Knowing Your Users and What They Want: Surveying Off-Campus Students About Library Services

Stephen H. Dew

University of Iowa

SUMMARY. In order to have a successful library program for off-campus students, librarians must understand who their students are and what they want. This paper will address the issues involved in conducting a user survey for off-campus students. The paper will cover details on developing a survey; it will discuss the logistics of sending and receiving; and it will examine one method of evaluation. This work is based on a student survey conducted by the University of Iowa Libraries during November 1998 and March 1999.

KEYWORDS. Library services, distance education, needs assessment, surveys

Communication with students should be a two-way street. In our teaching roles, and as the information experts within the academic setting, librarians tend to focus on disseminating the information that we think our students need. We talk at length to students about library services; we give presentations to them about all kinds of information resources; and we develop Web pages full of information just for them. Although we certainly should emphasize our teaching duties, occasionally we need to reverse roles, listen instead of talk, and let the students tell us a few things.

[Haworth co-indexing entry note]: "Knowing Your Users and What They Want: Surveying Off-Campus Students About Library Services." Dew, Stephen H. Co-published simultaneously in *Journal of Library Administration* (The Haworth Information Press, an imprint of The Haworth Press, Inc.) Vol. 31, No. 3/4, 2001, pp. 177-193; and: *Off-Campus Library Services* (ed: Anne Marie Casey) The Haworth Information Press, an imprint of The Haworth Press, Inc., 2001, pp. 177-193.

The user survey is a well-established research methodology for librarians. The first library surveys were conducted in the 1920s (Gothberg, 1990), and over the years, the survey has become a standard method of learning about academic library users. Although the large majority of the surveys conducted by academic libraries have focused on on-campus students (Clougherty et al., 1998; Berger, 1994), a couple of recent studies reported at the 8th Off-Campus Library Services Conference focused on off-campus students (Cassner and Adams, 1998; Rose and Safford, 1998; Schafer, 1998). In addition to the published evidence supporting the usefulness of user surveys, distance-education librarians are also advised by their guidelines to survey off-campus users regularly. In the ACRL Guidelines for Distance Learning Library Services (1998), the tenth "Management" recommendation suggests that librarians regularly survey distance learning library users in order to "monitor and assess both the appropriateness of their use of services and resources and the degree to which needs are being met." This presentation will address the issues recently faced by one institution, the University of Iowa Libraries, as it conducted a survey of its off-campus students.

The University of Iowa (UI) did not begin from scratch when it considered conducting an off-campus user survey. The UI survey instrument was based on a previous survey conducted by a sister state institution, the University of Northern Iowa (UNI) (Rose and Safford, 1998). UNI completed its off-campus survey in 1992, and shortly afterwards, cooperative efforts by the three Regents universities in Iowa (UI, UNI, & Iowa State University) culminated in the formation of the Inter-institutional Library Committee on Distance Education. During committee meetings, the three institutions shared information about their distance education activities, including information on the UNI user survey. Representatives from UI and ISU easily recognized the value of the information gained from UNI's survey. The committee ultimately recommended that UI and ISU follow up by conducting similar surveys, thus allowing for a comparison and sharing of data between the three Regents universities. During the summer and fall of 1998, UI library staff modified the survey instrument for our needs. We attempted to keep it as similar as possible to the UNI survey, but several questions were revised to better reflect technological advancements since 1992 (such as the growth of the Internet and its importance for distance-education library services). The revised survey instrument was pre-tested on a group of graduate students, and a few minor revisions were made. According to Hafner (1998), pre-testing the survey is quite important. It helps clarify some questions, provides a preview of the kind of answers one can expect, and supplies the researcher with experience in tallying the results.

Since the survey would require the use of human subjects, the UI Libraries had to obtain permission from the University's Human Subjects Office. Many universities require such a review in order to protect the welfare and confidentiality of the respondents. Since this review can take time and may require adjustments in the survey, it is recommended that contact with the Human Subjects Office occur as early in the planning process as is possible.

For any survey, sample size is of course critically important–the larger the size of the sample, the more accurate the picture of the target population. Although recommendations vary, many researchers consider a ten-percent sample to be a minimum (Clougherty et al., 1998). For the UI survey, the logistics involved in determining the sample size and mailing of the surveys required the cooperation of many people. Library staff members worked with a variety of personnel from the Center for Credit Programs and the School of Management in order to work out the details. The School of Management supervises the UI off-campus MBA program, and the Center for Credit Programs manages all other off-campus programs. The Center for Credit Programs developed a random sample that included fifty percent of the students enrolled in their degree-granting programs, resulting in a sample total of 506 individuals. The School of Management developed a random sample that included twenty-five percent of the students enrolled in the off-campus MBA program, resulting in a sample total of 200 individuals. The total survey sample, therefore, consisted of 706 individuals.

The mailing consisted of the survey instrument (Appendix A), a cover letter (Appendix B), and a stamped return-envelope addressed to the Coordinator of Library Services for Distance Education (me). Due to financial and time constraints, we decided not to attempt to follow up on students who did not respond to the survey. Following up on non-respondents helps increase the ultimate response rate and the overall relevancy of the data. However, it also increases the cost and time involved, while decreasing the privacy of both respondents and non-respondents. Believing that we would be able to get useful information from a one-shot mailing, we decided to send out the survey with no follow up for non-respondents. In our cover letter (Appendix B), however, we could assure each potential respondent, "Your participation in this survey is completely confidential. No names are associated with individual responses."

Staff concluded that two separate mailings were necessary–one mailing for students enrolled under the Center for Credit Programs and one for students enrolled under the School of Management. In November 1998, the survey instruments were mailed to all individuals enrolled under the Center for Credit Programs, and in March 1999, the survey packages were mailed to students enrolled in the MBA distance-education program. Responses were received throughout the spring semester, with the last response being received in June.

For any survey, the response rate is critically important–the larger the response rate, the more accurate the picture of the target population. Although recommendations vary, many researchers consider a forty-percent response rate to be a minimum in order to judge that the results are accurate (Clougherty et al., 1998). In the UI survey, 272 students returned the instrument, resulting in a response rate of 38.5 percent, just shy of the forty-percent minimum. If we had just ten more respondents, we would have broken the forty-percent barrier. Since we had no method of following up on our non-respondents, however, we were actually fairly pleased with the 38.5 percent rate of return. In our view, that figure is essentially forty percent, and therefore we believe that the results of the survey can be judged to be a legitimate reflection of our students.

There are several statistical packages on the market that one can use to tally the results of surveys: SAS and SPSS are probably the two most popular. For the UI survey, we used "SPSS 8.0 for Windows." With SPSS, data entry was fairly simple, although time-consuming. Data manipulation, however, was both quick and easy. By June 1999, all of the returned surveys had been processed, and we were ready to manipulate the data. The written comments to the survey's two open-ended questions (21 and 22) were compiled and analyzed separately.

Analysis of the data revealed some interesting results for UI librarians to ponder, such as:

Personal Characteristics

30 percent are thirty years old or younger, while 70 percent are older than thirty.

80 percent are unwilling to drive more than fifty miles for library services.

Coursework and Library Use

90 percent have been required to write a research paper for at least one class.

65 percent have used library resources for their class projects.

70 percent use public libraries for some of their information needs.

30 percent use public libraries as their primary information source.

50 percent use academic libraries as their primary information source.

Connectivity

85 percent have convenient access to the World Wide Web

85 percent have access to email

75 percent have convenient access to a FAX machine.

Library Services

Probably the most useful information obtained from the survey concerned a list of library services. Students were given the option of checking all services that they believed were important, and they were asked to rank their top three choices. The overall rankings were as follows:

1.	Web and/or e-mail reference services	71.3 percent
2.	Remote access to full-text databases	65.1 percent
3.	Home delivery of books and articles	60.7 percent
4.	Access to Internet resources	54.8 percent
5.	Toll-free number for reference	49.3 percent
6.	Remote access to UI, ISU, UNI catalogs	49.1 percent
7.	Interlibrary Loan/Doc-Delivery service	43.8 percent
8.	Remote Access to Electronic Indexes	43.3 percent
9.	Borrowing Agreements with Libraries	37.9 percent
10.	Guides to doing library research	30.9 percent
11.	Computer-assisted instruction	27.9 percent
12.	Librarian-provided instruction	20.2 percent

Generally, reference services, electronic services, and document delivery services were ranked high, while user education services were ranked lowest.

Open-Ended Questions

The Survey also had two open-ended questions. The first question asked, "In your own words, what library and/or informational needs do you have for University of Iowa courses that are not being filled currently?" The final question asked for "Comments?" Ninety-six students answered the first question, and seventy-three replied with comments. Responses to both questions varied considerably, but a general trend could be ascertained. Approximately one-third of the respondents were concerned about obtaining more access to electronic resources, and one-third were concerned about document-delivery services.

The statistics reported in this presentation have concerned the total sample of all distance-education programs at the University of Iowa. Through SPSS, we easily produced statistics for the student sample from each of the degree-granting programs, and that information was useful for understanding the needs of the individual off-campus programs. For instance, MBA students were far more concerned about obtaining access to Internet and electronic resources, while Library Science students were far more concerned about document delivery services. The differences between the programs were not great, however. There were no radical divergences of opinion. Summaries of the compiled statistics were shared with the Center for Credit Programs, the School of Management, the relevant departments, and relevant library staff. In some cases, the survey results were put to use immediately.

For example, the survey results were used to develop a new document-delivery service for distance-education students. Even though students were informed that there might be a fee involved, sixty-percent of the students ranked document-delivery as an important library service (third among the twelve services listed). In response to this obvious demand, a library working-group was established during the spring of 1999 to investigate the possibility of establishing a special document-delivery service for distance-education students. Using the survey results and other information, the working group recommended that students be given the ability to request that books be delivered by UPS and articles be delivered by fax or mail. The working group recommended a general fee of three dollars for each request, with the article request having an additional charge of ten-cents-per-page for pages eleven and higher. Later, when the library administration and the campus provost considered the proposal, it was clear that the supporting evidence provided by the survey results were key in their deliberations. The proposal was accepted in August, and the document-delivery service was launched at the beginning of the fall semester 1999.

The survey results were also used to implement a library-sponsored toll-free telephone reference service. At the time that the survey was distributed, the library was piggybacking on another department's toll-free telephone service. The Center for Credit programs has had a toll-free number for many years, and in November 1998, the Center agreed to let the library use that number when helping distance-education students. The shared service always required call transfers, however, and this occasionally resulted in some confusion for the students and staff. After the survey revealed that fifty-percent of the students ranked a toll-free telephone number as an important library service (fifth among the twelve services), the library administration supported the establishment of a separate toll-free number for distance-education library services. The new telephone number was operational by July. It was promoted through letters, handouts, Web pages, etc., and during the fall semester of 1999, it proved to be a popular method for obtaining reference assistance.

Several new library initiatives have been supported by the survey results that showed a large desire for more Internet resources. In addition, since the survey shows that eighty-five percent of our students have convenient access to the World Wide Web, a significant portion of our distance education students have the potential of benefiting from any improvement that we make to our Web-based resources. In one of the new initiatives, over the summer of 1999, library staff developed a "Library Services for Distance Education" Web site in order to better support library services for off-campus students (Appendix C). For each degree-granting program, the "Library Services for Distance Education" home page provides a subject link to a list of the most relevant electronic resources, and in addition, the Web site also provides access to special document-delivery, reference, and consultation services. In addition, for some of the degree-granting programs (especially business and nursing), the survey results are being used to support the co-funding of special, subject-oriented resources. Finally, the survey also showed clear support for more full-text databases. In response to the obvious off-campus and on-campus demand for full-text information, the UI Libraries recently purchased access to EBSCO-HOST. As other electronic resources are investigated, library staff members will seriously consider the information gained from the distance-education survey.

The usefulness of each survey is limited by time, however. It is only a snapshot of the views held by particular distance-education students at the time that the survey was distributed. Things will ultimately change, of course, and in this technological age, things can change very quickly. In order to keep informed about student opinions, the survey should be revised and repeated as frequently as possible. The UI Libraries are committed to conducting a survey of distance-education students at least every two years. Although surveys being repeated closely will no doubt show some continuity in student concerns, there will probably be some changes as well.

Distance education librarians should recognize that library staff members are empowered by the knowledge gained from surveys. Significantly, surveys will give us statistical information that we can use whenever we appeal to library and university administrators for new resources and services. Even more importantly, each survey will enlighten us about our students and reinforce our understanding of their evolving concerns for library resources and services. From the survey, we learn who our students are and what they want. How we react to that knowledge, however, is up to us.

REFERENCES

Association of College and Research Libraries. (1998). ACRL guidelines for distance learning library services. *College & Research Libraries News, 59,* 689-694.
Bao, X. (1999). Challenges and Opportunities: A Report of the 1998 Library Survey of Internet Users at Seton Hall University. *College & Research Libraries 59,* 535-543.
Berger, K. W., & Hines, R. W. (1994). What Does the User Really Want?: The Library User Survey Project at Duke University. *Journal of Academic Librarianship, 20,* 306-309.
Cassner, M., & Adams, K. (1998). Instructional Support to a Rural Graduate Popula-

tion: An Assessment of Library Services. In P. S. Thomas & M. Jones (Comps.), *The Eighth Off-Campus Library Services Conference Proceedings, Providence Rhode Island, April 22-24, 1998* (pp. 117-131). Mount Pleasant, MI: Central Michigan University.

Clougherty, L., Forys, J., Lyles, T., Persson, D., Walters, C., & Washington-Hoagland, C. (1998). The University of Iowa Libraries' Undergraduate User Needs Assessment. *College & Research Libraries, 59*, 572-584.

Fowler, F. J. (1993). *Survey Research Methods* (2nd ed.). London: Sage Publications.

Gothberg, H. M. (1990). The Library Survey: A Research Methodology Rediscovered. *College & Research Libraries, 51*, 553-559.

Hafner, A. W. (1998). *Descriptive Statistical Techniques for Librarians* (2nd ed.). Chicago: American Library Association.

Losee, R. M., & Worley, K. A. (1993). *Research and Evaluation for Information Professionals*. New York: Academic Press.

Rose, R. F., & Safford, B. R. (1998). Iowa Is Our Campus: Expanding Library Resources and Services to Distant Education Students in a Rural State. In P. S. Thomas & M. Jones (Comps.), *The Eighth Off-Campus Library Services Conference Proceedings, Providence, Rhode Island, April 22-24, 1998* (pp. 231-237). Mount Pleasant, MI: Central Michigan University.

Schafer, S. (1998). Student Satisfaction with Library Services: Results of Evaluation Using Focus Groups. In P. S. Thomas & M. Jones (Comps.), *The Eighth Off-Campus Library Services Conference Proceedings, Providence Rhode, Island, April 22-24, 1998* (pp. 231-237). Mount Pleasant, MI: Central Michigan University.

Van House, N. A., Weil, B. T., & McClure, C. R. (1990). *Measuring Academic Library Performance: A Practical Approach*. Chicago: American Library Association.

APPENDIX A

**University of Iowa Libraries, Survey of Distance-Education Students
Survey Instrument & Summary of Results for All Programs**

272 responses from 706 surveys mailed out, 38.5% returned

Personal Characteristics

1. Student Status	Percent
Graduate	56.3
Senior	17.6
Junior	20.6
Sophomore	2.2
Freshman	3.3

2. Gender	Percent
Male	34.2
Female	65.8

3. Age	Percent
18-21	.7
22-30	28.5
30+	70.7

4. Degree Seeking	Percent
Yes	100

5. Degree Program	Percent
BLS (Liberal Studies)	36.4
BSN (Nursing)	7.4
BSW (Social Work)	.4
MBA (Business)	28.0
MLS (Library Science)	4.4
MSCS (Computer Science)	1.1
MSECE (Electrical Engineering)	1.5
MSN (Nursing)	3.7
MSW (Social Work)	13.2
PHD (Pharmacy)	4.0

6. Willing to Drive Distance for Library Resources	Percent
Less than 50 miles	86.5
50-100 miles	11.2
100-200 miles	1.2
200+ miles	1.2

7. Willing to Drive Distance for ICN site (fiber optic TV classroom	Percent
Less than 50 miles	82.7
50-100 miles	15.8
100-200 miles	1.2
200+ miles	.4

Coursework

8. How many courses have you taken from the UI in recent years that have been taught in an off-campus setting?

Courses Taken from UI	Percent
0	2.2
1	17.8
2	13.4
3	11.9
4	9.7
5	4.5
6	9.3
7	3.0
8	4.5
9	3.7
10+	20.1

9. How many of your University of Iowa off-campus courses have required the preparation of papers/reports/presentations?

Courses Requiring Paper	Percent
0	9.7
1	19.0
2	16.4
3	10.4
4	7.5
5	5.2
6	6.7
7	3.4
8-9	7.5
10+	14.2

10. How many of your off-campus courses have required the use of library materials?

Courses Requiring Library Use	Percent
0	34.7
1	13.4
2	13.1
3	9.3
4	6.7
5	4.1
6	3.7
7	3.0
8-9	4.1
10+	7.8

If you answered "0" to this question, please go to question 15.

11. For those courses that have required the use of library materials, which libraries or types of libraries have you used (check as many as apply)?

Use of Libraries	Percent
U of Iowa Libraries	34.7
UNI Libraries	2.8
ISU Libraries	4.0

APPENDIX A (continued)

Use of Libraries	Percent
Other Academic Library	62.5
Special Libraries	22.2
Public Libraries	68.2
Personal Library	47.7
Instructor Materials	33.5
Area Education Agency	5.7

12. Which type of library have you used most frequently to complete the requirements for an off-campus course?

Type of Library Used Most	Percent
Academic	47.2
Public	29.0
Special	10.2
Personal	13.6

13. How satisfied have you been with the adequacy of the <u>collections</u> of the library you have used the most?

Satisfaction with Collections	Percent
Very Satisfied	24.0
Somewhat Satisfied	56.6
No Opinion	7.4
Somewhat Dissatisfied	8.6
Very Dissatisfied	3.4

14. How satisfied have you been with the adequacy of the <u>services</u> of the library you have used the most?

Satisfaction with Service	Percent
Very Satisfied	33.7
Somewhat Satisfied	46.9
No Opinion	9.1
Somewhat Dissatisfied	8.0
Very Dissatisfied	2.3

Library Services for Distance Education

15. Most useful services	Rank 1, 2, 3
Which of the following library services do you believe would be most useful as a student enrolled in off-campus courses? Please check any services you feel are important on the left and rank your top three choices on the right.	

1. Web and/or e-mail reference services
   71.3

        1. 15.1
        2. 17.3
        <u>3. 9.6</u>
         42.0

2. Remote access to full-text databases
   65.1

        1. 22.4
        2. 11.8
        <u>3. 11.8</u>
         46.0

3. Home delivery of books, photocopied articles, or other information materials (may involve a charge to students)
   60.7

1.	9.2
2.	11.4
3.	8.1
	28.7

4. Access to Internet resources
   54.8

1.	10.3
2.	9.2
3.	5.1
	24.6

5. 800 number for reference service
   49.3

1.	7.0
2.	5.1
3.	7.0
	19.1

6. Remote access to the UI, ISU, or UNI library catalogs
   49.1

1.	5.9
2.	7.0
3.	8.1
	21.0

7. Interlibrary loan/document delivery services
   43.8

1.	4.8
2.	5.1
3.	10.7
	20.6

8. Remote access to electronic indexes and abstracts
   42.3

1.	4.0
2.	6.3
3.	6.6
	16.9

9. Borrowing agreements with libraries where courses are taught
   37.9

1.	2.6
2.	4.0
3.	4.8
	11.4

10. Guides to doing library research in a subject area
    30.9

1.	2.6
2.	2.6
3.	6.6
	11.8

APPENDIX A (continued)

11. Computer-assisted instruction (in conducting library research)
    27.9

1.	1.5
2.	1.8
3.	2.2
	5.5

12. Librarian-provided instruction (in person or over the ICN)
    20.2

1.	2.2
2.	2.9
3.	.7
	5.8

Connectivity

16. Access to Electronic Mail	Percent
Yes	85.2
No	14.8

17. Do you have convenient access to the following?

Access to World-Wide Web	Percent
Yes	83.8
No	16.2

Access to Sending FAX	Percent
Yes	73.8
No	26.2

Access to Receiving FAX	Percent
Yes	73.8
No	26.2

Please check off the software and hardware noted below that are available on the workstation that you use for completing assignments.

Windows 95 or better	Percent
Yes	83.4
No	16.6

MacOS 7.5 or better	Percent
Yes	4.8
No	95.2

Windows 3.1	Percent
Yes	13.7
No	86.3

High Resolution Color Monitor .... Percent
    Yes 66.8
    No 33.2

CD-ROM Drive .... Percent

    Yes 75.3
    No 24.7

Keyboard .... Percent
    Yes 93.4
    No 6.6

Mouse .... Percent
    Yes 91.9
    No 8.1

28.8 or higher modem or Direct Internet Access .... Percent
    Yes 76.4
    No 23.6

18. How helpful would it be to have information describing library services, resources, and policies for off-campus students? .... Percent
    Very Helpful 33.7
    Somewhat Helpful 46.9
    No Opinion 9.1
    Probably Not Helpful 8.0
    Not Helpful at All 2.3

19. Best format for information on library services .... Percent
    Print 45.2
    Electronic 49.4
    Both 5.3

20. Interest in on-campus orientation by librarian .... Percent
    Yes 29.8
    No 70.2

Library Needs

21. In your own words, what library and/or informational needs do you have for University of Iowa courses that are not being filled currently?

22. Comments?

APPENDIX B

Cover Letter for Off-Campus Student Survey, University of Iowa Libraries

Dear Student:

You will find a survey packet from the University of Iowa Libraries enclosed with this letter. The purpose of the survey is to assess the effectiveness of the information services that are currently available to distance-education students, as well as the potential for improving those services. **We are aware that you are very busy with your academics and other matters, but we hope that you take time to respond.**

Your participation in this survey is completely confidential. No names are associated with individual responses. You were chosen to participate in this survey through the use of a random selection process, and each off-campus student had an equal chance of being selected. **Your participation in this survey is completely voluntary, but it is crucial to the success of our project. Your response will give us an idea of how well we are currently meeting your information needs, and it will help us improve future services.**

The University of Iowa Libraries is committed to creating a learning environment that encourages quality research and scholastic achievement. Your participation in this survey provides us with the type of feedback required to achieve this goal. In addition, should you later have a question about library services or need assistance with any library matter, please feel free to contact me. My university address, telephone number, and e-mail address are provided below.

It will take you approximately five-to-ten minutes to complete this survey. Please return the completed survey in the self-addressed stamped envelope enclosed in this mailing.

Thank You,

Stephen H. Dew, Coordinator
Library Services for Distance Education
100 Main Library
University of Iowa
Iowa City, IA 52242-1420
Tel: 800-272-6430
FAX: 319-335-5900
Email: stephen-dew@uiowa.edu

APPENDIX C

University of Iowa Libraries, Handout for Distance Education Students

LIBRARY SERVICES FOR DISTANCE EDUCATION STUDENTS

Student ID Card Required.

The University of Iowa Libraries offers Distance-Education Services to all students enrolled in the degree-granting programs directed by the Center for Credit Programs and to all students enrolled in the off-campus MBA programs directed by the School of Management. In order to qualify for these services, students must obtain a "**University of Iowa No-Picture ID Card.**" They can obtain forms to request the ID cards from the Center for Credit Programs and the School of Management.

Distance-Education Library Services Homepage.

http://www.lib.uiowa.edu/disted

This Homepage provides access to library resources and services that support distance education. The Homepage includes links to the following:

Short-Cuts to Electronic Resources by Subject.

For each degree-granting program (business, computer science, education, electrical engineering, liberal studies, library science, nursing, pharmacy, and social work), the Homepage provides a link to a list of the most useful electronic resources and databases. Some databases provide lists of articles and books by subject, keyword, author, etc., while other files provide information, such as full-text articles, statistics, or business information. In order to access some databases, your Web browser must be configured to work with the Libraries' Proxy Server. Links are provided to online instructions describing how to configure it properly. In addition, for access to restricted databases, you will be prompted for a "Login/Password." In such cases, on the first line of the "Login/Password" box, type in your student identification number (usually your social security number), and leave the password line blank.

Access to OASIS.

The Homepage includes a link to OASIS, providing users with access to the University of Iowa's online library catalog as well as several other electronic resources. The other resources in OASIS include several subject indexes (such as **ERIC**, the education database) as well as the online catalogs of a number of different libraries, including the Big Ten universities, Iowa State University, and the University of Northern Iowa. In addition to Web access, OASIS also can be accessed by telephone modem (**319-335-6200**) and by direct telnet (**oasis.uiowa.edu**).

Document-Delivery Services

- **Articles:** Distance-education students have the option of having articles mailed to any address that they provide or faxed to any fax number that they provide. For articles of ten pages or less, the charge is **three dollars** ($3) for each article. For articles over ten pages, there is an additional charge of **ten-cents-per-page (for pages eleven and higher)**.
- **Books:** Students also have the ability to request that books be sent by UPS to any address that they provide. The charge is **three dollars** ($3) for each book. Students are responsible for returning books to the Main Library or Hardin Library before the due date, and they may use any delivery method that they prefer (mail, UPS, hand-delivery, etc.). Renewals are possible.

Requests can be submitted electronically. Forms are available from a link on the Distance-Education Library Services Homepage. For students enrolled in programs that have made financial arrangements with the Libraries, total costs will be charged to the program account. Otherwise, total costs will be charged to the student's University bill.

Reference Services: Email and Toll-Free Telephone

Without leaving home or office, students can ask for help or advice from library staff. Any student who needs help finding information for a class project or help with research strategies should contact Stephen Dew, the Coordinator of Library Services for Distance Education. Web-based email forms are available on the Homepage. Otherwise, Dr. Dew can be contacted at the following: **1-877-807-9587, stephen-dew@uiowa.edu**

From Isolation to Cooperation: The Changes that Technology Creates in Institutional Culture

Steven Dunlap

Golden Gate University

SUMMARY. The use of technology in higher education has caused departments to interact with each other in new and different ways. Librarians can manage this transition better with an understanding of what the other departments must do as well as recognizing that librarians often know as little about other departments' work as the personnel elsewhere in the institution know about librarianship. Although each institution will have its own unique situation and personalities, the experience at Golden Gate University's Libraries managing the implementation of remote access to databases provides an example of what takes place when previously independent departments interact in new ways, and also tells a tale of one librarian learning diplomacy and forming alliances.

KEYWORDS. Library services, distance education, interdepartmental cooperation

Golden Gate University is a private institution with a college, graduate school and law school. The University Library serves the college and the graduate school. A separate law library serves the law students. The curriculum that the University Library supports consists mostly of business and public administration along with Telecommu-

[Haworth co-indexing entry note]: "From Isolation to Cooperation: The Changes that Technology Creates in Institutional Culture." Dunlap, Steven. Co-published simultaneously in *Journal of Library Administration* (The Haworth Information Press, an imprint of The Haworth Press, Inc.) Vol. 31, No. 3/4, 2001, pp. 195-206; and: *Off-Campus Library Services* (ed: Anne Marie Casey) The Haworth Information Press, an imprint of The Haworth Press, Inc., 2001, pp. 195-206.

nications, Computer Information Science (CIS) and Operations Management. Electives in the undergraduate programs constitute the only purely humanities and social science courses offered. The University focuses on "adult" or "returning" students who work full-time and desire evening classes and accelerated programs. The traditional 18- to 22-year-old student studying full time and living near campus make up a small minority of the total student body. Just less than half the total number of students attend classes in the university's regional campuses throughout California (and one in Seattle). In the fall of 1997 CyberCampus, a distance education project that functions as a regional campus, started to offer courses through the World Wide Web. In the late Spring of 1998 the University Library and the Law Library added the "Web Access Management Module" to the Innopac on-line catalog the two libraries share. During the period from about 1994 to the present other departments in the university experienced rapid technological change as well. The university staff and faculty have struggled to make the best use of the new equipment and software and continue to work on integrating the new technology into the class instruction and work processes in the most effective and efficient manner possible. This does not prove as easy as one would expect.

Prior to the 1993/1994 academic year the university's schools, academic and administrative departments, and the libraries functioned largely independently of each other. The first large-scale cooperation between the libraries took place when the staff of the two libraries selected the Innopac on-line catalog that the two libraries would share. Starting in the 1995/1996 academic year the library staff started to transfer records from the Registrar's office's newly installed registration database into the Innopac's patron database. This process excluded regional students and library staff continued to check out books to regional students manually through our document delivery service. The infrequency of the regional student's borrowing of materials made bar coding their ID cards a low priority. However, we planned to use the barcode as a "PIN" to enter full-text databases. By the Spring of 1998 the introduction of remote access to those full-text databases made the issue of barcodes for regional campus students more urgent and led to a close cooperation between the Registrar's office and the Library.

In the Summer of 1997 the library staff received an invitation to attend meetings with the staff of the nascent CyberCampus. Prior to

CyberCampus the University Library had to rely on the Computing Services Department, known officially as the Office of Information Technology or OIT. Unlike OIT the CyberCampus staff provided training to the librarians on a one-on-one basis. For example, I learned how to configure CGI (Common Gateway Interface) files to make a Web-based form for regional and CyberCampus students to use to make document delivery requests. As a result the librarians could provide better support to CyberCampus students as well as to other regional students. CyberCampus stands as one of the better examples of inter-departmental cooperation to date, but the factors influencing the positive outcome included the eager willingness of both parties to participate, the dynamic and strong personality of the head of the CyberCampus program and the fact that both parties received tangible benefits from the cooperation. Without these three factors the librarian will have to find other ways to encourage the inter-departmental cooperation necessary to provide the services students now demand.

Remote access to databases also interested the School of Taxation, since we could restrict access to databases by type of student. The School of Taxation had a good relationship with the principle tax database vendors who gave a very generous discount for access to their databases but only for students taking the tax research class. When we acquired the capability of automating the process of authenticating students into the databases ourselves, we relieved the vendor of the labor of issuing individual passwords for each student in the class each of 5 terms a year. But this required much "behind the scenes" work on the part of the library. But demand for Web access to full-text databases, a necessity for CyberCampus, an improvement for the School of Taxation and generally demanded by all, forced all parties to cooperate with each other in rather unpredictable and fluid circumstances.

We live in an age of ever increasing demands, and the technology to fulfill them continues to lag behind our students' expectations. Our students had complained about having to go to the library to do their research for the two years leading up to the Spring of 1998 when we initiated remote access to databases by means of the Innopac's "Web Access Management" module, or WAM. The difficulties we had with the implementation of the WAM module require another paper to describe. The technological advance we received in 1998 with the acquisition of the WAM module of the Innopac system led to my working closely with the Registrar, CyberCampus, and the School of Taxation. In each interaction I learned important lessons about how each department worked, how technology affected the school or department and how best to manage inter-departmental cooperation. Here I limit my discussion to the logistical problems we faced as part of the implementation of remote access to databases.

Golden Gate University has two libraries: one a Law Library serving primarily the Law School and the other a "General" Library serving primarily the business and technology programs. Both libraries suffered from inadequate staffing levels that made a labor-intensive OPAC module implementation quite challenging. My collection development duties suffered as a result of my participation in the WAM implementation but the regional students had come to demand remote access to databases. I agreed to assist with the transfer of records from the Registrar's system to the Innopac patron database and to make sure that all regional campus students had barcodes issued to them. Placing barcodes on student ID cards makes the most sense and most other institutions handle the distribution of barcodes by placing them on students' ID cards. Thus, from June of 1997 to May of 1999 I worked closely with the University's Registrar to place library barcodes on student ID cards and mail them to the regional campuses or the students.

My job takes me to the regional campuses about one quarter of my total workdays. I speak to students in their classrooms and often take them to the small on-site libraries that contain small "core" collections and the computers necessary to search databases via the World Wide Web. I use these opportunities to make announcements and to teach students how to do research on full-text databases. Starting in the Summer term of 1997 (May and June), a year before we actually had remote access to databases, I brought sheets of barcode stickers with me on my visits in the hope that I could single-handedly perform a retrospective ID card bar coding project. Looking back on that time in my life I often ask myself, "What was I thinking?!"

Many students never received an ID card; many without cards had attended classes for years. Others had lost or misplaced their cards. The lack of any need to use their cards (since they never entered the library in San Francisco, they did not need an ID card to show for admittance) led to a somewhat lackadaisical effort on the part of the Registrar's Office to make them for regional campus students. The

Golden Gate University student ID card remains just a plain piece of plastic, without a picture, color-coded for grad, undergrad and law student. As soon as I realized my predicament I contacted the Registrar, David Smith, and we put our heads together. He agreed to send newly made ID cards to the library for bar coding.

I enjoyed working with David Smith, a tall, skinny, chain-smoking Englishman from Liverpool who lacked the pretenses that can make an academician difficult to deal with. I explained my predicament to him, pointing out that my class visits had revealed that the majority of students did not have ID cards and mentioned the mess that individual requests created. I could supply him with a list of currently enrolled students who did not have barcodes attached to their records. His office would create ID cards for them. Although I thought my plan had elements of simplicity and fairness I quickly realized that, despite his pleasant disposition, if I were to march up to our Registrar with a laundry list of demands that would create more work for his department I may not succeed. I needed to give him something. I made the following proposal: the Registrar's Office would issue a whole lot more ID cards than they ever had to before but the library would mail them instead of returning them to the Registrar after we bar coded them. I offered our staff time and postage in exchange for his office's participation in my retrospective patron bar coding project.

David Smith and I worked out the details of the project "as we went along." Since students who lacked a barcode in their student records most likely did not have an ID card I did a "create lists" on the Innopac, with the criteria of student type, non-San Francisco Location, future expiration date and a barcode less than 2. Smith offered to create labels for my assistant and me to work with. Once I had the list described above I used the "list" function of the Innopac to e-mail a list of student ID numbers to myself. Once received I used a macro I created in MS Word to format them as a list with carriage returns separating each one, saved it as a plain text file and e-mailed it to David Smith. This was the format the Registrar asked for to facilitate the creation of mailing labels that my assistant affixed to the library's envelopes. After the Registrar's office delivered the ID cards my assistant (and sometimes the circulation staff) bar coded them and then my assistant stuffed my form letter along with the ID card into each envelope bearing an address label. I would visit a given campus before initiating this process each term, allowing me to barcode the ID cards of those students who had them.

Thus, I had won a valuable ally for the library and I had worked out a tedious but efficient system for eliminating the backlog of "cardless" students. I patted myself on the back and breathed a sigh of relief in summer of 1997. That proved very premature. We hit the first snag in the Fall Term. Most Golden Gate University business students work full-time and attend classes part-time. In the regional campuses this type makes up at least 99% of the students. In addition, the students can "miss" a term or two without loss of matriculation. I expected my "create lists" routine described above would find a few hundred students currently registered without barcodes attached to their records. I actually found over 1300 such records.

At first I did not realize we had a problem. The Registrar's office has a heavy workload the first week of a term but then they can turn their attention to producing ID cards. This did not happen as planned. Over 1300 students in need of newly bar coded ID cards overwhelmed the Registrar's office. However, since we did not yet have remote access up and running we had no immediate crisis. I expected we would work our way through the backlog in time. I told students to expect delays but reassured them that by the time we were ready to open access to full-text databases we would have the ID card production under control. During the Spring 1998 terms the Registrar's staff made a valiant effort to process the backlog but the number of new students or those returning from taking a couple of terms off brought plenty of new names into the pool of those requiring a new bar coded ID card.

Starting in the late Spring of 1998 we brought the Web Access Management (WAM) module on-line and instructed students to use their barcodes as PINs to log in to the database of their choice. This is where the fun began. Although it took the Registrar's Office and the library about three weeks to produce and barcode all the needed ID cards, I felt that with each large batch we processed the backlog would continue to shrink. But the terms beginning in the late summer and fall of 1998 brought over 700 student records without barcodes. This proved too large a number for the Registrar's office to make cards for in a timely manner.

To complicate matters further, a bureaucratic problem outside the control of either David Smith or myself prevented the mass production of ID cards for about three months: funding for new ID cards for regional campus students dried up. The Registrar's office could make a card only upon receiving a student's request during the Fall terms of 1998. But early on, in 1997, I discovered that dealing with individual requests for ID cards did not work very well. The Registrar's Office created an ID card each time a student called to complain that he or she had still not received an ID card. My desk piled high with duplicate and triplicate cards. This created a record-keeping problem. I could not tell whether a given card was a replacement or an unnecessary duplicate, as the Registrar's office did not keep track of the card production. Calling students did not work well because the original card could be in the mail and not yet received. When I bar coded each card and sent it off (less work then keeping track of who got a card and when) students would discard the second card and then call me to complain that the barcode on their (earlier) card was invalid. I had other work to do and the process of keeping track of who asked for a card constituted a very labor intensive clerical task that neither I nor anyone in the Registrar's office wanted to do.

At the onset of our collaboration I explained to the Registrar the duplicate card phenomenon and showed him the resulting pile of cards. He and I agreed that I would be the single point of contact for students to request ID cards in order to bring some order to the process. At least with me sorting through the requests we could reduce or eliminate the duplicate and triplicate cards. I could also verify to the Registrar's Office whether or not a student had received an ID card since the barcode in our record for a student indicated that we had mailed (or handed) a bar coded card to them. David Smith appreciated the fact that the library, by means of systematically bar coding ID cards, could help keep track of who had been issued an ID card.

The halting of the production of ID cards for three months pretty much eliminated our headway through the backlog. Students objected (some quite vociferously) to having to go to a Regional Campus in order to do their research. My boss, the Dean of the Library, argued for separating the process of issuing the barcode from the process of issuing the ID card and e-mailing the student the number from the barcode sticker. I argued against this. The students would lose a barcode sticker far more frequently than a card. Also, we had a "service" which we provided the Registrar's office: helping them keep track of who had been issued a card (if the record had a barcode, the student was supposed to have received a card). I also did not want to maintain a file of barcode stickers awaiting ID cards.

We initiated a policy of producing cards for CyberCampus students before any other campus since they had no regional facility and thus had only remote access to databases. However, the demand from all the other regional campuses for remote access to databases reached fever pitch in the middle of the Spring 1999 term. I wrote an e-mail message describing the difficulty the Registrar's office had in producing ID cards along with a plea for increased funding, if only for temporary workers to help that office get through the backlog. But after consulting with the Dean of the Library and the Assistant Vice President to whom the library reports as a result of this e-mail message, I had to separate the production of ID cards from the issue of barcode stickers. The process they decided on constituted a complete and total divorce: the students would be responsible for putting the sticker on an ID card and the students would have to make a request for an ID card separately from the barcode.

My collaboration with CyberCampus started in the Summer of 1997 with a meeting between the library staff and the CyberCampus development team. The Head, or Provost, of CyberCampus had a great deal of energy and enthusiasm for the new medium. He also understood the benefits to his department of collaboration with librarians. We received training and advice from the CyberCampus development team. In particular, a CyberCampus programmer created a Web-based form for regional campus students to use to make a document delivery request from the library and I learned how to configure CGI-bin scripts in order to modify this Web page. Later, when the library's Web pages changed directories, I was able to use these skills I acquired to configure the cgi-bin script on our home page that allows a user to search our Web site by keyword. I did the same for the home page of my intellectual freedom Web site.

CyberCampus employs software called "Well-Engaged," created by The Well and running on The Well's server. The classes take place by means of "conferences" in which each student posts to the "class" and all members of the class participate and read each other's posts. Unlike the old-style correspondence course in which a student interacted only with the instructor, this model more closely resembles a traditional in-person class since all students interact with each other in addition to the professor. In the Summer of 1998, shortly after we introduced remote access to databases, I asked for a conference, run much like a class, on CyberCampus called "Ask the Librarian." I put messages into the conference providing information on various services the library provided and had a folder called "Questions and Answers" for the students to interact with us. A librarian from the Reference Department and I have moderator privileges for this conference and one or both of us check it each day.

The library's relationship with CyberCampus proves the great success story of cooperation. CyberCampus has received better library service for its students. The librarians received training that improved the library's Web site and service to all students. Through the "Ask the Librarian" conference we had better access to students who otherwise would have had to call us on the phone or gone without reference assistance entirely.

The School of Taxation has long had a relationship with the Tax databases CCH (Commerce Clearing House) and RIA (Research Institute of America). The Dean of the School of Taxation, in consultation with the library staff, decided to use the CCH tax database as a pilot project to determine the feasibility of using the library's WAM module for tax students. Unlike the rest of the databases that the library handled, CCH did not want remote access for the entire University population. All vendors have expressed the desire to restrict remote access to currently enrolled students (excluding alumni), but CCH went an additional step by specifying that only students enrolled in the graduate tax research class could have remote access to their database. Fortunately, the WAM has the flexibility to allow access by "patron type." The librarian creates patron types and assigns them a numerical label (0 = non-law student, 1 = doctoral student, 2 = faculty, etc.). After I created the entry necessary I then edited an entry for access to CCH allowing only tax research students, staff and faculty to search the CCH database from outside of a university building. In return, CCH allowed Web access to the database for computers inside of a university building. We opened up remote access through the Web to the "in-house" university community and handled the remote access authentication for the tax research class students.

We experienced problems with this plan right away. We first had to identify the students in the research class. Then my assistant or I had to change each student's patron type manually. For about 50 students this should not prove difficult. But we did not always receive class rosters for all the sections of this class taught at all locations. I also lacked the knowledge to interpret the class rosters correctly. Once I changed the patron type on a large list of students and then, grumbling, changed many of them back after I had seen some of the same names on a long list of "drops" at the end of the list, and did not realize that the "drops" had moved from one section of the same class to another. One term a regional campus director failed to send me the roster for this class. She "thought it was all done by computer." But a few phone calls and explanations later, the process of setting up tax students for remote access became routine.

The "proxy server problem" proved more intractable. CCH used JavaScript in all of its Web pages. With the introduction of JavaScript on over half of our commercial databases, in the summer of 1998 Innovative Interfaces released a "proxy server" to handle pages with JavaScript. Without the proxy server JavaScript buttons do not appear and the browser handles other JavaScript functions as applications to be downloaded. The proxy server resolved these problems but gave rise to new ones. The process of configuring one's browser for a proxy server looked easy to me, but I have had years of experience dealing with arcana of computers and the Internet. Many of the University's students and the majority of the tax students had little or no experience using the Internet except for surfing on the graphical browser that came installed on their computers. Many students (not just tax students) made mistakes configuring the proxy server, or did not configure it at all. Add to this the incompatibility of the proxy server with AOL and I had my work cut out for me. All the difficulties with the proxy server we could resolve by training the students and improving the instructions on our Web pages. But the one problem that we could not resolve lay entirely outside of our control.

Network security measures often block proxy servers. Much to our chagrin the majority of our tax students were practitioners upgrading their skills and qualifications that expected to use their workplace computers after hours to complete their research assignments. The JavaScript and frames in the CCH database Web interface made searches from home (even with 56K modems) excruciatingly slow. My e-mail box quickly filled, and reference librarians, at a loss for answers, transferred puzzled tax students to my office. I created a Web page of "trouble-shooting tips and hints," but many found the number of possible problems daunting. Even after explaining the proxy server setup over the phone innumerable times, the fact that workplace security measures made the proxy server setup impossible continued to dog my every effort. Finally, in the Summer of 1999 the Dean of the School of Taxation decided to return to the "old" method of asking CCH to issue each individual student his or her own password for access to the CCH tax database.

When I proposed this paper I had three "success stories" showing the ways that technology led to the creation of or improvement of inter-departmental cooperation between the Library and the Registrar's office, CyberCampus and the School of Taxation. The lessons I have to report, although very different from what I planned, have value nonetheless. I discovered that neither the new technology nor my efforts to change practices and attitudes failed. In the case of student ID cards, tight funding did not permit the timely creation of ID cards for regional campus students. The result mentioned above constitutes only a partial retreat. A new "all-campus smart card" proposal could reintroduce the practice of having the Library and Registrar's Office collaborate on the creation and bar coding of ID cards in the future. We have a better idea of the costs involved as a result of our recent collaboration. Both departments take from this experience a more realistic understanding of what such an effort requires in terms of staff and funding.

In the case of remote access to the CCH tax database, workplace network security created an obstacle beyond the University's control. I nonetheless learned a great deal about organizing an effort to identify and modify batches of student records in the Innopac patron database. I found that Web technology, although versatile and enormously useful, has limits and that counter-measures meant for hackers detract from educational and perhaps other constructive use of the technology. I also found that the use of JavaScript on a database's Web interface proves unnecessary and creates more of an obstacle than a bridge between the end-user and the information. The fact that 7 out of 15 of our commercial databases work fine without JavaScript proves that for Web databases JavaScript constitutes a superfluous embellishment. As a direct result of our experience our collection development committee asks all database vendors whether the Web version of their product employs JavaScript and if it does we place that product at the bottom of our "shopping list." I strongly advise that other libraries consider doing the same.

 KALAMAZOO VALLEY COMMUNITY COLLEGE LIBRARY

In the last two years I gained a new appreciation for what other departments must do and the challenges they face. The other departments have learned that records they create have a use beyond their own department. In the Fall of 1999 I participated in an inter-departmental committee to evaluate the present use of technology in the University and to make recommendations to the University President for the future. Most of the participants indicated that the most beneficial aspect of the Task Force was its inter-departmental nature and as a result the Task Force will include recommendations to encourage the use of inter-departmental teams in the future. The experiences I have described gave the Task Force some concrete examples of the inter-departmental nature of technological change and furthered understanding of the costs and benefits of such cooperation.

Now You *Can* Get There from Here: Creating an Interactive Web Application for Accessing Full-Text Journal Articles from Any Location

John Felts

University of North Carolina Greensboro

SUMMARY. This paper will focus on the process of creating an interactive World Wide Web application that allows patrons the ability to access and retrieve full-text journal articles from any of nearly 7,500 unique electronic journal titles, which are delivered to their computer desktops, without geographic constraints.

KEYWORDS. Library services, distance education, Web page development, full-text journal articles

INTRODUCTION

What can be more frustrating to an off-campus patron than to search diligently through online databases for journal literature on a research topic, to carefully constructing a bibliography on any desired titles, then to be provided no means of access to the full-text articles? And isn't it a shame to neglect putting such a wonderful resource at your patrons' fingertips: full-text journal articles delivered to their desktops upon request, free of charge and available twenty-four hours a day, seven days a week, without geographic limitation.

[Haworth co-indexing entry note]: "Now You *Can* Get There from Here: Creating an Interactive Web Application for Accessing Full-Text Journal Articles from Any Location." Felts, John. Co-published simultaneously in *Journal of Library Administration* (The Haworth Information Press, an imprint of The Haworth Press, Inc.) Vol. 31, No. 3/4, 2001, pp. 207-218; and: *Off-Campus Library Services* (ed: Anne Marie Casey) The Haworth Information Press, an imprint of The Haworth Press, Inc., 2001, pp. 207-218.

However, given the daunting array of publishers, vendors, journal title lists, interfaces, and file formats with which the library must contend, attempting to provide reliable, user-friendly access to full-text electronic journals has proven as problematic to the library as these journals are beneficial to the patron. Due to the lack, in part, of a fast, reliable, cost-effective vendor solution, the University of North Carolina Greensboro's Jackson Library decided to build its own World Wide Web interface for providing access to our full-text electronic journal holdings (http://library.uncg.edu/ejournals/).

IDENTIFYING THE PROBLEMS

Through surveys and informal communication with our patrons, student demand for full-text electronic journal articles was determined to be a high priority. Not only are e-journals highly popular to our student population because of their accessibility and ease of use, but they serve as a crucial research component in the Library's effort to support its growing distance education population. Having decided that a reliable and efficient means of access to electronic journals should be created, several technical and non-technical issues and questions presented themselves:

Technical Issues

1. Will we create several lengthy WWW lists, as so many other institutions are doing, or will we attempt to create a searchable, more interactive site?

The sheer number of titles to be listed would make static WWW pages not only very cumbersome for patrons to browse, but would make ongoing maintenance a significant problem. Theoretically, there would be static pages to include:

- Alphabetical title access
- Separate title access for each letter
- A multitude of subject-oriented pages
- Publisher's list

Not only would regular updating and maintenance of the site be tedious and unwieldy, but, because of the numerous pages in place, highly prone to human error and therefore inaccurate.

2. Will we integrate electronic journal titles into the existing library catalog, or create a separate site?

The traditional library catalog is not designed to handle the very dynamic, rapidly changing environment of electronic journals, and allows access to only a single record at a time, causing global changes and quick additions, deletions, or other updates to be very time-consuming. Additionally, we felt that applying Library of Congress subject access to these titles would be unnecessarily Byzantine and would not best serve the students' needs. A WWW page that would provide broader subject access to those disciplines and broad subject areas relating to our University's academic units was considered more appropriate. Also, we did not wish to undertake this project by placing limitations on content or functionality from the project's inception, which would have occurred had we attempted to use our integrated library system as the search and retrieval mechanism for providing access to our growing electronic journal collection.

3. If the library catalog is not to be used in creating this site, then how will we integrate a freestanding, WWW-based e-journals site within the catalog?

Tough questions. But given the limitations of our catalog and the burden already carried by the Library's technical services staff, it was decided that this would be an Electronic Resources Department project and that we desired a more dynamic, interactive, and easy-to-manage system than our catalog could provide. Honestly, lack of integration with the library catalog continues to be an ongoing challenge, with no clear solution in sight.

4. How will the multitude of inconsistent file formats for e-journals be solved and supported?

File format issues may seem somewhat trivial, but due to the many formats in which e-journals are written: .dvi, .hdvi, .tex, .txc, .ps, .eps, .pcf, .gz, .tar, and .rif, which require such programs as GhostView, CarlView, TeX, and LaTeX viewers; as well as DVIWin, TkDVI, and xDVI; gzip, unzip, eZIP, CCZip, PKzip, and WinZip; PCFView, Real-Page, and IBM Techexplore; to name a few, appropriate software combined with the provision of adequate support for this software must be in place from the site's inception.

5. How will remote access be provided to this electronic journal collection?

Since access to electronic journals is of particular value to distance education students, we felt it especially important to make the World Wide Web the default delivery protocol and considered the WWW browser to be the optimum and conveniently free software tool for delivering this content to students, regardless of geographic location.

Non-Technical Issues

1. Given the myriad electronic journal resources available from pub-lishers, vendors and aggregators, full-text databases, and cover-to-cover full-text journal sites, what would be the selection criteria for choosing electronic journal titles, and who would make these deci-sions? Would only those titles with dedicated access and dedicated URLs be included in this site, such as those titles from Project MUSE, JSTOR, and The Ideal Library?

The preliminary set of selection criteria that were put into place at the beginning of this project and that are still being used as rules of thumb with minimal alteration are:

- The resource must be free to the user
- At least fifty percent of the content must have full-text
- An archive of the electronic journal title should be available
- No "rolling" archives; the beginning date should be static, yet the archive, in its entirety, should grow
- The resource must be consistent with the University curriculum
- The e-journal must be in a format that is sustainable and capable of being supported by the Library

We believed that to ignore those titles found in aggregate databases, as many libraries currently do because of their less convenient means of access, would deprive our users of access to the literally thousands of available titles. Therefore, vendor title lists were downloaded and integrated into our catalog.

2. It was decided to add these resources, and the freely available, sometimes less scholarly publications found on the WWW (frequently

typified as "E-Zines") on a case-by-case basis, to be determined by the maintainers of the e-journals site. We also decided that publications available by trial access of less than six months would not be incorporated. After the e-journals site was in production for less than six months, it became apparent that this length of time was insufficient. Since a publication would be available for a brief period of time, then removing it would cause a high level of student frustration. This review period was changed to a year, then ultimately discontinued, as it became obvious that few vendors or publishers were allowing long-term access on a trial basis.

IDENTIFYING THE SOLUTION

We identified a number of solutions that would provide us with real-time database connectivity through a WWW interface, and evaluated each of these according to its functionality, design, and overall ease of use.

Allaire's Cold Fusion
Several conference presentations had indicated that Allaire's Cold Fusion was a very good software solution for creating WWW-based database interactivity. At this time, it was also evident that there was at least a discernible learning curve in running the software, in addition to being a relatively expensive product.

Perl Scripts
With a multitude of free Perl scripts available on the WWW that could be customized and run through CGI, using Perl was a distinct possibility. However, because we were not extremely conversant in Perl, and because we are a part of a campus network that has proven a difficult environment in which to develop due to security issues, we decided to seek a faster, easier solution.

FrontPage '98
At this time, FrontPage was becoming a viable solution for creating an interactive WWW site, but as this was the '98 version, there was a proven record of this software being very

intrusive to WWW servers, which was causing significant problems for Web masters.

Active Server Pages (ASP)

Our department already possessed a growing interest in connectivity to a customized database, mounted on a World Wide Web server, and accessible through the user's WWW browser of choice. We had a working knowledge of Microsoft Access as a relational database program, and had experimented with HTX/IDC as a way to generate an on-demand database query, which would result in an HTML table. This had proven a workable solution. Also, Microsoft had recently rolled out its Active Server Pages technology as a more powerful, robust extension of HTX/IDC, and this scripting environment was already proving itself a viable possibility for the development of interactive, real time database transactions across the Web. We also saw it as a growing, evolutionary product for not only WWW-enabled database development, but also as a tool for building WWW-based surveys, end-of-course assessment tools, and other real-time interactivity within our existing WWW environment.

Not coincidentally, our department was already using Windows NT as our network operating system, out of which IIS came bundled, which we use as our WWW server software. The Active Server Pages, which are a component of the ActiveX Data Objects (ADOs) and bundled with the IIS Web server software, integrates smoothly with Microsoft Access and other Office applications, which were already in production in the Library. In addition, the ASP scripts are essentially HTML, with enough Structured Query Language (SQL) and Visual Basic Script (VBScript) evident to call the necessary ADOs, query the database, and order the responses. Ultimately, this proved to be the path of least resistance and our obvious choice for creating the functionality we desired in an electronic journals search, retrieval, and display mechanism.

CREATION AND IMPLEMENTATION

To begin, a database containing electronic journal titles, dates of full-text coverage, originating sources, and other essential information was created using Microsoft Access. For development purposes, only a few records were imported into the database. The most important process in converting the database from a static to dynamic one also happens to be one of the easiest. Saving the database as HTML invokes a Help Wizard that automates this conversion process and creates the Active Server Pages that are ultimately used for the real-time querying of the database. The steps are:

1. Select the table that contains all of the data records
2. Select format type as Dynamic ASP
3. Choose the radio button labeled "Dynamic ASP (Microsoft Active Server Pages)"

On the WWW server, the ODBC Data Source Name (DSN) must be created. First, one has to be mindful of the NTFS permissions, since users do require read/execute permissions to use this database. One possibility is to create a Guest user account, which can then be assigned as the default user in this directory and to whom can be assigned read/change permissions. The other steps for creating and applying a Domain Source Name (DSN) to your database are as follows:

1. Go inside the Control Panel on the WWW server
2. Click on the ODBC icon
3. Click on the System DSN (Domain Source Name) tab
4. Click the Add button and select the Microsoft Access Driver (*.mdb)
5. Type the desired name for the database in Data Source Name

Incidentally, a username/password challenge can also be created in these advanced properties, should there be a need. Associate this DSN with the e-journals database by browsing through the various directories on the server. This tells the server that the DSN has access to the Database Access Component native in IIS 4.0. These Database Access Components contain the ADOs, which are the set of objects that are used to establish connectivity to a database as well as retrieve and order data through creating the necessary Recordset objects. These are the fundamental object-oriented components that allow the scripts to communicate with the server, which then talks to the database, then back again. Fortunately, these components are embedded in IIS, and minimal Structured Query Language (SQL) and Visual Basic Script

(VBScript) is required to create the interactivity between user and database. The SQL generally handles the querying of the database, while the VBScript is generally used for handling the output and formatting the information retrieved from the database. One of the nicer features of Active Server Pages is that the portions of the script that are run on the WWW server are embedded in the HTML code of these ASP scripts.

Once the functionality is working, the database must be populated. Since the database tables have been created, importing the data becomes the last order of business in creating the e-journals database. Generally, this is a tedious but simple process. The largest part of the actual data in the database originates from the product source lists found at various database vendor sites. These vendor-created source lists are generally available in ASCII and Excel spreadsheet formats, but unfortunately these are the only available resources for indicating full-text electronic journal holdings. It would be virtually impossible to check thousands of individual titles for accuracy and veracity.

There is one online database provider, however, that makes no provision for downloading and ultimately importing titles from their source lists. Ebsco Publishing only provides these title lists in HTML and .pdf file formats, which are extremely difficult to manipulate, given the markup code and other non-ASCII characters that surround the actual text. In order to accomplish importing these titles into the database, the following procedures had to be followed:

- View the source code of each WWW page for each database, which in one case consisted of eighty-two separate HTML pages
- Copy and paste this HTML code into one very large Word document
- Identify portions of this HTML code that appeared each time a new journal title was entered
- Perform a global search and replace these HTML tags with commas or tabs, to create a delimited file
- Import this file into a spreadsheet program
- Clean up the data in the spreadsheet for importing into the database

Again, this problem was not the norm, but does illustrate some of the issues that can occur when relying solely on the data provided by database vendors or other third parties as the sole authority for e-journals holdings.

REMOTE ACCESS

A vital component for providing title-level access to full-text electronic journals is the ability to provide remote access to these e-journals. Certainly, providing access to those full-text publications available in various and myriad WWW sites and online databases, but then omitting actual access to the journal article would severely impede the overall efficacy of the site. In order to access these journal articles without the user being confined by domain restrictions, Microsoft Proxy Server was used in conjunction with several Perl scripts for creating remote access.

After a user queries the e-journals database through the WWW interface, dynamically created search results pages indicate the journal title (formatted in hypertext), the originating source, as well as the full-text dates of coverage. However, instead of the journal title pointing to its actual WWW content page, which generally would not provide access to these titles from off-campus, a Perl script is called. This script was copied from a free resource on the WWW and customized to work within our environment, and is used to identify whether a user is coming from within the UNCG IP domain, or from outside this domain. Upon running this routine, the user is either granted immediate access to the selected resource provided they are on-campus (fulfilling the licensing agreement with the majority of our vendors), or if off-campus, the user is sent to a local instruction page describing how to configure the proxy server.

Before the proxy configuration instruction page is called, however, another script is run that identifies the type and version of WWW browser that is attempting to access the title. Since each browser has its own unique proxy configuration, the configuration directions are then dynamically customized and delivered to the user based on the browser being used. The users then simply follow the instructions for configuring their browsers to access the Library's proxy server, where they can then proceed to any remote site, regardless of their location. The Perl scripts that identify whether a user is on or off-campus, and the script that identifies browser type, are both written to carry the actual electronic journal URL as an argument across each script. This allows the users, upon completing their browser proxy configuration, to proceed directly to their intended site without having to recreate previous steps. By first accessing the local proxy server, the user is recognized as coming from the proxy server's on-campus IP number, upon which the remote database or electronic journal site grants access. Although requiring that the users configure their browsers, the proxy server has proven to be an effective means for allowing off-campus access to IP-limited WWW sites.

CONCLUSIONS

It became evident during the first few months of production that several benefits had arisen as a result of choosing Active Server Pages as the solution for providing access to our collection of electronic journals. Initially, we did not have to learn a new program, which saved considerable time in the site's development cycle. Since the applications, platforms, and scripts were essentially a bundled technology, creating and refining the various parts of the database proved very easy, due in part to the interoperability of these components. In addition, given that Active Server Pages has behind it the significant influence of Microsoft, ASP is almost certain to be an ongoing, thriving, and highly developed technology. This has already been proven true as witnessed by the software's evolution to version 2.0, in addition to the myriad books, WWW sites and journal articles that discuss various solutions for Web page development using ASP pages.

Some of the issues that developed over time and have proven themselves to be disadvantageous concern issues of scalability and database performance. Although the total number of records can negatively affect performance when using Microsoft's Access RDBMS, we have found that Access simply does not share well with both other applications and services as well as with connectivity. When multiple connections were made to the electronic journals database, performance has been adversely affected, albeit marginally. It has also been documented that malicious codes and programs have been passed to WWW servers that utilize Active Server Pages. However, since there are those who persistently attempt to exploit security weaknesses in Microsoft platforms and products, and given the relatively low occurrence in which these attacks have actually been successful, security does not appear to be a more significant problem than with other similar technologies and platforms. Applying Microsoft service packs and security patches will further diminish the occurrence of successful security intrusions against NT and IIS.

Although the proxy server offered an efficient means of accessing resources from off-campus and at that time was one of the few viable possibilities for allowing remote access, this solution requires that the users manually perform four steps in configuring their browser. These four steps have proven to be a technological hurdle many users are not equipped to handle. Since configuration not only requires users to enable their browsers to access the proxy server, but also requires disabling this configuration to access non-Library WWW sites, our users have experienced some confusion. We are currently testing other alternatives for simplifying remote access, namely EZ-Proxy, which requires virtually no user interaction other than simple password authentication.

THE FUTURE

Several enhancements and refinements are envisioned as we look toward improving our full-text electronic journal collection. Many of these we can achieve ourselves, but others rely on vendors and publishers of electronic journals to take a larger responsibility in the provision, licensing, and dissemination of these materials.

Primarily, we foresee integrating electronic document delivery into the e-journals collection to expand our collection from immediate, "just in case" access to the 7,500 journals we have available, to over 25,000 titles that would be available "just in time." Commercial document delivery companies such as the Reveal service, the Institute of Scientific Information's Document Solution, CINAHL, and Sports Discus are either currently in production or being considered as viable alternatives to interlibrary loan and the expense of ongoing journal subscriptions. We also envision giving the users more control over their interface, making it customizable to suit their own needs. Once again, Active Server Pages provide an excellent environment for this approach, since cookies can be created and pushed to each user which allow users to create and save preferences to their personalized e-journals site.

Ultimately, we hope to see a vendor step forward and offer a global interface for electronic journals. This product would allow users not only the ability to search a journal or sets of electronic journals, but also provide administrators a mechanism for ordering e-journals in an a la carte, title-by-title fashion. Ideally, this administrative module would allow an integrated means of licensing these titles through a central interface, rather than negotiating with each publisher or aggregator, then paying a surcharge to the electronic access provider. Until this occurs, Jackson Library's electronic journals site has proven to be a scalable, efficient, and user-friendly solution for providing on-campus and off-campus access to full-text electronic journals.

Straddling Multiple Administrative Relationships

Lois Gilmer

The University of West Florida

SUMMARY. Okaloosa-Walton Community College and The University of West Florida share the Fort Walton Beach Campus in a 2 + 2 approach to higher education in Florida. This paper explains how one library can serve two institutions with different missions when one institution provides the facilities, the other institution provides the management, and both institutions provide resources and personnel.

KEYWORDS. Library services, 2 + 2 programs, shared services

INTRODUCTION

A long-term educational partnership exists between Okaloosa-Walton Community College and The University of West Florida in Florida's 2 + 2 approach to higher education. In the Fall of 1981, a cooperative degree program began in response to a need for closer coordination between the lower division courses offered by the community college and the degree programs offered by the university in the Okaloosa County area in and around Fort Walton Beach. The two institutions established a joint center in 1983 in a vacated elementary school building. Based on a formal memorandum of understanding, both institutions remained mutually exclusive, with policies and procedures of both institutions modified to facilitate coordination.

[Haworth co-indexing entry note]: "Straddling Multiple Administrative Relationships." Gilmer, Lois. Co-published simultaneously in *Journal of Library Administration* (The Haworth Information Press, an imprint of The Haworth Press, Inc.) Vol. 31, No. 3/4, 2001, pp. 219-224; and: *Off-Campus Library Services* (ed: Anne Marie Casey) The Haworth Information Press, an imprint of The Haworth Press, Inc., 2001, pp. 219-224.

The relationship flourished and exists today on a 156-acre campus which began operations in 1992. With the new campus came many changes, however. Permanent faculty and additional support staff were added, and administration of the facility changed from the university to the community college. The university, however, remained in charge of the Library. The community college took over the administration of copier service for the entire campus, including the Library. The community college is also in charge of the AV program, which had been a university responsibility in the Library at the temporary center.

FORT WALTON BEACH CAMPUS LIBRARY

Due to the changes in campus operations, changes in library policies and procedures had to take place. Several proposals and documents were written relative to the library program. A reciprocal borrowing agreement was entered into on a trial basis and then on a permanent basis. Then an agreement was made to exchange library cards, making the community college cards compatible with the university circulation system. Eventually these documents were merged into one memorandum of understanding relative to library services provided on the branch campus. The Memorandum of Understanding between The University of West Florida and Okaloosa-Walton Community College Relating to Operation of the Fort Walton Beach Campus Library is divided into three major sections: Introduction/Background; Mission/Philosophy; and Policies/Operational Guidelines.

The Policies/Operational Guidelines section is by far the longest section in the Memorandum of Understanding. It is based on the *ACRL Guidelines for Branch Libraries in Colleges and Universities,* accommodates the different missions of the community college and the university, and relies heavily on the documents *Guidelines for Two-year College Learning Resources Programs* and *ACRL Guidelines for Extended Campus Library Services.* The Memorandum and this paper relating to the many fences one must straddle in order to make it work include the elements prominently outlined in the Guideline for Extended Campus Library Services: management, personnel, resources, services, finances, and facilities/equipment.

MANAGEMENT

A university librarian who reports to library administration on the parent campus in Pensacola approximately 55 miles away provides management of the branch campus library. The Fort Walton Beach Campus library director is subject to the same meetings, job assignments, evaluations, promotion, and committee assignments as the librarians who are assigned to the parent campus. Considerable travel between campuses is necessary, especially for committee work, and there is much interaction with each department head in the parent campus library. E-mail, voice mail, and FAX are also used. Recently NetMeeting was installed in both libraries to reduce travel time and expense.

Management of the branch campus library also includes contact with departments besides the libraries on both parent campuses–payroll, financial aid, graphics (for copier service), etc. It is extremely important that the branch campus library director be aware of the best resource people to help with problem-solving and that she/he be able to handle with grace any delays or political posturing that might be encountered in the process. Organization and tact are two very important qualities for the person who is always "in the middle." Managing a library that serves two institutions gives new meaning to the phrase "middle management."

In order to help fulfill the mission of the community college and to be aware of the programs offered and resources needed, it is necessary to keep in touch with the Director of the Okaloosa-Walton Community College Learning Resources Center and/or the outreach librarian and the various department heads. Each quarter the Fort Walton Beach Campus Library Director meets with other area librarians who provide library service for the various other community college sites in their service area of Okaloosa County and Walton County.

In order to provide as seamless an operation as possible for the two institutions sharing the branch campus, considerable coordination is needed with the chief administrative officers, cashiers, building maintenance, and other personnel. When deciding upon intersession library hours, for example, both institution's calendars must be consulted and the recommendation passed through both administrative offices before a decision can be considered final.

PERSONNEL

Support staff is provided for the library by both institutions, and they are cross-trained on each institution's operational methods and procedures as appropriate, providing assistance to all library patrons. Two permanent library technical assistants (one from each institution) have been in place for years, and another part-time university position is stable, but there is constant turnover among both institutions' student assistants, on whom the library must rely heavily. Training, therefore, is an ongoing, complicated process.

The Fort Walton Beach Campus Library Director recommends and evaluates all of the support staff, according to the hiring institution's methods. She/he also approves time sheets and leave forms. Five different kinds of time sheets are prepared four times per month.

RESOURCES

Due to the wide range of courses offered (basic education to the doctoral level), resources cover all areas of the Library of Congress classification system, some to a much greater extent than others. Each parent institution provides library materials to support the courses offered by that institution. Resources include reference works, circulating monographs, serials in hard copy and microform, CD-ROMs, and on-line databases, some with full text. Full Internet capability is available.

Selections are made based on the collection development policies of both institutions. Materials are stamped by the purchasing library and then cataloged and added to the database by The University of West Florida. A shelflist indicating ownership of materials is kept within the branch library. All materials are shelved as one collection and shared by all library patrons.

Online resources from the Florida State University System library network are available to patrons. The library is not equipped to access the statewide community college online resources, although the community college catalogs may be searched. A statewide distance learning initiative is providing some online sources common to both the community colleges and the state university system.

SERVICES

On site circulation, reserve, reference service, and bibliographic instruction are available during hours comparable to the library hours on the parent campuses six days a week. Services are automated almost to the same extent as they are on The University of West Florida parent campus. Daily van service from both campuses provides document delivery through reciprocal borrowing and intercampus/interlibrary loan. Students may request loans online or in person in the library. Monies collected for intercampus/interlibrary loan materials and transparencies are deposited by library staff with The University of West Florida branch campus cashier.

Students may also renew or return to the branch campus materials circulated from the parent campus libraries. Careful records must be maintained to verify the return of materials. Some university materials may be checked in on the branch campus, while others from special university libraries may not. Lacking the circulation system of the community college library, materials from that campus may not be checked in. There are, therefore, three procedures for returning materials checked out in other libraries and returned to the branch library.

FINANCES

Since The University of West Florida provides management for the branch library, the University through an Expense Budget provides day-to-day operating expenses. The University also provides budgets for personnel and materials. These budgets are expended through coordinated efforts of the branch library director, university library administration, acquisitions and serials department heads, and the controller.

The college controls funds allocated by the community college for use in the Fort Walton Beach Campus Library. Standing orders for materials are kept up-to-date, and other materials are ordered at the request of the branch library director, the community college teaching staff, or the acquisitions librarian. Materials needed are sometimes purchased with end-of-the year funds.

FACILITIES/EQUIPMENT

The two-story 20,000 square feet library and most of its furnishings, equipment, and utilities belong to the community college. Computers were placed in the new building by the community college as furnishings. Since that time, they have been upgraded and a local area network installed by the university. It was agreed in the Memorandum of Understanding that as it becomes necessary to replace or upgrade computers, both institutions have the responsibility of paying a proportionate share of the costs based on student FTE of the previous year, unless the upgrade or replacement is related to one institution's automation software. In that case, the institution requiring the change will bear the entire cost. Computer technicians for both institutions on the branch campus provide service for the computers, if a hardware problem is encountered. University library automation personnel must investigate library software problems. The community college provides maintenance contracts on most other machines in the library.

SUMMARY

It might seem that working in a branch campus library means working in isolation. While it is true that one does experience isolation at times, in order to keep such an operation running smoothly, especially when there are two institutions involved, daily contact must be maintained with one or more of the institutions and local administrators. A myriad of other resource persons are consulted on an as-needed basis.

Librarians' Changing Role in Distance Education: Need for Training

Dinesh K. Gupta

Kota Open University (India)

SUMMARY. Distance education is a learner-centered system of education. The librarians engage in developing and delivery of services in distance education relevant to both content and process. Librarians need to recognize the role of modern information technologies as learning resources in students' learning pursuits. This represents a major shift from a conventional model of the library-centered didactic style to a more learner-centered and task-based facilitating style. This change needs effective training of the professionals engaged in distance librarianship. The paper analyzes the present day role of librarians in distance education in India; discusses the rationale for the training of librarians involved in distance education; and finds out the areas of training, and methods and strategies that are to be adopted in the distance education institutions in the country.

KEYWORDS. Distance education, librarians, India

INTRODUCTION

In the past few years, higher education has seen drastic changes due to potent social and technological forces outside the control of Library and Information (L&I) professionals. Higher education is undergoing a paradigm shift from an instruction-oriented model of learning to a

[Haworth co-indexing entry note]: "Librarians' Changing Role in Distance Education: Need for Training." Gupta, Dinesh K. Co-published simultaneously in *Journal of Library Administration* (The Haworth Information Press, an imprint of The Haworth Press, Inc.) Vol. 32, No. 1/2, 2001, pp. 225-231; and: *Off-Campus Library Services* (ed: Anne Marie Casey) The Haworth Information Press, an imprint of The Haworth Press, Inc., 2001, pp. 225-231.

learner-centered model based on the access to learning resources and students' initiatives. Moreover, new technologies have increased the academic productivity and have brought a change in the pedagogy and curriculum content. Open and distance learning, characterized as flexible and more responsive to the demands of learners, is the manifestation of the new learning environment. This new environment, especially with respect to the delivery of appropriate information and knowledge to the learners at a place and time of their choice, contributes to a dramatic revolution in the role of library professionals. The revised role of the L&I professionals needs some kind of training to work with the new clientele, new resources and new environment. In this paper an attempt has been made to study the existing patterns of library services in open and distance learning institutions in the country; to look into the revised role of the library professionals in distance mode; to examine the need of training for new entrants and persons involved in distance library services; and to suggest some strategies and methods to train library professionals in distance library institutions in the country.

LIBRARY SERVICES IN DISTANCE EDUCATION: ROLE AND PATTERN

The role of the library and its services in campus-based education is well established. Similarly, in distance education, library facilities and services ought to occupy a key role in the students' learning process through:

- motivating all categories of learners to get the most benefit from open learning;
- a suitable form of imparting education to them;
- informing learners regarding educational opportunities through open university;
- its educational programs and components of each program;
- making information available regarding tools and sources, learning packages in print and nonprint form;
- assisting learners to make the most effective use of library services available to them;
- sharing resources with other agencies involved in educational guidance; and,
- supporting counselors/tutors in successfully completing counseling/tutoring sessions.

To provide library and information access to distance learners, open universities have a network of libraries. Open universities have two categories of libraries, namely, the library at the university headquarters, and the library of the study center. The latter is mainly established at the college where the study center is located and the college librarian acts as the librarian to the study center library. These libraries function only on weekends and contain mainly study materials, text books, audio-visual facilities, etc.

L&I PROFESSIONALS: A REVISED ROLE

The role of the library services is to contribute to the excellence of the distance and open learning through creation of learning and study environments to support the teaching, research, and personal development of support staff and learners of the institution, by facilitating access to the sources and collections of the information, both internal and external to the university, through the professionalism of its services and expertise in exploitation of enabling technologies. In order to make the role of the library services effective, the library and information professionals must support students' learning pursuits through particular attention to both the contents and process of acquiring information and its use, whose traditional role is largely confined to selecting and indicating the location and availability of resources to the user. As such the librarian is becoming an intermediary between the learners and the information resources. He must have the capability to use these resources to facilitate learning for the individual learner or in a group. He has to provide password and access control, assisting in intermediary searching, producing subject guides and gateways, and working as a mediator between the end user and the world's recorded knowledge.

He also has to serve the learners who want to have remote access and will make the use of a variety of networks to access the collection of other networks. With greater end user searching becoming the norm, the librarian's role changes from intermediary to facilitatory, in which he requires the ability to communicate, ability to determine and implement appropriate instructional strategies, and ability to design and develop self-learning tools for the clientele. Under such circumstances the librarians need to be constantly updated and trained in not only the use of various media but also in their acquisition, storage and retrieval to support every learner in his learning pursuits.

NEED FOR TRAINING

The development and spread of distance library services has implications for the curriculum in library and information science schools and continuing professional education. But, there is also no Library and Information Science (LIS) school in the country which has included this emerging aspect in their syllabi. Even open university and distance learning institutions offering library science courses have not come forward and have not included such kinds of services in their syllabi. More so, the STRIDE (staff training of the IGNOU), the premier agency involved in training manpower working in distance education in the country has done nothing so far in this regard, even after more than 5 years of its existence.

The librarian/assistant librarian of the college where the study center of the open universities or distance learning institution is located act as the librarians at the study center. But, they have been traditionally operating under a set of rules, regulations, bureaucratic models and institutional guidelines, wherein information seekers (students in the case of academic libraries) come to the library to use resources in a multiple format. But, contrarily in distance education, resources and services must be adaptable to the learner's convenience and pace rather than providers' convenience. Moreover, librarians working in traditional set-ups are not conversant with the use of multi-media and with the independent learning environment in which the distant learner learns. As a result they are unable to motivate students for independent learning and facilitate work in such an environment.

While distance educators have focused their development and decision making on using technology to improve the delivery of instruction, library professionals have focused on collection and increased access through the use of electronic devices. With this background the delivery systems for education have evolved from print media to telecommunications and electronic media. Instruction is delivered through interactive video via communication satellites, and through computer mediated communication such as e-mail, computer conferences, electronic bulletin boards and on-line databases, overcoming the time and distances barriers. Similarly, libraries which until recent years were especially stacking print material, have now begun to acquire electronic media like CD-ROMs and multi-media packages. The quality of electronic media is likely to increase substantially and it is clear that libraries will have to prepare themselves for conversion into electronic libraries, commonly referred to as digital libraries. Thus, there is much need to put both the distance learning and the libraries close together so as to build a meaningful relationship in the delivery of education, both campus-based and through distance mode. This task can be achieved only through effective training in both the areas.

Training in distance library services is a concern even of users. In a recent study conducted by the author (although it deals with the entire library system of an Open University), the following suggestions were give by users relating to training of the library staff:

- "Library staff must be trained so that they can provide proper information regarding the literature available."
- "Library staff should be pertinently trained and ably supervised."
- "Library staff should be courteous and helping."
- "There is a shortage of skilled manpower. It should be well equipped with trained persons, so that the library can function in an efficient manner."
- "Trained and efficient staff should be approved."
- "Polite and harmonious behavior of the librarian is very much essential to attract distance learners."

These responses to users are very pertinent and advocate for proper training for the professionals involved in distance library services.

METHODS AND STRATEGIES

When we talk of training, it could be at two levels; to start with, there is formal training and education. At the formal level the professional development courses can be useful for the people who need to maintain the specialist skills which is certainly required at the time of recruitment. For this LIS schools must design and implement curricula which prepare graduates for distance library services through (a) incorporating at least one to two units of distance librarianship in the courses on the Academic Library System, and (b) a complete optional paper on

Distance Library Services and Systems, introduced as an optional paper at the Master's level program, which should cover the following areas:

- Introduction to DE system
- Characteristics of DE library system and services
- Development of libraries as learning resource centers
- Digital libraries and their application in DE systems
- Information sources
- Services in digital library environments: online reference services; interaction through e-mail, list servers and bulletin boards; online document delivery services; Internet-based information services.

Secondly, there could be various short-term courses, training programs and workshops, for persons working in DE library services. This can be done at two levels: at the national level and at the university level. At the national level, the STRIDE should design and develop specialized courses and short-term programmes to upgrade the skills of the personnel working in the Open Universities and distance education institutions. Further, every open university and distance education institution must start training programmes for the librarians having traditional backgrounds and get involved in support services at study and regional centres.

The next part of training people working in libraries in open and distance learning is induction into the environment of independent and distance learning, which in many ways is different and unique. For this persons can be invited for a short time to work and learn the acquired knowledge that can be used at his/her workplace.

CONCLUSION

It is very clear that in the learner-centred or student-centred learning, library facilities are extended to the clientele according to their convenience in regards to time and space. This requires new roles for the persons working in the delivery of such services in the traditional set-up, and new tools for support and collaboration, which will largely depend upon the effectiveness of the education and training provided to new entrants and persons working in the delivery of library services to distant learners.

REFERENCES

Appaove, P., & Sansen, L. (1988). Profile of the distance education user. *Research in Distance Education, 1*(3), 14-15.

Association of College and Research Libraries. (1986). Guidelines for extended campus library services. *College and Research Library News, 47*, 189-200.

Bazillion, R. J., & Connie, B. (1992). Technology and library users automation outreach: Library services to off campus students. *Journal of Distance Education, 7*(2), 67-75.

Canadian Library Association. Library Services for Distance Learning Interest Group. (1993). *Guidelines for library support of distance education in Canada.* Ottawa: The Association.

Faulhaber, C. B. (1996). Distance learning and digital libraries: Two sides of a single coin. *Journal of the American Society for Information Science, 47*(11), 354-356.

Gupta, D. K. (1997). Library And Information Access To Distance Learners: The Role Of Information Technology. In A. L. Moorthy, & P. B. Mangla (Eds.), *Information technology applications in academic libraries in India with emphasis on network services & information sharing: papers presented at the fourth national convention for automation of libraries in education and research* (pp. 40-42). Ahmedabad: Information and Library Network Centre.

Gupta, D. K., & Jain, S. L. (1996, July 22). Open university and library: Concept and relationship. *University News, 34*, 9-11, 17.

Closing the Gap:
Using Conferencing Software
to Connect Distance Education Students
and Faculty

Mary M. Henning

University of Wyoming

SUMMARY. Distance programs utilize various strategies and technologies in an attempt to keep students and faculty connected. Express mail delivery, telephone and conference calls, electronic mail and compressed video sessions have all been used with varying degrees of success. This paper discusses the use of a novel Desktop Video Conferencing (DTVC) product, CU-SeeMe, and offers an analysis of its effectiveness in providing distance instruction and library support to a cohort of medical technology students embarked on the clinical rotation phase of their program at the University of Wyoming. We conclude that the potential benefits of this low cost technology outweigh the inconveniences of working with an immature technology.

KEYWORDS. Computer mediated conferencing, distance education, library services

Students and faculty involved in distance education programs in rural states and regions face common problems. They are separated by long distances across prairies and over mountain passes bridged by often-treacherous roads. Distance programs utilize various strategies and technologies in an attempt to keep students and faculty connected.

[Haworth co-indexing entry note]: "Closing the Gap: Using Conferencing Software to Connect Distance Education Students and Faculty." Henning, Mary M. Co-published simultaneously in *Journal of Library Administration* (The Haworth Information Press, an imprint of The Haworth Press, Inc.) Vol. 32, No. 1/2, 2001, pp. 233-246; and: *Off-Campus Library Services* (ed: Anne Marie Casey) The Haworth Information Press, an imprint of The Haworth Press, Inc., 2001, pp. 233-246.

Express mail delivery, telephone and conference calls, electronic mail and compressed video sessions have all been used with varying degrees of success. Wyoming is a case in point.

Wyoming towns are relatively few and far between. In a 97,914 square mile area, 453,588 people live. Contrast this with our neighbor to the south, Colorado, with slightly more area, 104,091 square miles but nearly 4 million inhabitants, or the state of Oregon with 97,073 square miles but nearly 3 million people. Wyoming has at least 262 towns and cities but only 6 or 7 can boast of populations over 10,000. (Usually the altitude is greater than the population listed on the city limit signs.)

The University of Wyoming, the Cowboy State's only four-year university, is located in the southeastern corner of the state in a town called Laramie. Laramie is 45 miles from Cheyenne, 65 miles from Ft. Collins, Colorado, 148 miles to Casper, 383 miles to Jackson Hole, 249 miles to Gillette, and 294 miles to Sheridan. Our roads are good but our winters are long and treacherous, making it difficult and time consuming to travel across the state.

Consequently, UW has an active distance education program with students scattered all over the state. These students receive formal classroom instruction through compressed video, telephone, and correspondence courses, both online and through the U.S. Mail. They are well served by these programs, but educators in all disciplines recognize the ever more pressing need to personalize instruction and enhance contacts with the growing number of students who inhabit today's virtual campuses.

Desk Top Video Conferencing (DTVC) technologies appear to offer another solution by combining elements of audio, video, electronic mail, word processing, and presentation software to enhance long distance communication and learning.

WHAT IS DESKTOP VIDEO CONFERENCING?

To baby boomers familiar with images of Dick Tracy barking into his wrist radio-television communicator device and Captain Kirk negotiating face-to face with alien beings from the bridge of the Starship Enterprise, the concept of real time synchronization of full-motion video images with live audio seems only natural. We knew it was only a matter of time before we would have to check our look in the mirror prior to answering the phone. Thanks to recent advances in real-life technology that time is just around the corner.

Desktop video conferencing (DTVC or DTV) emerged as an experimental technology early in the 1990s. With funding and cooperation from the National Science Foundation and other organizations, Cornell University led the field in research and development of the technology necessary to produce the first Internet-based videoconferencing product. In 1993 CU-SeeMe was created. According to a White Pine news release, "the software was designed to be used for desktop videoconferencing over the Internet and TCP/IP networks, and consists of desktop clients for Microsoft Windows and Macintosh, and a server-like component (a Reflector). With the UNIX-based Reflector technology, CU-SeeMe provides group videoconferencing" (CU-SeeMe World, n.p.).

By 1993, researchers were already studying the unique characteristics of communication behaviors of work groups using video-conferencing software "designed for small groups to meet across distance for the purposes of exchanging information, generating ideas, solving problems, and making decisions" (Duin, 1994). While sociologists and efficiency experts were imagining the applications for videoconferencing, the technology continued to develop.

Don Labriola of *PC Magazine* observed in a 1995 review of desktop video conferencing products that in as little as 12 months time there had been significant advances in the quality and functionality of personal videoconferencing products on the market. He characterized 1994 software as being hampered by "inadequate communications, high prices, mediocre output quality and limited software" (Labriola, 1995). Some of these problems still plague even the newest releases, but prices have gone down while performance has risen. Currently, if your existing PC workstation meets the minimum standards described below, you could begin videoconferencing for as little as $99.00 with the purchase of a software and video camera package from White Pine. Add the microphone of your choice for $25-$200 and you have assembled a complete personal videoconferencing workstation for less than $300.00. Compare this with the considerable expense of installing a compressed video classroom or a one-to-many videoconferencing system such as the White Pine ClassPoint product and you begin to see why DTVC software presents an innovative alternative to conventional methods of one-on-one contact with outreach students.

CU-SeeMe is certainly not the only game in town. According to experts at *Digital Horizon,* an online newsletter focusing on new computer technologies, there are currently more than 70 desktop video conferencing products vying for the DTVC crown worn so long by CU-SeeMe and Microsoft NetMeeting. The editors of *Digital Horizon* maintain that the development of DTVC is analogous to the amazing metamorphosis of clunky old mainframe computers into the ever present desktop PCs and predict that DTVC, "will impact business on a scale similar to e-mail and the Internet" (Desktop Video Conferencing [DVC], 1996).

CU-SEEME PRO

According to the White Pine Web Page, "CU-SeeMe Pro is the easy and fun way to keep in touch over the Internet" (http://www. wpine.com/). The software description lists the following features:

- CU-SeeMe software is easy to install and configure with a step-by-step Setup Assistant Conference Companion [that] lets you locate associates, friends, or family online and call them without needing to know their IP addresses.
- Directory Service lets you see a list of all of the users published on a particular ILS server, whether they are using CU-SeeMe Pro, CU-SeeMe Version 3.1.2, or Microsoft® NetMeeting™.
- The Favorites List can locate other CU-SeeMe users and Microsoft® NetMeeting™ users as well, and place calls to those users. You may view up to 12 video images simultaneously.
- It features integrated T.120 data collaboration for sharing applications, whiteboard, and file transfer for multi-user collaboration during conferences.
- You have a choice of video and audio codecs for best performance over a variety of network speeds H.323 compatible;
- It lets you make point-to-point calls to users of Microsoft NetMeeting, Intel ProShare and other H.323 clients.

SYSTEM REQUIREMENTS: HARDWARE AND SOFTWARE

In order to get started with CU-SeeMe® ProV4.0.1, you will need to have the following hardware and peripherals in place:

- Windows® 95/98 or Windows® NT 4.0; a Pentium processor, requires 133 megahertz (MHz); a minimum of 166MHz is recommended for H.323 connections; 32 megabytes (MB) of RAM; 10MB of hard disk space; Current release 4.0;
- For network connections you will need a TCP/IP (Winsock compliant IP address), requires also: 33.6Kbps (minimum modem, LAN, Cable, or ISDN connections (56Kbps recommended for H.323 connections), PPP for dial-up connection.
- In order to send video, choose a desktop color video camera and a video capture card or a digital camera. To send audio, you'll need an external microphone and a 16-bit (minimum) sound card and drivers. Speakers or headphones are required to receive audio. Price: $99.00 retail, $89.00 if ordered from the manufacturer.
- The software is available for Windows® 95/98, Windows NT® and Macintosh.

CU-SEEME COMES TO THE UNIVERSITY OF WYOMING LIBRARIES

In August of 1998, University of Wyoming Libraries (in partnership with Sheridan College Library) and Denison Memorial Library of the University of Colorado, agreed to participate in a special communications project to test the capabilities and uses of DTVC. The project's goal was to enhance learning outreach, and general communications in the rural states of Wyoming, Colorado, and Nebraska. Workstations and DTVC software were provided through a generous grant from the National Network of Libraries of Medicine, Midcontinental Region. (NN/LM MR)

The NN/LM has a special interest in promoting the teaching and use of its brainchild, Pubmed, which utilizes the giant medical database, Medline. UW Libraries are part of the network of resource libraries that the NN/LM works with to help disseminate medical information throughout the United States. Part of the UW Libraries' responsibilities as a resource library are to help advance the educational aims of the NN/LM, especially with regard to our rural constituents.

Although the project officially came to a close in April of 1999, testing at UW continued as the technology evolved and ways to use it were fine-tuned. Faculty members in such diverse departments as Medical Technology, Communications and Mass Media, History, and

Nursing have expressed an interest in exploring how they might use this technology to keep students and faculty connected outside the classroom.

In May 1999 I initiated discussions with Jim Thompson, clinical coordinator for the UW Medical Technology program. Faculty in the Medical Technology program previewed a CU-SeeMe test conference and felt that their students participating in clinical rotations "on the bench" might benefit from a more personal connection with their instructors back on the Laramie campus. With this in mind, we implemented a pilot collaboration to do our part to help close the gap between distance education students and their teachers. Students who were already assigned to Sheridan medical facilities where our second DTVC workstation was installed were selected for the project.

Medical Technology students doing clinical rotations are placed with cooperating medical facilities in various parts of the state. Each student works on clinical case studies and reports weekly on his or her practicum activities and progress through the program. This weekly communication takes the form of e-mail messages and phone conversations as needed. Case studies and other text materials are mailed to the students in the field.

We proposed to swap these weekly e-meetings for an initial series of three one-on-one video conferencing sessions lasting no more than 30 minutes each. Jim or another faculty member would engage one or two students at the remote sites in virtual face-to-face discussions and presentations of clinical case studies on medical technology topics accompanied by sessions on library support services and bibliographic instruction, including Medline and other healthcare databases. The collaborative features of the CU-SeeMe software would be used to send text materials and review case studies with the students. Faculty would use the computer workstation located in my office at the main library of the University as well as a workstation provided by the Medical Technology Department located in another building on campus. Both workstations are equipped with identical DTVC software and hardware. Off-campus students were connected through a workstation equipped with compatible software located at the Griffith Memorial Library on the Sheridan College campus in Sheridan, Wyoming. Debbie Iverson, the library director, has the second UW DTVC workstation set up in her office and has been facilitating testing on that end.

We decided early on that we would concentrate on a White Pine software product called CU-See Me. At the time that we began testing the software, CU-See Me had better video and audio capabilities than NetMeeting, but lacked the collaboration features (application sharing, file transfer, whiteboarding) that the Microsoft product offered. Additionally, White Pine had announced that an upgrade with the collaboration features was in the pipeline, so we decided to continue testing while we learned the ropes and then upgrade to the new, improved version. In August the upgrade to CU-SeeMe Pro was installed on both workstations.

BUT DOES IT DO WINDOWS? FUNCTIONALITY TESTING

Testing at workstations in Coe Library on the Laramie campus and at Sheridan College Library (the two Wyoming sites) focused on the following activities and issues:

- Installation and testing of the hardware and software. What combination of available hardware and software is most appropriate for distance education? How does the existing communications infrastructure affect the application?
- Integration of library support services and instruction into course content and presentation of course materials. How does the spontaneous nature of the medium affect structuring and scheduling of online discussion sessions? What is the best mix of library instruction and course content?
- Evaluation and analysis of technical effectiveness and contribution to student learning and satisfaction. Can the software deliver what it promises? Does it enhance the delivery of library instruction and course-related materials? Does it facilitate student learning?

THE CONFERENCES

Session I (Two Students)

Jim Thompson, the clinical instructor and outreach coordinator, came to the first session prepared with an agenda of orientation items to discuss with students and a case study on a floppy disk that he planned to transfer to the students using the collaboration feature of the software. Debbie Iverson on the Sheridan end welcomed the students, oriented them to the workstation environment, and initiated the call. Our expectation was that the students would be able to manipulate the various features of the program after a short orientation provided by Debbie Iverson. We were also able to explain how to make adjustments to audio and video during the conference.

We went into the first conference with two very basic goals: we wanted to make the connection with acceptable audio and video levels and we wanted to be able to transfer a file and share the contents. This seems quite elementary, but we had learned that successful use of a feature in one conference would not necessarily guarantee its replication in the next one.

In this conference, feedback howl was our biggest obstacle. It was determined that audio on the Laramie end was the culprit. I experimented with microphone and speaker placement at the suggestion of a computer technology expert we had invited for backup. We tried to put as much distance between the mike and the twin speakers as possible to minimize the feedback (a coworker in the office next door said it sounded like a bull elk bugling to its mate.) The speakers were also turned around to face away from the mike with the volume adjusted down as low as possible. CU-SeeMe features an "audio tuning wizard" to help fine-tune the audio settings. Setting the squelch level to reflect the amount of background noise at each workstation is important.

We did finally reach a point where the two students in Sheridan and the instructor in Laramie could see and hear each other. After a couple of false starts, the instructor was able to invoke the collaboration features and transfer a file to the Sheridan site. The student at the keyboard was able to open and display the file but we were unable to transfer control of the mouse to the instructor. He had to direct the student to scroll through the document as he went through the points he wanted to cover.

Session II (One Student)

Once again our conference goals were to use the features of the software as designed. This turned out to be a very frustrating session for several reasons. For some unknown reason we have been unable to call out from the UW workstation. There was no problem accepting a call either from the Sheridan workstation or from other CU-SeeMe users, but our efforts to dial out were met by an error message stating that the other party was not responding to our call. In an attempt to improve the connection, our very helpful library tech support aide had downloaded a "patch' from the CU-SeeMe WebPages that was supposed to fix certain audio and video glitches. When that failed to squash the bug he reinstalled CU-SeeMe Pro after removing the older version of CU-SeeMe. Neither approach worked so Sheridan continued to initiate the calls.

A bright note was the participants' enhanced ability to move around the conference window and adjust the settings. At one point at the Sheridan location, increasing the video quality setting produced clear, beautiful, and very fluid video that had us cheering on the Laramie end. The instructional interchange between Linnea, the student in Sheridan, and Jim was smoother and less self-conscious as well.

Session III (One Student)

Once again we were unable to invoke the collaboration features even though only a few minutes prior to this conference I had successfully used the whiteboarding function in another call. We collectively gnashed our teeth about this for a few minutes because Jim needed to send a new case study to Linnea in Sheridan. Just before Linnea arrived for the session we realized that we could go into Microsoft Word, open the case study file, copy and paste the text into the chat box in the conference window in CU-SeeMe, then edit the text to remove system-supplied screen prompts.

Our cut-and-paste job was certainly not as sleek as a file transfer or application sharing, but it produced a text that Linnea and Jim could easily work with and review simultaneously. The rest of the conference went smoothly; video and audio quality were acceptable (alas, no miraculous video this time), the interaction between Jim and Linnea was markedly more natural, and Linnea walked away from the "office meeting" with a clean copy of her current assignment.

CAN YOU SEE ME? CAN YOU HEAR ME?
PROBLEMS ENCOUNTERED AND HELPFUL HINTS

These sessions taught us a number of things about the conferencing process.

- Conferencing is surprisingly exhausting. Not only are the participants learning how to use a new software tool, they are also learning a new communication style. It's not easy to watch, talk, and type chat at the same time!
- Experience in manipulating the mechanics of Windows NT allows the user to move much more comfortably through a conference. The CU-SeeMe program itself is very straightforward to use in terms of mechanical navigation. The manual is equally straightforward to the point of being simplistic. No advice is offered for troubleshooting or setting up the placement of microphone, speakers and camera. Jim Thompson remarks that the manual, "is miserably underdeveloped in regards to detail of operation and the options available to the instructor" (J. Thompson, personal communication, December 2, 1999). White Pine, take note!
- Some individuals are uncomfortable with seeing their own images on the screen. It is possible to resize or blank the video windows entirely to minimize the distraction. Earlier descriptions of similar problems prompted writers to recommend that gesturing and moving around onscreen be kept to a minimum. Backgrounds should be plain and uncluttered to improve video quality. In previous test conferences we struggled with placement of the tiny video camera. At one point after exchanging what was to become our ritual opening line of "Can you see me, can you hear me?" I asked Debbie Iverson if the camera angle was satisfactory. I quickly readjusted the location of the mini-cam after learning that I had been sending nice clear video of the top of my head and of my office's acoustic ceiling in the previous conferences. You will also become more aware of personal mannerisms and any facial tics you may be prone to as bandwidth slowdowns freeze your features in mid-twitch.
- While interactions take place in very nearly real time, there is a noticeable time lag in audio response. Words can be clipped and quite often participants will overlay one another's conversation resulting in frequent requests to repeat words or phrases. It's best to speak deliberately and pause briefly after each sentence. Use the backup text chat feature if you think it will help.
- Poor connections may interfere with initiating collaboration features. Local network traffic may affect the amount and speed of

transmission that directly affects the quality and clarity of video and audio. The collaboration features are especially bandwidth intensive and our computer specialist speculated that the incomplete connections that deprive us of collaboration abilities are the system's response to too much traffic.

- Mechanical issues with peripheral hardware such as microphones may make or break your conference. Microphone/speaker feedback has been the most enduring and least endearing problem we have faced. We started out with inexpensive headsets that we hoped would be lightweight and unobtrusive. Participants spent a lot of time fidgeting with the flimsy headsets and tripping on the cords. Individual headsets also limited the number of persons who could participate comfortably in a conference. We switched to more sensitive (read expensive) omnidirectional microphones that enabled us to converse hands-free, but intensified the feedback problem. In addition to the howling of the feedback loop, participants could hear their own voices echo back while talking. This is quite distracting and might discourage novice users.

But . . .

- Don't be afraid to practice. If you are working with a partner institution, you will probably have already set up a conference schedule, but try to make additional calls. Look at your DTVC directory and pick someone to call. During initial functionality testing of the DTVC workstation in Debbie Iverson's office at Griffith Memorial Library, Sheridan College, Debbie and I joined a NetMeeting call in progress from an office group in Port Lincoln, Australia. Testing was informal, to say the least, but the boys from "Down Under" cheerfully went through their paces as we worked our way through the audio and video features (and glitches) of the program. A caveat, however, for making and accepting unsolicited DTVC calls: use your business directory instead of the personal page and exercise caution with calls from people using monikers like "MsSexyPants" or "BigBoy!"
- Cultivate flexibility. If something doesn't work, try another approach. Ask other DTVC users and your technologically adept associates what has worked for them in terms of microphones, workstation configuration and program adjustments. Look at your workstation setup, move the camera and the microphone

around. We borrowed a directional microphone and discovered that it worked better in a small office area than the omnidirectional microphone we had been using in terms of feedback reduction.

- In addition to suggesting that we switch to a directional microphone to reduce feedback from the speakers, our technology support person recommended going up to 128MB of system memory and upgrading to a video card with 8 or 16 MB of video memory to enhance video and audio performance.

Little things may make a difference too. While we were wrestling with the ongoing problem of howling feedback from the speakers, my student assistant observed that the microphone was set up on the bare wooden surface of the desk and suggested putting it on a mat of some kind. I slipped a handy foam coaster under the microphone and was pleased to note that the feedback lessened to some degree.

- Be of good cheer. Keep in mind that you are working with a developing technology. Glitches happen. The CU-SeeMe advertising campaign features a cute little white doggie with its paws on the keyboard and its eyes on the image of its beloved master who beams from the monitor as if to show us how easy it is to video-chat. In real life, two librarians, a university instructor, an information technology specialist and two college students were unable to correct technical problems that cropped up during a session.
- However, the conference participants remained cautiously optimistic about the process. Jim Thompson comments," the collaborative real-time tools potentially offer advancements over the e-mail communication mode traditionally used by our program in out-reach instruction" (J. Thompson, personal communication, December 2, 1999). Linnea, the distance student, notes that, "the idea of video conferencing over the computer lines is promising for the future. The immediate feedback is a big advantage over e-mail" (L. Hood, personal communication, December 2, 1999).

WHAT TO BUILD WITH THE NEW TOOL?

The corporate world has been quick to pick up on ways that DTVC can be used to build bridges between clients and the home office, but what can we do with this new tool in our libraries? So far the conferencing software at Coe library has been used to conduct virtual "office hours" meetings between student and teacher as an extension of classroom activities. The intent behind the original NN/LM equipment grant was to provide opportunities to expand instruction in Pubmed databases. In addition to the bibliographic instruction sessions I offer to classes in the health sciences, I also meet one-on-one with students who drop by my office or make appointments for individual assistance. DTVC is not really comfortable for use with more than a couple of students at a time, but it lends itself admirably to individual contacts with students. In the upcoming series of conferences with Linnea and Rebecca in Sheridan, I plan to offer a mini-tutorial on health science databases including Medline, and to make sure that they are aware of the UW Libraries outreach services that are available to them.

Since I am also the coordinator of our health science information and fee-based services unit, I can draw on the corporate model for ideas on how to increase our client base for research services and document delivery. Certainly the medium is well suited for long distance committee meetings with other librarians across the state, or collaborative grant writing sessions. As the pool of DTVC users grows, there will be more opportunity to personalize contacts with our clients and respond to their information needs

CONCLUSION

Earlier in this paper I posed the following questions: Can the software deliver what it promises? Does it enhance the delivery of library instruction and course-related materials? Does it facilitate student learning? The short answer to all of these questions is, *not yet.* I'm also reminded of a recent question from one of my colleagues. She wondered how CU-SeeMe was better than the efficient way that she currently handles reference questions from our outreach students, which involves combining a phone call with access to online databases and e-mail. Aside from eliminating the additional cost of the long-distance phone call and providing a face-to face contact, DTVC is certainly clunkier and less reliable. DTVC still suffers from the problems of a "young technology overcoming the obstacles that go with the territory-immature standards, price/performance issues, and underpowered support technologies" (Labriola, 1995). So why bother?

DTVC technology is evolving so rapidly that in the 4 months that I have been working with it, CU-SeeMe has already introduced a new version followed by an update to address specific audio and video bugs. It will only get better. Even now, despite the aggravation of working with an imperfect product, our initial goals were accomplished and the clinical instructors had enough confidence in the potential of the medium to arrange to continue the weekly conferencing sessions with the two Sheridan students for the remainder of their rotation. Warts and all, DTVC technology offers the potential to provide enhanced communication and connectivity between distance students and their teachers for a relatively low cost. I do believe that the time and effort involved in testing, learning, and thinking creatively about DTVC is worthwhile and will eventually result in the kind of seamlessly synchronous interaction that we take for granted in science fiction movies.

REFERENCES

CU-SeeMe World Web Page. No date. Available: http://www.cuseemeworld.com/news/cu-rights.asp [11/29/99].

Desktop Video Conferencing (DVC). (1996, September). *Digital Horizon, 1*(1). Available: http://www.broadband-guide.com/news/dnewssept96/dh [11/29/99].

Duin, A. H., Mason, L. D., & Jorn, L. A. (1994). Structuring distance-meeting environments. *Technical Communication, 41,* 695-708.

Labriola, D., (1995, April 25). Hardware–Desktop videoconferencing: Candid camera. *PC Magazine, 14*(8), 221-236.

White Pine Web Page. No date. Available: http://www.wpine.com/ [09/23/99].

Education for Provision of Library Services to Distance Learners: The Role of the LIS Schools

Heidi Lee Hoerman

University of South Carolina

Kevin A. Furniss

Winthrop University

SUMMARY. As distance education (DE) and its support needs proliferate, schools of library and information science (LIS) need to address the education of librarians for the provision of DE services. This paper discusses current efforts of LIS programs in this regard, difficulties of establishing curricular units in this area, and steps the profession can take to ensure that education for DE services becomes an integral part of all LIS curricula.

KEYWORDS. Distance education, library school curriculum

INTRODUCTION

Over a third of American colleges and universities answering a 1995 survey indicated that they provide distance education (DE) opportunities; the same survey indicated that up to sixty percent would

[Haworth co-indexing entry note]: "Education for Provision of Library Services to Distance Learners: The Role of the LIS Schools." Hoerman, Heidi Lee, and Kevin A. Furniss. Co-published simultaneously in *Journal of Library Administration* (The Haworth Information Press, an imprint of The Haworth Press, Inc.) Vol. 32, No. 1/2, 2001, pp. 247-257; and: *Off-Campus Library Services* (ed: Anne Marie Casey) The Haworth Information Press, an imprint of The Haworth Press, Inc., 2001, pp. 247-257.

be offering DE programs by 1998 (United States, National Center for Education Statistics 1997). Although no one knows the exact number of higher education institutions involved with DE as the year 2000 opens, the explosion of opportunities for Web-based curricular efforts, unknown in 1995, suggests that a similar survey done today would find even greater numbers of colleges and universities involved in distance programs. DE is here to stay.

When planning for DE programs, too few institutions take into account the needs for information services of distance learners. Librarians are rarely involved in the planning process, and the complications inherent in providing effective access to information are often underestimated (Pease & Power, 1994). Costly issues must be taken into consideration: availability of resources and copyright constraints, access to appropriate technologies, and training of librarians, faculty and students (Interinstitutional Library Council 1995). To fully address the information needs of distance learners in the planning process is to fully face costs of effective DE programs. This is an unpleasant and unwanted factor often avoided by those doing the planning.

Librarians who are invited to participate in planning for DE programs find themselves asked to make estimates of the costs for a level of service wholly new and somewhat mysterious to them. It is among the things they "didn't learn in library school." The question that then arises is, "What should be the role of library and information science (LIS) programs in educating librarians about DE services?"

LIS PROGRAMS AND DE

Ironically, LIS schools have offered DE options to their students for a long time but are only now coming to the realization that DE services should be included in their curricula. In 1994, no LIS program offered a course dedicated to DE service provision nor had any offered continuing education (CE) programs in the area (Kascus, 1994). LIS programs offer entire masters programs at a distance but provide the resulting librarians with no direct education for provision of distance services. LIS programs face the same problems as other DE efforts: how to provide appropriate curricular support at a distance, especially reference services and access to the journal and monographic literature. Perhaps, if the schools offered courses in DE services, it would awaken them to better address the problems faced by their own students.

The University of South Carolina (USC), for example, first embraced DE in 1937, when Havilock Babcock, an important author and professor, said, "Surely a state supported institution such as the University cannot discharge its full obligation by ministering merely to the needs of the relatively small group who can establish residence on campus. A forward-looking aspiring University should say to the citizens who sustain it: 'Our campus is the State. If you can't come to the University, then the University . . . will come to you'" (College of Library and Information Science, 1999). The USC College of Library and Information Science's (CLIS) first DE efforts were to provide on-site courses around the state in 1976; CLIS has been delivering education via television broadcast since 1982. Since that time, total CLIS enrollment in televised courses has exceeded 17,000. In recent years, enrollment in televised courses has produced over sixty-percent of credit hours generated. Despite the important role of DE at CLIS, a course for DE services is only now under development. CLIS also has a well-established schedule of CE workshops but the first on this topic was offered only recently.

DE services must compete with all the other topics that demand curricular attention. The emphasis on information science (some would say to the detriment of library science) in some programs has, for the most part, left such practical matters as services to distance learners "out in the cold." Only recently have some institutions developed courses or workshops that emphasize distance services.

In considering the addition of a new focus to the already full curricula of LIS programs, several factors must be taken into consideration. Does sufficient knowledge (theory and practice) exist to inform the curriculum? Who needs to learn about DE service provision? What faculty will teach DE services courses and how will all faculty be made aware of the issues? Where should DE services fall in the curriculum and what types of curricular offerings should be made? Finally, what information should be included in a course or workshop on DE services?

WHY EDUCATION OFTEN LAGS BEHIND PRACTICE

LIS programs, as graduate programs in universities, must look to the value structure of universities for their identities and their missions. One of the problems faced by graduate LIS education is the need to balance the demands of the universities for concentration on research in graduate education with the demands for concentration on craft knowledge appropriate to professional education. Baskett argues that although craft knowledge in professional education has been devalued in favor of scientific theory, universities are starting to "rediscover the value of field-based knowledge" (1993).

Field-based knowledge for an emerging issue like services to distance learners is only beginning to be formalized by research and publication. Librarianship is a field that must rely on practitioner generated research to advance. The practitioners whose positions emphasize distance services are few and those who produce research on the topic are fewer. With the rapid expansion of DE students' demands and the explosion of options for services, the DE librarian-practitioner has little time to perform the research necessary to create a core of formalized knowledge for the educator to share with students. The state-of-the-art is very difficult for educators to impart to students if they cannot find out what the field-based knowledge is.

The traditional model for learning by professionals held that knowledge was handed down by experts in formal settings, leaving the professional to adapt this knowledge for practice (Baskett 1993). This is still an important model for LIS education but it is a model that underestimates the importance of the knowledge that is created during practice. It assumes that knowledge created as part of practice cannot be generalizable theory and thus is not suited for graduate education. Knowledge must be formalized through research reports. This introduces an unavoidable delay between the time knowledge is created *in situ* and its inclusion in the graduate curriculum.

Although research on distance services in libraries is in its infancy, the work of the participants in the Off-Campus Library Services Conferences is an important effort to increase knowledge in this area. Education for provision of distance services can draw from two other areas with larger bodies of literature, in the meantime. DE has long been a topic of research and publication in the field of education. This knowledge can form the basis of an understanding of the needs of DE students. The literature of our own field, LIS, has also produced much formal knowledge that can inform DE services.

ALL LIBRARIANS NEED EDUCATION
FOR DISTANCE SERVICES

With the expansion of DE comes an expansion in demand for library services. The model of the university student taking a course designated as a distance course using services designated as distance services at the library of the institution hosting the course is only one of many. Those residing on campus and using the library locally may take DE courses. Similarly, commuting students taking local courses may use distance library services.

Demands for distance services from libraries come not only from those who are identified as DE students. Increasingly, students, faculty and staff expect to have full access to library services wherever they may be performing their studies. If students enrolled in distance courses have access to specialized reference and interlibrary services, the argument goes, why not offer those services to all students? What used to be identified as the normal college student, the 18- to 22-year-old living on campus, is no longer the norm. Students of all ages and walks of life need access to materials to support their learning and may find it difficult to get to the library (Ehrmann, 1998). The "library without walls" is becoming an expectation among students. Why should they come to the library? Why can the library not come to them?

Finally, as Dugan points out in his article on "victim libraries," students seek services to support their educational needs from the libraries closest to them, what Kascus calls "'silent partners' in the educational process" (Dugan, 1997; Kascus, 1994). Forty to seventy percent of DE students rely on their local public libraries to provide academic library services. "There is still the tendency for the students to ignore the services offered by the main campus and turn up instead in the most convenient and familiar library in their neighborhood or area of employment" (Pease & Power, 1994). Graduates of LIS programs find positions of all types in a wide variety of information centers. Some, of course, will become academic librarians providing services to distance learners enrolled at their own institutions. These form a very small number of graduates, but this does not vouchsafe the rest from finding themselves providers of DE services.

Most discussions about the need for librarians to be educated for distance service provision have concentrated on reference, bibliographic instruction and interlibrary loan services for academic libraries. But librarians responsible for all aspects of library activities must take into consideration the need to support distance services. Collection development officers need to be aware of the DE course offerings, taking into account the need to access curricular support materials for those courses at a distance. Acquisitions and serials librarians must take into consideration the special licensing issues involved with providing access off-campus. Catalogers must consider off-site use of the catalog. Furniss and Kariel recommend enriching the bibliographic descriptions with tables of contents to stand in lieu of shelf browsing, for example (1998). Preservationists must be involved with establishing the standards for protecting library materials sent to distance learners. Finally, administrators must be aware of the fiscal and staffing implications of providing distance services.

FACULTY FOR DISTANCE SERVICES EDUCATION

Faculty in library and information science need to know more about distance information services both as teachers of distance learners and as teachers of those who will provide services to distance learners. The faculties of schools of LIS are rather small; the median number of faculty in ALA-accredited MLIS programs is about ten. Schools attempt to provide education for the full range of library and information service roles their graduates undertake. Everything from cataloging to children's services, from networked information to government documents, must be covered in the curriculum. Education for providing distance services must compete with other topics for the attention of the faculty. Few schools have faculty with expertise in this area.

Faculty often must teach in areas new to them. It is rare the LIS professor who teaches only in areas in which he or she has previous practical experience. Teaching requires constant learning on the part of faculty both in terms of new information in their core fields of expertise and information for teaching new topics. For many faculty, distance service provision is a new and foreign topic. Here we link back to the problem of little formalized (published) research. One of the prime ways faculty gain knowledge in new areas is by reading the published literature of those areas. Not only is there little published research establishing the theories underlying quality distance services provision but, as the course Web page for Ilene Frank's course reads:

"Textbooks (Hint: There isn't one!)" (Frank, 1999). It is difficult to teach in areas in which one has not experience with "authority" when it is difficult to gain access to authoritative information by those who do have experience.

A strategy used by many library schools is to augment the full-time faculty with the use of adjunct instructors drawn from the "real world" of libraries. These instructors often have specialized information not held by the faculty and are commonly used to teach in such specialized areas as preservation, law librarianship, and distance services provision. One of the problems with relying on adjunct faculty to teach specialized courses is that the knowledge in those courses becomes marginalized. The isolation of adjunct faculty from the full time faculty means that their concerns are not voiced in faculty meetings. They tend not to be part of the planning process. It is not as easy for them to have informal conversations with the regular faculty about the place of their subject in the overall curriculum and in the courses of those other faculty. They tend to have fewer resources devoted to the teaching of their courses. Their courses tend to be offered less often.

Faculty awareness of DE services and production of publications in this area can be increased by practitioners teaming with LIS faculty on research projects. Faculty often obtains mastery over a topic by doing research and writing about it. This paper, for example, resulted from the collaboration of an experienced DE services practitioner and a faculty member with DE teaching experience. Another way to increase faculty understanding of the issue would be to invite LIS faculty to participate in the Off-Campus Library Services Conferences. Finally, in a more general way, DE services practitioners can keep faculty aware of their "real world" through informal communications including e-mail.

LEVELS OF EDUCATION FOR DE SERVICES IN LIS PROGRAMS

Education for DE services can appear in the LIS curriculum in a variety of forms. Most obvious is the elective course devoted wholly to DE services. Such a course has been offered by Ilene Frank at the University of South Florida (Frank, 1999). Sandy Slade developed the first draft syllabus for a course on DE services and distributed it widely via e-mail (Slade, 1998). A course is being developed for

USC's CLIS and will be presented at the Ninth Off-Campus Library Services Conference. It is expected that more schools will develop and offer such courses.

Newly minted librarians often apply for positions for which they have no direct experience. And many libraries hire such librarians. An interviewee for a position including cataloging, for example, may say, "No, I have no cataloging experience but I took a cataloging course." Hiring agencies expect students who have taken specialized courses to have the knowledge needed to start to become proficient in specialized areas. Selection of particular courses by students can also indicate a special interest in a topic that employers value. As more positions require provision of services to distant learners, an elective course on distance services provision will serve the same purpose for the job applicant who lacks direct experience.

DE services also need to be a topic covered generally throughout the MLIS curriculum. As access to higher education through DE becomes greater in even the most rural of communities, the demands for library support will increasingly burden rural libraries where only half of those titled "librarian" hold the masters degree from ALA-accredited programs (Barron, 1995). Education for provision of DE services is particularly important for these librarians. Courses and workshops on DE services, themselves offered by DE, can serve this population.

Specialized electives often have difficulty attracting sufficient numbers of students. MLIS students are faced with a wide variety of elective courses to choose from. These courses would also be of interest to post-masters students. At USC, the DE services course is being developed as the school starts a large two-state (Georgia and South Carolina) cohort of specialist degree ("masters-plus-30") students. It is expected that many of the registrants in the course will come from this specialist cohort.

Although taking an elective course on DE services after the master's degree is clearly a form of continuing education, the more usual model for continuing education (CE) is the short workshop. LIS programs have often been criticized for failing to provide continuing education programs and Kascus found that no schools offered CE workshops on distance services (Kascus, 1994). USC has for many years had an active program of continuing education workshops and USC's Dan Barron developed and delivered a workshop entitled "Distance Learning Workshop: Teaching and Training in Distributed

Learning Environments" in 1999 (Barron, 1999). Barron's workshop, itself a DE offering, was available to anyone anywhere who wished to take it. USC has also made its grant writing CE workshop available for free on the World Wide Web and expects to use DE technologies to further expand access to its CE offerings (Hoerman, 1999).

WHAT TO INCLUDE

It may seem odd to discuss what to include in a course on DE services at the very end of an article such as this, but this order parallels the planning process for offering a course. First, the need is perceived. Next, a faculty member strives to obtain some level of mastery over the topic; the development of a course is normally faculty driven, not administratively directed. The type of offering (course, workshop, etc.) is determined and proposed to the program's curriculum committee and administration. Finally, the actual content of the offering is developed. The order differs somewhat between the development of workshops and the development of courses. Workshops can often be approved with little formal discussion while courses can require the design of a completed syllabus before approval. Campus- or university-level approval for offering the course must be obtained, and that university approval is not sought until the program is committed to offering the course if approved.

"Conversations about continuing education for librarians usually revolve around the functional responsibilities we are assigned" (Stebelman, 1996). Therefore, the types of things that need to be included in courses and workshops for DE services comprise the full range of public and technical services concerns in libraries. In addition, a DE services course should address the history of DE and relevant educational and learning theories.

CONCLUSION

Despite the long need for DE services by libraries, LIS programs have only recently started to include DE services provision in their curricula. As more and more DE students expect to obtain information services from more and more libraries, the need for librarians who understand the many complexities of DE services will increase. Thus it is imperative that LIS programs include education for DE services in the curricula for all their students. It is encouraging that some schools are starting to offer courses and continuing education workshops in this area but more schools need to do this.

Practicing off-campus services librarians should continue to produce formal literature in the area of DE services and should strive to increase the awareness of LIS educators of the needs in this area. DE services articles need to be published in a wide variety of publications, not only those devoted strictly to DE services nor even those devoted strictly to academic librarianship. Papers on the topic should appear in sources read by all the types of librarians who deal with this issue and that is, for all intents and purposes, all librarians.

REFERENCES

Barron, D. D. (1995). Staffing rural public libraries: The need to invest in intellectual capital. *Library Trends, 44*(1), 77-87.

Barron, D. D. (1999). *Distance learning workshop: Teaching and training in distributed learning environments.* Retrieved December 5, 1999 from the World Wide Web: http://www.libsci.sc.edu/Dan/pfgde/pfghome.htm.

Baskett, H. K. (1993, July/August). The nanosecond nineties: Challenges and opportunities in continuing professional education. *Adult Learning, 4*(6), 15-17.

College of Library and Information Science. University of South Carolina. (1999). *Distance education.* Retrieved December 5, 1999 from the World Wide Web: http://www.libsci.sc.edu/program/disted.html.

Dugan, R. E. (1997, July). Distance education: Provider and victim libraries. *Journal of Academic Librarianship, 23*(4), 315-318.

Ehrmann, S. C. (1998, January 9). Libraries and distance learning. In *Distance Education in a Print and Electronic World: Proceedings of the OCLC Symposium, ALA Midwinter Conference 1998, New Orleans, LA.* Retrieved December 5, 1999 from the World Wide Web: http://www.oclc.org/oclc/man/10256dis/print.html.

Frank, I. (1999). *Library Services to Distance Users, Summer Session May 10-July 16, 1999.* Retrieved December 5, 1999 from the World Wide Web: http://www.lib.usf.edu/~ifrank/distance/course.html.

Furniss, K. A., & Kariel, D. (1998). Library catalogs, the World Wide Web, and serving the off-campus user: Boon or bust? In P. S. Thomas & M. Jones (Comps.), *The Eighth Off-Campus Library Services Conference Proceedings, Providence, Rhode Island, April 22-24, 1998* (pp. 155-158). Mount Pleasant, MI: Central Michigan University.

Hoerman, H. L. (1999). *Go for that grant.* Retrieved December 5, 1999 from the World Wide Web: http://www.libsci.sc.edu/cern/heidi/ (password available from CE coordinator at USC CLIS).

Interinstitutional Library Council, Oregon State System of Higher Education. (1995, March 10). *Library support for distance education programs.* Retrieved December 5, 1999 from the World Wide Web: http://www.ous.edu/dist-learn/library.htm.

Kascus, M. A. (1994). What library schools teach about library support to distant students: A survey. *American Journal of Distance Education, 8*(1), 20-35.

Pease, B., & Power, C. (1994). Reference services for off-campus students and faculty. *Reference Librarian, 43*, 43-62.

Slade, A. (als@uvic.ca)(1998, August 20). *DE services course syllabus.* E-mail to H. L. Hoerman (hoerman@sc.edu).

Stebelman, S. (1996). Taking control of continuing education: The formation of a reading group at George Washington University. *Journal of Academic Librarianship, 22*, 382-385.

United States. National Center for Education Statistics. (1997, October). *Distance Education in Higher Education Institutions: 2. Distance Education Course Offerings.* Retrieved December 5, 1999 from the World Wide Web: http://nces.ed.gov/pubs98/distance/chap2.html.

Planning for Distance Learning:
Support Services and the Library's Role

Jon R. Hufford

Texas Tech University

SUMMARY. The article examines the role that student support services plays in planning a distance learning program, especially the services offered by a university library. The content of the paper is based on the experience the author acquired as a member of Texas Tech University's Distance Learning Council. The Council's efforts to plan a program that will include strong support from the Library are discussed.

KEYWORDS. Library services, distance education, student services

A transformation is occurring in how universities teach students. New technology, changes in the composition of student bodies, with adults, minorities, women, and foreign students participating in ever increasing numbers, and distance learning are major components in this transformation. The University Continuing Education Association recently published a report titled *Lifelong Learning Trends: A Profile of Continuing Education* (1998). This report describes several of the trends bringing about this transformation. One trend is the great potential of the adult population in the United States for participation in distance learning. According to the Association's report, distance learning has become an appealing alternative for working adults with career and family responsibilities who want to enhance their educa-

[Haworth co-indexing entry note]: "Planning for Distance Learning: Support Services and the Library's Role." Hufford, Jon R. Co-published simultaneously in *Journal of Library Administration* (The Haworth Information Press, an imprint of The Haworth Press, Inc.) Vol. 32, No. 1/2, 2001, pp. 259-266; and: *Off-Campus Library Services* (ed: Anne Marie Casey) The Haworth Information Press, an imprint of The Haworth Press, Inc., 2001, pp. 259-266.

tion. Other trends include the fast and consistent growth of jobs in occupations requiring more education, and the increased number of American households that have access to technology-based instruction (*Lifelong Learning Trends,* 1998).

Universities are facing challenges and are offered opportunities in this new learning environment. One of the challenges is that, although greater demands are being placed on universities, resources have not grown proportionally. Given this situation, a plan of action can go a long way towards narrowing the gap between new demands and available resources. The planning should have a long-term strategic approach that includes an analysis of the environment, making strategic choices, and setting and prioritizing goals. A liberal dose of imagination and action are also required. Throughout the entire planning process, it is vitally important that the university faculty and staff responsible for the program focus on key elements of the new learning environment. Some of these key elements are recognizing the need for new educational systems and correctly identifying constituents that the distance learning program will serve. Other key elements include developing exemplary support services for the constituents, developing a good technical infrastructure and a cooperative network for sharing information and experiences, and having in place skilled staff (Pohjonen, 1997).

Another challenge is that views on education, learning, and information technology change quickly in today's environment. In fact, the life span of electronic learning environments that are dependent on particular technologies is becoming shorter all the time. Some of these environments are already out of date when they are introduced to the public. The rapid growth of knowledge and technology is responsible for this short life span. Because of this rapid development, universities must learn to plan better and respond faster. Also, they must spend sufficient amounts of money, time, and staff talent during the developmental phase of a distance learning program (Pohjonen, 1997).

More than anything else, the success of a distance learning program depends on the distance learning courses offered. A significant factor contributing to the success of these courses is the ease with which students can accomplish the library research needed to complete the assignments their professors give them. Library personnel are expected to assist distance students in several ways. In general, the goals of a comprehensive library support program for distance education should include reference services, information literacy instruction, and document delivery services. The successful implementation of these goals depends on library staff projecting its traditional ethos of service to the patrons to also include distance learning students.

With the intention of meeting the challenges and benefiting from the opportunities associated with the transformation that is taking place in higher education, the Texas Tech University administration formed the Telecommunications Infrastructure Fund/Distance Education Vision Committee in the fall of 1996. In an effort to encourage a sense of involvement and commitment at all levels across campus, faculty from various departments, departmental chairpersons, associate deans, directors, and a vice-provost were asked to participate as members of the Committee. The Committee's assigned task was to develop a vision statement for the future of distance learning at the University. The main theme of the Committee's final report (May 27, 1997) was that, by early in the next century, the University should become a national leader in changing the paradigm of higher education through distance learning (Texas Tech University, 1997, part 2).

The "Vision" Committee recommended in its report that a permanent administrative unit be created that would be responsible for insuring the university's ability to achieve this position of leadership. More specifically, the unit would be responsible for facilitating the development and delivery of distance learning and for fostering collaborative distance learning relationships with educational institutions throughout West Texas. The report recommended that the unit concentrate on four areas: distance learning infrastructure and operations, distance learning program development, coordination and support, and information services and technologies. The unit would insure that the academic components of the institution were equipped and supported at the level necessary to provide their constituencies access to and the benefit of "cutting edge" distance learning and information technologies. Further, the unit would interface with other academic units on campus, respond to the inter-institutional distance learning challenges within Texas, and take advantage of new developments in distance learning and information technology which impact the University's mission.

The University President accepted the Committee's recommendations and, late in 1997, appointed the Vice-Provost for Outreach and Extended Studies to be the administrative officer responsible for the unit. At the same time, the President accepted the recommendation that a Distance Learning Council be created to advise the Vice-Provost and to assist in providing strategic direction for the distance learning program. The Council became a standing body with representation from each of the major academic and service units of the University. It is presently responsible for developing policies that will define distance learning priorities and activities. When completed, these policies will guide the overall development and implementation of distance learning at Texas Tech University (Texas Tech University, 1997).

In addition, the Distance Learning Technology Committee was created as a standing subcommittee of the Council. This Committee is responsible for the development of recommendations for system computing and network standards and design, distance learning classroom design, interactive video systems design, and satellite and other alternative delivery systems. The Committee is also responsible for coordinating the review, evaluation, and demonstration of new technologies for potential adoption and application in the distance learning programs of the University. The Council can appoint additional standing and/or ad hoc committees when the need arises.

Early in 1998, the chair of the Distance Learning Council set up working committees to address its responsibilities. Each council member is assigned to one of these Distance Learning Council committees. Each committee has undertaken to study its assigned area and then write a report that will include recommendations for its area of responsibilities. Working committees are in place to address student services and course management, faculty issues and programs, and institutional relations and issues. Although it is likely that these committees will sit indefinitely, it is unclear at this time whether they will continue to exist once all the reports are completed.

An area frequently neglected in the development of distance learning programs is student support services. Support for students at a distance includes registration, enrollment, and transcript services; access to student advisors; academic counseling; and financial aid services. Also included are such services as access to library and research materials, bookstore services, timely receipt of instructor materials for courses, technical support, and communication with other students.

The Distance Learning Council decided early on to make student support services an important part of Texas Tech University's distance learning program. Several members of the Council identified library services as being especially important. The fact that the Associate Dean of the University Libraries and the Libraries' Coordinator of Library Instruction are members of the Council has helped to reinforce this belief.

With this in mind, the chair of the Distance Learning Council established the Student Services and Course Management Working Committee. The Committee's members include the University's Director of Extended Learning, who is serving as chair, the Libraries' Associate Dean and its Coordinator of Library Instruction, the Director of the University Transition Advisement Center, and the Associate to the Vice President for Student Affairs. Some of the Committee's more important responsibilities are developing an inventory of potential constituents to be served, defining their characteristics, identifying the elements of the learning context for constituents, identifying market forces driving educational requirements, developing approaches for providing service, and developing uniform guidelines for support services for distance students. These responsibilities will serve as a framework for writing the Committee's report.

The Student Services and Course Management Committee began its work in February of 1998 and has met several times since. The Committee recognizes that thorough and careful policy development is a key component of a successful distance learning initiative. Its rationale is that all too frequently the toughest distance learning policy questions remain unasked. Also, some issues may seem minor at first and thus receive minimal consideration. Yet later on these issues often become major stumbling blocks to a successful distance learning program. Asking the really tough questions early in the policy development process can go a long way towards avoiding potential policy pitfalls and contributes to the quality, rigor, and strength of a distance learning program. With this in mind, the Student Services and Course Management Working Committee has approached its responsibilities in a deliberate manner.

On several occasions, the Committee has discussed the issue of what should be the appropriate level of service for distance learning students. It decided that Texas Tech University's distance learning student must be offered the same level of service quality that on-campus students receive. The Committee is acting on the assumption that it is critical for a program's student service policies to be developed with quality service to the distance students always in mind. Committee members have found it helpful when discussing policies to work through the steps that students must take to learn about courses and programs, enroll in them, participate in the classes, and successfully complete a distance learning course or program. The Committee is firmly convinced that strong student service policies can greatly increase a distance learning program's chances for success.

Another issue that the Committee discussed is whether a single department or office should handle all questions from distance learning students who may have difficulties in any number of critical areas, including computer-related connection problems, registration glitches, undelivered textbooks, or advisement options. Would a single office serve the students best? If so, which office should be responsible? Or should there be a central office or clearinghouse that refers students to other offices or departments for specialized assistance?

More than anything else, the success of a distance learning program depends on the distance learning courses offered. A significant factor contributing to the success of these courses is the ease with which students can accomplish the library research needed to complete the assignments their professors give them. Library personnel are expected to assist distance students in several ways. In general, the goals of a comprehensive library support program for distance learning should include reference services, information literacy instruction, and document delivery services. The successful implementation of these goals depends on library staff projecting its traditional ethos of service to the patrons to also include distance learning students.

The Libraries are well positioned to support distance learning at Texas Tech University. The primary means of providing library services to the University's distance students is through Internet access to the Libraries' Web site. The University's Academic Computing Service provides Point-to-point Protocol (PPP) accounts for access to Web-based electronic resources requiring user validation/IP addresses. The cost of these accounts to distance learning students is $45.00 per semester plus long distance phone charges. Telnet access to the Texas Tech University Libraries' online catalog and several other databases are also available.

Several resources that provide valuable services to distance students are available on the Libraries' Web site. A link on the site introduces distance students to all the services available to them. A portion of this Distance Learning site is also available as a printed handout. The Web site also provides access to reference assistance. Distance students can submit questions on the site and expect to receive answers either on the same day the questions were submitted or the morning of the next workday. Additional links provide current news about the Libraries, a staff directory, and links to Internet resources compiled by the Libraries' subject librarians. The staff directory includes e-mail links to subject librarians and other staff personnel. There is also a tutorial available on how to conduct library research and online forms for requesting delivery of University-owned material and interlibrary loans. Both the library-owned and interlibrary loan materials that are requested using the forms can be mailed or faxed to a distance student's home or office. Finally, distance students have access to scanned materials placed on reserve by instructors at the Electronic Reserve link on the Libraries' Web site, and there are countless full-text resources available on the site and throughout the Internet.

Other existing services include an 888 toll-free phone number, customized library instruction, express delivery of Library materials, and the establishment of a Library team that coordinates distance learning services. Distance students who want to avoid purchasing a bar-coded Texas Tech University ID card can ask the Library to mail them a library card with a barcode. The bar-code number is necessary for access to all databases requiring user validation. Also upon request, a TexShare library card will be mailed to distance students. This card permits the holder to borrow books from other Texas academic libraries.

Apart from the services already available, the Texas Tech University Libraries will have additional ones made available to distance students in the near future. The Libraries will soon have a proxy server that will provide direct access to Web-based databases restricted by Internet Protocol (IP) addresses, thus bypassing the need for a Texas Tech University Point-to-point Protocol (PPP) account. Students will then be able to use America Online (AOL) or other Internet providers to access all Web-based resources supplied by the Texas Tech University Libraries.

Another service that will be implemented soon is desktop (computer to computer) delivery of articles to patrons from Texas Tech University Libraries and interlibrary loan sources. Renewal of books, requests for "recalls" of books and other material checked out to someone else, and accessing personal borrowing information, such as information on books currently checked out or overdue items, are other services that will be made available in the next few months.

As was pointed out earlier in this article, the strategic approach required in planning a distance learning program should include an analysis of the environment, making strategic choices, setting and prioritizing goals, imagination, and action. The university faculty and staff responsible for the distance learning program must recognize the need for new educational systems, correctly identify constituents, develop adequate support services, develop a good technical infrastructure and a cooperative network for sharing information and experiences, and acquire skilled staff. Also, universities must respond to new developments quickly and be ready to spend sufficient funds for development.

A university library's role in this strategic planning is to provide the best possible support for distance learning courses. A significant factor contributing to the success of the courses is the ease with which students can accomplish the library research needed to complete the assignments their professors give them. Generally, the library support that makes success possible includes reference service, information literacy instruction, and document delivery services. Ultimately, the successful implementation of these services depends on library staff projecting their traditional ethos of professional service to the patrons to also include distance learning students.

Texas Tech University, with strong support from the Library, has taken a strategic approach in planning its distance learning program. The formation of the "Vision" Committee that authored a vision statement, the establishment of a distance learning administrative unit with a council to assist and advise it, and council committees that are developing recommendations for defined areas in distance learning are developments that reflect careful planning and determined action. When completed, the committee reports will include the results of such activities as environmental analyses, making strategic choices, and setting and prioritizing goals. Texas Tech University has made a commendable start in planning its new distance learning program.

REFERENCES

Lifelong learning trends: A profile of continuing higher education (5th ed.). (1998). Washington, DC: University Continuing Education Association.

Pohjonen, J. (1997). New learning environments as a strategic choice. *European Journal of Education, 32,* 369-377.

Texas Tech University. Telecommunications Infrastructure Fund/Distance Learning Vision Committee. (1997). *A vision for distance learning at Texas Tech University.* Unpublished manuscript, Texas Tech University.

Partners in Emerging Technology: Library Support for Web-Based Courses

Jamie P. Kearley
Karen S. Lange

University of Wyoming

SUMMARY. This paper discusses how the University of Wyoming Libraries have worked in partnership with the larger institution and its Outreach School to develop a strategic plan for the future of distance education at the University of Wyoming. This collaboration insures that distance learners receive comparable library services to on-campus learners. The authors focus on how the World Wide Web is utilized to provide library services to students, in particular to online students.

KEYWORDS. Distance education, library services, World Wide Web

INTRODUCTION

Approximately ten years ago, the off-campus library literature began to stress the importance of library participation in planning and collaborating with the institution's distance education program. Kascus and Aguilar (1987) were some of the first librarians to address this topic. In their study, they concluded that "librarians should become an integral part of the planning process and that programs should not be allowed to become operational without the provision of adequate library support. Collaboration between the distance education office

[Haworth co-indexing entry note]: "Partners in Emerging Technology: Library Support for Web-Based Courses." Kearley, Jamie P., and Karen S. Lange. Co-published simultaneously in *Journal of Library Administration* (The Haworth Information Press, an imprint of The Haworth Press, Inc.) Vol. 32, No. 1/2, 2001, pp. 267-280; and: *Off-Campus Library Services* (ed: Anne Marie Casey) The Haworth Information Press, an imprint of The Haworth Press, Inc., 2001, pp. 267-280.

and the library is essential and libraries need to establish a viable presence for off-campus programs" (p. 97).

In 1995, the Oregon Interinstitutional Library Council submitted a paper to the state's System of Higher Education calling for the need to make libraries part of the planning process when developing distance learning programs. This document noted that "too often the critical need for library and information services receives insufficient attention both in terms of policies and procedures, and as a cost which must be included in a program's budget" (p. 1). The paper noted this problem is not confined to Oregon, but exists nationwide. The *ACRL Guidelines for Distance Learning Library Services* (Association of . . ., 1998) support this position and recommend that "institutions take responsibility for involving the library administration and other library personnel in the planning, developing and adding or changing of the distance learning program from the earliest stages and onward" (p. 691). More recently, Slade and Kascus (1998) emphasized the importance of library collaboration and participation in distance education programs as one of four trends in the area of library services for distance learners.

The University of Wyoming (UW) Libraries have a long history of cooperating with the Outreach School to provide library services to distant learners. This paper will examine that history of collaboration in the planning process and will also describe how as a consequence of collaboration, UW Libraries have responded to enhance library services to distance learners using the World Wide Web.

BACKGROUND

Established as a land grant institution, the University of Wyoming has provided off-campus education to its citizens for well over 100 years, and was the first university east of the Missouri River to offer correspondence courses. In the 1890's and on into the early 1900's, professors rode the train to reach their students.

Beginning in 1926, a university-owned airplane shuttled faculty to and from remote sites. Eventually, due to rising costs and increased demands to offer on-site courses, the university began to investigate the technological aspects of delivering courses remotely to multiple sites simultaneously. By the 1970's, UW was using audio teleconferencing to reach students, and in 1992 began delivering compressed video courses. Initially seven sites were connected to the statewide compressed video network. Today there are 24 sites throughout the state.

In 1983, the Libraries' director had the foresight and wisdom to reallocate a library faculty position devoted to planning and implementing library services designed to meet the needs of off-campus learners and faculty. This resulted in the formation of the Library Outreach Services office. From its inception, the department has collaborated with the institution's off-campus program. We have worked jointly to write cooperative agreements between the University and Wyoming's community colleges. These agreements specify the services available to UW students at the community colleges' libraries, computer labs, and other facilities. The School of Extended Studies, the administrative unit of the University's distance education program, and Library Outreach Services have worked cooperatively to conduct needs assessments, promote off-campus programs throughout the state, provide access to the libraries' resources, and, most recently, to participate in the outreach planning process.

Similar to other distance education programs across the country, the University's program continues to grow at an astonishing rate. For example, in 1994, 2,423 students were enrolled in degree programs, but by 1998 enrollment had soared to 6,115 students. The number of audio-teleconference courses grew from 75 in 1994 to 174 in 1998, and compressed video courses, which totaled 22 in 1994, had increased to 86 by 1998.

Due to the expansion of distance learning programs and increasing enrollment, the Libraries are also experiencing greater demands for document delivery, access to more electronic databases and full-text articles, and assistance with reference and research questions. Only by working cooperatively with our distance education program administrators and engaging in the strategic planning process can we even begin to resolve the issues that will ultimately impact the Libraries' ability to serve distance learners.

STRATEGIC PLANNING PROCESS

As UW's distance education program became more complex, administrators, faculty, staff, and students all expressed concerns about the program's overall administration and organizational structure. In response to questions and misunderstandings surrounding our off-campus program, the Outreach Council was established in 1992 under the direction of the Associate Provost for Academic Affairs. The purpose of the Council was to serve as an advisory body by providing input and direction for the existing program. The council consisted of representation from all of the academic colleges, including the Libraries, extension offices, business assistance center, cultural outreach, and student support services, such as information technology, registration, and financial aid.

A major outcome of the Outreach Council's work was the identification of specific issues and concerns regarding the delivery of off-campus courses. The issues ranged from program administration, costs, staffing, faculty compensation, and student support services to outdated equipment, marketing, and external pressures such as the Western Governors University (WGU). By 1997, it was apparent that some concerns could not be resolved without the involvement and commitment from other administrative units. Therefore, the Council recommended an institution-wide strategic planning initiative that would critically review the University's distance education program, and determine a course of action that would guide them into the next millennium.

Coincidentally, the University's planning process fits the model outlined in an article by Hache (1998), entitled "Strategic Planning of Distance Education in the Age of Teleinformatics." He identifies five elements or components that comprise the strategic planning process. The elements are: (1) preparatory steps of planning, (2) gathering of information and analysis, (3) strategic choices, (4) implementation of the strategy, and (5) evaluation and control of the strategy. We have therefore organized UW's outreach strategic planning activities around these five elements.

PREPARATORY STEPS OF PLANNING

The Outreach Council universally adopted two assumptions. First, given the number of unresolved issues that had come before the Outreach Council, it was determined that a campus-wide planning effort was inevitable. Secondly, participation in the proposed planning effort had to be expanded to include individual units and departments who would be directly effected by changes.

By Fall 1997, the University president directed the Associate Provost of Academic Affairs/Dean, School of Extended Studies and Public Service with the responsibility of identifying individuals who would be invited to participate in the planning process. This led to the formation of five task forces with 9-14 members per group. Each task force was asked to examine a specific aspect of the distance learning program and submit a report with their observations and recommendations. The designated task forces were:

- Outreach Technical Support
- Development and Delivery of Internet/Web Courses
- Academic Planning and Budgeting
- Outreach Student Services
- Non-Credit/Enrichment/Extension Programming

The Libraries had representation on three of the five task forces–Planning and Budgeting, Outreach Student Services and Outreach Technical Support. For all three groups, the Libraries' task force members submitted documentation that either (1) raised questions about the level of commitment and support for offering library services (costs, funding, technology), (2) provided statistics and anecdotal information, or (3) offered suggestions and recommendations for strengthening the University's overall distance education program.

GATHERING OF INFORMATION AND ANALYSIS

The task force members immediately focused on gathering information, sifting through an enormous amount of documentation, and listening to the testimonies of stakeholders who represented the University community as well as interested citizens throughout the state. This process was exhaustive and time-consuming. Over a four month period most groups met four to five times per month for two to four hours each.

Off-campus academic program directors met with the task forces. Their presentations were thorough; they were well prepared to answer hard questions about program costs, enrollment figures, staffing, faculty compensation for developing off-campus courses, program quality issues, and so on. Statistics, costs, and program self-assessments were put on the table for members to question, probe, and ponder.

Stakeholders at all levels, both on- and off-campus, were asked to evaluate the quality of UW's distance education program. One task force mounted a survey on the Internet to give students, faculty, and staff an opportunity to comment and make suggestions for student support services, including the library, financial aid, registration, admissions, and computer support.

Finally, the task force members began to conceptualize and articulate the problems and concerns that had previously seemed so vague and untouchable. Values and beliefs were clarified. Mission and vision statements evolved and the groups reached a consensus on the issues and recommended actions. Interestingly, the one theme that became apparent in each of the task force reports was that we should cooperatively focus on the concept of "one university–one student body." This conclusion supports another of Slade's and Kascus's (1998) predictions that there will be a blurring (and perhaps complete disappearance) of the boundaries between on and off-campus student services.

Each task force submitted a report at the end of January 1998. By March a combined report, "A Vision for the Future of University of Wyoming Outreach," was delivered to the president. The report noted that initially 79 administrators, faculty, academic professionals, and staff from throughout the University were involved in the preparation of this planning document.

STRATEGIC CHOICES

The "Vision" report continued to move on through an extensive and rigorous review process. The president convened the University's Executive Council to discuss the mission, values, objectives, proposed management, and organizational changes iterated in the report. The president also requested input from throughout the campus and beyond. Finally, a letter from the president was delivered to the Associate Provost summarizing his recommendations for implementing the proposed "Vision" document.

In some cases, the president recommended that we take action immediately, such as to reorganize the School of Extended Services and Public Service and to rename it the Outreach School. He also recommended the Outreach School take immediate action on developing Web-based courses. Due to funding availability and programmatic circumstances, a decision was made to investigate the feasibility of offering Web-based courses before the strategic plan was officially adopted.

IMPLEMENTATION OF THE STRATEGY

This phase included the final preparation of the strategic plan and set the stage for implementation of the action items. As the Outreach "Vision" document underwent revisions and clarification, the University embarked on another strategic planning effort–an academic planning process which included all of the University's academic programs. An abbreviated version of the "Vision" report was incorporated into the overall University "Academic Plan." Thus when the "Academic Plan" was adopted by the University's Board of Trustees in July 1999, it accepted the outreach program's plan. It also adopted a new vision statement for UW's distance education program which reads as follows:

> The State of Wyoming is the campus of the University of Wyoming. The University has one faculty and staff, one student body and one set of academic programs. Teaching, research and service are the mission of the University regardless of location. The University recognizes that its "one student body" is composed of a wide variety of students whose needs differ. The University is committed to providing all student support services essential for success, regardless of where the student is located. The University will share the expertise of the faculty and staff with the citizens of the state, through instruction, community service and application of research. (p. 25)

The strategic plan is dynamic and fluid, and yet it keeps us on course and makes us accountable for the changes that will occur in the next 3-5 years. Included in this plan are the mission and vision statements, goals/actions, staffing implications, estimated costs, and timelines.

In fall 1998, the first steps were taken toward the establishment of a virtual university. The Outreach School contracted with eCollege.com (formerly RealEducation), a Denver-based private firm specializing in the development and delivery of Internet courses. On campus faculty were recruited to share in this new endeavor and by January 1999 the

University went online with 10 Web-based courses and approximately 150 students. Now 22 courses are offered through UW Online.

EVALUATION AND CONTROL OF THE STRATEGY

On-going evaluations and assessments will keep us focused on the actions identified in the plan. The Outreach School is currently measuring the effectiveness of online courses. In addition, the School is conducting a statewide needs assessment to determine what programs need to continue and what new programs should be considered. The Outreach School's staff and other units involved with the delivery of off-campus services will also be used as sources of ongoing input and feedback.

UW LIBRARIES' RESPONSE TO STRATEGIC PLANNING

Having been involved throughout the planning process, we knew Library Outreach Services would be participants in the venture of Web-based distance education. In fact, we have long operated under the assumption that it is imperative that all distance learners receive the same educational and research opportunities as on campus students. Therefore, once the development of Web courses commenced, we immediately began to consider how best to serve this new group of distance learners. We quickly concluded that the current outreach services of bibliographic instruction, personalized reference and research assistance, access to databases, and document delivery would be offered to online students, just as they are to all distance learners.

TRANSITION TO THE VIRTUAL LIBRARY

Fortunately, advances in communication technology in recent years have enabled the University of Wyoming Libraries to expand the availability of information sources and services beyond the campus library buildings. Initially the Internet permitted remote patron access to online catalogs via a telnet connection. Then the advent of the World Wide Web facilitated the creation of a Library Outreach Services Web homepage with descriptions of services, access to online catalogs, a limited number of Web-accessible databases (as these were created by vendors), searching guides, and an electronic request form to order materials. Thus we were able to create a virtual library environment for patrons regardless of location. The virtual library has been of tremendous benefit to distance learners. This has been especially true for distant learners in Wyoming where population is sparse, distance between towns is considerable, and only one four-year university exists in the entire state.

Recently the UW Libraries expanded the walls of the library even farther with the implementation of proxy serving. Proxy serving verifies the patron's affiliation with the University and grants access to password protected Web-accessible databases. Distance learners are now able to use UW Catalog Plus, the desktop gateway to library resources used in-house, thus making the full range of electronic library resources available. UW Catalog Plus expands the number of available databases to over 400 and includes bibliographic, statistical, informational and full-text databases, as well as an online encyclopedia, directories, and newspapers. The subject coverage is extensive: business, education, arts and humanities, science, government, law, medicine, and engineering.

Of equal importance from a librarian's perspective is that proxy serving allows us to serve one student body as opposed to a divided body of on campus and off-campus learners. Prior to proxy serving, a librarian had to determine first whether the individual was affiliated with our University and then the location from which they were searching the library databases, i.e., a computer in a Wyoming community college library which used a recognizable IP or a home/office computer which needed a username and password. This was necessary so that the librarian could determine which databases were accessible to the students and whether they would be utilizing a telnet or Web version. It is a tremendous relief to a librarian who works at a reference desk and with off-campus students to be able to respond in a consistent fashion to a reference query regardless of the students' geographical location.

Having reached this juncture we felt we were in a good position to extend our services to Online UW students. However, two challenges became apparent. How best to promote Library Outreach Services and how to manage library instruction. Both undertakings required cooperation with other entities to be successful.

PROMOTION OF LIBRARY OUTREACH SERVICES

First, we approached eCollege.com, formerly RealEducation, the Web developers of the Online UW virtual campus. We expressed our desire to extend Library Outreach Services to Online UW students and found they were eager to collaborate in this endeavor. At the outset we knew the Library needed a presence on the Online UW campus and a way to communicate with students. The initial problem was to determine the best point of contact with students. In discussions with eCollege.com we concluded that the point of contact would be the student's homepage since that is the beginning point for entering class. Consequently eCollege.com added a link from the student's homepage to the UW Catalog Plus Web page, and a link to "Ask a Librarian," our electronic reference service.

The next step was to publicize the range of our services. This was accomplished by adding a section, "Using the UWYO Library," to the Student Orientation Course for all Online UW students. "Using the UWYO Library" outlines:

- the purpose of the electronic library
- cost of services
- how to get a library card
- how to get help from a librarian
- how to obtain a password
- how to request materials
- how to cite sources used
- a brief description of the difference between the electronic library resources and those found by searching the Web.

Promoting library services to faculty took a different direction. Each semester eCollege.com meets in person with current and potential Online UW faculty. At these meetings, the Outreach Librarian is always present to promote services and to answer questions. In addition, by the beginning of the second semester of Online UW, a flyer was sent to faculty alerting them to new library services and new features of UW Catalog Plus. The plan is to continue this approach in working with faculty.

LIBRARY INSTRUCTION

Library instruction presented a different challenge. Individual research consultation with a librarian was already available to distance learners by a toll free telephone number or by e-mail. The new challenge was to develop a process for group instruction. It has been relatively easy to meet with a class for the purpose of library instruction in audio-teleconference, interactive video, and on-site classes. In these synchronous learning environments, faculty and students meet at the same time, although not necessarily in the same location. However, it was obvious that bibliographic instruction would have to be adapted for the online environment, which has no meeting time for the class. In the asynchronous environment of online classes, faculty and students come to class whenever it suits their personal needs. Therefore, there is not a single time to communicate with a group of students. The only common point of instruction for online students is the Web.

The need for class instruction was apparent from the inauguration of Online UW, because a graduate level educational research class was offered in the first semester. The professor of this course had included a unit on developing a research topic which she asked us to critique. However, it did not cover database searching nor any information about Library Outreach Services. The immediate short-term solution was to compose an instructional memo, which was e-mailed to class members. The memo detailed Library Outreach Services, directed students to the subject appropriate databases, explained how to request materials, and how to contact a librarian for assistance. The class memo did not address the basics of database searching for two reasons. First, as graduate students we assumed they had some prior searching experience and secondly, we were concerned that an exhaustive memo would be so lengthy that students would not bother to read it.

A comprehensive online research tutorial appeared to be the logical long-term solution to group instruction for Online UW students. Given that Online UW students, other distance learners, as well as on campus students were all conducting their library research from UW

Catalog Plus, a universal online tutorial was in order. Thus we contacted the reference librarians to inquire whether they would like to collaborate in developing the tutorial. A committee of three worked in partnership to ensure that the final product would suit everyone's needs. The committee discussed: (1) the research needs of distance students versus on-campus students, (2) topics to be included, (3) whether the tutorial should be interactive, and (4) on whose server the tutorial should reside. We also looked at a variety of existing Web library research tutorials. We concluded that: (1) the research needs of distance students were the same as on campus students, (2) a generic tutorial with universal information was needed to avoid having to constantly update the information, and (3) we would use lots of examples, but not design an interactive tutorial because we were in the process of switching to a new integrated library system and to new versions of SilverPlatter and First Search. Furthermore, we determined that we wanted a tutorial that was easy to navigate, did not use frames, had a variety of entry points so students could control their learning, and used minimal text on each screen so scrolling would not be required. Contents of the tutorial include:

- UW Catalog Plus
- Database Basics
- Using Database Wrangler (a locally developed meta-database)
- Finding Books
- Finding Articles
- Finding Full-text
- Searching the Web
- Writing papers
- Online searching guides

The completed tutorial went live Spring 2000. The intent is to work with Online UW students and faculty to evaluate the effectiveness of the tutorial.

WORKING WITHIN THE LIMITATIONS OF TECHNOLOGY

While advances in communication technology have vastly improved our ability to serve distance learners, the technology is not without flaws. Authentication via proxy serving opens databases hitherto inaccessible to remote students, however it is a complicated process to initiate. Currently we encounter the following problems:

- AOL users cannot utilize proxy serving.
- Internet Explorer 4.5 for Mac cannot be configured for proxy serving.
- Some students cannot identify which browser their ISP utilizes.
- The state of Wyoming moved all public schools and community colleges to a new high-speed network with a firewall that does not take kindly to proxy serving.
- Students who successfully gained access to databases one day will contact us the next to say it is not working so connections are not entirely stable.
- Students forget the username and password they established.

The format of the Online UW virtual campus created by eCollege.com uses frames which means that the full UW Catalog Plus screen is not visible, making it necessary to scroll left and right, as well as down. The UW Catalog Plus URL is not visible on the online student's homepage and the cache does not hold a search history, making navigation problematic.

CONCLUSION

The literature and our experience confirm the benefits of establishing an ongoing cooperative relationship between the library and the institution's distance education program. Librarians need to be assertive in pursuing this relationship. They must be prepared to convince program administrators that the library has the tools, expertise, and resources to serve distance learners.

In conclusion, a comprehensive library outreach program can be used by the institution as a strong marketing tool for its distance education program. The University's "Academic Plan" noted that, "An example of an effective partnership is the partnership between the School and the University Libraries." It further states that "this partnership adds a level of quality which is often unavailable in distance learning programs, and which is equal to services anywhere in the world. It is an accomplishment of which the University should be proud, and should continue to support" (p. 9).

REFERENCES

Association of College and Research Libraries. (1998). ACRL guidelines for distance learning library services. *College &Research Library News, 59*, 689-694.

Hache, D. (1998, Summer). Strategic planning of distance education in the age of teleinformatics. *On-line Journal of Distance Learning Administration* [Online], 1 (2). Available: http://www.westga.edu/~distance/Hache12.html.

Kascus, M., & Aguilar, W. (1987). Problems and issues in providing library support to off-campus academic programs: A pilot study. In *Shaping a cohesive agenda: Next steps: Proceedings of the 7th National Conference on Adult and External Degree Programs, October 7-10, 1987, Memphis, Tennessee* (85-103). Co-sponsored by The Alliance and American Council on Education. (ERIC Document Reproduction Service No. ED 321-625).

Oregon Interinstitutional Library Council, Oregon State System of Higher Education. (1995). *A report for distance education programs* [Online]. Available: http://www.osshe.edu/dist-learn/library.htm.

Slade, A., & Kascus, M. A. (1998). An international comparison of library services for distance learning. In P. S. Thomas and M. Jones (Comps.), *The Off-Campus Library Services Conference Proceedings: Providence, RI, April 22-24, 1998* (pp. 259-297). Mount Pleasant, MI: Central Michigan University.

University of Wyoming. Office of the Vice-President for Academic Affairs. (1999, August 30). *University of Wyoming Academic Plan, 1999-2004.* [Online]. Available: http://uw-docs.uwyo.edu/theplan/UW-Plan.htm.

University of Wyoming. Office of the Vice-President for Academic Affairs. (1999). *Academic Plan: The Outreach School (School of Extended Studies and Public Service), Draft Report.* Laramie, WY: University of Wyoming.

Library Instruction for the Next Millennium: Two Web-Based Courses to Teach Distant Students Information Literacy

Kimberly B. Kelley
Gloria J. Orr
Janice Houck
Claudine SchWeber

University of Maryland, University College

SUMMARY. The library staff, in conjunction with the Graduate School of Management and Technology (GSMT) and Undergraduate Programs (UGP), developed two online courses. The first, for GSMT, was an online, fee-based, self-paced, required course for all incoming graduate students at the University of Maryland, University College (UMUC). The second, LIBS 100, was an elective, for-credit course. The process of designing, testing, and delivering the graduate course is described. In addition, a comparison of the two course design processes is briefly reviewed. Finally, the initial survey data assessing the students' perception of the value of the graduate course is also included.

KEYWORDS. Library instruction, online courses, distance education

THE UNIVERSITY AND DISTANCE EDUCATION

The University of Maryland University College (UMUC), established in 1947 as the College of Special and Continuation Studies

[Haworth co-indexing entry note]: "Library Instruction for the Next Millennium: Two Web-Based Courses to Teach Distant Students Information Literacy." Kelley, Kimberly B. et al. Co-published simultaneously in *Journal of Library Administration* (The Haworth Information Press, an imprint of The Haworth Press, Inc.) Vol. 32, No. 1/2, 2001, pp. 281-294; and: *Off-Campus Library Services* (ed: Anne Marie Casey) The Haworth Information Press, an imprint of The Haworth Press, Inc., 2001, pp. 281-294.

within the University of Maryland, became a separate university in 1970. The University now represents one of 11 degree-granting institutions of the University System of Maryland (USM). UMUC's long-standing mission remains the same throughout its history: to offer academic programs to the part-time working adult student regardless of time and place. Today's worldwide enrollment is over 70,000 students.

From the beginning, UMUC has provided access to academic programs regardless of time and place, extending programs and resources to part-time students on and off campus, stateside and around the world. The European and Asian Divisions were founded in 1949 and 1956 respectively. As technology has evolved over the last 50 years, so have the various means of course delivery. UMUC has strived to be on the cutting edge, utilizing each new technology to enhance "traditional" teaching and learning. UMUC continues to provide educational opportunities through both classroom instruction and distance technologies. In 1993, UMUC developed Tycho, a proprietary software for the online delivery of distance programs. Today 23,000 students study via this online application. Library services, too, have evolved and kept pace with the tremendous growth of UMUC's distance education programs and the accompanying technological innovations.

PROVISION OF LIBRARY RESOURCES AND SERVICES

The need for library resources and services to support academic programs was realized early on and equity of access to materials to distant students was a prime concern. In the 1950's courses would not be taught at any location unless adequate reference library materials were available. Many of the teaching sites were, and remain, military facilities. Course-related books were often placed at the military installation libraries for use by UMUC students. This option is still available at our teaching sites. During the 1960's and 1970's, in cooperation with the University of Maryland libraries, a bookmobile visited off-campus centers offering library books on loan. UMUC students could use the library at the University of Maryland College Park (UMCP) campus. By the late 1970's, UMUC had its own librarian to assist students with library-related matters. The UMUC librarian maintained two office locations, as is true today, at McKeldin Library

(UMCP), and at UMUC's location in the Center for Adult Education. Access to materials increased as new University of Maryland campuses were opened and extended library resources and services to UMUC students. UMUC students could also borrow books, obtain reference services, and use reserve materials. Because of the vast resources of the University of Maryland libraries, over nine million volumes, as well as the rich resources located in the Washington Metropolitan area, UMUC did not develop and operate its own separate library. UMUC's office of Library Services mission then, as now, is to facilitate access to library resources and services regardless of where the student is enrolled.

Instruction on how to locate and use the library resources began in the late 1970's when the UMUC librarian published a booklet to assist students in dealing with the complexities of university libraries. By the mid-1980's, the Office of Library Services offered a one-credit course, Introduction to Library Research, on the UMCP campus; traveled to teaching sites to offer in-class instruction on request; provided library sessions via interactive television; disseminated a video on how to search a library catalog; and conducted workshops on information retrieval skills in various topic areas. With technology came the online catalogs and by the late 1980's those with a PC and modem could gain remote access to the online catalog of the University System of Maryland to determine availability and location of books at the system libraries. Shortly thereafter, journal databases containing citations and abstracts became accessible through the online catalog.

EVOLUTION OF THE VIRTUAL LIBRARY

With the advent of the World Wide Web (Web), UMUC's Office of Information and Library Services quickly took advantage of the opportunities provided using this new technological tool. The Web is the gateway to UMUC's virtual library. Through the Web site at www. umuc.edu/library students can access over 60 Web databases, half of which are full-text; use e-mail, Web conferences, and Web forms to ask UMUC reference librarians for assistance or request materials through interlibrary loan; visit tutorials to learn more about library skills; view guides and bibliographies to both print and electronic resources on various topic areas; access the combined holdings of the University System of Maryland libraries and request books be delivered to a library or, if outside the state of Maryland, to a home address or place of work; and access required readings for online courses through our electronic reserves program. The full array of these resources and services, available via the Web, facilitates access to those materials that UMUCs' students studying at a distance need to successfully complete their course assignments. Access now is available whenever and wherever it is most convenient to the student. The advent of technology did not result in the need for less library staff, however, as many have suggested. Today, ILS has grown to twice the size it was in 1970 and further growth is expected as the University ventures further into online course delivery. We have found that online course delivery results in a greater need for human assistance, not less. Students seek assistance frequently and expect assistance to be readily available. Therefore, the University has responded by hiring more library staff and increasing the number of hours that librarians are available with the ultimate goal being 24/7 service for UMUC's global student population.

DEVELOPING WEB-BASED LIBRARY COURSES

Library instruction sessions were offered over the years at the request of the instructor. Depending on the faculty member, some students received bibliographic instruction (BI) while others did not. In 1993, the Academic Dean of the graduate school's introductory administrative courses, 601's, mandated that all 601 level courses must incorporate a library session into the curriculum. A schedule was established and each semester a UMUC librarian would teach a BI session in each of the 601 level courses. Most of these courses were taught on the UMCP campus or at one of our off-campus sites in Maryland. This arrangement worked well, ensuring that all new graduate students would receive library instruction during their initial coursework. However, beginning in the mid-1990's, courses were increasingly being offered in the online environment. It was no longer possible for the UMUC librarians to offer instruction to all 601 classes, only those taught locally in the classroom. Tycho allowed students to take courses anywhere in the world. The new delivery method offered the library the challenge and opportunity to meet the students' library instructional needs regardless of time and place.

The Web and development of UMUC's distance software provided the technological advances to enhance the instructional programs of the Office of Information and Library Services. Now interactive library courses could be developed to provide library skills needed for searching the new and increasingly complex Web databases. The undergraduate one-credit library skills course was converted to an online course in 1998. In early 1997, the Graduate School of Management and Technology approached our office requesting that we design a course that all graduate students, regardless of where they were located, could take and learn how to identify and use the library's online resources.

DEVELOPING UCSP 610: RESEARCH SKILLS FOR THE INFORMATION AGE

In June of 1997, the UMUC Graduate Council approved a proposal to create UCSP 610: Research Skills for the Information Age, a required, fee-based, pass/fail online course for all UMUC graduate students. It was the desire of the Graduate Council that the course be self-paced, self-assessed, and available anywhere and at any time. In order to achieve this goal, the course would have to be delivered via the Web on UMUC's proprietary software, WebTycho. Another unique requirement of the Council was that the course should not have a faculty member. In the view of the Graduate School, it would be prohibitively expensive to require all graduate students to take the course and also pay for a faculty member to teach the course. Further, the number of students taking the course would exceed 1,000 yearly and the Council was concerned that this would be too great a burden on a faculty member. Therefore, the Council asked the library staff to use the necessary technology to create a course that could deliver the course materials and test students on their learning of the course content without faculty intervention. In order to achieve this goal, the library staff realized we would need to work with the information technology (IT) staff to devise a testing program that could have students take the quizzes online, automatically record their grade for each module, allow the students to retake any or all of the quizzes in the event they failed any or all of them, and automatically submit the grade for the course once the student completed the seven modules. The specifications for the course were significant and we knew that we would have to use technology creatively to be able to create the library course to meet the Graduate School's requirements.

The Council also specified that students would be prevented from registering if they did not complete the course. Students could complete up to six credit hours before they were required to finish the course. The course specifications provided to the library staff included a time line in which the Library Services staff would have the course ready for preliminary review by the full time faculty in the Fall of 1997. The course would be updated based on feedback from the full time faculty and then reviewed by the adjunct faculty in the Spring and Summer of 1998. The course would then be delivered to graduate students in the Fall of 1998.

The Library Services staff course development team, which included Kim Kelley, Assistant Vice President, Gloria Orr, Director, Casey Grimmer, Electronic Services Librarian, and Janice Houck, Reference and Instruction Coordinator, met on June 19, 1997. During this meeting, the course development team created an outline for the course that included nine modules. Each member of the team took a few modules for initial content development. We agreed that each module would have exercises at the end that would give students the opportunity to use the resources being discussed. For example, the module on the library catalog would have exercises in searching the catalog. At the conclusion of the course, there would be a test reviewing the information presented in the modules.

We had a very short period of time in which to get the course ready, but fortunately, we were not starting from scratch. The content development for UCSP 610 grew out of several sources. Some of the modules were written just for the course, but many others came from previous publications, instruction sessions, and workshops offered through Information and Library Services (ILS).

First, we looked at the UMUC *Library Services Handbook*. The handbook was written and published by the staff at UMUC Library Services in 1995 and was a required text for all undergraduate UMUC courses. Sections taken from the handbook included the following: types of libraries, the search strategy, searching the library catalog, Boolean searching, call numbers, finding books, finding journal articles, and tips for using the library effectively. Information about using the Internet was also included in the Handbook, but by then it was out of date and discussed mainly online discussion groups (listservs), accessing library catalogs, USENET, Gophers, and only briefly mentioned the Web using Mosaic or Lynx.

After taking basic information from the handbook, we updated the content with the information currently being provided in our library instruction sessions and faculty workshops. ILS staff had already developed several sections about the Internet for a faculty workshop on searching the Internet. These sections included topics such as understanding Web addresses, using search engines, and evaluating Web sites. We were able to take these sections and turn them into portions of the online course. It was helpful that this information had already been "tested" through the faculty workshops, so we were able to refine the content based on previous feedback.

We also took information about searching Web databases from current library instruction sessions and incorporated this into a section of the course. During library instruction sessions, the librarian would point out which of the online subscription databases were recommended for doing research for that course. So for UCSP 610, we listed databases recommended for the various subject tracks in the graduate school. For example, the databases recommended for the Master of General Administration/Health Care Administration program included Health Reference Center and MEDLINE, while the students in the Master of Software Engineering program were advised to search Computer Database, INSPEC, and Microcomputer Abstracts. The exercises for that section asked students to do similar searches in two of the most popular databases: Lexis-Nexis Academic Universe and ABI/Inform.

As the team developed the modules, we shared the drafts with the other team members. In this course development, we did not work with an instructional designer or an editor. In weekly meetings, the team would gather to discuss changes to the modules. The team member responsible for that module would then incorporate the changes and everyone would review again. This procedure was followed for each of the modules, and we worked on all of the modules simultaneously in order to meet our impending deadline. We should also note that our other work, meetings, reference, instruction, and Web page development did not let up. Team members put in many extra hours to write their sections and review other modules.

The Fall 1997 version of UCSP 610 was in simple HTML format with a frame on the left side of each page giving access to the table of contents for the course, listing each of the modules. A Web conference was set up for the course so that faculty could post comments and questions.

FACULTY FEEDBACK

The feedback we received after the first version of UCSP 610 was unveiled to the full time faculty in the Fall of 1997 was significant and resulted in substantial improvements to the course. The comments of all the faculty were reviewed and then summarized by Claudine SchWeber, who was at the time the Director of Distance Learning and Instructional Technology. In general, the faculty liked the course and praised its ability to meet the varied needs of the graduate students within the content. However, they thought that there was too much focus on print resources and encouraged us to revamp the course with this in mind.

The first version of UCSP 610 included nine modules that focused on (1) copyright and plagiarism, (2) libraries, (3) call numbers, (4) catalogs and indexes, (5) library catalog, (6) finding journal articles, (7) research on the Web, (8) research process, and (9) effective use of library resources.

The faculty recommended that we switch the order of modules to begin with the module on searching the Web, and expand this into two or three modules. It was thought that this should be first, since it is the most important search skill to the GSMT and because this content was more "interesting" and less "librarianish." They further suggested that we combine the sections on the research process and the effective use of library resources into one module and place it at the end of the course.

The course development team was at first a bit incredulous that a "good" library course could be taught without starting with what most librarians considered the basics. However, we could see that we needed to take off our librarian hats for a moment and remember what was most important about the course. We realized that despite years of working in a "virtual" library environment, we were still tied to the traditional modes and functions of the library. Although it was all-important information, we could see that putting students to sleep with minutia about libraries would ultimately be detrimental to the course.

The faculty also recommended that instead of having one test at the end of the course, we incorporate shorter quizzes at the conclusion of each module. They wanted quizzes with six questions, and a pool of five different versions of each question so that the system could generate unique sets of questions for each student. This system ensured that students were not likely to get the same questions, and would therefore make it difficult to share answers. If the student failed to pass the first quiz by answering 4 out of 6 questions correctly, then he or she would take the quiz again, but they would get a new set of questions. This meant that we had to write a total of 35 questions for each module–6 questions with five different variations.

The Graduate school faculty and administrators were also very concerned that students not be able to skip over the course content and go directly to the quiz. They asked the technical developers to require that the students go through the modules and complete the exercises for each module before they could get access to the quiz.

Based on these comments, the course development team made the revisions to the course content. By the end of January 1998, the revised course was available in the same basic HTML format. Part-time faculty then reviewed the content during the Spring 1998 semester.

In the Summer of 1998, the work of putting the course into the WebTycho software began. We had fairly typical problems once this process started. The WebTycho technical developers took our ASCII text files and converted them into HTML format. In the process, there were some editorial and cosmetic changes that were needed. In addition, the course was in a completely new format, requiring bleeding-edge programming. The technology available that would make it possible to program the course so that completing the exercises would be required before being able to access the quiz for a particular module was Javascript. As the course was used in subsequent semesters, we found many browser incompatibilities as the Javascript versions conflicted. The WebTycho programmers promised that the course would be ready by a certain date. However, the date was inevitably delayed. As a result, these set backs would delay testing and ultimately, delayed the start of the trial and the course delivery in subsequent semesters. In many instances, the technical developers would be so late getting things up that the librarians working on the content would work feverishly as soon as we were given access to new versions of the course to review, check for errors, and get change requests back to the developers. As a result, we learned that a course with a significant technological component needed more lead time for changes than other courses we have delivered via the Web.

DELIVERING THE COURSE

The course went live in the Fall of 1998. It was immediately obvious that the majority of students were having no problem taking the course. However, it was also clear that the underlying technology for the course was creating significant problems for students who did not have more current versions of the browsers Netscape or Microsoft Internet Explorer (MSIE). For students using America Online (AOL), taking the course was near impossible. Students using lower end versions of these browsers experienced numerous problems with the course content. The inability of the browsers to handle Javascript caused students to have problems ranging from a completely blank screen to Javascript error messages that confused and upset them. Although we had thoroughly tested the course, it was impossible to anticipate the wide divergence in students' browsers and the resulting difficulties these caused. Before the launching of this course, the Library Services staff was not intimately familiar with every version of Netscape, AOL and the MSIE browsers. After delivering the course for a single semester, we became experts in identifying which versions of the browsers caused problems and were incompatible with the course. In an effort to meet the Graduate School's requirement to have a "facultyless" course, we utilized the latest technologies, most notably Javascript. The result was that the course could not accommodate wide divergence in browsers. In order to participate in the course, students needed later versions of their Web browser or the course was not accessible to them. This was one drawback of using new technologies. On the other hand, we do emphasize the need for students to keep up-to-date and it is one of our cross-curricular initiatives that students be computer literate. Further, we specified up front which browser we wanted students to use to complete the course. An unexpected outcome of the course is that we have been instrumental in introducing new graduate students to newer technologies and as a result, these students are better prepared to meet the Graduate School's computer requirements when they complete our course. We have also learned that Javascript is more temperamental then we thought. It is not as browser-independent as we thought it would be and it is less robust than we would like.

We also found that the volume of students accessing the course simultaneously caused difficulties initially. The technology underlying the course had difficulty processing the test results when hundreds of students were online simultaneously. As might be expected, many of the students waited until the last few weeks of the semester to complete the course, after their other courses were complete, and as a result, when they simultaneously tried to complete the quizzes, they sometimes overwhelmed the system. Students were particularly upset if their test results were lost because of the volume of use.

Once the course was launched, we immediately identified the technical problems that needed to be fixed. One lesson we learned is that the online quizzes worked much more effectively when we rewrote the program to have the students submit each quiz after they had submitted all of their answers. In the original course construction, we had the program submit each answer individually and provide a grade of pass or fail. This was unwieldy and once we altered this, the students did not experience any further difficulties taking the online quizzes. The majority of the problems we identified with the course revolved around the online testing. Once they were solved, we found that the course went fairly smoothly. As of Fall 1999, we had offered the course over three semesters, and the Javascript error remains the major technology problem students experience. Our solution is to have these students download a newer version of their browser. To date, we have not yet found a solution to this problem that works for all of the students taking the course.

The existence of technical problems resulted in two outcomes. First, we systematically fixed the problems and now have a robust, stable course delivery. Second, the existence of the technical problems was a strong motivating factor in the decision to have a faculty member, who is a UMUC librarian, monitor the course and provide students assistance with any problems they might experience with the course. The sheer volume of students taking the course requires that at least one person monitor the course to assist with problems or questions. This has been a good decision. Although there are hundreds of students taking the course, only a small percentage need assistance. The faculty member is able to assist students with their technical problems and coordinate their solutions with the IT staff. Also, having a faculty member is essential because of the nature of the course content. The course emphasizes the evaluation of Web resources and the use of

UMUC's proprietary Web databases. The databases we offer and the Web sites we use from the Internet change frequently. Therefore, there is a need for constant updating. The faculty member teaching the course is also responsible for updating the content as needed. This is necessary to ensure the Internet links are working, that the sites used are still relevant, and to ensure that new resources are included in a timely fashion. Further, we occasionally change the quizzes and the faculty member is responsible for monitoring the quiz questions and changing them as the need arises. When a librarian agrees to be the faculty member, she is paid extra for her time and effort. We do not expect full-time staff to teach a course as part of their regular duties. The librarian signs a separate contract for teaching and is paid a stipend based on her faculty rank.

EVALUATING THE COURSE

Although we thought that the course content might also cause students to comment or ask questions, we found that the students have had little to say about the content itself other than they find it extremely valuable to have this information at the beginning of their graduate school career. Students are vocal in their opinion that a required, non-credit course is an unfair burden. However, they also quickly change their opinion once they actually complete the course. We have conducted a survey of the students and have found the following about their opinions of the course. First, the majority of students surveyed (N = 222), 56.3%, report that the library course is their first online course. That is important because it means that the library course introduces students to online study. This has pros and cons. On the one hand it is a manageable course and therefore, offers a less threatening way to learn about asynchronous study. On the other hand, it means that the faculty member must deal with novice students who tend to have more technical issues than students who have already taken one or more classes in an online environment.

In addition, based on the survey results, we know that 80.7% of the respondents strongly agreed (29.3%) or agreed (51.4%) that they were better able to conduct research as a result of taking this course. Also, 81.9% of the respondents strongly agreed (39.6%) or agreed (47.3%) that the information they learned in the course will help them in their graduate work. When asked whether the exercises accompanying the course material helped students understand how to get resources from the Web, 89.2% strongly agreed (34.4%) or agreed (54.8%) that the exercises were helpful in learning about doing research for Web resources. We also asked students whether they thought the course was self-explanatory. Of a total of 98.2% of respondents who thought the course was self-explanatory, 51.4% thought it was very self-explanatory and 46.8% thought it was self-explanatory. When asked whether they liked learning in an online environment, 78.7% responded strongly agree (44.8%) or agree (33.9%) to this question. Therefore, we found a high acceptance of this mode of delivering instruction, which was unexpected.

We were also interested in learning how long it took students to complete the course. The initial results indicate 79.8% completed the course in less than 10 hours. Of those, 36% completed the course in less than five hours. As a result of these findings, we are confident that the course requirement is not too burdensome and requires a reasonable amount of time to complete.

We intend to survey the students taking the course every semester. The preliminary data are very encouraging, but we want to continue to monitor the course to improve the content and ensure students are not experiencing too many technical problems.

CONCLUSION

The library staff created an online course for the Graduate School in a very short time period. Although we were skeptical of student acceptance of a course that was fee-based, required, and non-credit, we have been pleasantly surprised at the feedback from students and the initial survey data. After the completion of UCSP 610, we completed a second course, LIBS 100, where we had an instructional designer. We found the method of course development for LIBS 100 resulted in a more polished product and gave us the chance to incorporate multimedia which was not possible with the graduate course, primarily because there was not enough time. However, LIBS 100 is an elective whereas UCSP 610 is required. Further, we were able to hire an instructional designer because the library had special grant funds for this purpose. Typically, the library has had difficulty paying for an instructional designer for course development. The fact that UCSP 610 is required has been pivotal to its success and ensures that all entering graduate students have a minimum level of knowledge of library research before they progress too far in the Graduate School. It has been an invaluable tool in reaching the graduate students and working on developing their information literacy. Further, the design of the course makes it possible to handle a tremendous volume of students without the need for constant intervention. As a result, we reach a wide audience without a heavy burden on the library staff or the faculty member. All in all, it has resulted in fuller integration of the library into the curriculum of the Graduate School and a self-contained, Web-based course that has high acceptance among the student body. The synergy between the library staff and the Graduate School, and the effort committed to testing, both before and after the course went live, were essential elements in ensuring its relevance to the Graduate School's needs and its ultimate success with the student body. The model we used at UMUC may be of use to other universities seeking a means to deliver high quality library instruction to a scattered student population who need anytime, anywhere access to their course materials, who may have limited access to a traditional library, and who need to develop skill and knowledge about online resources and services available to them through their university.

All Hands on Deck:
Navigating the Political Waters
of Off-Campus Library Programs

James J. Kopp

Lewis & Clark College

SUMMARY. Libraries are immersed in politics, from the "office politics" that take place within libraries to the "real" politics associated
with local, state, and federal jurisdictions and mandates affecting libraries. Off-campus library programs include not just those politics associated with libraries but by their very nature extend into deeper political waters that are critical to their establishment and success. This paper
examines the political shoals, currents, and rip tides associated with off-
campus library programs and suggests that awareness and involvement
are key ways to avoid running aground.

KEYWORDS. Library services, distance education, politics

INTRODUCTION (A MARITIME METAPHOR)

At the time when this paper was being proposed in early 1999, an
event took place just off the coast of Oregon that provided not just a
real focus of a study of the role of politics in a complex situation but
an opportunity for a metaphorical analysis of how politics work in a
number of situations. The event was the plight of the cargo ship, the
New Carissa, which on the night of February 4, 1999 ran aground near

[Haworth co-indexing entry note]: "All Hands on Deck: Navigating the Political Waters of Off-Campus
Library Programs." Kopp, James J. Co-published simultaneously in *Journal of Library Administration* (The
Haworth Information Press, an imprint of The Haworth Press, Inc.) Vol. 32, No. 1/2, 2001, pp. 295-308;
and: *Off-Campus Library Services* (ed: Anne Marie Casey) The Haworth Information Press, an imprint of
The Haworth Press, Inc., 2001, pp. 295-308.

Coos Bay, Oregon, creating a potential environmental disaster for the sensitive coastlands of Oregon. In the hours, days, weeks, and even months following its grounding, the *New Carissa* incident became a beacon for politics on the local, state, national, and international level as issues of not just environmental concerns came to the fore, but those elements at the core of politics became intertwined–ownership, territories, and boundaries. Who's to blame, who's in charge, and who's going to pay were just the beginning of questions and concerns that surfaced in the political waters lapping at the side of the *New Carissa*.

As the events surrounding the *New Carissa* continued–from efforts to pump the oil from the split hull of the vessel to attempts to burn the fuel oil in the massive storage tanks, from a lengthy process to pull the separated bow out to sea which resulted in a snapped tow line that sent the bow adrift where it ended up ashore at Waldport, Oregon, to a second effort to pull the bow to sea and scuttle it in international waters–the political immensity of the crisis loomed larger. Nearly a year later the stern of the *New Carissa* still is on the beach at Coos Bay after initial efforts to pull it to sea have been thwarted by bad weather, heavy seas, and an almost seemingly insurmountable obstinateness of the ill-fated ship to let loose its grip of the Oregon beach. It was not just the real politics associated with this event that inspired it as the impetus and initial focus of this paper but the metaphorical nature of the saga of the *New Carissa*. For politics, like this seemingly haunted ship, has a way of defeating efforts to overcome it and ends up on our institutional "shores" at the most inopportune time. When it was thought to have been "towed to sea," it often reappears like an unwanted, burned-out hull. Thus the ballad of the *New Carissa* (which indeed has found its way into rhyme and song) offers a fitting departure to sail into the political waters of off-campus library services.

The politics of off-campus library services, in some ways like the *New Carissa* incident, are complex in part because players from multiple jurisdictions (including international ones) are involved but also because the services offered cut through several "depths" of politics on the inter- as well as intra-institutional level. The intent here is not to suggest that off-campus library services have run aground but, on the contrary, to suggest that "all hands" be on deck to be alert and aware of the power, problems, and even potential of politics that will keep such programs from having the same fate as the *New Carissa*.

THE POLITICAL SEA
OF OFF-CAMPUS LIBRARY SERVICES

Politics, like the ocean, exists on multiple levels. As we look upon it, we see only the surface that extends as far as the horizon with waves that may become dangerous in a tempest or deadly in a typhoon. Surface politics are those that we can easily see and identify and which, like the sea, are subject to the ebb and flow of forces beyond our control. Below the ocean's surface, however, a whole different world exists and in politics too, a different world exists immediately below the surface. It is a fascinating environment but one filled with unexpected perils as well as significant opportunities. To venture into that realm you need to know, understand, and appreciate the creatures, currents, and crevasses of this environment. Throughout the ocean are uncharted, unsuspecting, and irregular phenomena that add to the mystery and danger of the undersea world. In a political sense, these are those things we might not necessarily feel are political in nature but which in a moment can whisk us away to some fathomless depth or send us off-course to be marooned like some stranded castaways. In this analysis of the political seas of off-campus library service, we will explore first these more abstract political undercurrents and then move up through the multiple layers of sub-surface politics and then reach the surface of the "real" politics.

UNDERCURRENTS

Some aspects of politics flow deep below the surface, not readily apparent but sometimes just as treacherous as more visible political hazards. Often there is not much that can be done about these elements but an awareness of their existence is important. Some of those that are particularly of note in the off-campus library services seascape are presented here.

POLITICS OF LANGUAGE

One such undercurrent is the politics of the language we use in describing the services we provide and the environment in which these services are provided. Robin Tolmach Lakoff notes in *Talking Power: The Politics of Language in Our Lives* (1990) that, "All language is political; and we all are, or have better become, politicians" (p. 2). Lakoff explains that there are special languages within different professions that serve to reinforce the powers of interrelationship within these professions and thus create an internal bond as well as an external barrier. Librarianship certainly is no exception to this as our language, comprised of acronyms, initialisms, and various idiosyncratic meanings for common words, sets us apart and creates not only linguistic "boundaries" but political ones as well. Individuals and institutions can latch on to words, phrases, or terminology with an allegiance as strong and binding as political beliefs.

Consider the term "off-campus library service" itself. Each of these words is loaded with political potency. "Off-campus," for instance, is a term tied to this conference out of tradition (and thus with some political overtones) but it is not a term found extensively in use. Even though it still adequately and accurately reflects the nature of such programs, other terms have been adopted in its place. With the change in 1998 in the Association of College and Research Libraries (ACRL) Section from Extended Campus Library Services to Distance Learning Section, a reflection of the politics of language associated with this phrase can be highlighted, not just because "distance learning" appears to be the politically "correct" term but also because a political process of sorts (within a professional organization) was involved in the name change. But what of "off-campus" and "extended campus," not to mention the debate between "distance education" and "distance learning?" There are advocates and supporters of each of these terms, many of whom will stand firmly behind their words of choice. Even the word "library" can conjure up various feelings of a political nature, ranging from the definition or description of what "library" is to whether there indeed needs to be a "library" at all in its traditional sense. Service is a word that those of us in library land are fairly clear about, but it is a word that is unclear to those outside the profession and thus potentially politically problematic. The point here is that the language of off-campus library services (or whatever you choose to call it) is fraught with political undercurrents. Be aware and cautious of the language you use in different settings. The "first impression" given is often that of the language used. It can either assist you on your way or pull you under.

POLITICS OF VIRTUALITY

Elsewhere I have addressed the politics associated with the "virtual collection" (Kopp, 1997) and, in a broader fashion, the politics of the "virtual library" (Kopp, 1999). In these analyses the multiple levels of politics are explored in dealing with the entities (real or imagined) that have been labeled "virtual," primarily because of the increased utilization and reliance on information technology for access and delivery of information and service. For the off-campus library service programs, this is a critically important aspect of such programs and some of the key aspects of the politics of virtuality as they relate to such programs will be addressed here.

"IT" POLITICS

Ever since libraries have adopted computer technology, if not before, there have been territory and ownership issues involved with control and operation of such activities. Veaner (1974) examined the "Institutional Political and Fiscal Factors in the Development of Library Automation, 1967-1971" and identified a number of issues as the basis of political tension between libraries and, as he labeled them, computer facilities. As libraries and computer facilities evolved over the next twenty-five years, and Information Technology (IT) became a more common label for "computer facilities," many of the same political issues remained. Further compounding the situation were the discussions, debates, and, in many cases, actions associated with convergence, integration, or merger of libraries and IT operations. Although cooperative and collaborative efforts appear to have been successful in many cases in the last two decades of the twentieth century, the political realities of IT and libraries continue to play a role in academic institutions. For off-campus library programs, which rely heavily on effective and efficient use of technologies, they often are at the core of such political situations. Moreover, with access from and delivery to another institution, which is often the case, the IT politics become more complex as there may be two (or more) separate IT operations in the mix. The potential for significant political parlaying in such situations is great and close and careful monitoring of the political situation is called for.

WEB POLITICS

The World Wide Web offers one of the most sophisticated and widely available tools for delivery of off-campus library services but the Web, although a great resource for all, has become a political battlefield in many academic institutions. With the visibility that the Web offers, the control of the Web presence has become a hot and often divisive political issue on many campuses. Again, off-campus library programs which already must balance the needs and demands of on-campus libraries, departments, and administrators, as well as off-campus personnel in the same categories, may feel particularly caught in a tangled Web of politics. It is an environment fraught with potential political perils and caution, care, and diplomacy (if not neutrality) are advised.

CONSORTIAL POLITICS

The resurgence of library consortia in the 1990s, largely due to the increased opportunities made available by the Internet and the World Wide Web (Potter, 1997), have been a boon to off-campus library programs in many cases. However, library consortia by their nature are very politically charged as multiple institutions are represented with the anticipated issues of ownership, control, and territory coming into play. The role of the off-campus library program of one or more of the participating institutions (or, not all that uncommon, an off-campus library program offered at one of the consortium institutions by a non-consortium school) can be a focal point for political tensions within the consortium and thus for the off-campus library program as well. Measuring the impact of such programs on consortial arrangements and services (including database licensing) is an important step in alleviating potential political hotspots.

INTRA-LIBRARY POLITICS

Although "office politics" are all around us and are dealt with on a daily basis, we tend to consider them more as necessary nuisances than anything major on the political radar. In most cases this is true, but they are included here as potential significant undercurrents because they can quickly grow in intensity and lead to some rough waters. This is particularly the base in an off-campus library program in which one or more areas of a library (for instance, public services and systems) may be more directly involved in the off-campus programs than another area (such as technical services). It bears to monitor the overall political barometer within a library (or libraries at larger institutions) as these small ripples might quickly grow into tidal waves.

THE DEPTHS OF ACADEMIC POLITICS

The most challenging and, for many librarians, uncharted waters are those associated with the broader environment in which our libraries exist, academics. Allen Veaner writing in *Academic Librarianship in a Transformational Age* (1990) makes it plain and straightforward: "The academic workplace is highly political and strongly elitist, an island of exclusivity in an openly democratic society" (p. 29). Veaner's important study (subtitled *Program, Politics, and Personnel*) presents a number of observations that highlight the difficult role of libraries and librarians in the academic political arena. At one point (p. 29) he notes, "Librarians contemplating a career in administration require a clear understanding of the political realities of academic life." Later (p. 125) he identifies one of these realities that place libraries in a difficult position: "Unfortunately, with very few exceptions, academic library administrators are virtually held incommunicado from the area where persons in the major positions exercise their political powers." Whitson, Cottam, and Van Arsdale (1991), in one of the relatively few examinations of politics in the off-campus library service arena, make similar observations in a presentation in *The Fifth Off-Campus Library Services Conference Proceedings* (even introducing their statements with the same telltale word–"Unfortunately"):

> Unfortunately, libraries too often find themselves in a corner because parent institutions establish outreach, distance education programs and then inform the libraries that library resources and services will be expected. While the vice-president may not inform us of outreach programs, we are at fault as librarians for not being more active and visible on campus. (p. 326)

Veaner, as well as Whitson et al., provides suggestions for addressing the political role librarians should play in the academic political arena and those will be discussed below. First, some of the types of issues off-campus library programs might encounter in the murky water of academic politics will be explored.

MISSION POLITICS

Although one would like to think that the mission of an institution is the guiding beacon for all programs, resource allocations, and general directions of that institution, it is remarkable to see how often a single sentence or paragraph mission can be manipulated (call it "mission spin") to meet the needs and interests of various constituencies. This can, in turn, lead to widely different camps that believe they each are tied to the mission of the institution (as they probably are, in their views) but with significantly different agendas and courses of action. For libraries in general and for off-campus library service programs specifically, it is imperative that the missions for these programs be tied consistently and directly to THE mission of the institution. That means that a clear understanding and directive from the top administrator must be in identified (and documented) and that the libraries not place an allegiance to some "faux mission" of another academic program area or department.

RESOURCE POLITICS

Clearly much of the politics in the academic environment (as in most situations) center on who gets the money and how much. Again turning to Veaner (1990) for a summation of the importance of politics in the resource allocation struggles, he notes:

> We reaffirm that the basic strategy for obtaining library resources is identical for getting any limited resource people compete for: political knowledge and political alliances. On campus, a library administrator must sense the strength and directions of the various academic forces and know which programs are in the ascendancy and which in decline. Off campus, especially in publicly funded schools, knowledge of the higher education policies and priorities of the appropriate state or provincial agency is essential. (p. 198)

Librarians have a history (and perhaps even an expectation) of not being "players" in the game of resource politics. Although there have been and continue to be strong leaders in academic libraries who strive to be involved in necessary resource politics, there often is a perception that libraries need not be at the table. Constant vigilance and persistence to be "in the game" is important. There is more to resource allocation than politics but it cannot be overlooked. As Veaner (1990) points out in his discussion of resource allocation, "The resources will go to the cleverest constituencies, to those who both make the most rational sounding arguments and play the best politics" (p. 203). This is particularly important for off-campus library service programs that can often be viewed as tangential to the already tangential aspects of the library.

CURRICULAR POLITICS

A significant aspect of Resource Politics centers on programs and courses offered, with resources being allocated to those that are deemed to meet the mission of the institution (and thus tied to Mission Politics). Curricular politics can take on many appearances, from broad issues associated with "centers of excellence" within the academic programs to nitty-gritty issues such as library materials and services for a new course. Curricular development, without question the purview of faculty in academic departments and programs, should have involvement by librarians as access to information resources and services are a critical element in course or program development (or should be). However, too often the role of the library is viewed as a rubber stamp on a new course request form. Getting involved in the curricular development process is perhaps one of the most difficult political hurdles to overcome but it is an important one. For off-campus programs where access to and delivery of information is mission critical, this is even more of an imperative.

COLLECTION POLITICS

The politics of collection development have been examined by Ferguson (1994), Kopp (1997), and others. The whole process of collection development is filled with aspects that are a feeding ground for political issues, largely because aspects of "ownership" are involved. In the depths of academic politics, the notion of ownership of the collection (or even the library) often can be a sticky issue with faculty. (If you want to test this notion, just consider cancellation projects or weeding activities!) Collection development politics in the off-campus library environment become more complex as issues of developing separate collections come into play and, as might also happen, cooperative collection development with other institutions to support the off-campus programs might be established. Kopp (1997) posits that a multi-dimensional matrix is required for addressing the politics of cooperative collection development (p. 96). It is suggested here that some additional layers of complexity are required for capturing the potential political possibilities in collection development for off-campus library programs.

ACCREDITATION POLITICS

The accreditation process increasingly has been discussed in the literature of off-campus library programs. Papers on the topic have been presented at conferences (Gilmer, 1995) and have been included in general studies of this important aspect of academic existence (Abbott, 1994). Although politics technically is verboten in a formal accreditation process, it comes into play in many levels of this activity, from the standards set by regional accreditation bodies, to selection of site visitors, to the methods of presentation being made by the institution "under fire." As off-campus programs and the library materials and services needed to support them have become increasingly visible and important in such accreditation activities, the politics of accreditation have become more evident for such programs.

STATUS POLITICS

Issues involved with promotion and tenure, continuing appointment, collective bargaining, and other aspects of the status of personnel at an institution are hotbeds for politics in the academic setting. How library personnel fall within these schemes presents even further opportunity for political factors to come into play. And when off-campus library programs are added to the mix, the complexities are likely to be compounded further. Getting promotion and tenure committees (or comparable groups) to understand and appreciate library activities in general is a Sisyphean task, but adding off-campus library service programs presents further educational and political challenges.

POLITICS AT THE SURFACE

The "real" politics at the national, state or provincial, and local levels, especially as they deal with support of libraries in those categories, is well documented in the library literature. Josey and Shearer's *Politics and the Support of Libraries* (1990) is still a very thorough examination of the widespread nature of the political arenas as they relate to libraries. For academic libraries and off-campus library service programs, the examinations of the political environments of the community college library, the private academic library, and the multitype library system are of particular note. Although these areas of politics are vast, and like the sea seem to go on endlessly, there are more clearly defined parameters and procedures in place. In the maritime metaphor, there are often channel markers, buoys, and beacons one can use to navigate safely through these waters. That does not mean that such navigation is easy and the underlying political hazards and obstacles can still create problems.

STAYING AFLOAT ON THE POLITICAL WATERS

One of the keys for smooth sailing, keeping ahead of the storms, and avoiding dangerous waters is to become familiar with the forces that present potential problems. Paying attention (and heed) to the political environment is critical to success, let along survival. We cannot ignore politics or, as Mara Niels (1990) notes, " . . . view politics as a dirty business that is nevertheless necessary in order to accomplish major initiatives like implementing new technology in the library" (p. 408). Veaner (1990) presents similar views when he notes that " . . . the librarians for whom politics is a dirty word inherit a Weltanschauung that fails to appreciate political realities" (p. 126).

Whitson et al. (1991) stress that librarians in off-campus library programs need to "speak out and be heard" (p. 326) and to become active participants in the decision-making process.

In addition to educating ourselves about the political realities as well as understanding the way politics plays out within our institutions as well as outside of it, there are more proactive efforts that can be achieved. Veaner (1990) and Whitson et al. (1991) offer some similar advice on how to become a more active and effective political player. Key to both sets of recommendations is building alliances, but to do so with an understanding of the environment and the potential for success or failure. As Veaner (1990) notes, "The well-constructed political alliance will do more to put a program into place than all the intellectual merit in the world; correspondingly, an alliance with a loser is a guarantee of failure" (p. 198). Alliances, as Whitson et al. (1991) point out, can take a variety of forms including "technological connections, institutional arrangements, operating policies with shared authority and joint responsibility, and contractual relationships" (p. 327). For alliances to be effective and appropriate, Veaner (1990) sets forth the following methods:

- Make regular, frequent, personal calls on influential department chairs and faculty members; build strong bridges.
- Quickly remove bureaucratic obstacles between the library system and its most influential users – the faculty.
- Try to keep the library neutral territory; avoid taking sides in other people's battles.
- Maintain a careful balance of library support among academic departments.
- Participate vigorously in the work of campus committees.
- Be visible and be heard at meetings of the academic senate or similar governing body.
- Get together with faculty and administrators on a social basis.
- Set up or help to organize academic events based on school and library strengths, such as lectures, readings, or concerts relating to programs and collections (p. 199-200).

Although Veaner suggested these methods primarily for on-campus situations, their importance in the off-campus environment is even more substantial and the list of individuals, departments, and programs with which to build alliances is also more substantial.

Another form of building alliances is collaboration with external groups. Whitson et al. (1991) recommend collaboration with colleagues in distant libraries, particularly of value in programs located near or servicing remote locations. Similarly, involvement in library consortia has advantages from political perspectives (keeping in mind that there will be consortial politics to address with such involvement). Professional involvement in such activities as the Off-Campus Library Services conference and the ACRL Distance Learning Section are ways to collaborate with others as well as to enhance your education on issues related to the politics involved in these matters.

None of these activities come without an impact on time, energy, and other priorities. But it should be a priority to become aware and involved in the politics of off-campus library service programs. It takes time and effort to be involved in the political process but the results are often the difference between smooth sailing or running aground.

REFERENCES

Abbott, T. E. (1994). Distance education and off-campus library services: challenges for the accreditation process and librarians. In E. D. Garten (Ed.) *The Challenge and practice of academic accreditation: A sourcebook for library administrators* (pp. 77-89). Westport, CT: Greenwood Press.

Ferguson, A. W. (1994). Collection development politics: The art of the possible. In P. Johnson and B. MacEwan (Eds.) *Collection management and development: Issues in an electronic era* (pp. 29-41). Chicago: American Library Association.

Gilmer, L. C. (1995). Accreditation of off-campus library services: comparative study of the regional accreditation agencies. In C. J. Jacob (Comp.) *The Seventh Off-Campus Library Services Conference Proceedings* (pp. 101-110). Mount Pleasant: Central Michigan University.

Josey, E. J. & Shearer, K. D. (Eds.). (1990). *Politics and the support of libraries*. New York: Neal-Schuman.

Kopp, J. J. (1997). The politics of the virtual collection. *Collection Management, 22,* 81-100.

Kopp, J. J. (1999). Running into walls in a wall-less world: The politics of the virtual library. *Advances in Library Administration and Organization, 16,* 177-194.

Lakoff, R. T. (1990). *Talking power: The politics of language in our lives*. New York: Basic Books.

Niels, M. (1990). Politics of the library of the future. *The Electronic Library, 8,* 408-411.

Potter, W. G. (1997). Recent trends in statewide academic library consortia. *Library Trends, 45,* 416-434.

Veaner, A. B. (1974). Institutional political and fiscal factors in the development of library automation, 1967-1971. *Journal of Library Automation, 12,* 51-65.

Veaner, A. B. (1990). *Academic librarianship in a transformational age: Program, politics, and personnel.* Boston: G. K. Hall & Co.

Whitson, D., Cottam, K., & Van Arsdale, W. (1991). Library outreach services: A vision of the future. In C. J. Jacob (Comp.), *The Fifth Off-Campus Library Services Conference Proceedings, Albuquerque, New Mexico, October 30-November 1, 1991* (pp. 319-335). Mount Pleasant: Central Michigan University.

New Partnerships for New Learning

Firouzeh Logan
Erin McCaffrey

DePaul University

SUMMARY. This paper describes a model program at DePaul University of partnering the Library with an academic department, specifically the School for New Learning. This department was established solely to serve the non-traditional adult student and lifelong learner. The historical background of adult education, the development of the School for New Learning, the shared goal of the Library and the department, the history and development of the partnership, the role of the library liaison, and how the partnership has changed the curriculum and library programs are discussed. Future ideas for the direction of this partnership are examined.

KEYWORDS. Adult education, library services, library liaison

In the year 2000, the idea of including inquiry in a liberal arts education curriculum is not new. However, back in 1972, the School for New Learning (SNL) at DePaul University in Chicago was among the pioneers in designing a successful program with inquiry at its center. DePaul was responding not only to reports from the Carnegie Commission on Higher Education that called for new ways to address the needs of non-traditional age students, but also to its Vincentian mission. This mission includes a call to "Vincentian personalism," or attention to the needs of individual students

University administrators were convinced that in serving adult

[Haworth co-indexing entry note]: "New Partnerships for New Learning." Logan, Firouzeh, and Erin McCaffrey. Co-published simultaneously in *Journal of Library Administration* (The Haworth Information Press, an imprint of The Haworth Press, Inc.) Vol. 32, No. 1/2, 2001, pp. 309-318; and: *Off-Campus Library Services* (ed: Anne Marie Casey) The Haworth Information Press, an imprint of The Haworth Press, Inc., 2001, pp. 309-318.

learners within DePaul's own humanistic tradition, "DePaul could advance to the forefront in higher education by being boldly experimental" (Rury & Suchar, 1998, p. 309). Howard Sulkin, from the University of Chicago, and an assistant, Marilyn Stocker, were hired and given total freedom to develop a new program (Rury & Suchar 1998). Today, the program flourishes at all six DePaul campuses and has also taken a global perspective in its approach to education. It has formed partnerships with organizations all over the world and offers classes in Hong Kong, at Allstate Insurance Company, and to steelworkers in Northwest Indiana (SNL, 1999c, p. 1). SNL offers courses with a global focus, provides for travel courses, and has served as a model for programs in South Africa. In November 1998, the Council for Adult and Experiential Learning named SNL one of six "Best Practice" institutions in the United States and Canada (SNL, 1999b).

SNL has gone from graduating two students in 1975 to 281 in 1998, and currently has 2,130 students enrolled. It seems that SNL has truly moved from "the marginality and isolation of a school that saw itself as both experimental and embattled into engagement with the larger academic community" (Rury & Suchar, 1998, p. 312). SNL has also has become a veteran center for continuing experimentation. This article examines this model program and describes how the role of the library evolved within it.

HISTORY OF ADULT EDUCATION

American concern for adult education is older than the United States. The early colonists realized that self-government would require an educated citizenry, and they also desired to expand commercially and industrially. Thomas Jefferson and others who understood how crucial adult education was to the infant nation established institutions such as the University of Virginia as early as 1819. Nonetheless, in the United States the term *adult education* did not appear in the professional vocabulary until 1920 (Knowles, 1994). As the movement matured, the vocabulary expanded to include terms such *as continuing education, non-traditional student,* and *lifelong learner.* Whatever the terminology, it is clear that in the last thirty years, adult education has moved from the periphery of the educational ethos to its center.

Universities were originally intended to preserve knowledge, but their purpose gradually shifted to cultivating morally responsible leaders. College was viewed as a way to bring "a higher tone to the public mind" (Knowles, 1994, p. 32). Today, most modern universities continue to pursue the goals of transmitting existing knowledge and cultivating future leaders. However, change is afoot. And this change is fueled by a 20th century phenomenon, namely that "the time span of cultural revolution has for the first time in history become compressed into less than the lifetime of an individual" (Knowles, 1994, p. 272). That is, generations no longer live in conditions that governed past generations. The rapid pace of social and technological change dictates that adults must engage in self-improvement for reasons that range from entertainment to survival. One result of this phenomenon is that neither the needs of the individual nor the needs of society as a whole are best served by an educational system that merely transmits knowledge. The focus of education must shift from transmitting knowledge to fostering the individual's capacity to learn. Researchers in adult education theorize that this is best achieved through a lifelong process of inquiry.

Many adult education programs have been engaged in this process for decades. However, adult education institutions have historically been attached to agencies established for other purposes and thus have held a slightly inferior status in the academic hierarchy. Now that it is increasingly clear that education must allow for the creation of new culture, teaching how to understand what is not yet known, adult education programs once ignored are being dusted off and examined, new ones developed, and some even emulated by more traditional programs. If learning is to be a lifelong adventure, then program designers must provide not only adult learners, but also young learners, with the tools to engage in this process of inquiry. "Like it or not, we live in a age when knowledge itself is continually being shaped and recast to new purposes, and research methodology–formal inquiry–is emerging as a critical body of knowledge in its own right, and constantly changing itself" (Rury, 1996, p. 187).

OVERVIEW OF THE SCHOOL FOR NEW LEARNING

The School for New Learning (SNL) at DePaul University is best described as an interdisciplinary, competence-based liberal arts college for adults age 24 years and older. This program "was one of the first university-wide efforts in the nation to address and serve the needs of the adult student" (Firestone, 1987, p. 4). The school was established in 1972 as a separate degree-granting college of DePaul University with its own dean. Then, in 1984, a master's program was designed for experienced practitioners who worked in new or rapidly changing fields or those who wanted to take existing fields of practice in new directions. To keep the school dynamic and responsive to change, the program designers mandated regular self-examination and evaluation. Moreover, early on it was recommended that classes be taught away from the traditional campuses. SNL was the first DePaul program to be offered in the Chicago suburbs.

In the early stages of adult education, both curriculum and teaching methods were borrowed from traditional schools. However, Howard Sulkin and his associates were well aware that adults were different from the youth for whom those traditional programs were designed. They designed a program to meet the needs of students who (1) usually had less time available for their studies, (2) brought more resources to the learning transaction, and (3) came to school with a clearer purpose for learning. The non-traditional curriculum recognizes that adult students bring knowledge and experience to the table. It is therefore less concerned with transmitting knowledge and more concerned with developing critical skills.

Students design their own programs with help from their advisory committee and may accelerate their progress toward a degree by using experience as well as previous course work for academic credit. Students choose the members of their Academic Committee after completing the Foundations of Adult Learning (in the undergraduate program) or Learning Plan Research and Development (in the graduate program). The student, his or her faculty mentor, and a professional advisor make up the Academic Committee. The professional advisor offers expertise and guidance in the student's field of interest. (DePaul librarians have occasionally served as professional advisors to students in SNL whose career goal was librarianship.) Students with the help of the advisor and faculty mentor proceed then to create competencies for their Individual Focus Area to fit their professional and personal goals.

Rather than earn a degree in the traditional manner of hours of credit earned, students are assessed on competency in five domains, each of which is comparable to a discipline found in a traditional liberal arts program. In light of this non-traditional program, faculty members have had to develop new approaches to teaching and advising. SNL instructors' teaching load incorporates the time spent outside the classroom advising and working individually with students. "[T]he role of the instructor is less one of providing subject matter expertise and more one of modeling effective learning behavior" (Justice, 1997, p. 32). Faculty members are seen as both role models and mentors for students.

In developing a program that would accomplish all of this, the SNL founders made certain assumptions (Firestone, 1987, p. 7):

- The School should develop the whole person, including skills and attitudes as well as knowledge.
- Student growth should be recognized in terms of competence rather than in terms of course accumulation.
- Students should be able to receive "credit" for appropriate learning gained through prior experiences, regardless of the nature or timing of those experiences.
- The School should equip adults to engage in constructive, self-directed lifelong learning.
- Students should bear the major responsibility and authority for designing and completing their own degree programs.
- The School should provide appropriate counseling and other support services so that the students may exercise their academic responsibilities fully and efficiently.
- The School should de-emphasize administrative rigidities and emphasize flexible scheduling.

FORMAL INQUIRY AND THE ROLE OF THE LIBRARY

Underlying these assumptions was the notion that adults must possess certain skills in order to survive, adapt, and advance in an ever-changing environment. The core skill in this inquiry-driven program is the ability to do formal research. "The School for New Learning has made research–labeled 'formal inquiry'–a central facet of liberal education, or as SNL puts it, a part of being an educated adult in contemporary society" (Rury, 1996, p. 188). The program's Lifelong Learning competence framework is composed of the only series of courses that is required of all students, and it is within this framework that the Library and the School for New Learning partner in teaching students a wide range of research methodology.

If inquiry or research is the "central facet" of SNL's program, then the Library also has a central role to play: providing both students and faculty the tools with which to proceed with the secondary research aspect of this inquiry. The Library and SNL have a shared goal: to provide students with skills for lifelong learning. Given the multidisciplinary and non-traditional design of the SNL program, faculty are not expected to know or even be aware of all of the resources each student needs and has access to–this is the responsibility of the librarian. Therefore, faculty members serve as advocates for librarians and library resources. The Library, in turn, tries to communicate an understanding of and commitment to the SNL program to the students.

INTEGRATING LIBRARY INSTRUCTION
AT THE SUBURBAN CAMPUSES

The Library did not become a full partner in this venture from the very beginning; it was a somewhat reluctant participant at first. The very first contact was made in 1978. A library research workbook that had been designed for traditional, first-year English composition students was made available to SNL students. For many years, this workbook sat in a three-ring binder at the reference desk. Students photocopied the exercises and were required to complete them at one of the Chicago campuses. Even though the workbook was modified over the years, it was not a convenient tool or particularly suited to the needs of adult students.

In the early 1990s, because of the SNL program, efforts were made to establish a greater library presence at the suburban campus locations. Once in place, librarians initiated contact with the instructor of each course offered at the suburbs as a public relations strategy. Suburban campus librarians simply introduced themselves to classes and offered basic library orientation. This did not quite meet student needs as perceived by the librarians. The next organized effort involved collecting syllabi from the courses offered in the suburbs to assess which involved library research and at what level. This allowed librarians to target courses that were the most logical venue for bibliographic instruction and to assist in curriculum development (Bean & Klekowski, 1993). This led to developing course-integrated bibliographic instruction.

Two courses were considered for the first tier of the undergraduate program: Foundations of Adult Learning and College Writing. Both of these courses are taken early in the undergraduate program and are part of the Lifelong Learning Area. This area "focuses on the essential skills students need to become productive adult learners" (SNL, 1999a, p. 7). Foundations of Adult Learning is required for all students. The course is taught by a full-time faculty member who becomes the student's faculty mentor throughout that student's time in the SNL program. The competence statements fulfilled in this course are, "can use one's ideas and those of others to draw meaning from experiences" and "can design learning strategies to attain personal and educational goals" (SNL, 1999a, p. 7). College Writing is not required for all students. Those who successfully complete the writing portion of the SNL proficiency exam may waive the course. An adjunct faculty member generally teaches this course. The competence statement fulfilled in this course is, "can write clearly and fluently" (SNL, 1999a, p. 7).

After several years of targeting both classes and too often teaching the same students within the same year, it was decided that Foundations of Adult Learning would be the only targeted course for the first tier of bibliographic instruction. The second tier of bibliographic instruction was designed for the Research Seminar course, a required research methods course. Students "learn to identify a set of research questions, define hypotheses, perform a critical analysis and review of existing research literature on a topic, and to outline their own proposed methodology for studying it directly" (Rury, 1996, p. 190). The competence statement fulfilled in this course is, "can pose questions and use methods of formal inquiry to answer questions and solve problems" (SNL 1999a, p. 7). Students in this course "become intimately familiar with the library (especially the periodicals) and with the protocols of various research traditions" (Rury, 1996, p. 190).

Although the classes were targeted in formal instruction planning, contact between the Library and SNL was neither routine nor organized. Because SNL is an interdisciplinary program without an identifiable subject area, it does not have a regular bibliographer or separate collection development funds. Rather, a library liaison gathers SNL faculty purchase requests and mediates with subject bibliographers to acquire the needed material. Not until 1992 did the Library develop the goal of fully integrating the Library into the SNL program. It became the priority of the liaison librarian at the time, Paula Dempsey. After a particularly successful instruction session for a Foundations class, Paula had discussions with the department about formalizing the relationship. She redesigned the workbook, creating a much more appropriate assignment that, to the delight of suburban students, could be completed at any academic library. The Library was responsible for getting the workbook published and sold through the University bookstores. Bibliographic instruction also became a regularly scheduled affair for the two targeted undergraduate classes (P. Dempsey, personal communication, November 5, 1999).

The final goal was targeting the Master of Arts program. The M.A. in Integrated Professional Studies is composed of the Focus Area, Liberal Learning seminars, and the Learning Plan Research and Development and Learning Plan Review courses. It was decided to give bibliographic instruction during the Learning Plan Research and Development course, which is the first course in the M.A. program. Here, students explore "the aims of graduate education with particular focus on the program of study leading to a Master of Arts in Integrated Professional Studies" (SNL, 1999d, p. 9).

Today, librarians provide bibliographic instruction most consistently in SNL courses. The Library targets other courses in other departments, but no other department gets the consistent attention that SNL does. The Library can offer instruction to almost 100 percent of the targeted courses. The library liaison to SNL usually teaches all of the off-campus classes and tries to teach at least one course at each suburban campus location throughout the academic year. The Suburban Reference/Instruction librarians teach the remaining courses. The partnership is becoming strong enough that the current liaison to SNL, Arlie Sims, was invited to visit Hong Kong in 1999 to provide bibliographic instruction to SNL students at the International Bank of Asia. The director of SNL's Hong Kong program thought library representation would be beneficial to the students and sought support from the deans of SNL and the College of Commerce, which also has a program in Hong Kong (A. Sims, personal communication, October 15, 1999). As a result of the trip, the Library designed a Web page specifically to meet the needs of these international students.

As technology has advanced, the workbook has once again evolved—from a physical item to an online Library Research Tutorial (LRT). The LRT was designed to offer greater flexibility for SNL students in the suburbs, in Hong Kong, or anywhere else they are taking classes. Currently, two of the six assignments must be completed in an academic library, and the remaining four assignments can be completed online. Arlie Sims participated in meetings and discussions for SNL curriculum planning in 1999, and the LRT was updated to meet SNL's new technology requirements.

Just as SNL undergoes regular evaluation, so does the Library. Once again, the Library is reassessing the LRT to make it more of an interactive research guide and to ensure that DePaul's SNL students do not burden other area academic libraries with their assignments. There is also discussion underway now to have a librarian assigned to each Foundations of Adult Learning class. Much like the faculty member is an advisor and mentor, so would the librarian be a resource for the students in that class throughout their SNL program. The classes targeted for instruction are also being evaluated to decide whether it would not be more productive to shift instruction from Foundations of Adult learning to College Writing. What is not under discussion is putting less time and energy into this partnership. The partnership between SNL and the Library has truly benefited the students, faculty, and the librarians involved.

CONCLUSION

It is often remarked that teaching an adult student is a learning experience for those doing the teaching. The teacher becomes a co-learner and a collaborator in this process of inquiry. This partnership with SNL has allowed the Library to expand its horizons and experiment with creative approaches to research. It has also provided a model for partnerships with other departments interested in preparing students for lifelong learning. Collaborative partnerships have been an integral part of the success of SNL, and the Library can learn much from their example.

The Library must make the partnership a priority and have librarians whose priority it is to further the partnership that achieves the goal. Ideally, the goal is that the university as a whole would be an educative community in which everyone is "always partly a teacher and partly a learner; highest social approval would be reserved for those activities and those persons concerned with improving the quality of human competence" (Knowles, 1994, p. 279). In reality, the goal can at least be that all the partners (students, faculty, and librarians) become facilitators and resource persons of lifelong learning.

REFERENCES

Bean, R., & Klekowski, L. M. (1993). Course syllabi: extracting their hidden potential. In C. J. Jacob (Comp.), *The Sixth Off-Campus Library Services Conference Proceedings, Kansas City, Missouri, October 6-8, 1993* (pp. 1-9). Mount Pleasant, MI: Central Michigan University.

Firestone, B. (1987). *The School for New Learning: A time tested model of the future.* Chicago: DePaul University.

Justice, D. (1997). Facilitating adult learning in a liberal education context. *Liberal Education, 83*, 28-33.

Knowles, M. S. (1994). *A history of the adult education movement in the United States.* Malabar, FL: Krieger Publishing Company.

Rury, J. L. (1996). Inquiry in the general education curriculum. *JGE: The Journal of Education, 45*(3), 175-196.

Rury, J. L., & Suchar, C. S. (Eds.). (1998). *DePaul University: Centennial essays and images.* Chicago: DePaul University.

School for New Learning. (1999a). *Bachelor of arts degree program guide.* Chicago: DePaul University.

School for New Learning. (1999b, Summer). *Common Knowledge, 11*, 1.

School for New Learning. (1999c, Fall). *Common Knowledge, 11*, 2.

School for New Learning. (1999d). *The master of arts program in integrated professional studies.* Chicago: DePaul University.

Services to Distance Learners: Planning for E-Reserves and Copyright

Susan Lowe

University of Maine System Network (UNET)

Joyce Rumery

University of Maine (Orono)

SUMMARY. This paper focuses on the outreach to over 3,000 students taking classes at over 80 locations within the State of Maine, as well as students taking classes nationally via the Web through the University of Maine System Network (UNET). The discussion will briefly note the wide range of collections and services available through the University of Maine System's digital library and the Off-Campus Library Services Office. In particular, the discussion will center on reserve services for students at remote locations, using traditional paper copies and particularly electronic reserves, and the copyright issues that surround the e-reserve service.

KEYWORDS. Library services, distance education, reserves

In November 1985, the University of Maine System Board of Trustees charged the president of the University of Maine at Augusta with the responsibility for preparing a proposal for the "development of a community college concept throughout the University of Maine System with particular attention towards policies and procedures governing access to the university for older, part-time and commuter stu-

[Haworth co-indexing entry note]: "Services to Distance Learners: Planning for E-Reserves and Copyright." Lowe, Susan, and Joyce Rumery. Co-published simultaneously in *Journal of Library Administration* (The Haworth Information Press, an imprint of The Haworth Press, Inc.) Vol. 32, No. 1/2, 2001, pp. 319-330; and: *Off-Campus Library Services* (ed: Anne Marie Casey) The Haworth Information Press, an imprint of The Haworth Press, Inc., 2001, pp. 319-330.

dents" (University of Maine System Board of Trustees, 1981). One of the committees formed as a result of that charge was the Task Force for Off-Campus Library Services. The task force prepared the planning document which formed the basis of the current service.

The Task Force early on recognized the need for a librarian to handle the operation of the Off-Campus Library Services program and to provide all library services to students, faculty, and staff of the program. This individual would be responsible for setting up the services, maintaining the contact with other campuses, maintaining contact with the local libraries involved, and providing instruction in the use of the services developed for the distance student as well as bibliographic instruction sessions (Task Force for Off-Campus Library Services of the Community College of Maine, 1987). The off-campus librarian was hired in 1989 to implement the program.

UNIVERSITY OF MAINE SYSTEM NETWORK (UNET)

As the Community College matured, it moved from being administered by a single campus within the University of Maine System to being governed by the Chancellor's office and having its mission broaden to include a wider variety of technologies for the delivery of distance courses. With the transition from a single campus administration to a system administration have come name changes which include the Education Network of Maine (ENM) to the current University of Maine System Network for Education and Technology Services (UNET).

UNET is the organizational umbrella under which the distance classes take place. Formed with the merger of the University System's Computing and Data Process Services (CAPS) and distance learning technologies and services (Education Network of Maine), UNET provides the University of Maine System community with a single point of service for current and emerging information technology and support for distributed learning. UNET provides statewide access to college courses and degree programs through interactive television, video and computer conferencing and the World Wide Web. Students can participate in classes from home or at more than 100 sites statewide. Nine regional university centers offer a range of support services, including skills workshops, career counseling and advising.

Approximately 3,000 students of every age and from every region of the state enroll in distance learning courses and programs, but women who live in Maine's rural communities make greatest use of the Network's services. Surveys of students show that the majority are over the age of 30 (60 percent), female (74 percent), and typically travel a distance of 10 miles to the ITV classroom, compared with the 31 miles it would have taken to commute to the nearest University campus.

Interactive television is the primary medium of course delivery, but courses also are delivered via the World Wide Web, computer conferencing, videotapes, and other technology. Computer conferencing and the Web allow students and faculty to correspond regardless of time and distance. Audio conferencing brings guests from anywhere in the world into the college classroom. Voice mail, fax notes, and electronic mail all help to expand the diversity and range of communication available to students. Students may choose from 22 degree and certificate programs at the associate, bachelor and master's levels and more than 130 courses each semester (http://www.unet.maine.edu).

MARINER (HTTP://LIBRARIES.MAINE.EDU)

Students at the University campuses, at all off-campus Centers and Sites, or from home via the Web have access to Mariner (Maine Academic and Research Initiative for Electronic Resources), the University's gateway to electronic information on the global network. Mariner provides the access to URSUS, the UMS online catalog, to periodical literature, to electronic journals, to the Virtual Reference Shelf, to subject guides, to special collections, to other libraries' catalogs, and to electronic reserves. It also provides access to resources to assist users such as Web search engines, subject trees, courseware, Usenet, ftp and software, and to meta-search engines. This networked information is created and maintained by librarians at the seven campuses of the University of Maine System Libraries and its affiliated libraries.

Mariner allows the off-campus student to locate and use the same resources as a resident student at any of the campuses and provides access to those local and remote databases required by specific courses. In addition, the students may have access to subject guides or course guides specific to their field of study. Since licensing restrictions apply to some of the commercially produced indexes and databases, some of those resources are available only to students registered at a particular campus. To allow access to these resources, if the patron is connecting from an off-campus location, they may be required to enter their name and library card ID number in order to use these resources.

Reference, interlibrary loan and document delivery services for extended campus students are provided through the Off-Campus Library Services office.

URSUS

The primary online resource residing in Mariner is URSUS (University Resources Serving Users State-Wide), the shared catalog of the participating Mariner libraries including the University of Maine System libraries, the Maine State Library, Bangor Public Library, and the Law and Legislative Reference Library. URSUS indexes the majority of the print and non-print materials for the libraries, including books, serials, microforms, sound recordings, maps, government documents, and other audiovisual formats. The combined collections total over one million bibliographic records and over two million volumes. In addition to a bibliographic description of each item, URSUS provides location and status information. This is a valuable resource for the distance learner since most of the books and documents can be requested electronically online with a valid library card and those items can be delivered to their local campus, Center or Site. All of the libraries except the Bangor Public Library participate in this electronic request function.

The URSUS catalogue also provides the access to both the paper and electronic reserves collections for classes taught from any of the University of Maine System campuses.

OFF-CAMPUS PRINT RESERVE COLLECTIONS

The general purpose of a reserve is to ensure availability for all users of limited copies of material that are required reading for a course, material that is in great demand, or requires the availability of hours provided by the library. Reserve requests are generated by faculty to give all of their students in a class access to required readings to supplement the lectures and the textbook. For the courses offered through UNET, the reserve collection is considered a temporary collection supporting those courses.

In 1989, from the start of the off-campus library services (OCLS) program, reserve materials to support distance education courses presented unique problems for off-campus library services staff. Funding was available from the off-campus library services budget to actually purchase multiple copies for faculty of reserve materials (books monographs, reprints) or to pay any copyright costs for the multiple copies needed to be placed at Centers and Sites. It was the reserve process itself that proved to be most difficult to manage. The OCLS office had to have a timely list from faculty of the reserve material needed for their classes, estimate the number of copies needed so that the material could be ordered and received in time for the beginning of the semester, determine the locations where students would be participating in the course, and catalogue and check out the material to the appropriate Center/Site in time for the beginning of the semester. At that time, thirty copies (30) usually were sufficient to cover the number of reserve items needed for a particular class.

Providing reserve material on a multiple site basis quickly became a very expensive item in the budget and a logistical and bookkeeping nightmare. In some instances, more copies were needed than had been ordered and had to be rush ordered; in others, too many copies were ordered and the extras had to be returned. In some cases, the class was canceled and all items had to be returned to the distributor.

It was found that students rarely used the reserve readings provided or that items were borrowed and never returned. The staff time for ordering, the expense of the materials, and the loss and difficulty in tracking materials all proved to be determining factors to rethink the whole reserve process.

Currently, if a faculty member wants a copy of a book on reserve, he/she must provide sufficient copies to the OCLS reserve librarian in time for distribution to Centers and Sites. Copies of articles or chapters from books are copyright cleared using the Copyright Clearance Center and distributed from the OCLS office. There is a set limit on the number of pages that are copied without expense for faculty members for a course. Typically, in an academic year, print reserves are distributed for approximately forty (40) courses.

Print reserves still present logistical problems, so alternative options, especially e-reserves, were seen as a viable option. On-campus, as well as off-campus, faculty were asking for the ability to use digital materials in support of their coursework and looked to the library system for leadership in this area.

SYSTEM-WIDE DIGITAL LIBRARY COMMITTEE

Campus librarians had already begun work on providing access to digital information and understood the need to take the library beyond the physical walls and to make materials available when the libraries were closed. The response to the need for electronic access to the reserve collection was recognized as another service that would add significantly to the digital library. The University of Maine System libraries felt that in order to provide an e-reserve system, adequate safeguards and policies needed to be in place to ensure that copyright laws and national guidelines were followed. The Library System also wanted assurances that access restrictions were put in place to limit uncontrolled copying and dissemination of copyrighted material.

As a result of discussions in late February of 1998, the Library Directors requested that a system-wide Digital Library Committee be developed to guide the development of a digital library for the University of Maine System libraries. The Digital Library Committee, with recommendations from the Library Directors and the System Librarian, developed several task forces to work on various aspects of the digital library. Those pertinent to this discussion would be the Copyright Task Force and the Electronic Reserves Task Force.

COPYRIGHT TASK FORCE
AND ELECTRONIC RESERVES TASK FORCE

It is difficult to discuss one task force without the other since both of their missions were so intertwined. The implementation of a system-wide electronic reserves system relied on a copyright statement endorsed by University and Library administrations; the copyright statement depended on a clear understanding of electronic reserves in a digital environment and the Digital Millennium Copyright Act

(DMCA) as it pertained to distant education. The charges for both task forces are outlined below.

The Copyright Task Force's charge was "to recommend to the University of Maine System a copyright statement, guidelines, and associated Web documents for publication on Mariner." In addition, the Task Force was to "monitor national copyright legislation and recommend revisions to the Mariner Web as appropriate" (University of Maine System Libraries, 1998).

The Electronic Reserves Task Force's charge was "to implement and maintain an electronic reserves system for the University of Maine System libraries." The task force was "to design a system that provides easy, direct creation of documents for faculty, and provides easy, direct access to electronic documents for students" (University of Maine System Libraries, 1998).

Membership on these two task forces consisted of the off-campus librarian and staff from access services and circulation drawn from four of the seven campuses. Discussions centered on both of the issues in the charges: electronic reserves and copyright.

Before the first face-to-face meeting, task force members independently investigated online resources and Web sites which dealt with both copyright and electronic reserves to find models which would provide both copyright statements and guidelines for managing electronic reserve systems. They found that there is much information available with an especially helpful Web site at Columbia University, "Electronic Reserves Clearinghouse: Links and Materials on the Web" (http://www.columbia.edu/~rosedale/) that compiles links on copyright and e-reserves. Before any definitive set of guidelines could be drafted, the task force realized that it needed answers to some very specific questions:

- Would the library offer both print and electronic versions for reserve?
- What types of material would be entered into the e-reserve collection?
- journal articles
- book chapters
- photographs/slides
- movie clips
- sound clips

- instructors' sample tests
- instructors' course notes
- instructors' exercises/problem sets
- instructors' syllabi
- Was it possible (according to licensing agreements) to place a full-text article from one of our databases or e-journals on e-reserve?
- Would an item be posted pending copyright clearance?
- Who would obtain the rights for copyrighted material–the library or the faculty member?
- Who would pay for the rights for copyright material–the library or campus department?
- How would the copyright notice and additional language against further electronic distribution be displayed?
- What new equipment and training would be needed for the e-reserves service?
- What changes were needed in staffing?
- What format of the e-reserve document would provide seamless, faster delivery with high quality output?
- How would we limit access to the e-reserves–at the class level, the individual student level, or at the document level?
- How would off-campus students be notified of a class e-reserve?
- How would usage be tracked?
  - per document use?
  - by discipline or subject area?
  - for copyright-protected documents?
  - a combination of the above?
- What would be the process for payment of copyright charges?

The library directors and other library staff system-wide provided input on the questions posed by the task force. With input from staff, the task force made recommendations for streamlining and focusing the e-reserves process and procedures. Also, the library system was able to develop standards of practice for dealing with copyrighted material in the electronic reserve system and reduce concern about the legal implications of the system. The resulting recommendations and revisions were as follows:

- Revise the Mariner page on electronic reserves procedures to meet the requirements of the different campus libraries,

- rather than develop system-wide procedures for tracking the use of copyright material and its associated paperwork, it is best left to the local campuses to develop procedures to verify that copyright was obtained and to track paperwork,
- faculty would obtain copyright and pay the associated costs for material not falling under the fair use guidelines for electronic reserves systems as defined by ALA,
- the library would provide faculty with templates and publisher information for obtaining copyright clearance,
- the library would offer faculty the option of linking to the library's e-reserve from their course homepage or linking to the course homepage from e-reserves,
- agreed on a short electronic copyright statement for e-reserve documents,
- developed a draft copyright policy for the library system which is pending approval from University legal counsel,
- agreed on system-wide guidelines for the e-reserves system, and
- provided opportunities for librarians in the System to attend workshops and training on the DMCA and copyright.

ELECTRONIC RESERVES

The resulting e-reserves service provides online access to course materials for both on-campus and off-campus students. The University of Maine System Libraries make selected course reserve materials available for students to read at any time, from any location through URSUS via the Web. Students may access electronic reserves that are in Portable Document Format (PDF) with the proper software (Adobe Acrobat Reader) and a computer connected to the University of Maine System network or to another service provider. Some documents may be in html format and require a Web browser for viewing.

URSUS lists all material on reserve and also indicates those items that are available in electronic format. Using URSUS, faculty and students are able to access a centralized source to read their reserve materials from remote locations. Patrons can access the reserves by course number, course name, or instructor. It also lists reserves by title and gives the circulation status of those on traditional reserve, lists those items that are on e-reserve, and gives the notation of "electronic access" to those items. If working from a browser, the student can click on the item and the document will load. Reserve requests from faculty are submitted using the on-line form, by mail, or in person.

Even though the groundwork had been laid for the e-reserves system, this did not mean that the actual implementation of the e-reserves system went smoothly. We did encounter problems.

- Copyright clearance requires sufficient lead-time so that material would be cleared before the semester starts. Often, this was overlooked.
- Publishers were slow to grant or refused to grant clearance for e-reserves.
- The associated copyright costs for electronic reserves were often prohibitive.
- Faculty were reluctant to obtain their own clearances.
- Some departments could not afford to pay the copyright costs associated with electronic reserves.
- Librarians found that lengthy material had to be broken into smaller parts so that the document would load more quickly for users, but made retrieval confusing.
- The system required Adobe Acrobat Reader for viewing documents. Therefore, students working from home or at off-campus Centers or Sites had to download Adobe before viewing the documents. Many were uncomfortable with the downloading process via their modems, not only because of the time it took, but also their own level of knowledge about the downloading process was at times minimal. (The use of html formats as another option for e-reserves is being explored and may offer some solutions to the off-campus students in particular.)
- Remote students with modem access especially had problems with the load time for the document itself. Those using low-end technology were forced to travel to regional University Centers or a campus for faster access.

Librarians found that access through the Online Public Access Catalog (OPAC) was awkward for staff and student retrieval. Librarians found that the students were sometimes confused about the multiple clicking required to get to the document; there was also some confusion about the use of Adobe, particularly concerning the printing of the document; the slowness of retrieval from off-campus; and the break-up of longer documents.

- The current e-reserves system in use does not generate status reports.

The library system has observed a recent trend in reserve usage. Many faculty both in their on-campus courses as well as off-campus are circumventing using the library's e-reserve services. Those with course homepages or using course presentation software are using this technology to link students directly to readings required for the course. Faculty find that using course presentation software allows students to maneuver through screens with which they are familiar, they do not have to leave the environment where they are working, and many times documents can be viewed in html format with a browser rather than pdf which uses Adobe reader.

CONCLUSION

The work of both task forces was essential since it increased the level of awareness and understanding about electronic reserves and copyright at the eleven libraries of the UMS. Since the e-reserves were a new venture for us, we wanted to understand all of the implications related to the production and product. Copyright had to be addressed from the beginning of the project and in the context of the ongoing paper reserves. The DMCA did not address the electronic reserves issue and we continue to rely on fair use, but copyright is a topic that is ignored at the peril of the library and its parent organization.

E-reserves must be constantly reevaluated and every effort must be taken to respond to the changes in technology and to the needs of the faculty and students. Attempting to make the retrieval work for everyone, no matter what their hardware, is unreasonable (we cannot work towards the lowest common denominator electronically), but looking for the best means to get the resources to the off-campus student remains the highest priority.

E-reserves also need to be strongly promoted to the administration and faculty of the University System. Those faculty who are currently scanning their own materials into pdf or html format may be unaware of the reserve services offered by the campus libraries and would willingly turn that process over to the library staff or would like the additional access point from URSUS.

Although we have accomplished much, we also need to continue to explore the ways to make e-reserves more easily used by both faculty and staff. We need to check for ways to use authentication for the individual courses, explore better modes of scanning and retrieval, and continue searching for software answers to our questions. We also need to have statistics that will give us information about the use of the e-reserves so we can make informed decisions about the current use and our future direction. Although the work is not finished, we feel that the achievement of the goal of a process and procedure to provide electronic access to reserves has been accomplished.

We were anticipating that the questions regarding distance education, electronic resources, and the DMCA would have been addressed and answered by the legislature by this point. We were only able to go so far in providing information to the libraries in the system and University faculty since it is not addressed in the law. The next step will be to see what the legislature requires pertaining to distance education and electronic resources and then work on responding to those requirements.

REFERENCES

Task Force for Off-Campus Library Services of the Community College of Maine. (1987). *Preliminary report.* Augusta, ME: University of Maine at Augusta.

University of Maine System Board of Trustees. (1981). *Report of the Community College Study Committee.* Unpublished manuscript, University of Maine System.

University of Maine System Libraries. (1998). *Electronic reserves task force charge and copyright taskforce charge.* Unpublished manuscript, Orono, ME: University of Maine.

Doctoral Dissertations at a Distance: A Novel Approach from Downunder

Peter Macauley
Anthony K. Cavanagh

Deakin University Library, Australia

SUMMARY. The model suggests that librarians can assume the role of co-supervisor to ensure that the literature review of a doctoral dissertation is comprehensive and relevant. Librarians can also assist research students, make sure their supervisors are kept abreast of new information resources in their research disciplines, and act as a mentor to both student and staff member in library matters. The model was developed in recognition of the special support needs of off campus research students who are disadvantaged by isolation, time and distance. It is anticipated that adoption of the model will lead to increased rates of completion, higher standards of research, an improvement in information and literacy skills of research students and supervisors, and reduced isolation for off campus researchers.

KEYWORDS. Distance education, library services, doctoral students, doctoral dissertations

INTRODUCTION

Providing proactive library support to students and academic staff is a major priority for Deakin University Library. The cornerstone of this service is the Library's existing liaison program in which individual liaison librarians are designated as a contact point for Deakin Univer-

[Haworth co-indexing entry note]: "Doctoral Dissertations at a Distance: A Novel Approach from Downunder." Macauley, Peter, and Anthony K. Cavanagh. Co-published simultaneously in *Journal of Library Administration* (The Haworth Information Press, an imprint of The Haworth Press, Inc.) Vol. 32, No. 1/2, 2001, pp. 331-346; and: *Off-Campus Library Services* (ed: Anne Marie Casey) The Haworth Information Press, an imprint of The Haworth Press, Inc., 2001, pp. 331-346.

sity students and staff. The liaison focus for academic staff and higher degree (doctoral or research) students is based on developing a one-to-one relationship in which individual needs can be met at the time of need. Developing this relationship is not always easy with research students who may be isolated as a result of their part-time or off campus status. In addition, these students must come to terms with a proliferation of new electronic resources and services. This paper describes an enhanced model for aligning the liaison program with the strategic initiative of Deakin University to attract and retain doctoral students, and places an emphasis on the special needs of the off campus research student. The new model is based on extending the role of the liaison librarian to be a partner in collaboration between doctoral student, academic supervisor, and librarian.

THE CHALLENGES OF INFORMATION LITERACY FOR RESEARCH STUDENTS IN THE ELECTRONIC AGE

Scholarly communication has certainly changed in the 1990s and, in many ways, the 1990s appear to have been the decade of "do it yourself" or "self service." Consistent with this trend, end-user searching of bibliographic databases has increased significantly. End-user searching refers to the direct access to databases by researchers in contrast to the mediated searching normally carried out by a librarian or information specialist. Among information workers the term "dis-intermediation" is used to describe the diminishing role of the inter-mediary associated with the electronic information environment (Edwards, Day & Walton, 1996, p. 357). Access to online public access catalogues (OPACS) from desktops also became possible and then commonplace in the last decade. This enabled researchers to check from the convenience of their desk, laboratory or home, their own library's holdings and in some cases, to electronically order materials to be sent directly to them. It also allowed an interface to hundreds of library catalogues globally. This electronic browsing could enable serendipitous discoveries to be made and represents a source of intellectual empowerment for online researchers. The 1990s brought networked full-text databases; making not just abstracts but whole journal articles available to the desktops of researchers. This has been a boon to all students and academics with appropriate access, but especially for research students studying off campus. Access to copies of papers within seconds of their being published electronically has sig-nificantly enhanced the usefulness of end-user searching. This has dramatically changed the way in which bibliographic searching is carried out as librarians rarely undertake searches for researchers. This has a number of implications for information literacy training.

The superimposing of the World Wide Web on scholarly commu-nication places a heavy emphasis on the need for users to develop information skills from the earliest stages of their research. This is especially so as the Internet is a huge and unstructured mass of infor-mation (Small, 1997, p. 41) and even the most unsophisticated search can often yield an abundance of apparent riches. As the proliferation of information continues unabated, researchers will, even more, re-quire access to relevant information and will need to know how to do this themselves. It is in this important aspect of information literacy that librarians can assist both research students and their supervisors.

THE OFF CAMPUS RESEARCH STUDENT–
WHO ARE THEY AND WHAT CHALLENGES DO THEY FACE?

Possibly because external doctorates are only a relatively recent phenomenon in Australia, there is almost no discussion in the litera-ture of the library needs and requirements of such students. Indeed, as Pearson and Ford noted in their important study, *Open and Flexible PhD Study and Research* (Pearson and Ford, 1997, p. 2), "The litera-ture on flexible or distance learning at the Ph.D. level is sparse and recent in Australia." Much of the earlier discussions on alternative means of delivery of postgraduate education has focused on postgrad-uate coursework and the special (and different) needs of the research doctoral student was hardly considered until the pioneering work of Evans (1995), later developed in Evans and Green (1995), Evans and Pearson (1999) and in the study *Open and Flexible PhD Study and Research* (Pearson and Ford, 1997). Evans and co-workers placed emphasis on the critically important role of the supervisor in the suc-cessful management of these students and the newly emerging "pro-fessional doctorate" students but also stressed that entrenched institu-tional attitudes and practices needed to change. Evans and Pearson (1999, p. 191) describe the situation thus:

> . . . a fundamental aspect of future postgraduate research in Australia rests on research students who complete their work in

"flexible" or "mixed-mode" study . . . . We would suggest that there will need to be some important policy and planning initiatives to create the best possible conditions to ensure that the research conducted is of high quality and addresses the relevant scholarly, professional and national needs. Especially, this will require a greater understanding of the diversity of the research student's needs, interests and contexts spanning a broader range of social, economic and geographical circumstances. . . . In the future, there will be proportionally fewer "young" students prepared to commit themselves to full-time study/research . . . . University staff will find themselves dealing with someone as old or older than themselves, who juggle work and family commitments alongside their research, and may well earn more than their supervisors.[1]

The shift in perspective required of supervisors and universities (libraries, computer centres, research office, etc.) is quite significant and means dealing with students more as colleagues or partners than as juniors or "students."

From this analysis, it may be seen that the off campus research student is typical in some ways to the off campus undergraduate–they tend to be older than their on campus fellows and they are juggling the conflicting requirements of work, family, and study. But, less typically, they are often professional people with many years of experience and accumulated knowledge who are returning to study. As established and motivated professionals, they are seeking "greater flexibility in the conditions of learning and researching" (Evans, 1995). They may well prefer to study at home or their workplace may be the site of their research. In either case, they still require supervision and access to the facilities of the institution–the library and the culture of an intellectual community.

A discussion of the issue of the "quality" of research degrees completed off campus is beyond the scope of this paper. However, given the caliber of many of the professional applicants and the fact that sixteen of the thirty-six Australian universities accept external doctoral candidates and all have provision for part-time enrollment (Pearson and Ford, 1999, p. 20), there is little reason to expect that doctoral qualifications gained externally are in any way inferior to those gained on campus. The Library within the student's home institution will thus still be expected to support the student, but given the more demanding needs of research students, there are special additional considerations that may not apply in the case of library support for undergraduates. These include the following:

- The need for interlibrary loans (Cavanagh and Lingham, 1994).
- The generally much higher cost for the library to support research students (Cavanagh and Tucker, 1993).
- A much greater reliance by these students on computer and information technology for contact with their supervisor, the library, and for conducting much of their own research.
- The "gap" in their knowledge of new library computer systems and services–Web-based catalogues and online bibliographic and full-text databases, for example.
- Lack of access to much of the specialized software that is required for doctoral studies and access to University networks.
- The difficulty of training /teaching them to use these services if they rarely come on campus.
- Their lack of access to the informal networks which operate in the on campus situation and which are often an important source of information on resources and privileges available.
- Their mobility if they are involved with fieldwork and the potential difficulties this poses for the library with delivery of resources.

In this paper, we will concentrate on just a few of these issues and discuss the development of a strategy to enhance library support research or doctoral students and their academic supervisors. It stresses collaboration between library staff, the student, and the supervisor to try to ensure that both student and supervisor are aware of library resources and know how to use them efficiently. It also establishes a library "contact" who can act as a mentor or adviser to the student, in much the same way suggested by Evans for their supervisor. A pilot study has been established to implement and evaluate the effectiveness of this program.

ELECTRONIC RESOURCES–TRAPS FOR THE UNWARY

Some researchers, especially inexperienced ones, can fall into a common trap explained by Manoff (1996, p. 221): "Many users believe that if they have searched an electronic index they have searched the entire world of information. If it's not in the computer, they assume that it must not exist." This view is echoed by Herrington (1998, p. 383) who commented that "library users attribute much authority to information obtained from a computer; if it was created on a computer, exists in a computer, or came out of a computer, some will view it as more valid, up-to-date, and credible than a print format." Reinforcing this argument, Simpson (1998, p. 8) says:

> People who extract *some* useful bibliographic entries from a database may easily be able to persuade themselves that they have exhausted the resources of the available universe. If this point has relevance to use of the computerized library catalog, it must be even more germane to the vastness of the Internet, where even the most inept of searches usually produces an embarrassment of riches.

This has implications for information literacy. Firstly, often only mainstream literature is generally accessible from electronic databases. Secondly, whilst technology can produce greater access to information, especially for students at a distance, it can also restrict access to relevant information. That is, with the trend toward large multi-disciplinary commercial database producers, if something does not make money such as some "fringe" material, it does not get published (Manoff, 1997, n.p.). Put another way, you cannot get virtually everything via the virtual library, and if you do not pay, you get virtually nothing. Specialist knowledge of marginal literature is crucial for research students, and librarians are well placed to assist users to locate it. The attractiveness of the virtual library, especially for off campus students, and the ease with which *some* information can be obtained places an unrealistic over-confidence in what may be delivered. Disintermediation can actually be a disservice to virtual library users. It lacks the human interaction and spontaneity of a real conversion or reference interview with an information professional and discourages users from seeking professional advice.

DEVELOPING COMPETENCIES
FOR INFORMATION SKILLS DEVELOPMENT

Coinciding with the massive changes in technology and growth in information in the past decade are the changing demographic characteristics of the candidates, who are often returning to university and may be accustomed only to traditional information seeking techniques. Even those who are professionals and are researching in their field of work may not be familiar with many of the tools available and may not have updated themselves on the latest electronic services. Both Alire (1984) and Fabiano (1996) have discussed the difficulties facing doctoral students and concluded that their return to study often reveals substantial gaps in their knowledge of information gathering procedures, which is exacerbated by the new electronic technologies. As many as one half of the students in Alire's sample recognised this deficiency while Fabiano (1996, p. 167) found clear evidence that the methods and resources used by students in conducting research reflected inadequate information skills. Nor is their plight helped by the frequent observation that supervisors *assume* that their graduate students have mastered the art of using the library and its services and rarely consider that it is one of their responsibilities to ensure that their students are given the necessary assistance and instruction in information searching and retrieval (Dreifuss, 1981; Madland, 1985; Behrens, 1993; Cavanagh, 1994). Reluctance to ask for assistance and the absence of traditional information networks available to on campus students also compound the problems for the new off campus student.

Librarians know that many academics do not use anywhere near the number of information services available to them, nor do they all have the necessary skills or techniques to use those resources. It can thus be argued there is also a skills gap between the academic's perceived library skills and the academic's library skills observed by librarians. Interviews with academic staff and supervisors on their library knowledge frequently reveals that while they know sources, they are often relatively inarticulate when asked about specific information (Zaporozhetz 1987, p. 54; Behrens, 1993). In reality, supervisors often lack the necessary information skills and this bears out Bruce's findings that "whilst exhortations to students and supervisors focus on the importance of reviewing the literature in research, in practice, candidates appear to receive little assistance from their supervisors." She further states, "research candidates, apart from the assistance they receive from their library, fend for themselves" (Bruce 1991, p. 103). The comments of Bruce have been backed up by Macauley's study on distance education research students. He found only 26 percent of respondents were given any guidance on how to carry out a research project as an off-campus student from their supervisor when they began their thesis (Macauley 1997, p. 191).

A partial reason for the apparent inability of at least some supervisors to help their students make better use of available resources is the complexity of the modern electronic technology. Barry (1997, p. 227) explains: "the skills required of an academic in an electronic age appear to be of a different magnitude from those that were required in a wholly traditional information age . . . . As we continue to make the transition from a traditional to an electronic age, the need for information skills intensifies." Later in the same paper, Barry (1997, p. 236) goes on to say, "we cannot expect academics to train new researchers in skills they have not yet achieved themselves." Supervisors tend to pass on their own library techniques to their students, techniques they have often learned from their own supervisors, sometimes many years ago. The passing down of old skills and outmoded techniques by supervisors, according to Delamont, Parry and Atkinson (1997) is what is called "pedagogic continuity." They argue that pedagogic continuity "is a key to understanding the intergenerational transmission of knowledge and skills" (Delamont, Parry & Atkinson, 1997, n.p.). Of course, pedagogic continuity is not always a negative concept; supervisors can pass on their positive traits as well and it must be stated that many academic staff are highly competent users of the new technologies.

The lack of guidance given has implications for others, including library staff who must then fill in some of the gaps left by the lack of consultation by supervisors. These above observations support the contention that the research student population is often ill prepared to conduct advanced library or information research and may require assistance additional to that which is currently being provided by supervisors.

A STRATEGY TO ENHANCE THE INFORMATION LITERACY SKILLS OF RESEARCH STUDENTS AND THEIR SUPERVISORS– THE DEAKIN UNIVERSITY PILOT STUDY

The above brief review of the literature reveals that both supervisors and their students may be able to benefit from a library initiative developed at Deakin University. It proposes that an experienced librarian be allocated to a "supervisory team" early in the student's candidature. This three-way collaboration between candidate, supervisor, and librarian enables the librarian to become a "partner" in the work and places them in a position to be a "mentor" or guide to both the student and the supervisor. The scheme is seen as a way of improving information literacy by formally collaborating with researchers and information professionals, and endeavours to assist researchers with their methods of scholarly communication in a period of rapid information growth (Macauley & McKnight, 1998). Research candidates probably have the greatest information requirements of all students; consequently they have the greatest need for information literacy skills. A prime example is that of the review of relevant literature which is nearly always a standard chapter of a thesis or dissertation, although the necessity of its being a "single chapter" at the beginning of a thesis is often highly unpopular with students (Phillips 1996, p. 200). The preparation of the literature review often causes considerable anguish, especially as it is supposed to be undertaken very early in a student's candidature when they are often still finding their way and are unsure of research procedures.

By introducing this model, we hope to achieve:

- More and faster doctoral completions as students are receiving expert assistance at the literature review phase.
- Higher standards of research as background research will be comprehensive and new developments can be monitored while the thesis is being prepared
- Research students and academic supervisors with well-developed information literacy skills
- Enhanced collection development within the library as librarians are closer to the research interests of the university's academics and postgraduate students
- Reduced isolation for researchers, as the research liaison librarian and all the specialised information services of the library will be actively promoted to the student.

Typical duties of a librarian on a supervisory team vary, but could include:

- providing reader education including one-to-one sessions
- assistance with electronic access to library resources

- assistance with bibliographic packages, e.g., EndNote
- undertaking in-depth database searches including citation searches
- provision of publisher awareness services, e.g., DA Recommender
- recommending relevant quality journals (especially refereed)
- establishing and maintaining current awareness services in the research area
- advising on bibliographic style
- recommending other libraries with relevant substantial holdings and facilitating access
- attending meetings with academic supervisors and students
- identifying relevant electronic lists, newsgroups, conferences, etc.
- occasionally browsing on behalf of research students (traditional and virtual methods) to identify new information resources
- with other supervisors, targeting students at risk (of failing) and providing support and assistance
- educating the supervisors in information literacy skills
- participating in electronic conferencing (e.g., FirstClass)
- becoming a pro-active partner within the research culture.

The pilot study involves Deakin University's five Faculty Liaison Librarians plus two other librarians including one of the authors (Macauley) who helps oversee the project. Faculty Liaison Librarians are allocated, on average, two higher degree research students, normally with different supervisors. Of course, their liaison role encompasses many more research students, but not at such an intensive collaborative level. The students involved include Ph.D., professional doctorate (Ed.D.), and master's by research candidates. Students are chosen by supervisors to take part and most are in the very early stages of candidature. Candidates include full-time, part-time, on-campus, and off-campus including overseas students; some are new to research whilst others already have research degrees and published their work. Supervisors were suggested by Heads of Schools and include relatively new academics to those at professorial level. The pilot study has been totally optional for students and supervisors taking part.

SUPPORT AND COMPETENCIES

The Library has developed a Research Skills Module (http://www.deakin.edu.au/library/reschsk.html) that supports the pilot study.

In addition to information links to assist researchers, the Web site also provides information on thesis writing and on the literature review process. The module has proven to be a great adjunct to the personal relationships and direct assistance of the pilot program. To maintain consistency of service, standard IT, bibliographic management, requesting service, and information retrieval competencies were identified. A checklist of competencies for higher degree students and their supervisors (http://www.deakin.edu.au/library/hdrchecklist.html) was developed to ascertain the information literacy competencies of each student and supervisor involved in the pilot study. The primary purpose of the checklist is to establish the specific training requirements of each individual in order to tailor and deliver relevant and personalised tuition. After training is completed, there is subsequent self-assessment of competency levels. The process is predicated on improving competencies in the defined areas.

An expectation of the scheme is the development of information literacy skills, not only for the candidates, but also for the supervisors. It is hoped those newfound skills will be transferred to new generations of students and academics through pedagogic continuity.

EVALUATION OF THE PILOT STUDY

Formal ongoing evaluation of the pilot project is an integral part of the process. At this early stage feedback has been informal, yet very useful. Without doubt, the students involved greatly appreciate the one-to-one relationship, with one doctoral candidate stating, "you're the only one that cares about me." The student found the individual contact a "lifesaver" which is a mixed blessing; it is positive feedback for the Library but it reinforces the contention that some supervisors do not appear to be as supportive as the candidates would like. Another student said, "this should be done by everyone" and added, "it has made me reflect on my [lack of] information skills." Referring to the wealth of knowledge being disseminated in a one-to-one information literacy session, a professional doctorate student exclaimed, "why don't we know all about this stuff?" Further investigation found that much of the information she didn't know about was actually provided in various formats such as in published guides sent directly to students or accessible via the Web. Quite simply, *students often do not read what they are sent,* an observation backed up by an earlier study on off-campus research students (Macauley, 1996, p. 58). Feedback from academic staff so far has been positive, although some academics feel it is only the students who need the information skills training and not themselves. Interestingly, the majority of the academics involved in the project admitted to having information skills gaps at the initial briefing sessions, but when it comes to actually undertaking any training, they can rarely be pinned down to do it!

The librarians involved have found the program to be a success, but acknowledge that building the relationship with the students, and to a lesser extent the academics, can be a slow process. Once the participants experience the benefits of the collaboration, the relationship tends to blossom. Another obvious concern is if the program proves to be a success, how will the small number of librarians be able to cope with a possible large number of students and supervisors. One librarian was reluctant to be taking on some of roles that should realistically be in the supervisor's domain, although the program has direct benefit to supervisors in (hopefully) updating their knowledge; this knowledge can then be passed on to the students. Certainly the approachability of librarians may influence this. Another librarian concerned about one of his students undertaking a Ph.D. in education, who had not heard of the ERIC database, exclaimed, "they don't know what they don't know!" The overwhelming issue was that personal communication was the key, especially when dealing with the specialised interests of research students and their supervisors.

OTHER ISSUES AND FUTURE POSSIBILITIES

There is certainly the question of spoon-feeding research students with this model. While some may question the degree of the librarian's involvement in the research process, as Cavanagh and Lingham (1994, p. 119) have stated, "the student, in the end, is the one who must put the material together and write the thesis." Moreover, a central aim of the whole pilot is to help the students to become self-sufficient in their gathering of information and be better informed of what additional material is available.

There are a number of other issues and considerations to be taken into account before adopting this model. For instance, are librarians appropriately trained and have they the necessary experience to add value to the supervisory process? Are libraries sufficiently resourced to take on these additional responsibilities? Are research candidates, academics, and librarians willing to take on this new model of supervision?

The challenge ahead is in mainstreaming the model in a period of contracting staffing resources, increasing options for flexible course delivery and possible increase in numbers of higher degree students. The enigma is that the success of the pilot study to attract and retain students may result in increased demand for places and untenable workloads to meet the demand on liaison services.

CONCLUSIONS

Although librarians often point to the academic staff as obstacles to information literacy, citing their inexperience in library use and their reluctance to change their pedagogical styles, librarians in many cases are not doing their part either (Bodi, 1992, p. 72). Despite what librarians have to offer academic staff and students, says Bodi (1992, p. 72), "they have managed to keep their expertise largely a secret." Collaboration between researchers and librarians can assist candidates and supervisors to stay informed in specific fields and can assist in filtering the proliferation of information in a controlled and structured manner. Most importantly, librarians are trained in interpreting how library users can make better use of the library and its services. In addition to this, librarians can help academics and students keep abreast of new technological developments, especially in information science. Librarians, as experts in electronic (and print) bibliographic fields, have a role to play by adding value to the information. One of the challenges for librarians is to keep distance education students and their supervisors up to date with technological developments whilst they are researching, and train them to have an open mind about what will continue to be a rapidly changing future.

A shift has occurred in scholarly communication and therefore information literacy in recent decades. Electronic communication has significantly gained prominence; end-user online searching by research students and academics has all but replaced intermediary searching by librarians or information specialists; electronic sources available in homes and offices are becoming an alternative to visiting libraries; electronic publishing is growing at a fast rate; and the Internet continues to provide new forms of scholarly communication.

The proliferation of information, combined with increased accessibility to electronic scholarly communication for research students, especially those at a distance, has led to a situation where researchers may suffocate in an informational morass. Instead of enhancing access to information, disintermediation may actually reduce access to relevant, comprehensive and quality information. Disintermediation may also lull both doctoral candidates and their supervisors into a false sense of security regarding their levels of information literacy. In some instances the information skills gap is perpetuated via pedagogic continuity and it is hoped the program mentioned in this paper may assist in reversing this contention. The major strategy suggested to overcome these problems is to form a three-way partnership between the doctoral candidate, their supervisor(s) and an experienced librarian that combines the various talents and strengths that only disparate experts can achieve.

NOTE

1. A fascinating reaffirmation of this situation was given by Barker who completed a Ph.D. in his seventies: ". . . here I was seventy-years-old with the aforementioned working history saying 'How do you do' to an obviously energetic young woman from the Faculty of Education half my age. We eyed each other and started work. Eight years later we have published and presented several joint papers even though our core academic interests differ" (Barker 1999, p. 148).

REFERENCES

Alire, C. A. (1984). *A nationwide survey of education doctoral students' attitudes regarding the importance of the library and the need for bibliographic instruction.* Unpublished doctoral dissertation, University of Northern Colorado, Greeley.

Barker, R. (1999). Towards a sustainable relationship between supervisor and student. In A. Holbrook and S. Johnston (Eds.), *Supervision of postgraduate research in education* (pp. 147-152). Coldstream, Vic.: Australian Association for Research in Education.

Barry, C. A. (1997). Information skills for an electronic world: Training doctoral research students. *Journal of Information Science, 23*(3), 225-238.

Behrens, S. J. (1993). Obstacles for user education for off-campus students: Lecturer's attitudes to library skills. In C. J. Jacob (Comp.), *The Sixth Off-Campus Library Services Conference Proceedings: Kansas City, Missouri, October, 6-8, 1993* (pp. 11-23). Mount Pleasant, MI: Central Michigan University.

Bodi, S. (1992). Collaborating with faculty in teaching critical thinking: The role of librarians. *Research Strategies, 10*(2), 69-76.

Bruce, C. S. (1991). Postgraduate response to an information retrieval credit course. *Australian Academic & Research Libraries, 22*(2), 103-110.

Cavanagh, A. (1994). The role of libraries in off-campus study. In T. Evans and D. Murphy (Eds.), *Research in Distance Education 3* (pp. 91-102). Geelong: Deakin University Press.

Cavanagh, A. K., & Lingham, B. (1994). Library services for external postgraduate and overseas students. *Distance Education, 15*(1), 112-127.

Cavanagh, A. K., & Tucker, J. (1993). Costing of off-campus library services. In C. J. Jacob (Comp.), *The Sixth Off-Campus Library Services Conference Proceedings: Kansas City, Missouri, October 6-8, 1993* (pp. 59-72). Mount Pleasant, MI: Central Michigan University.

Delamont, S., Parry. O., & Atkinson, P. (1997). Critical mass and pedagogic continuity: Studies in academic habitus. *British Journal of Sociology of Education, 18*(4), 533-549.

Dreifuss, R. A. (1981). Library instruction and graduate students: More work for George. *RQ, 21*(2), 121-123.

Edwards, C., Day, J., & Walton, G. (1996). Disintermediation in the year 2010: Using scenarios to identify key issues and relevance of IMPEL2 eLib Project. In *Online Information 96: Proceedings of the International Online Information Meeting* (pp. 357-361). London: Learned Information Europe.

Evans, T. (1995). Postgraduate research supervision in the emerging 'open' universities. *Australian Universities Review, 38*(2), 23-27.

Evans, T., & Green, W. (1995). *Dancing at a distance? Postgraduate studies, 'supervision,' and distance education.* Paper presented at Annual Conference of the Australian Association for Research in Education, Hobart, 29 November, 1995. Launceston, Tas.: University of Tasmania.

Evans, T., & Pearson, M. (1999). Off-campus doctoral research and study in Australia: Emerging issues and practices. In A. Holbrook & S. Johnston (Eds.), *Supervision of Postgraduate Research in Education* (pp. 185-206). Coldstream, Vic.: Australian Association for Research in Education.

Fabiano, E. (1996). Casting the 'net': reaching out to doctoral students in education. *Research Strategies, 14*(3), 159-168.

Herrington, V. J. (1998). Way beyond BI: A look to the future. *The Journal of Academic Librarianship, 24*(5), 381-386.

Macauley, P. (1997). Distance education research students and their library use. *Australian Academic & Research Libraries, 28*(3), 188-197.

Macauley, P. (1996) *Is the home institution library needed? The information needs of Deakin University distance education higher degree by research students: a user-centred approach.* MAppSc Thesis, Charles Sturt University, Wagga Wagga, NSW.

Macauley, P., & McKnight, S. (1998). A new model of library support for off-campus postgraduate research students. In *Quality in postgraduate research: Managing the new agenda: Proceedings of the 1998 Quality in Postgraduate Research*

Conference (pp. 95-106). Adelaide: The Advisory Centre for University Education, The University of Adelaide.

Madland, D. (1985). Library instruction for graduate students. *College Teaching, 33*(4), 163-164.

Manoff, M. (1997). *Cyberhope or cyberhype? Computers and scholarly research.* Available: http://libraries.mit.edu/humanities/manoff.html.

Manoff, M. (1996). Revolutionary or regressive? The politics of electronic collection development. In R. P. Peek & G. B. Newby (Eds.), *Scholarly publishing: The electronic frontier* (pp. 215-229). Cambridge, Massachusetts: MIT Press.

Pearson, M., & Ford, L. (1997). *Open and flexible PhD study and research.* Canberra: Evaluations and Investigations Programme, Higher Education Division, Department of Employment, Education, Training and Youth Affairs.

Phillips, E. M. (1996). The quality of a good thesis. In O. Zuber-Skerritt (Ed.), *Frameworks for postgraduate education* (pp. 197-212). Lismore, NSW: Southern Cross University Press.

Simpson, A. E. (1998). Information-finding and the education of scholars: Teaching electronic access in disciplinary context. *Behavioral & Social Sciences Librarian, 16*(2), 1-18.

Small, M. (1997). Virtual universities and their libraries: A comparison of Australian and North American experiences. *Advances in Librarianship, 21*, 25-46.

Zaporozhetz, L. E. (1987). *The dissertation literature review: How faculty advisors prepare their doctoral candidates.* Unpublished doctoral dissertation, University of Oregon, Eugene.

Innovative Methods
for Providing Instruction
to Distance Students Using Technology

Paul R. Pival

Calgary Health Trust

Johanna Tuñón

Nova Southeastern University

SUMMARY. Bibliographic instruction is one of the major challenges facing libraries that support distance students. Most libraries have neither the budget nor staff to send librarians to all places students might be located. This paper will examine three innovative methods tried at Nova Southeastern University for providing quality bibliographic instruction to distance students: one synchronous, another asynchronous, and the third combining features from both synchronous and asynchronous methods of delivering instruction.

KEYWORDS. Library instruction, distance education, library technology

INTRODUCTION

Bibliographic instruction (BI) is one of the major challenges facing libraries that support distance students. Most libraries have neither the budget nor staff to send librarians to all places students might be located. This paper will examine the Einstein Library's recent efforts

[Haworth co-indexing entry note]: "Innovative Methods for Providing Instruction to Distance Students Using Technology." Pival, Paul R., and Johanna Tuñón. Co-published simultaneously in *Journal of Library Administration* (The Haworth Information Press, an imprint of The Haworth Press, Inc.) Vol. 32, No. 1/2, 2001, pp. 347-360; and: *Off-Campus Library Services* (ed: Anne Marie Casey) The Haworth Information Press, an imprint of The Haworth Press, Inc., 2001, pp. 347-360.

to find technological methods for delivering library instruction to distance students that does not require meeting face to face with students. Three innovative technologies for providing quality bibliographic instruction to distance students will be examined. Each technology will be examined for its usefulness for delivering library instruction in a distance setting, and the advantages and disadvantages of each will be discussed.

BACKGROUND

Nova Southeastern University is a large private academic institution located in Fort Lauderdale, Florida. A pioneer in the field of distance education, NSU has been providing instruction "at a time and place convenient to students" since the early 1970s. NSU enrolls over 15,000 students with about one-half of its students in distance programs. There are field-based programs at 79 sites in Florida, 66 sites in other states, and 13 international sites, as well as a growing number of online programs where students attend virtual classes. The majority of NSU's distance programs are at the graduate level (both masters and doctoral) in the fields of education, business, psychology, and computer science.

Instruction is offered in various formats depending on the academic program. In some programs students meet on a regular basis at cluster sites for face-to-face instruction. Other programs operate almost exclusively online. In the latter, students meet on campus for an orientation at the beginning of each semester and then complete the rest of the semester asynchronously. Many of NSU's academic programs provide some combination of these methods. It has been a major challenge for the library to deliver consistent bibliographic instruction to students in programs where classes are delivered in such a variety of modalities.

The Einstein Library has actively supported these distance programs with document delivery and bibliographic instruction for the past eight years (Tuñón & Pival, 1997), and the library has learned many valuable lessons along the way. NSU began to consider technology solutions for instruction (1) after it became apparent that the Einstein Library did not always have sufficient librarians to travel to all the field-based sites in a timely manner and (2) in response to the newer academic programs where students met exclusively in virtual environments. Because NSU's academic programs used so many different models for delivering distance education, librarians at the Einstein Library have been experimenting with both synchronous and asynchronous instructional delivery systems (Tuñón & Pival, 1997; Pival & Tuñón, 1998, Tuñón, 1999) for a number of years.

COMPRESSED VIDEO

In 1996 and 1997, librarians explored the possibility of using compressed video as a means of delivering library instruction. Because of the cost of the compressed video equipment, this solution was not feasible for programs meeting at sites where equipment was not already in place. At that time, there were only two NSU academic programs where compressed video technology was being used to deliver instruction (primarily in a lecture-based format) to remote sites within the state of Florida, Las Vegas, and Puerto Rico. The Einstein Library provided instruction to the Graduate Teacher Education Program (GTEP) while the university's Health Professions Library handled the training for students in pharmacology.

While adequate for classroom-type instruction, Einstein librarians found two problems with compressed video: one technical and the other logistical. The technical problem manifested itself in difficulties with displaying computer screens. The technology did work well for displaying PowerPoint presentations and for viewing instructors and classes at either end. It did not, however, work well for displaying an online search, particularly when the compressed video had to display a series of rapidly changing computer screens. Secondly, bright colors on PowerPoint slide presentations tended to bleed–particularly shades of red. Once the librarians removed many of the animated transitions and bright colors, the slide presentations transmitted better, but they were also much less visually appealing.

The library might have been able to overcome the technical problems, but the logistical problem proved more difficult to address. The roadblock proved to be scheduling the compressed video equipment. The Einstein Library had negotiated to integrate bibliographic instruction into one of GTEP's required research classes. This particular research course, however, was one of the few courses where all instruction was delivered by instructors at the sites, not through compressed video. The problem was that, although the compressed video equipment was not being used for the research class, it was being used for delivering other regularly scheduled GTEP courses. Consequently, the Einstein librarians decided in 1997 that compressed video was not a viable option for delivering bibliographic instruction.

NETMEETING

A new type of software known as groupware started to show promise in 1997. Groupware, also known as collaborative or remote meeting software, was originally designed for the corporate world to facilitate meetings between home and branch offices. This type of software often supports file sharing, synchronous chat rooms, and whiteboards. Participants at both ends can collaborate on projects and have discussions without being required to be in the same physical location. Microsoft's NetMeeting software is one example of groupware that is rapidly gaining popularity. NetMeeting could be easily adapted to academic environments by providing live bibliographic instruction to distance students. The software allowed a librarian to run "canned" presentations (such as a PowerPoint slideshow) or display live Web pages to a remote audience. Unlike other software packages such as CU-SeeMe (Folger, 1997), NetMeeting also had the advantage of being able to be transmitted to two or more simultaneous locations. Unlike compressed video, NetMeeting gave students at the receiving end the ability to take control of the software to conduct searches. This allowed students to demonstrate their search techniques at both ends and to receive input from the instructor. NetMeeting only provided full audio for point-to-point transmissions but not for multi-point transmissions. For the Einstein librarians, one of the most attractive features of NetMeeting was that it was free and required only standard computer equipment and Internet connections to run. Although it was not without problems, NetMeeting offered a truly cost-effective method for delivering bibliographic instruction to students in the field, particularly when compared to compressed video.

The library used NetMeeting for its first experiment with delivering remote library instruction to distance students in 1997. Classes are offered at each site five times a year in eight-week blocks. Some classes are conducted live at the cluster sites while others were conducted remotely via either Audiobridge (a moderated conference call service) or compressed video. The library chose to implement this remote instruction with GTEP at seven of GTEP's 11 sites. The GTEP program made a commitment to having the necessary resources at the sites: computer labs with Internet connections, technology support staff, Audiobridge conference call capability, and LCD projectors.

Before the library decided to go ahead with this project, Einstein librarians arranged for several trial connections to the remote sites. The intention was to test how many sites could receive instruction simultaneously. The remote sites used Microsoft NetMeeting 2.1 for Windows95, running on a Gateway P166 with 32 meg of RAM. The library was showing a slide presentation using Microsoft PowerPoint and online (Web) databases via Netscape Navigator 4.01. The on-campus connection was a T-1 connection; the receiving sites were dialing in via modems at 28.8 or 33.3 bps. The preliminary trials revealed the following:

- The transmission of both audio *and* data over the Internet slowed the transmission times for sites using modem connections.
- The quality of point-to-point audio transmissions over the Internet was less than ideal.
- NetMeeting could not reliably handle more than four simultaneous sites even when the library only used the software to transmit visual data (no audio).
- The transmission of PowerPoint slides with elaborate transitions or design slowed the transmission of data.
- The system worked best when computers at all the sites were set at the lowest display settings (640 by 480 pixels). This was because the receiving sites were displaying through LCD panels or projectors, and some could not handle higher screen resolutions.
- Using Microsoft's public server had limitations. Its server was slow and non-NSU individuals were free to access the sessions. When NSU set up its own NetMeeting server, transmissions improved and also ensured privacy for NSU activities.

Because of these findings, the library team opted to use Audiobridge, a commercial telephone conferencing system, for transmitting audio (voice) to the remote GTEP sites. This meant that each site had to provide *two* telephone lines: one for the modem connection and one for the Audiobridge connection. Each site also had to provide a speakerphone so that all the students at the site could hear and interact with the librarian/instructor.

The library team decided to limit instruction to a maximum of three to four sites at a time and to keep the initial trials with GTEP classes short and simple. The librarians doing the sessions stuck to the basics of show and tell and did not make use of the collaboration feature during the initial set of training sessions. The library team decided to spread the implementation over several weeks and to have librarians be present at the GTEP sites as observers. This permitted the library to formatively evaluate the training adjustments based on both student input and the library observers' input and allowed sufficient time for librarians to make any necessary adjustments.

Because the success of implementing NetMeeting depended heavily on the cooperation of staff at the GTEP sites, the library wanted to ensure the GTEP staff knew what was expected of them. Consequently, the library asked the GTEP Program Director to send a memo to the technology staff and cluster coordinators at the various GTEP sites. Each GTEP site needed to provide (1) a person to set up equipment and make the initial NetMeeting connection, and (2) a facilitator to escort the class to the room in which instruction was to be received, to distribute library documentation, to act as a moderator during instruction, and to collect evaluation sheets after the sessions.

The Einstein Library began delivering remote library instruction to GTEP sites in April of 1998. Librarians ran the trial presentations at the five sites with scheduled research classes during that session, and spread the training over three weeks. Librarians were also physically present at each trial site during the first two weeks. These librarians were there simply as observers or "flies on the wall." They were only to step in if there were major technical difficulties, but fortunately, that did not become necessary. Students were instructed to address all questions and interactions to the NetMeeting presenter from the main campus.

At the end of the trials, the library team evaluated NetMeeting as an alternative for delivering library instruction. The librarians had been prepared to go back to traveling to the sites to deliver BI if the results had been unsatisfactory, but training via NetMeeting was well received. During the initial trials, a total of 59 students at five sites received instruction via NetMeeting. All the participating students indicated that they felt this was an acceptable method of receiving basic library instruction. Equally important, 100% of the participants also felt that future classes would benefit by receiving instruction in this format.

The presenters learned several lessons in the process:

- Keep things simple at first. Only use NetMeeting's sharing capabilities after mastering the basics.
- Keep the training segment relatively short. Observers noted that students grow weary of just watching the screen while listening to a "disembodied voice." Students participated more when the content of the instruction was more relevant. In order to make the training more relevant, the Einstein librarians would ask students to suggest topics for the online searches being demonstrated.
- Have a backup computer ready to deliver instruction.
- Use the lowest screen resolution (640 by 480 pixels) at all sites.
- Be sure to write, e-mail, or telephone people at the remote site a few days before the presentation to ensure that all is ready and that they are comfortable with the procedures to be used.
- Verify that the Internet Service Providers used at the remote sites will not drop connections if the machines are seemingly inactive for an extended period.
- Pause regularly during the presentation to ask if students have any questions. This is important since the presenter has no visual clues for judging whether students are grasping the concepts being introduced and demonstrated.

Librarians upgraded to NetMeeting 3.0 in 1999. Version 3.0 had a new and less intrusive interface, new security features, and better application sharing. One of the few potential drawbacks to this technology solution was that it only worked with the Windows platform. Fortunately, none of the GTEP sites used Macintosh equipment for their labs so this was not a problem for us. One new feature that the Einstein librarians added after the initial trial was the transmission of a video image of the librarian at the beginning of each instructional session. Students liked seeing who was speaking to them. The video image was too small to provide anything other than a visual cue for students, but it did help personalize the remote instruction. Librarians hope to have cameras added at the receiving sites in the future so they too can receive visual cues. Without a camera at the sites, the presenter has no idea when the sites are quiet whether the connection has been lost, students are intently following along, or students have all fallen asleep or tiptoed away!

Since the initial trials, the Einstein Library has continued to deliver remote library instruction to the GTEP sites. Librarians provide on-site BI once in the fall and once in the spring. They use NetMeeting when there are scheduling conflicts. Librarians have used NetMeeting to deliver 24 sessions to GTEP sites during 1998 and 1999 to a total of 389 students. This has saved the library approximately $8,000 in travel expenses over the two years. Using NetMeeting also made it possible for the Einstein Library to ensure that students received training even when there were not enough librarians available to travel to each site. The students' evaluations of NetMeeting were satisfactory. The satisfaction level of NetMeeting sessions was 4.34 on a 5-point scale, which was above the university's minimum level considered satisfactory of 4.0. However, when compared to student satisfaction levels for face-to-face training of 4.75, it was clear that students still preferred face-to-face instruction when possible. Site administrators at the cluster sites also indicated to the Einstein librarians that students much preferred face-to-face training to training via NetMeeting.

STREAMING MEDIA

A new technology called streaming media offered the Einstein librarians a new method for delivering library instruction to distance students. Streaming media uses the Internet to deliver instruction to remote students asynchronously. It allows users to view multimedia presentations on the desktop without having to wait for a file to download from a server. After a very brief pause while the initial data is being buffered, audio and video are delivered directly to the desktop in a continuous stream as content is downloaded and decompressed "on the fly." This allows users to view live events as well as large packaged presentations that would otherwise cause prohibitively long downloads over typical communication networks. As a result, students see and hear the presentation "live" without having to wait for the download to their hard drives. The quality of both the visual and audio portions of the presentation is quite good. Streaming media has the advantage of being able to use an Internet connection that operates at virtually any speed to deliver high-quality audio and video content directly to the desktop. The current application leader, RealNetworks, produces software that interfaces with Microsoft PowerPoint to create a slideshow that can be delivered, with full audio (voice and/or music), over the Web in a streaming format.

Streaming media has several advantages over more traditional self-paced tutorials. Lectures can be videotaped and the tape digitally converted to a streaming format, allowing instructors to deliver a high-quality lecture an infinite number of times. It is also possible to deliver a live lecture or seminar across the Internet to a large audience. The financial gains that can be realized with this technology are obvious. No longer do instructors need to travel to meet students, and the same lecture can be delivered to an unlimited number of students simultaneously or on-demand, or viewed as often as is necessary for the student to grasp the content. The distribution of the files is much quicker than through any of the other means described earlier. Also, production time is minimal because only one file needs to be created to serve the entire class body. This means that there is no delay in mailing the materials to students, and broadcast time does not need to be scheduled. Just as importantly, students are ensured of viewing the most up-to-date version of the information since they are obtaining the information directly from the information's source. For example, if a telephone number changes in a library presentation, the librarian can simply change it on the slide and re-publish the presentation to the Web. The RealMedia player also has the advantage that it is free for students to download. There is no cost to the student associated with this form of instruction, and only a small cost to the library for the RealPresenter plug-in to convert PowerPoint to streaming media. The major drawback of streaming media is that there is no interactivity between the conveyor of information and the recipients. Presenters, however, can overcome this by using streaming media in conjunction with synchronous methodologies to incorporate interactivity into their instructional strategies.

The real impetus for NSU to experiment with streaming media came in late 1998 when the School of Business and Entrepreneurship (SBE) decided unilaterally to deliver its technology course only online. This impacted the Einstein Library because library instruction was already integrated into this particular course. Up until that time, Einstein librarians had delivered the training in person at the remote sites. The advent of the Virtual MBA program, however, presented problems. Students in the Virtual MBA were scattered throughout the world, and were only accessing instruction online. This meant that there was no opportunity for a librarian to address students in a live setting, even during an initial orientation. Because students did not gather at sites, it also meant that NetMeeting was not an option for delivering library instruction.

Because the MBA program had made the decision to use Web pages for delivering all instruction, librarians in the Einstein Library concluded that they too would have to use Web-based instruction. The library team decided to use this opportunity to try streaming media, particularly for information that had originally been delivered in conjunction with PowerPoint slides the librarians had used at site-based MBA training sessions. The librarians decided to break the instruction into several small modules consisting of approximately five to eight slides and three to five minutes in length. This was done to ease the production of the files, and it also allowed students to view instruction that was relevant to the information they needed at that time rather than require them to view an entire instructional presentation to get one specific piece of information. The librarians decided to use each PowerPoint streaming module as the cornerstone for an instructional module on a specific topic. For instance, one five-minute module dealt with the differences between scholarly publications and popular literature. Each module would also include links to a variety of Web pages that would supplement the streaming media module. In addition, students were required to complete three performance-based assignments that they emailed to the MBA program and to complete an online test that included both true and false and multiple choice questions. Each question on the test provided an optional link that referred students back to the appropriate pages when they needed help. Students had to score at least 80% on the test, but they were allowed to take the test as many times as was necessary to finally show that they had gained some kind of mastery of the content.

The streaming media technology was fairly easy to implement. Because some staff already had familiarity with the product, RealNetworks was chosen for the trials. The Einstein librarians used a plug-in purchased from RealNetworks that allowed a narrated MS PowerPoint presentation to be converted to a streaming media data file. Because the staff did not have access to a streaming media server, they also decided to produce the files for the lowest common denominator, a network connection over a 28.8 kbps modem.

At the time this was written, streaming media had not proven to be a very successful method for delivering instruction. The lack of interactivity proved to be a significant drawback that the Einstein librarians have so far not been able to overcome. Although the Einstein Library never surveyed students on their use of this technology, student usage statistics indicated that MBA students were not accessing the streaming media information anywhere near as often as they were accessing the static Web pages. The Web pages in the first module were accessed three times as often as the first streaming module. The fact that student rates of accessing later streaming media pages dropped precipitously seemed to indicate that students did not want to use streaming media. In the library's formative assessment, the librarians concluded that they had to do something about just having a voice "droning on" and that more interactivity was needed.

WebCT

In the fall of 1999, Programs for Higher Education (PHE), one of four doctoral education programs in the Fischler Graduate School of Education and Human Services (FGSE&HS), expressed interest in offering a one-credit library course to help their distance students. Programs in Higher Education is a program for college and university administrators and faculty interested in earning a doctorate of education (Ed.D.) that is delivered in a distance-learning format. Most of the classes offered by PHE are site based, but the program has also started to offer some optional courses via WebCT (*Web Course Tools*), a software/server package that provides customizable courseware tools. At the time this paper was submitted, the library WebCT course for PHE was still in development.

Originally designed at the University of British Columbia, WebCT is a Web-based instruction (WBI) program that allows instructors to create customized course Web pages on a secure server. NSU liked that instructors could quickly create customized pages by using pre-defined WebCT templates. Faculty and staff did not need to have knowledge of HTML (Hypertext Markup Language) in order to be able to make use of the software's advanced programming features. Second, because the pages can be housed on a separate secure server, detailed statistics on student use can be collected. For instance, an instructor can find out how often a particular student logged in to the course pages and how many times the student visited particular pages. Thus, instructors can easily track whether students are accessing optional readings or not. Finally, WebCT software supports both synchronous and asynchronous learning though easily integrated tools such as chat rooms, bulletin boards, email, and online quizzes. Because WebCT allows the instructor to have control over the course design, the instructor can opt to use any or all of these features. As a result, Nova Southeastern University began actively using and supporting WebCT in 1998 by providing a university server and offering training to interested faculty and staff.

In the fall of 1999, librarians in the Einstein Library started working with Programs in Higher Education (PHE) on the library's course using WebCT. Although WebCT had been used for some time by the Fischler Graduate School of Education, this was the first occasion that the library had tried to use it to deliver bibliographic instruction. The librarians working on the course design decided to focus on providing students with a series of course-integrated Web pages and tutorials for self-paced instruction (Alberico & Dupuis, 1996). The librarians coupled these resources with performance-based assignments. This module of library instruction had already been successfully implemented by the Einstein Library when the library had begun integrating library instruction into the curriculum of another NSU doctoral education program (Tuñón, 1999). The librarians developed Web pages and tutorials for each module with the idea that students would use these resources to complete a series of online assignments. The course was designed so that the librarian responsible for designing and "teaching" the course would also correct the assignments and provide the students with individual feedback about search strategies and choice of databases. Providing one-on-one feedback to each student was considered critical to the success of the process. The Einstein librarians have learned from past experiences that students need directed feedback from the instructor for this kind of asynchronous library instruction to be successful (Tuñón, 1999).

Along with one-on-one asynchronous communication between instructor and students, Einstein librarians also planned to use the Web-board function in WebCT to encourage student collaboration. The librarians planned to have small-group work on the Web board where students would develop group strategies for focusing their search on some aspect of higher education. By including small group active learning that focused on how to use online resources as the literature has suggested (Allen, 1995; Cleary, 1998; Dabbour, 1997), the librarians hoped to encourage "an interactive, access-based approach focused on active learning and critical thinking" (Nahl-Jako-bovits & Jakobovits, 1993, p. 73).

So far, the Einstein librarians have found WebCT easy and versatile to work with, but they also have concerns about applying the model throughout the university. The problem is not with WebCT as a course tool but rather with the fact that there are insufficient librarians to use this as a model for all NSU programs. Teaching courses and providing students with detailed one-on-one feedback is very time intensive, and the Einstein Library only has four librarians responsible for providing all bibliographic instruction to NSU's 7,000+ distance students. Although the librarians anticipate good results with this approach, they also believe that this model may be too labor intensive for the library to use for delivering instruction to students in all of NSU's distance programs. It should be noted, however, that a formative evaluation of this course had not yet been completed at the time this paper was submitted. The presenters expected to provide more concrete conclusions at the time they delivered this paper in Portland in the year 2000.

DEMONSTRATIONS

Time will be allowed at the Off-Campus presentation for either a live or "canned" demonstration with screenshots of each of the implemented technologies.

CONCLUSIONS

Finding new and effective methods for delivering library instruction to students in distance education programs will become an increasingly pressing problem as new methods for delivering distance education continue to evolve. Compressed video, collaborative groupware, streaming media, and Web-based instruction all are technologies that offer certain advantages, but each also has inherent limitations. No one technology provides a "silver bullet" that solves all of the instructional needs for the Einstein Library. Librarians searching for technology solutions for their bibliographic instruction needs will need to experiment and use each technology, as no one of these technological solutions is the right choice in all situations.

REFERENCES

Alberico, R., & Dupuis, E. A. (1996). The World Wide Web as an instructional medium [Instructive session]. In L. Shirato (Ed.), *The impact of technology on library instruction: Papers and session materials presented at the twenty-first National Library Instruction Conference held in Denton, Texas, 5 to 6 May 1995* (pp. 27-35). Ann Arbor, MI: Pierian Press.

Allen, E. E. (1995). Active learning and teaching: Improving postsecondary library instruction. *The Reference Librarian, (51/52)*, 89-103.

Cleary, J. S. (1998). Asking the right question: Formulating effective search strategies for electronic databases (BI vignettes). *Research Strategies, 15*, 199-203.

Dabbour, K. S. (1997). Applying active learning methods to the design of library instruction for a freshman seminar. *College & Research Libraries, 58*, 299-308.

Folger, K. (1997, April) *The virtual librarian: Using desktop videoconferencing to provide interactive reference assistance.* Paper presented at Association of College and Research Libraries 8th National Conference, Nashville, TN. http://www.ala.org/acrl/paperhtml/a09.html.

Microsoft NetMeeting: http://www.microsoft.com/windows/netmeeting.

Nahl-Jakobovits, D., & Jakobovits, L. A. (1993). Bibliographic instructional design for information literacy: Integrating affective and cognitive objectives. *Research Strategies, 11*, 73-88.

Pival, P., & Tuñón, J. (1998). NetMeeting: A new and inexpensive alternative for delivering library instruction to distance students. *College & Research Library News, 59*, 758-760.

RealAudio Streaming Media: http://www.real.com.

Tuñón, J. (1999). *Integrating bibliographic instruction for distance education doctoral students in the Child and Youth Studies Program at Nova Southeastern University.* Ft. Lauderdale, Florida.

Tuñón, J., & Pival, P. (1997). Library services to distance students: Nova Southeastern University's experience. *Florida Libraries, 40*, 109,118.

WebCT: http://www.webct.com.

Indonesia Electronic Library Design Plan for Supporting a Distance Learning Environment

Lamhot S. P. Simamora
Firman Gunawan

Divisi RisTI PT TELKOM Indonesia

SUMMARY. Indonesia is answering the need for a more skilled work force by using distance education and technology to reach more students. This paper describes the development of an electronic library to support these students by member libraries of the Indonesia Distance Learning Network.

KEYWORDS. Distance education, electronic library, library services, Indonesia

INTRODUCTION

Indonesia is entering the global era that requires qualified human resources in order to be able to live and compete with others. The long crises that Indonesia is facing now are pushing us to produce skilled human resources. Much still has to be done in the effort to develop the intellectual life of the Indonesians in order to be able to survive in the global era full of challenges. One approach for achieving this goal is Distance Learning, that is, utilising technology to cover more students. The number of distance learning providers is increasing in Indone-

[Haworth co-indexing entry note]: "Indonesia Electronic Library Design Plan for Supporting a Distance Learning Environment." Simamora, Lamhot S. P., and Firman Gunawan. Co-published simultaneously in *Journal of Library Administration* (The Haworth Information Press, an imprint of The Haworth Press, Inc.) Vol. 32, No. 1/2, 2001, pp. 361-369; and: *Off-Campus Library Services* (ed: Anne Marie Casey) The Haworth Information Press, an imprint of The Haworth Press, Inc., 2001, pp. 361-369.

sia with some of them joining the Indonesia Distance Learning Network (IDLN). As this number increased, the need for learning resources increased too. The learning resources may be used as a common resource and can easily be accessed without leaving home or workplace. One of these learning resources is the electronic library.

This electronic library will integrate IDLN members libraries and offer library service in Technology for Distance Training and Education in a standard codification and interface. The electronic library will include many kinds of information such as references (books, magazines, journals, bulletins, papers, etc.), library transactions, library members, public service, library statistics and partners. Security is also another aspect to be concerned about when designing this electronic library.

There are two big teams involved in designing this library. The first team is assigned to designing and building the application, while the second team is assigned to managing and maintaining the electronic library system. We realise much data takes a big role in building this library. All IDLN members joining in this library should have a uniform database structure. In the library transaction process we already defined a 3-step scenario for users: searching, transaction and delivering.

Going toward the implementation of this electronic library, we defined two phases. The first phase will concentrate on designing the technology (hardware and software), building applications (user classifications, data structure), coding and data entry. The second phase will concentrate on building the system: procurement, installation and testing. This second phase will be built step by step. The first installation will be done in the IDLN head office in one Local Area Network, then the Wide Area Network will be expanded to IDLN member libraries.

The next phase for our electronic library is creating partnerships with other institutions or libraries in order to have larger learning resources. By having this integrated electronic library, the distance learner may improve his/her skills and he/she can overcome culture, economic and geographic problems, which are still big problems for achieving better skills and education in Indonesia.

TELKOM DISTANCE LEARNING

Developing a Digital and Virtual Library system is dependent on the Distance Learning Development. And as we sought to support teaching and learning through distance learning, we need a learning resource center that can be accessed anytime and anywhere. The virtual library that developed in PT TELKOM is intended to support Distance Learning. TELKOM, especially Divisi RisTI, has developed three major distance learning technologies: Video conference based ISDN, Desktop Conference, and Web. Indonesia has an association consisting of organizations which have a great interest in Distance Learning Development. It is called IDLN (Indonesia Distance Learning Network). TELKOM also joined in this Organization. IDLN is concerned about the Library System in Indonesia. In Indonesia, libraries are not yet as good as in other countries. There are many conventional libraries with a conventional system. So, to migrate to virtual or digital can be done as quickly as we want, but we can't ignore that the technology is growing faster and faster. That's why IDLN and also PT TELKOM are trying to develop a system that bridges the technology and the library.

TELKOM DIGITAL LIBRARY

Information and telecommunication technology is growing so fast that it changes the way people live. Because of this progress, the research and information technology division of PT TELKOM INDONESIA (Divisi RisTI) has to continually rise to new innovative efforts for utilizing the technology to improve employee knowledge and the workforce. Those efforts are an absolute requirement for the organization, which always wants to improve the quality of human resources.

Distance learning application development almost cannot be separated from any learning resources that will always needed by the learner. Because of that reason, the progress in distance learning will always be followed by the development of learning resources that support distance learning applications. One of the most important of these is the information center where the learner or user can easily get the information that they are looking for or need to find. With the impact of information and telecommunication technology growth or integration, the information that was expensive and difficult to get in the past, is now very easy to obtain. But in order for the learner or user to find what they want among the millions of bytes of information, we need to classify those facts. With proper classification, people will not be confused when they look for information. Starting from this point, to support distance learning that develops in the PT TELKOM Indonesian environment and to make people find the information they want easier, the RisTI Division will develop a concept about the Library Information System and Learning Resource Center. There are two concepts that will be developed: First, the Web-based Library Information System, and second, an information center where the information can be put and collected in digital format, which we call the Virtual Library.

WEB-BASED LIBRARY INFORMATION SYSTEM

The library information system developing objective is to give effective, easy library information services to customers of library services. With this system people do not need to come to the library. They just need to sit in front of their computer and access the library information Web sites. Besides that, the library provider is easy to integrate into other Web sites (Figure 1).

Some important aspects should be considered in a Web-based library information system. Those aspects are services given by the library, data management, and security. Services are important for

FIGURE 1. Library Information System RisTI Division Concept

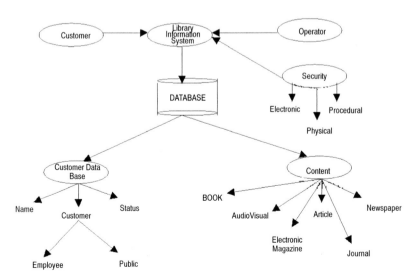

library operations. Through this aspect we hope that every information need of the customer will be fulfilled. This service will involve who is being served, who is the server, and what kind of medium will be utilized to bridge the client and the server. The services that will be provided in the Web-based library information system are report services, membership services, customer education services, promotion services, and production.

Data management consists of two aspects: First, customer data management and second, content management. Library customers should be categorized in some classification so this will be easier for the administrator of the library. Besides that, we have to consider content management in the library. Content will consist of the book, magazine, newspaper, article, journal, and audio-visual collections, and others. Data security is one of the important aspects that should never forgotten. Data security consists of three aspects: physical security, procedural security, and electronic security. Security is intended for libraries to avoid mismanagement and the security tools themselves can be the barcode system, Security Gate, ID Card, regulation, anti-virus usage, internal and external building security systems, and others.

Year 2000 was the year planned for the distance learning program take-off by Divisi RisTI PT TELKOM. We have to provide an infrastructure that will support the environment. That infrastructure, beside the distance learning system infrastructure, is also the networking. To strengthen the networking Divisi RisTI then joins to Distance Learning in Indonesia called IDLN (Indonesia Distance Learning Network). This organization has a regular meeting every month to discuss progress in every member environment. IDLN even sets up an international seminar every year. IDLN also sets up some workshops and training. One of the workshops is about the electronic library. In that workshop we hope that every IDLN member will build their own electronic library. And after that the library information system of every member should integrate their library so we will have a big network in the IDLN environment. The Divisi RisTI tries to develop a library information system in the RisTI environment, then integrates into the library in the IDLN environment.

VIRTUAL LIBRARY

The virtual library is defined as the information center which collects information in a digital format. The virtual library is the library that never exists physically, but this library can collect or provide services provided by a conventional library.

Beside developing a Web-Based library information system, Divisi RisTI is trying to develop a virtual library which includes data and collections in a digital format. We can utilize the virtual library as the support system in the Web learning environment. We identify some aspects considered important in building the Virtual Library.

Data collecting and data processing are the aspects needed to classify the data in a regular structure. Data will be collected in several formats. Data consist of article, e-journal, electronic book, electronic magazine, white paper, audio-visual, presentation in MS-Word, PDF, HTML, PowerPoint, and other formats. After collecting data, we do data classification. Resouce data is classified according to author name, presenter name if the file is the presentation file, event if we get the information from any event like a seminar or symposium, or according to the topics and title. The data will be put in a data base system. To connect the system to the user we need some interface between the operator or administrator, the user or customer, and the system itself. Because of it we have to make several facilities like the registration facility, services, support, searching facility, and others (Figure 2).

Figure 3 describes the information searching flowchart in the virtual library. From the simple figure we can see that the flow starts from the searching process with the search engine facility. Users or customers can utilize the search engine facility to find the information they need based on topic, title, author, event, and others. After they pass that process and find what they are looking for, there will be a transaction process between the operator and user. After the two parties agree, then the delivery process begins. The delivery process is also on-line because the collection in the virtual library is put in the digital format so we can deliver the collection in the digital way.

The basic configuration of our virtual library is described in Figure 4. From the provider side we should have an access control facility to authorize the customer or user. The provider also should have a search engine facility to make it easier for the user to access and look for some information. To classify data, we should have an excellent content management system. And for operational needs, the provider should have an operator and administrator.

FIGURE 2. Data Collecting and Processing

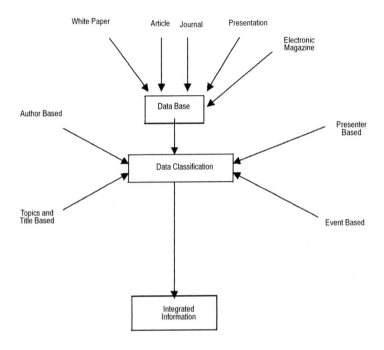

HUMAN RESOURCES

In order to develop these two concepts we need technical prepara-tion involving a feasibility study, comparative study, project team, and experts. Because of that we should divide human resources into two teams: First, the developer team and second, the operational team. For the developer team we will need:

- System Designer and Analyst
- Software Engineer
- Hardware Engineer
- Programmer
- Database Expert
- Network Expert

FIGURE 3. Global Concept of Information Searching

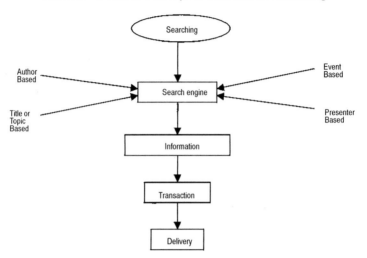

FIGURE 4. Basic Configuration

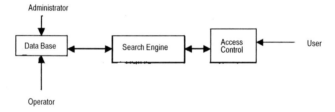

And for operational requirements we will need:

- Librarian
- Administrator
- Marketing and PR
- Technician
- Operator

We hope that the Web-based library information system and virtual library can be integrated so the TELKOM distance learning environment and others will have an integrated resource learning center with high capability.

IDLN ELECTRONIC LIBRARY PLAN

IDLN had a meeting in February 1999 to discuss Digital Library Design for the IDLN environment. In that meeting the members tried to define the Digital Library concept that will be adopted by all IDLN members. IDLN members agreed that to build a great system like this we have to pass two big phases.

In the first phase we must organise technical specifications including hardware and software, build a customisable application if we can't find any application in the market, handle classification and codification, prepare the human resources, and prepare the technical document and application manual, system evaluation, entry data. All will do this in each organization. The second phase integrates all the library systems into a network.

CONCLUSION

We hope that Web-Based library information system and virtual library development will support the distance learning process in the TELKOM environment. And TELKOM membership in IDLN is hoped to give a new spirit or new embryo to build library information system networking that will support the national distance learning environment.

In the first step we will build a digital library in the PT TELKOM environment. Especially for the Web-based library information system, we will start from the Divisi RisTI environment then broaden the network to other division libraries (particularly the training division). After that we will integrate our network with other IDLN member library systems.

For the virtual library we will start to collect the data, processing, and classification in the Divisi RisTI environment. Then we will design a data management system, and finally we can create a pure virtual library.

Virtual Desk:
Real Reference

Rhonda M. Smith
Stephanie F. Race
Meredith Ault

Florida Distance Learning Reference & Referral Center

SUMMARY. This paper will address the issues involved in establishing a statewide system of library support for distance learners and the ongoing challenges to be met. A primary consideration is how to establish continuity of service and provide an integrated experience for the user, despite contingent funding and distributed responsibility. Issues include selection of and access to electronic resources, improvements to Interlibrary Loan services, inter-library cooperative agreements, and providing and promoting reference services for students and faculty of multiple institutions.

KEYWORDS. Distance education, library services, statewide systems

Distance learning is a growing factor in higher education. The Florida Public Postsecondary Distance Learning Institute was created in July of 1996 to coordinate the state's response to this challenge. Their 1998 document, *Florida Postsecondary Distance Learning Scenarios,* projected a 41 percent increase in Florida student FTE by the year 2010 with 20-35 percent of students taking at least some courses at a distance. Having looked at the possibilities of leaving the development of distance education to existing institutions and of creating a new

[Haworth co-indexing entry note]: "Virtual Desk: Real Reference." Smith, Rhonda M., Stephanie F. Race, and Meredith Ault. Co-published simultaneously in *Journal of Library Administration* (The Haworth Information Press, an imprint of The Haworth Press, Inc.) Vol. 32, No. 1/2, 2001, pp. 371-382; and: *Off-Campus Library Services* (ed: Anne Marie Casey) The Haworth Information Press, an imprint of The Haworth Press, Inc., 2001, pp. 371-382.

distance education college or university, they elected to pursue a middle course. This called for increased coordination between the state's ten universities and 28 two-year community colleges and the creation of new, cross-institutional, support services.

It was recognized that the growth of distance education would have significant implications for libraries, both those of institutions providing distance education courses and the local libraries of distance learners. In this light, the Florida Distance Learning Library Initiative (DLLI) was established later in 1997. The goal of the Initiative is the cost-effective provision of enhanced library services to distance learners, which meet the information demands of their coursework and enable them to develop the information literacy skills necessary for lifelong learning. It is a partnership between the Community College System, the State University System, the State Library and public libraries, all of whose representatives sit on the Steering Committee.

Reflecting the orientation of the Institute, DLLI's strategy includes the establishment of new, statewide programs that leverage the value of services provided by existing libraries. This strategy was made more feasible by the existence of the Community College Library Association (CCLA) and the Florida Center for Library Automation (FCLA) serving the universities. Each of these groups already maintained a common catalog and had a staff and committee structure to deal with common concerns. Public libraries were also practiced cooperators with almost all of them belonging to one of six regional consortia and many local agreements in place.

The challenge was to firmly establish and coordinate the individual elements of such a distributed program. Different elements had different problems to deal with, but all occurred within the context of insecure funding and a less than optimally aware state legislature.

ESTABLISHING THE ELEMENTS OF THE INITIATIVE AND SECURING CONTINUING FUNDING

In fiscal year 1997-98, all DLLI funding came directly from the state legislature. The two million dollar appropriation was used for:

- subscribing to a common core of databases
- running two document delivery trials
- planning for reciprocal borrowing agreements

- opening a reference and referral center (RRC) and library user training service (LUTS)

In the following fiscal year, database subscription prices had increased to the point where $2,000,000 would not pay for renewal of the entire existing package. Direct funding from the legislature was specifically restricted to database subscriptions with no provision for other DLLI elements. These were continued with funds from various sources.

Though central funding was largely restored in the third year, the events of this period had a real effect on the development of the various services. One result was the cancellation of plans to set up a small central office for DLLI, leaving the administration of DLLI to fall into the general workload of steering committee members, and existing libraries, associations, and committees. The Reference and Referral Center took on the de facto role of clearinghouse for DLLI information but had no official status as such.

NEGOTIATING THE CORE ELECTRONIC RESOURCE SUBSCRIPTIONS

Annual negotiation of the databases to be included in the core electronic collection provides an example of the pluses and minuses of cooperation between institutions. In the first year, the core consisted of the Encyclopaedia Britannica Online and sixty-one databases from OCLC's FirstSearch. It was available on-site at the 38 public community colleges and universities and in participating public libraries. It was also available off-site to the faculty, staff and students of the community colleges and universities. This project was prompted by the demands of distance education, but made resources available to all users of participant libraries.

The educational rationale for the core electronic collection was to insure that all distance learners would have access to some online full text and have the ability to search major indexing and abstracting sources. Financially and practically it meant different things to different institutions. The State University System already subscribed to most of the FirstSearch databases included and provided off-site access to their students. For them, having a statewide group subscription meant some loss of control in exchange for a probable increase in buying power. For the community colleges, the package represented a major funding element and an enormous increase in the number of electronic resources available. For almost all community colleges, it provided the first electronic resources available off-site.

For public libraries, it came as a bit of a surprise–a plan most of them didn't know about until they were asked to press for it during the libraries' 1997 lobbying day at the state legislature. The case that was argued was that there would be distance learners without home computer access who would need resources not available at the public library, but that they could use the computers there to search and order items by ILL when necessary. Public libraries were well placed to provide additional services to distance learners and would also gain additional resources for the rest of their patrons.

The service was free to individual libraries, though they did have to bear the cost of any extra demands on equipment and staff time. Most public libraries did accept the electronic collection, but provision was very uneven. A few made it available only to staff. Some still had only or mainly pre-Windows dumb terminals, providing command line searching and text only. While many librarians and other staff members were enthusiastic, others were inexperienced and reluctant to promote the collection. Those with the most experience and the best equipment probably had the least to gain as they were already providing some other online sources that better met the needs of most of their patrons.

In the second year, because of increased charges from OCLC and *Encyclopaedia Britannica*, the package had to be cut and the various participants had to make compromises. It was fairly easy to agree to drop Medline and ERIC as these were available in other, free, formats. Difficult decisions were exemplified by the fact that the universities sacrificed MLA and the community colleges were unhappiest about losing Periodical Abstracts. The universities had more electronic collection money and a mechanism in place for negotiating their own group discounts, so they could fairly easily pick up MLA on their own. The community colleges had neither money nor mechanism so lost comparatively more.

In the third year, there was more money again, and most of the missing databases were restored, bringing the common collection back to fifty-nine. The universities also subscribed to ATLA Religion and Chemical Abstracts. Significantly, CCLA was by then organized to negotiate for the community colleges and added ERIC and Business Dateline. The wording of the appropriation had changed to require the State Library to assume the costs for any public library subscriptions and they decided on a package of only 13, eliminating the specialist academic indexes. By using password authentication provided by their community college or university library, students could still access the full academic package at public libraries.

PLANNING FOR RECIPROCAL BORROWING AND OTHER AGREEMENTS

Because DLLI is a cooperative program, agreements can be reached and effected only by the consensus of all participants. While the imperative of renewing online subscriptions impelled timely action in that area, other decisions have taken longer to make and cannot be said to have been fully or uniformly implemented. CCLA has always been a centralist body, with its administration taking the lead in devising and implementing the common programs of the community colleges, while the cooperation of State University System libraries has been through a participant committee structure. The decision not to fund a central office with an administrator dedicated to furthering DLLI projects almost exacerbated the tensions inherent in negotiations between bodies with such different traditions.

Universities and community colleges providing access to one another's students was one of the original stated goals of DLLI. The state university and community college libraries are open to all members of the public, so distance learners have always had on-site access to the resources of any other school. Beyond that, the university and community college systems each had reciprocal borrowing agreements covering their own members. There were also several local, cross-system agreements among groups of nearby universities and community colleges. Despite this experience, there was considerable reluctance to institute unrestricted lending to all patrons of both groups. Technical barriers also delayed the reaching of an agreement. Soon after a bridge had been built to allow the two computer systems to share patron information, the *Borrowing Privileges Agreement Information* (1999) was signed by all 38 institution presidents, agreeing to make some provision for reciprocal borrowing and setting the ground rules for fiscal responsibility, but leaving many details to be decided locally.

Some institutions have extended the same privileges available to their own students while others offer more limited service, for instance setting lower item limits or excluding non-book media. The technology requires that community college students have a 14 digit ID to use university resources, but four community colleges still use nine digit social security numbers. There have been some local workarounds, but no universal plan to deal with this problem. Not all of the institutions have formulated a detailed policy and very few are making their policies easily available to potential users.

The universities have taken the further step of negotiating an agreement to provide for the interlibrary loan of books to one another's students. Other materials have not presented a problem because most of the libraries will mail copies of owned and borrowed articles, and books from their own collections to their own distance learners. Only one library however, was willing to mail borrowed books, meaning that a distance learner needing a book would have to travel to the campus to collect it or, perhaps, borrow it through their public library. Though this agreement has been signed, it has not been uniformly adopted. Again, even where this service is available, it is not advertised.

Other cooperative agreements have included FCLA's providing a proxy server to allow university students off-campus access to additional, IP-authenticated subscription databases and CCLA's taking on the function of leading negotiations for groups of community colleges that wish to subscribe to the same databases. Talks have begun about providing reserve services where a large group of students taking a course from one school are based in the area of another institution. No general agreements have yet been reached, but the universities have all named a responsible librarian so that a faculty member asking about such provision can at least find the right person to talk to.

IMPROVING DOCUMENT DELIVERY FOR DISTANCE LEARNERS– BENEFITS FOR ALL ILL USERS

Document delivery was recognized as an important part of service to distance learners. Many schools already mailed books and articles to distance learners, usually under the auspices of the ILL department. Where they didn't, students were dependent on ILL services offered by public libraries. This was a potential source of steadily increasing costs for both provider libraries and those that have been called victim libraries (Dugan, 1997). In response, two document delivery trials were run in the first year. In the second year, one was not renewed and the other secured alternative financing.

The first, an experiment with patron-initiated, unmediated document delivery from a commercial source (UMI), was ended because of low use and because almost all of the ordered items could have been borrowed from other Florida libraries.

This finding underlined the value of the second trial, a project to improve interlibrary loan within Florida. The Tampa Bay Library Consortium secured the contract to administer a statewide courier service. Delivery was provided to all state system academic libraries and most public libraries. Librarians of all types reported that reusable bags and standard labels had greatly reduced the staff time needed, while delivery speed remained as good or better. Because first year funding came from DLLI, libraries' carriage costs were eliminated.

In the second year, the courier service was funded from Federal Library Services and Technology Act (LSTA) money, administered by the State Library of Florida, and CCLA and FCLA appropriations, covering costs for services to public libraries, community colleges, and universities, respectively. Third year funding for the service continued to include LSTA, CCLA, and FCLA money, but libraries were required to contribute $600 for each day of the week that they were scheduled for a van stop. Thus, costs varied from $3,000 for major academic libraries receiving Monday to Friday deliveries to $600 for small public libraries receiving only one delivery per week. The total number of libraries served was increased, but there were some changes within systems, altering which libraries received direct DLLI deliveries and which were served by local courier services from main or larger branches.

Independent academic libraries were also invited to join, based on the cost of adding extra stops on the courier route and many independent universities and colleges are now participants. Though independent schools benefit from the state sponsored administration of the program, their participation has also improved service for existing participants because their loans to and from the independent schools can now be handled in the same, uniform, time-, and labor-saving way.

While the courier service is sponsored by DLLI in support of distance learners, it has proved to be of general benefit to all libraries and types of library users. Contract costs are based on a fixed delivery schedule rather than actual packets exchanged, so the service is used for other loans at no incremental cost. More of the costs may be gradually passed back to libraries, but most will still have lower total costs for ILL than they had before the courier began.

THE DIRECT PATRON SERVICE ELEMENTS: REFERENCE AND REFERRAL AND USER TRAINING

From the beginning, the DLLI Steering Committee was committed to an element of direct patron service. It was agreed that all distance learners should have access to the services of academic librarians, but not all would be reasonably near an academic library. It was also recognized that many people were choosing distance learning for reasons that were not purely geographical. As the clear distinction between on campus courses and distance education began to blur, many students were choosing distance courses for scheduling purposes. They could be expected to need library services at odd hours, too. At the same time, the libraries of most of the schools beginning to offer distance courses had limited, traditional opening times and none were in a position to substantially increase their hours without further funding for that purpose. It was decided to try setting up a central service that would offer reference support online, by toll-free telephone, and be open long hours. A central user training service could coordinate library instruction for distance learners.

A proposal from the University of South Florida (USF) for the provision of reference and referral service was accepted by DLLI. The Reference and Referral Center (RRC) and Library User Training Service (LUTS) opened in late 1997, housed in the USF Tampa Campus Library. As a new service, the RRC had two things to do: to begin immediately to make the promised high level of service available over long hours, and to build awareness of the availability of the service.

The pattern of first and second year funding significantly affected how this was done. Midway through the first year, it began to seem likely that there would not be money from the legislature for a second year and that any other funding arrangements would probably be delayed until well into the new financial year. Continuing to provide high quality service for users, including maintaining staff coverage for advertised hours, was considered vital, so salaries for the existing librarians and LIS graduate assistants were prioritized. When the original LUTS coordinator left, the two services were merged under the Director of the RRC. While this was a desirable move from a service point of view, the consequent short-term savings were also an incentive. Further planned librarian positions were not filled. Development and promotional plans were scaled back for reasons of immediate finance and because there was no guarantee that the service would continue to exist.

These savings and a grant of $70,000 from the Florida Public Post-secondary Distance Learning Institute covered most of the expenses of the now-merged services through the fall of the 1998-99 financial year, though USF had to informally advance librarians' salaries for the final pay periods. Finally, with the financial year more than half over, $245,800 came from surplus funds held by the Florida Distance Learning Network, an older organization set up to provide and coordinate the use of a television relay network.

Because that body also included Florida-based, accredited independent colleges and universities, the RRC agreed to extend service to them. This provided a partial answer to the seeming anomaly, that some non-Florida residents were served, but Florida taxpayers were not eligible if they attended private schools. Though 35 institutions fell into this category, only a handful actually offered courses at a distance and most of these were already providing similar services. However, the RRC's hours and accessibility via toll-free telephone and electronic communication provided an additional resource for research assistance.

Planning for the 1999-2000 state budget had been underway, with good prospects for a return to direct funding for DLLI, even before the RRC was assured of sufficient funds to make it through 1998-99. The late arrival of most 1998-99 money did mean that there was a rollover available when 1999-2000 funds were allocated as expected, but were not available until November. Despite this temporary difficulty, the RRC entered the 1999-2000 financial and academic year with much improved prospects: funding was now recurrent and long-term plans could be made.

When the RRC was established, preparing to support the students of so many different colleges and universities across Florida was a daunting task. The goal was to provide individual advice, based on a knowledge of what resources were available to an individual, both as a distance learner of a particular school and as a resident of a particular locality. Library Web pages and online catalogs could provide much of this information, but not all libraries had Web pages and where they did, their content and organization varied widely. The RRC set out to collect and systematically present information in a way that would be easily usable by RRC staff answering questions or by patrons using the RRC Web site themselves.

An online directory of Florida public libraries and public academic libraries was created, with alphabetic and geographical indexes. Directory pages included standard fields such as hours, addresses, and phone numbers, and items likely to be of particular interest to distance learners, including the availability of public Internet stations and policies governing their use. Where available, they also provided direct links to online catalogs and specific information within library Web sites. Libraries were contacted to verify and augment publicly available information. These directory pages have been regularly maintained and improved in response to experience. New features have included information about databases available for onsite use at community colleges and direct links to off-site database access and remote service request forms for universities. When the RRC's services were officially extended to private academic institutions, directory entries were compiled for their libraries, too.

In the summer of the RRC's second year, more experience answering users' questions lead staff to write a series of brochures for the state universities, each combining information about the RRC with local information, which was often not available or not easily found on the university or university library's Web sites. The brochures provide an easy reference tool for RRC librarians, and are available direct to students and faculty in HTML and PDF formats. The systematic collection of service facts, such as the procedure for getting a library card or requesting a document, also helped members of the university libraries' subcommittee on services to distance learners to share examples of best practice and consider gaps in their own service policies.

The most challenging aspect of providing statewide reference service to distance learners has been making distance faculty and students aware of the service and building relationships with them. Question logs show a direct relationship between verbal contact with faculty and student use of the RRC. Students who receive direct instruction from RRC librarians are also more likely to use RRC services. Initially, RRC brochures were sent to academic libraries and distance learning administrators, asking them to inform their faculty and students about the service. Coverage was far from uniform—it was often difficult to determine who to contact or even if there was a good central contact. This mailing did result in a fairly satisfying response in terms of links to the RRC from library and distance learning Web pages, but very little contact from potential users. It seemed that the message was not getting down to the faculty level.

With limited staff and uncertainty over its future, the RRC choose to concentrate on developing a relationship with administrators or faculty who did respond. To provide students with an introduction to library resources, they offered to visit distance classes that had face-to-face off campus meetings or on-site orientations, and to participate in broadcast classes. Where a professor (or several students from the same class) contacted them, they prepared Web pages with library service information and links to suggested subscription databases and Internet resources. Depending on the level of collaboration, these ranged from the very general to suggestions for researching specific paper topics.

When the future looked more certain and additional staff had been hired, broader contact attempts were resumed. A survey of a sample of distance learning faculty was conducted in the summer of 1999, in an attempt to identify the kinds of courses where faculty were making assignments that assumed library usage. Faculty were also asked if there were differences in their assignments for on campus and distance courses. Unfortunately the response rate was so low, under 10%, that no conclusions could be drawn. Comments also gave the impression that responses came from faculty members who were either very enthusiastic and relatively aware of online resources or unhappy with the whole process of distance education.

Before the fall semester, letters and brochures were sent directly to all the identifiable distance learning faculty of selected programs. Again, the response was limited. Looking to the spring semester of 2000, plans called for a mass mailing to distance learning faculty and personally contacting institution and department level distance education coordinators. It was hoped that the latter would generate invitations to speak at faculty meetings and workshops.

Though use of the RRC remains low, it rose steadily over the first two years and quite spectacularly in the last semester of the second year. And there is every indication that the service is needed. Where a professor recommends the service, students use it. And where one student finds out about the RRC and contacts it for technical help or advice on a research assignment, others from the same class usually follow. Early user surveys showed a high level of satisfaction with the quality of service and it is encouraging that user comments continue to be very positive.

The provision of off-campus access to databases, improved cooperation between community colleges and universities and speedier document delivery all make vital contributions to distance education. The RRC's record of questions shows that students don't necessarily know about these possibilities and often need a high level of support to begin using them effectively. The staff have come to realize that having laid down a foundation of good service, achieving a high level of awareness among potential users is going to be a long-term, labor intensive task, but one that is very worth performing.

REFERENCES

Borrowing privileges agreement information. (1999 February 2). Tallahassee: Florida Center for Library Automation. Retrieved November 29, 1999 from the World Wide Web: http://www.fcla.edu/FCLAinfo/sus/borrowing_agreement.html.

Dugan, R. E. (1997). Distance education: provider and victim libraries. *The Journal of Academic Librarianship, 23,* 315-318.

Florida postsecondary distance learning scenarios. (1998). Fort Myers: Florida Public Postsecondary Distance Learning Institute. Retrieved November 29, 1999 from the World Wide Web: http://sun6.dms.state.fl.us/institute/scenarios2.html.

Florida distance learning reference & referral center. Tampa: Florida Distance Learning Reference & Referral Center. Retrieved November 29, 1999 from the World Wide Web: http://www.lib.usf.edu/distance.

Using a Web-Based MOO
for Library Instruction
in Distance Education

Joanne B. Smyth

University of New Brunswick

SUMMARY. This institution is in the process of establishing a graphical interface, Web-based MOO [Multi-User Dungeon, Object-Oriented], both to create a forum for synchronous library instruction and to serve as an online meeting place for off-campus students, who are otherwise without a learning community. This paper describes the development of that service and outlines its strengths and weaknesses.

KEYWORDS. Library services, distance education, library instruction, Web-based MOO

After a 1996 survey of our off-campus students revealed service in several areas to be lacking, UNB Libraries reaffirmed and strengthened its support to distance education students to meet the Canadian Libraries Association Guidelines (http://gateway1.uvic.ca/staff/sslade/guidelines.html). We developed a clearer sense of who we were serving, and looked at the particular needs of each cohort of users. The boom of Internet-based Library databases created an opportunity to design and implement a coherent venue for communicating with off-campus students. In 1996, our SilverPlatter databases were made available through the Web. Our Library catalogue has been available

[Haworth co-indexing entry note]: "Using a Web-Based MOO for Library Instruction in Distance Education." Smyth, Joanne B. Co-published simultaneously in *Journal of Library Administration* (The Haworth Information Press, an imprint of The Haworth Press, Inc.) Vol. 32, No. 1/2, 2001, pp. 383-392; and: *Off-Campus Library Services* (ed: Anne Marie Casey) The Haworth Information Press, an imprint of The Haworth Press, Inc., 2001, pp. 383-392.

via telnet since 1995, and through the Web since 1996. With the addition of other serials indexing, abstracting and full text services, we can now offer our off-campus students access to research tools that is similar to the access enjoyed on-campus. In the spring of 1999, we developed a Web site specifically for distance education students (http://www.lib.unb.ca/Services/DistEd/), including an online request form for book and article requests, which could feed inter-library loan requests directly into our Document Delivery Unit. Links from our Web site also enable students to e-mail requests for help with database use, and for troubleshooting with user access and other such annoyances to distance learners. These annoyances spring from new sources, constantly. Most recently, the introduction of proxy server access to some of our databases has confounded users. We continue to provide toll-free telephone contact with the Library, and routinely conduct subject-specific library instruction sessions, either on-site or through audio conferencing to groups of students. While we are still developing our services to off-campus students, we feel that we are approaching the "equitable library services" described in the CLA Guidelines.

In individual dealings with off-campus students, however, two issues became clear: one practical, the other, perhaps social. The first grew from the frustration students felt when conversing with Library staff, receiving instructions on how to access and use our online resources. Students, typically, have only one telephone line to their homes. After hearing a litany of "click there"-based instruction, they would disconnect the telephone, plug in a modem, turn on their PC, dial in, and hope they could remember where to click once our Library home page appeared. The need for an interactive forum for instruction in using our Web-based resources soon became clear.

The second issue sprang from a comparison of the way our on- and off-campus students used the Library. A half-hour of observing students in our Reference lobby demonstrates that students often use the Library in small groups, and rely on each other to strengthen their research efforts. In contrast, off-campus students generally work in solitude. Thus, they often find using the Library's resources more difficult than do the students who work with their peers. New Brunswick is a rural province: students in one course may live hours apart. UNB offers no synchronous 'chat' facility for its students. Indeed, our Computing Services policy discourages online chat. In effect, there is no "student union" for off-campus students.

In looking for a technological answer to the problems of library instruction at a distance, and filling the social void that distance education can produce, I began playing with the idea of using a MOO as a venue for student and library staff communication. The history of the MOOing is well described in Haynes and Holmevik (1998). In brief, MOOs (Multi-User Dungeon, Object-Oriented) began as a forum for players of Dungeons and Dragons-style gaming, wherein they could use their PCs to communicate in real time, by typing what they wanted their characters to do or say. Using a series of commands, players could describe scenarios, "move" through scenes, "pick up" or "examine" objects, "speak" to each other, etc. Leslie Harris describes the advantage of an object-oriented system:

> Object-oriented programming is a highly efficient form of coding that depends on the notion of 'inheritance.' A person programs a 'parent' object, which serves as the prototype for all other objects of its kind. Other people can then create a 'child' (or copy) of that parent, and the 'child' retains all the features of the original. Any changes made to the 'parent' object are automatically made to all its 'children' as well (such as an added feature, capability, verb, and so on). In addition, the 'child' object can be further customized (possessing capabilities that the parent doesn't contain), and it too can become the parent of other objects. (Harris, no date).

One does not need to know the programming code to create objects on a MOO. One simply copies existing, "generic" objects, and modifies them to suit particular purposes. Initially, the objects were game-related. However, the potential use of the MOO for educational purposes has begun to overshadow its genesis.

While interesting, it did not seem that a text-based MOO would provide any advantage over the use of a telephone in the delivery of library instruction to off-campus students. Library users would still have to make the leap from using the text-based MOO to using our Web-based resources. The immediacy of an entirely Web-based interface remained elusive.

I was introduced to graphical interface MOOs in the autumn of 1998, when UNB hosted the 4th International North America World Wide Web (N. A. Web) Conference, focusing on "The Virtual Campus." There, Mark Haas of Dakota State University presented *Moo in Your Face: Researching, Designing, and Programming a User-Friendly*

Interface, which chronicled his development of a graphical interface-MOO to complement a composition class. Haas describes the inadequacies of a text-based MOO, and posits that a Web-based graphical interface is more germane to the needs of the people using it. Haas and others designed a graphical MOO site using freeware, Pueblo from Chaco Communications–now Andromedia (http://www.chaco.com/). They found that a graphical interface spared the MOO from threatened obscurity as an outdated mode of communication. Further, they observed that their students were able to navigate through and use the MOO in significantly less time than had been required in a textual environment.

Intrigued, I sent out a query to DEOS-L, the Distance Education Online Symposium (LISTSERV@LISTS.PSU.EDU), asking if anyone had tried using a Web interface with a MOO for the purposes of library instruction to remote students. It seemed to be an obvious forum for integrating our Web-based resources with direct, synchronous communication with Library users. The responses were helpful and encouraging: although no one reported having used a MOO specifically for library instruction, many subscribers expressed a desire to hear how we fared if we chose to try. I was also referred to Diversity University, and to Isabel Danforth, who was said to be particularly helpful in teaching people how to use the MOO.

Diversity University (http://moo.du.org:8000/) is a MOO devoted to education. Established by Jeanne MacWhorter, it is a multi-disciplinary, completely cyberspace-based campus. DU is designed for classroom use, and is used by many colleges and universities to complement their various programs (http://www.du.org/dumoo/schoolslist. htm). It is a good place to begin experiencing a MOO: upon logging in, one is offered help with commands, maps, and other guides to use. One sees graphical clues to navigating, and is encouraged to explore the "campus" (see Figure 1). One login option integrates Web and telnet functions, so that users see a Web window and a live interaction window within the same screen.

This connection uses the Cup-o-Mud telnet applet, and works only on Java-enabled browsers. The screen, when at DU, is divided into three parts. The upper area is the Web portion, and can contain graphics, hypertext links to other Web sites, or text. The middle area is entirely textual, logs conversations and actions taken in the "room" and provides the text of notes or other communications. The bottom

FIGURE 1

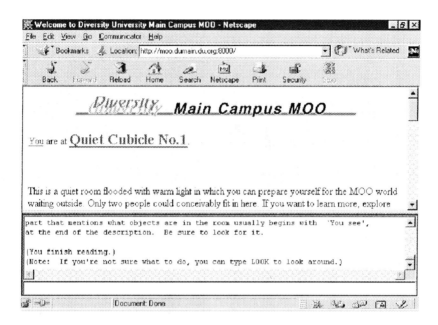

area is a single line, into which one can enter commands to speak, move, read, manipulate objects, etc. Using the MOO for the first time, one is overwhelmed by the foreignness of it all. One must use specific commands to do anything, registered users invent characters for themselves, and are sometimes difficult to know in a text-only environment (although there are some graphics for places and things in DU, people are described entirely verbally).

Eventually, I gave up on wandering rather aimlessly through Diversity University and contacted Isabel Danforth, asking her how I might learn to use the resources there for my specific purpose. She suggested that I enroll in Web-based courses, offered by herself and Diane Kovacs (p://www.kovacs.com), which would show how to use Diversity University MOO for distance education. These courses were offered at DU, and were an education in themselves; we gained a sense of the purpose of the MOO, along with learning how to create environments there and manage groups of students online in real time. By the end of the second course we had graduated to "builder" status, and were able to construct our own learning environments in our own "rooms."

There are four general classifications of people on the MOO: guests or players, who can communicate and move around, builders, who can use commands to change objects and create spaces, programmers, who can use advanced commands to control the MOO, and wizards, who administer the entire database (the language of gaming pervades even DU MOO).

Having acquired an elementary sense of MOO building, I considered what might be useful to our off-campus students: providing them with a meeting place, providing the capability for synchronous communication with Library staff, and providing some Web-based material that would be accessible through the MOO site for asynchronous library instruction, which some prefer. One can create "rooms" at DU, which are virtual places, filled with whatever objects one chooses to place there, and evoking whatever atmosphere one chooses to describe. I elected to begin with a place, the UNB Libraries Lounge. Since I was working in a chilly office on a raw Maritimes' March day, the Lounge was described as sunny, warm and, I hoped, inviting (see Figure 2).

A few key generic objects were soon added to the Lounge: tables and chairs, of course, notes, and slides, and a slide projector for view-

FIGURE 2

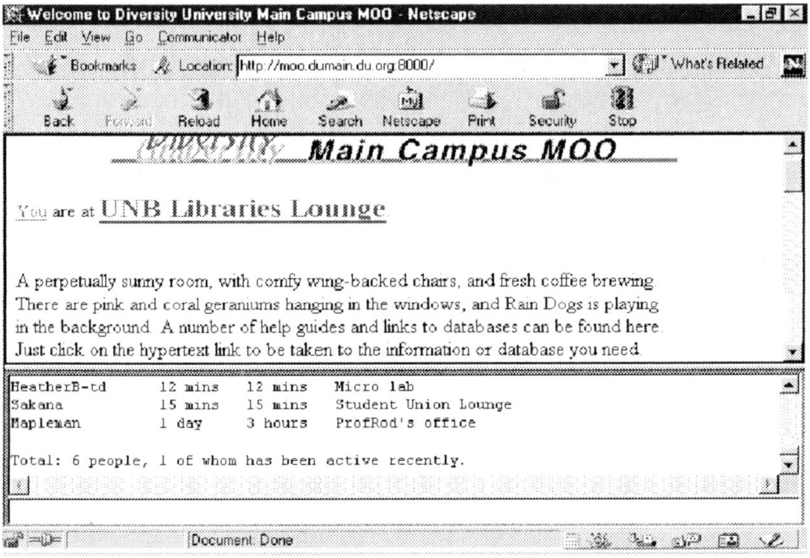

ing them. The notes contained hypertext links to other documents on the Web, tutorials describing how to use various databases, and help on various topics, from essay writing to online reference tools. These were intended for students' individual perusal. The slides were created for use with groups of students who would meet me at some designated time at DU. It is possible to force Web screens to appear on students' PC monitors by showing them "slides" that are connected to specific URLs. When such a slide is shown, it forces a second Web browser to open on each participant's PC. One can then re-size screens so that each is partly visible, or toggle between Web sessions, using resources on one, and communicating with others in the "room" with the other. All conversations in the MOO can be recorded, so that users can be reminded later of instructions given and sequences followed.

Builders not only create places and objects in the MOO, they also create groups of users (VSPOs or Visiting Student Person Objects), to create a class. These would, in the present case, be distance education students at the University of New Brunswick, who would meet on the MOO for library instruction with me, or to do group work with classmates. By creating VSPOs one has greater control over the group: each user is recognizable by name, and each user has abilities specified by the group builder. Entry into the MOO is controlled by passwords created by the group builder, so access can be limited to one's own cohort. Further, a group builder can, during instruction sessions, force a URL onto the screen of each person in the group, without having to create slides. Each VSPO's e-mail address can be registered, so that the conversation log and needed help files can be sent directly to him or her during a session.

I initially attempted to create text files of our various printed brochures, and set these up as slides on the MOO. However, file length became a problem: notes and slides have a finite file size, and mine consistently exceeded these. The advantages of translating these files into html format and placing them on the UNB Libraries' server soon became clear. Once we had established Web sites for the information in our printed brochures, I was able to create objects on the MOO which pointed to the sites' URLs. This way, we could have almost limitless information accessible through the MOO, without tying up MOO memory.

One such brochure describes our Electronic Information Sources, the online databases to which we have access through the Internet, and which are now accessible on- or off-campus. In creating an html file for this document, I incorporated links to the necessary login screens for each resource listed, and set up step-by-step guides to logging in to some of our more popular databases. The guides were fairly easy to create as Corel Presentations slides, saved as html documents. We also created an online guide to using our WebCat, QUEST. Of course, the Library's home page, and specifically, the site describing our services to distance education students, were also set up as URL links through the MOO Library Lounge site. The idea was to have this "room" emulate the physical space of our Main library's Reference Lobby as closely as possible, with ready access to needed resources and databases, synchronous contact with Library staff, and the chance to converse with fellow users.

Having built a "room" and arranged resources within, we still faced our greatest challenge. Finding students who are interested in learning to use the MOO has proven to be much more difficult than ever expected. We began by advertising casually, to faculty who held teleconferenced courses, some of whom expressed interest at the outset, but most of whom then found the constraints of time during the term made it necessary to exclude such extraneous activities. Our campus Computing Services Department had earlier established an Internet-based Presentation System for Courses (PSYCO), which provided students with access to course notes, assignments, and an asynchronous communication system, similar to a listserv. Some faculty members were content to use only PSYCO, probably aware of the spate of information systems juggled by our students, and unwilling to add to their burden with a competing system.

We began describing the MOO site while visiting remote sights for library instruction early in the school year. Students were enthusiastic, but somewhat timid about the commands needed to navigate and speak. Perhaps the point-and-click environment (see Figure 3) recently added to Diversity University will appeal to these students. We added one-page advertisements for the MOO to the packages of material sent to off-campus students. These too have failed to elicit much response.

Perhaps students' reluctance to use the MOO site stems from the site being hard to access without my assistance and intervention. Before they can use the MOO, they must contact me for a login and password, and to prearrange a time for library instruction. Distance education students are a self-reliant group, working with considerable time constraints, who may well reject a medium that demands yet

FIGURE 3

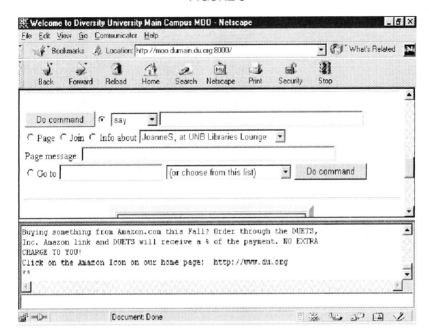

another lesson. Perhaps too, their inherent self-reliance precludes their seeking classmates on the Internet. However, many off-campus students complain in conversation (over the telephone) with me that they feel disassociated from the university community.

Diversity University provided us with tools and space to begin exploring the MOO as an educational resource. If UNB were to establish its own MOO site, we would be able to tailor it specifically to our students' needs, perhaps making the medium less visible, yet more directly accessible. We will continue to refine our Internet-based services and resources for our off-campus community, and examine ways to bring the Library to our users.

REFERENCES

Filby, A. M. (1996). Proposal for implementing multi-user database (MUD) technology in an academic library. *Internet Reference Services Quarterly, 1*(2), 75-95.

Haas, M., & Gardner, C. (1998) MOO in your face: researching, designing, and programming a user-friendly interface. In J. L. Shoecroft et al., *N.A. Web 98: The Virtual Campus*, (pp. 48-63). Fredericton, N.B.: University of New Brunswick.

Harris, L. (No date). *MUDs and MOOs: an Overview.* Retrieved February 2, 1999 from the World Wide Web: http://www.susqu.edu:80/ac_depts/arts_sci/english/ lharris/mudsmoos.htm.

Haynes, C., & Holmevik, J. (Eds.) (1998). *High wired: On the design, use, and theory of educational MOOs.* Ann Arbor: University of Michigan Press.

Slade, A. L. (1998). *Guidelines for library support of distance and distributed learning in Canada.* Retrieved November 25, 1998 from the World Wide Web: http://gateway1. uvic.ca/staff/sslade/guidelines.html.

Woods, J. C. (1998). EduMOOs: Virtual learning centres. *Technology Connection, 5*(2), 24-25.

Graduate Students' Perceptions
of Library Support Services
for Distance Learners:
A University System-Wide Study

Carol J. Tipton

Texas A&M University-Kingsville

SUMMARY. A survey was conducted in Spring 1999 to assess the library support services for distance learning within the Texas A&M University System. Graduate students actively enrolled at remote sites in one or more courses taught on the system's interactive video network were surveyed. Results of this survey provide insight for improving library services.

"People want what they want when they want it. They don't want something else, they don't want less than they want, and they certainly don't want it at some other time" (Forsha, 1992).

KEYWORDS. Surveys, library services, distance education

INTRODUCTION

The Texas A&M University System consists of nine universities, eight state agencies and a health science center, serving more than 88,000 students the system has a presence in all 254 Texas counties. Through its service mission the system reaches approximately 3.5 million people each year throughout the state. A statewide network,

[Haworth co-indexing entry note]: "Graduate Students' Perceptions of Library Support Services for Distance Learners: A University System-Wide Study." Tipton, Carol J. Co-published simultaneously in *Journal of Library Administration* (The Haworth Information Press, an imprint of The Haworth Press, Inc.) Vol. 32, No. 1/2, 2001, pp. 393-408; and: *Off-Campus Library Services* (ed: Anne Marie Casey) The Haworth Information Press, an imprint of The Haworth Press, Inc., 2001, pp. 393-408.

the Trans-Texas Video Conference Network (TTVN), which provides two-way, multi-point, digital videoconferencing and data transmission for academic and administrative use, connects the A&M System. TTVN began operating in 1990 with 12 network locations. It now serves more than 100 locations and provides dial-up services to video-conferencing facilities around the world.

Over 67 percent of the videoconferences from September 1997 to August 1998 involved university telecourses. Since system universi-ties maintain a high level of autonomy, primary responsibility for library support to students enrolled in telecourses and other distance learning courses lies with the library at the university in which stu-dents are enrolled. The libraries within the Texas A&M System partic-ipate in the TexShare program, a cooperative program designed to enhance library service to students, faculty, and staff of Texas state-supported institutions of higher education. The program provides state-wide licensing of databases, access to library collections, assistance in document delivery, and additional electronic resources. This com-bined buying power has resulted in cost reductions for electronic information subscriptions for many Texas academic libraries. Addi-tionally, the TexShare card program affords students and faculty ac-cess to the collections of all TexShare participants. Through the years, TexShare has been expanded to include private and community col-lege libraries and public libraries. Amigos Bibliographic Council, a nonprofit organization, has administered TexShare since 1996. This study was funded, in part, by a fellowship from Amigos.

Library support is an essential part of any academic program, in-cluding those offered through distance learning. Like their on-campus counterparts, distance-learning students need consistent access to li-brary resources to develop and broaden their understanding of their disciplines by researching a topic and incorporating the information into their coursework (Pettingill, 1995). The same constraints that motivate students to opt for distance learning also limit their ability to use the library; therefore, distance students must rely on the library support available at the remote site, interlibrary loan, or travel to the campus where the course originates. Since library collections and policies vary, students enrolled in the same class may not have access to the same resource materials. If distance-learning programs are to be credible and successful, the distance-learning student must have the same access to library support services as the on-campus student.

Research by Dillon, Gunawardena, and Parker (1992) on learner support found that the effectiveness of library services provided to distance students could be a significant barrier to those required to use the library.

To provide effective library support to distance students, libraries need to assess the needs of their users. The annual statistics reported by many libraries offer no insight on the quality of the service rendered because such measurers focus on the library's internal operations rather than on its "customers" or users. However, libraries exist to serve their users; only the users can justify the existence of a library. In this time of swiftly changing technology, it is important to know how library users perceive and utilize information, both those on-campus and at remote sites. Surveys of user satisfaction or dissatisfaction are important in identifying problems and issues faced by distance students in accessing library services and resources. Such assessment provides the basis for quality assurance and continuous improvement. Just as interest in distance learning is increasing, the focus on quality service or "customer satisfaction" in libraries has increased.

The purpose of this study is to determine the extent to which the general academic libraries of the Texas A&M University System serve the information needs of graduate students enrolled in distance learning telecourses within the system's member institutions. The study sought to determine the extent to which distant graduate students are aware of the library services offered to students at remote sites. Secondly, this study sought to determine the extent to which distant graduate students perceive that their information needs are met. It is anticipated that this study can offer insight for improving library services to distance students by identifying problems and issues faced by distance students in accessing library services and resources, thereby providing the basis for quality assurance and continuous improvement.

REVIEW OF THE LITERATURE

Kascus and Aguilar (1987) surveyed faculty and students at ten off-campus sites to determine their perceptions about the availability and adequacy of off-campus library services. Results indicated that students were uncertain of the library services available to them and made minimal use of libraries. In 1991, Jaggers, Tallman and Waddell conducted an assessment of how effectively the need for library materials was being met at Northern Arizona University. Results indicated students used materials provided by the instructors (82%), personal collections (68%), local schools (62%), and community college libraries (42%). Additionally, 85% of the respondents who used library services indicated that the materials they received were inadequate for the assignments (Jaggers, Tallman, & Waddell, 1991). In a similar study, Stasch explored where distance students look for information when they do not have access to the campus library. Respondents indicated that their selection of information sources was based on convenience rather than content (Stasch, 1994).

Craig and Schults (1993) investigated the effectiveness of bibliographic instruction to off-campus graduate students in a course in administrative and research methods for the Master of Science in Administration degree (MSA). The findings indicated that the library instruction component was of value to the successful completion of assignments and subsequent courses and the final research project. The researchers recommended that library instruction be evaluated at regular intervals.

In 1993, a survey was conducted at the University of Northern Colorado to assess the needs of faculty teaching off-campus and to provide faculty the opportunity to have input in the design of off-campus library services. As a result of this study, the following services were initiated: library use instruction; reference and referral; and document delivery (Lebowitz, 1993).

Eagan (1994) investigated the information gathering process of off-campus pharmacy students at the University of North Carolina at Chapel Hill. Results indicated that while the students use both print and electronic resources, they prefer electronic sources. However, they do not take advantage of the statewide access to the database system available by remote access. Recommendations from this study included the need for continuous marketing of library services in general, including the promotion of the statewide database.

Cassner and Adams (1998) conducted a study to assess the instructional support provided by the University of Nebraska-Lincoln libraries to a group of rural graduate students. The study included both a student survey and a faculty survey. Responses to both surveys indicated that library services and resources were not being utilized to their full potential. Suggestions for improving library services included improving the turnaround time for delivery of materials to students; increasing student and faculty awareness and use of library resources; and increasing communication between librarians and faculty.

The capacity to deliver services to distance learners is enhanced by the potential of technology; however, effective library services entail much more than simply providing access to the Internet. If no effective method of communication exists between libraries and distance students, such studies are of little value. Research conducted by the University of Minnesota Libraries indicated that for many distance students, the faculty member is the primary communication link to students for information about campus services, including those of the library (Butler, 1997). A critical factor in the effective delivery of library services to distance students is faculty awareness and involvement.

METHOD

The population for this study was graduate students at remote sites enrolled in telecourses taught through the Trans-Texas Videoconferencing Network (TTVN) within the Texas A&M University System in Spring 1999. The total population of 133 graduate students enrolled during the designated period was included in this study. Proctors at remote sites administered the survey. A letter of transmittal and an individual consent form accompanied each instrument. Participation was voluntary and precautions were taken to ensure the anonymity of subjects. The proctor at one site was not able to administer the questionnaire because the packet of surveys did not arrive until after the last class meeting. A cover letter, a questionnaire, an individual consent form and a stamped return envelope were sent to the students not surveyed in class. Two weeks after the initial packet was sent, a postcard was mailed to all non-respondents. Additionally, one instructor requested that a Web-based questionnaire be administered to her classes. Microsoft FrontPage was used to develop the Web-based questionnaire and an email was sent to the students enrolled in her classes to solicit their participation. A total of 102 or 76.69% of the questionnaires were completed and returned.

A survey questionnaire consisting of both open and closed-ended questions was developed based on a survey conducted by the University of Nebraska-Lincoln (Cassner & Adams, 1998). The questionnaire was designed to measure the graduate distance learners' satisfaction levels with library support services and library use patterns. A five point Likert-type scale was used for questions designed to measure general library use patterns and satisfaction. Also asked were a series of questions concerning computer and Internet access. Demographic information collected included gender, age, number of telecourses taken, number of telecourses that required the use of library services, and university originating the course. Additionally, respondents were asked the distance they lived from the university and the teleconference classroom.

Validity of the survey questions was established by using a panel of experts comprised of library faculty at Texas A&M University-Kingsville to review the items. Additionally, a group of administrators at Texas A&M University-Kingsville who had taken distance courses completed the questionnaire and remarked on items they found confusing or in need of more explanation. Based on this input, the survey questionnaire was revised and then administered to the targeted population in Spring 1999. Data were analyzed using the statistical software SPSS for Windows, release 7.5.

RESULTS

The first four questions were designed to solicit information about respondents' use of libraries in general. Questions 5-11 were designed to gain information pertaining to the library support from the university at which the students were enrolled. The remaining questions were designed to gather information about computer skills, the need for additional training and demographic information.

For question 1, approximately one-third of respondents indicated that they did not use printed resources (books 31.4%, journals 31.7%, and print indexes 36.1%). E-mail (41%) and the Internet (44.6%) were reported as being used very often. One-fourth (25.5%) reported using electronic databases for journal articles very often. Seventy-one (69.61%) of the respondents indicated that they did not use the TexShare card. Of these, two respondents commented that they had difficulties when trying to use their TexShare card at a private institution that has chosen not to participate in the TexShare card program. However, seven (53.85%) of the 13 students enrolled at Texas A&M University-Kingsville reported that they often or very often used their TexShare card.

Question 2 asked respondents to report where they obtained materials for their telecourses. Thirty-eight (38.4%) respondents reported they very often printed from the screen. Twenty-five (25.3%) of the respondents reported using other local libraries very often and 24 (24%) reported using materials downloaded from the computer very often. Sixty-six (66%) reported that they did not request materials from an Interlibrary Loan Office, and 76 (74.5%) reported that they did not use their TexShare card at other institutions.

For question 3, 73 (71.56%) respondents indicated that the proximity of the library to their home or workplace was often or very often a factor affecting their choice of a library. Convenient hours were often or very often a factor for 63 (61.76%) respondents. Sixty-two (60.78%) respondents indicated that "Library owns books I need" and "Library owns journals I need" were often or very often a factor. Forty-six (45.10%) reported that a courteous and helpful staff was a factor in their selection of a library.

In question 4, 21 (22.1%) respondents indicated that they very often used a 4-year college or university other than the institution in which they were enrolled. Fifteen (15.6%) indicated they used a public library very often. Thirty-six (36.7%) of the respondents enrolled at Texas A&M University, 4 (80%) of the students enrolled at Texas A&M University-Corpus Christi and 2 (15.38%) of those enrolled at Texas A&M University-Kingsville reported that they had not used the library at the institution at which they were enrolled.

Questions 5-11 pertained specifically to the library at the university from which the respondent had taken the majority of their telecourses. Forty-five (44.1%) reported using the online catalog and 46 (45.1%) used the online journal databases. However, 35 (34.3%) indicated that they had not used their institution's library services. Of these 14 (40%) have not needed to use these services, but 17 (48%) did not know how to get these services, and 18 (51.43%) did not know they had access to the services or did not know how to use the online services. Twenty-four (23.5%) respondents indicated that they had used interlibrary loan services in question 5; however, in question 6, respondents could select more than one method of submission so the total responses is greater than 24. The methods for submitting requests included: 13 by e-mail, 12 by fax, 3 by telephone, 7 by U.S. Postal Service and 14 through a Web page or online catalog. Responses to question 7 indicate that timely receipt of interlibrary loan items appears to be a problem. Only six (8.7%) individuals reported receiving library materials via fax. Responses to question 9 concerning the clarity and legibility of faxed materials indicate that this mode of delivery does not appear to be a problem. Of those respondents to question 11 who indicated that they had contacted library staff, 10 (10.5%) were dissatisfied or very disappointed with the service they received. Furthermore, 22 (11.6%) were dissatisfied or very disappointed overall with the library support services they received as distance-learning students, as indicated by responses to question 12.

Questions 12-16 gathered information about computer skills and the need for additional training. Eighty-one (81%) of the respondents use a computer at home for assignments and research while 17 (17%) use a computer at work. Ninety-five (95%) of the computers used by respondents have Internet access and 80 (80%) of the respondents indicated they have an account with an Internet Service Provider. Ninety-four (92.2%) of the respondents use word processing, software, 90 (88.2%) use databases software, 89 (87.3%) use spreadsheet software, 44 (43.1%) use the Internet, and 42 (41.2%) use e-mail for assignments and research.

In questions 16 and 17, 44 (43.14%) respondents reported that they often or very often felt the need for additional training in searching for materials for research papers and other assignments, while 20 (19.61%) reported that they often or very often felt the need for additional training in using an Internet browser.

Questions 18-24 were demographic in nature. The number of classes taken by respondents ranged from one to 17 with both a mean and a median of five classes. Similarly, the number of classes requiring the use of library resources ranged from none to 17 with a mean of 3.99 classes and a median of 3 classes. There appears to be no relation between student satisfaction and the number of classes requiring the use of library resources. Forty-eight (47%) of the respondents live more than 150 miles from the university at which they are enrolled but 87 (87.9%) of the respondents live within 50 miles of the remote classroom. As anticipated, the majority of the respondents were female (58.8%) and 41.2% males. The ages of the respondents ranged from 23 to 63. The mean age of 38.80 (mode 38) indicates that these are non-traditional students. Sixty-eight (66.66%) of the respondents were enrolled in education classes, 24 (24.5%) in engineering, three (2.9%) in agriculture, and five (4.9%) in English.

IMPLICATIONS

The findings indicate need for a follow-up focus group to better determine why students are not using library services and resources to their full potential. Based on the comments and responses, there appears to be a need for orientations to the services. Tutorials or other methods of instructions on searching methods should be considered. Additionally, a review of the procedures for accessing the online catalog and electronic resources is indicated. Finally, system libraries should consider providing a list of libraries that participate in the TexShare card program when disbursing TexShare cards.

REFERENCES

Butler, J. (1997, May). From the margins to the mainstream: Developing library support for distance learning. *LibraryLine: An Occasional Newsletter of the University of Minnesota Libraries–Twin Cities, 8*, 1-4.

Cassner, M., & Adams, K. (1998). Instructional support to a rural graduate population: An assessment of library services. In C. J. Jacob (Comp.), *The Eighth Off-Campus Library Services Conference Proceedings, Providence, Rhode Island, April 22-24, 1998,* (pp. 117-132). Mount Pleasant, MI: Central Michigan University.

Craig, M. H., & Schults, K. E. (1993). Off-campus students' perceptions of the effectiveness of library user education. In C. J. Jacob (Comp.), *The Sixth Off-Campus Library Services Conference Proceedings, Kansas City, Missouri, October 6-8, 1993* (pp. 73-77). Mount Pleasant, MI: Central Michigan University.

Dillon, C., Gunawardena, C., & Parker, R. (1992). An evaluation of learner support services in a distance education system. *Distance Education, 13*(1), 29-45.

Eagan, V. (1994). *Information needs, sources, and accessibility requirements of pharmacy students learning in off-campus settings.* Unpublished master's thesis, University of North Carolina at Chapel Hill.

Forsha, H. I. (1992). *The pursuit of quality through personal change.* Milwaukee, WI: ASQC Quality Press.

Jaggers, K. E., Tallman, E. M., & Waddell, W. D. (1991,). Library services to off-campus sites: An assessment survey. In C. J. Jacob (Comp.), *The Fifth Off-Campus Library Services Conference Proceedings, Albuquerque, New Mexico, October 30-November 1, 1991* (pp. 131-135). Mount Pleasant, MI: Central Michigan University.

Kascus, M. A., & Aguilar, W. (1987). Problems and issues in providing library support to off-campus academic programs: A pilot study. *Shaping a Cohesive Agenda: Next Steps: Proceedings of the Seventh National Conference on Adult and External Degree Programs, 7th, Memphis, Tennessee, October 7-10, 1987* (pp. 85-103). (ERIC Document Reproduction Service No. ED 321 625)

Lebowitz, G. (1993). Faculty perceptions of off-campus student library needs. In C. J. Jacob (Comp.), *The Sixth Off-Campus Library Services Conference Proceedings, Kansas City, Missouri, October 6-8, 1993* (pp. 143-154). Mount Pleasant, MI: Central Michigan University.

Pettingill, A. (1995). Distance education library services at Old Dominion University. In C. J. Jacob (Comp.), *The Seventh Off-Campus Library Services Conference Proceedings, San Diego, California, October 25-27, 1995* (pp. 303-316). Mount Pleasant, MI: Central Michigan University.

Stasch, M. (1994). *A survey of information sources used by students involved in distance education.* Unpublished master's thesis, San Jose State University.

APPENDIX

Below are the questions included in the survey questionnaire and the results. Since some questions allowed multiple responses; therefore, the number of responses per group will vary.

Library Support Services for Distance Learning
Survey of Graduate Students Enrolled in Trans Texas Videoconference Network Courses
Texas A&M University System

Question 1. How frequently have you used the following library resources for course-related research for TTNV courses? (Mark as many as apply)

	Very often	Often	Sometimes	Not often	Not at all	No response
Books (printed)	12	24	24	10	32	
Journals (printed)	21	11	25	12	32	1
Print indexes for journal articles	6	9	26	21	35	5
Electronic (online) databases for journal articles (e.g., Periodical Abstracts 2)	25	14	17	16	26	4
E-mail	41	19	8	6	26	2
Internet	45	20	13	1	22	1
TexShare card	6	9	6	6	71	4

Question 2. How frequently have you obtained books, journal articles, etc., you needed for TTVN courses from the following sources? (Mark as many as apply)

	Very often	Often	Sometimes	Not often	Not at all	No response
Requested materials via an Interlibrary Loan office	3	7	9	15	66	2
Borrowed from colleague or instructor	7	14	35	16	27	3
Used TexShare card at any college or university library	7	6	8	5	76	
Used local public library	14	9	28	13	37	1
Used other local library	25	14	23	5	32	3
Printed from screen (e.g., full-text materials or Internet)	38	22	15	9	15	3
Downloaded from computer to disk	24	22	16	11	27	2

APPENDIX (continued)

Question 3. How frequently do the following factors affect your choice of a library in terms of your TTVN courses? (Mark as many as apply)

	Very often	Often	Sometimes	Not often	Not at all	No response
Convenient hours	32	31	18	5	11	5
Close to home or work	48	25	7	5	14	3
Library owns books I need	34	28	17	8	10	5
Library owns journals I need	37	25	12	10	15	3
Staff is courteous and helpful	27	19	18	12	21	5
Other (Please specify)	12			3	8	79

Question 4. Please rate the frequency with which you have used the resources and services at the following libraries in support of your TTVN courses. (Mark as many as apply)

	Very often	Often	Sometimes	Not often	Not at all	No response
Texas A&M University	9	10	15	19	45	4
Texas A&M University-Corpus Christi		2		1	87	12
Texas A&M University-Commerce				2	88	12
Texas A&M University-Kingsville	3	5	5	1	79	9
Other 4-year college or university	21	15	18	9	32	7
Community college	9	13	15	9	49	7
Public library	15	9	29	11	32	6
Other (Please specify)	8	4	3		10	77

Question 5. Which of the following library services have you used while enrolled in TTVN courses?

Online catalog (to identify needed *books* or *journals*)	45
Online journal databases (to identify needed *journal articles*)	46
Reference services (to *ask questions* or get *help*)	28
Interlibrary Loan services (to *request materials*)	24
TexShare card (for *borrowing privileges* at other libraries)	22
None (Please mark which of the following best describe why you haven't used these services)	35
I have not needed to use these services for my courses	14
I did not know I had access to these services	9
I don't know how I can get these services	17
I don't know how to use online services	9

Question 6. If you submitted requests for library materials to the Interlibrary Loan Office, which methods have you used? (Mark as many as apply. If none, skip to question #10)

E-mail	13
Fax	12
Telephone	3
In person (at the library)	
Mail (U.S. Postal Service)	7
Web Page or Online Catalog	14
None (have not used the service)	29

Question 7: How frequently were materials you requested from Interlibrary Loan delivered in a timely manner? (Mark as many as apply)

	Very often	Often	Sometimes	Not often	Not at all	No response
Books	5	5	3	1	19	69
Journal article photocopies	5	10	2	1	17	67
Microfilm/Microfiche	1	3	1	19		78
Dissertation/Thesis	2	1		1	20	78

Question 8. Have you received library materials via fax?

Yes	6
No	64
No response	33

Question 9. If you answered yes to question #8, how frequently were the text and graphics clear and legible?

	Very often	Often	Sometimes	Not often	Not at all	No response
Text		6				86
Pictures		3	1			88
Charts		2	2		1	88
Tables		2	2		1	88

APPENDIX (continued)

Question 10. If you have contacted library staff, how would you rate your satisfaction with the service you received?

Very Satisfied	Satisfied	Neutral	Dissatisfied	Very disappointed	Not applicable	No response
15	21	7	3	6	34	16

Question 11. How would you rate your overall satisfaction with the library support services you have received as a distance-learning student?

Very Satisfied	Satisfied	Neutral	Dissatisfied	Very disappointed	Not applicable	No response
13	16	22	11	11	24	5

Question 12. Where is the computer you have used most frequently for the majority of your TTVN course-related assignments and research located?

Home	81
Work	17
Home of friend or relative	1
Library	
Computer lab	1
Other (Please specify)	
No response	2

Question 13. Does this computer have Internet access?

Yes	95
No	5
No response	2

Question 14. Which of the following types of software have you used for TTVN course-related assignments and research? (Mark all that apply)

Word processing	94
E-mail	42
Spreadsheet	89
Databases	90
Internet	44
Presentation Software (i.e., PowerPoint)	86

Question 15. Do you have an account with an Internet Service Provider (such as AOL)?

Yes	80
No	20
No response	2

Question 16. When preparing your research papers and other assignments for your TTVN courses, how frequently do you feel the need for additional training in searching for materials?

Very often	Often	Sometimes	Not often	Not at all	No response
19	25	38	12	6	2

Question 17. How often do you feel the need for additional training in using an Internet browser such as Internet Explorer or Netscape?

Very often	Often	Sometimes	Not often	Not at all	No response
9	11	27	24	29	2

Question 18. Please specify the number of courses you have taken via TTVN, including any you are taking during the current semester.

Number of courses	1	2	3	4	5	6	7	8	9	10	11	12	15	17	No response
Number of Respondents	18	12	6	13	10	11	6	10	2	6	2	2	1	1	2

Question 19. Please specify the number of TTVN courses you have taken that required the use of library resources and services.

Number of courses	None	1	2	3	4	5	6	7	8	9	10	11	12	17	No response
Number of Respondents	11	17	12	10	14	4	8	2	8	2	4	2	1	1	6

Question 20. What is your age?

Age Range	Number of Responses
Less than 25	2
25-30	19
31-40	36
40-50	31
Over 50	9
No response	5

APPENDIX (continued)

Question 21. What is your gender?

Female	60
Male	42

Question 22. From which university does the TTVN course you are presently taking originate?

Texas A&M University	84
Texas A&M University-Corpus Christi	5
Texas A&M University-Commerce	
Texas A&M University-Kingsville	13

Question 23. How close do you live to the *university* at which this TTVN course originates?

Within 50 miles	51-150 miles	151-300 miles	300+ miles	No response
5	46	45	3	3

Question 24. How close do you live to the TTVN *classroom* where you attend this course?

Within 50 miles	51-150 miles	151-300 miles	300+ miles	No response
87	11	1		3

Question 25. Comments:
Thirty of the respondents commented on library services. Of these 26 were negative, expressing frustration in trying to connect to online services, lack of orientation, and problems with getting needed materials. Six respondents commented on the transmittal mode of the course.

Reaccreditation at Nova Southeastern University: How Reaccreditation Can Create Opportunities for Improving Library Services to Distance Students

Johanna Tuñón

Nova Southeastern University

Paul R. Pival

Calgary Health Trust

SUMMARY. Reaccreditation offers academic libraries concerned about improving library services to distance students with an important opportunity to obtain support from their academic institutions. Nova Southeastern University (NSU) Libraries provides a case study of how one library has used the reaccreditation process to increase both the administration's cooperation and funding for document delivery, online resources, bibliographic instruction, and local library resources to distance students.

KEYWORDS. Distance education, library services, reaccreditation

Obtaining reaccreditation is always a challenge for any academic institution, and the process can be even more challenging for institu-

[Haworth co-indexing entry note]: "Reaccreditation at Nova Southeastern University: How Reaccreditation Can Create Opportunities for Improving Library Services to Distance Students." Tuñón, Johanna, and Paul R. Pival. Co-published simultaneously in *Journal of Library Administration* (The Haworth Information Press, an imprint of The Haworth Press, Inc.) Vol. 32, No. 1/2, 2001, pp. 409-424; and: *Off-Campus Library Services* (ed: Anne Marie Casey) The Haworth Information Press, an imprint of The Haworth Press, Inc., 2001, pp. 409-424.

tions offering distance education. Not surprisingly, librarians faced with the process often feel apprehensive as they begin to prepare for reaccreditation. Nevertheless, reaccreditation can also be a valuable experience for academic libraries interested in providing library services to distance students because it provides an important opportunity for them to obtain support from their academic institutions that those institutions would otherwise be reluctant to provide. Libraries can use the standards set by accrediting agencies as a tool to improve the level of support provided by their academic institutions. The Nova Southeastern University Libraries provides a case study of how one institution was able to use the reaccreditation process to obtain the university's cooperation and funding to improve document delivery, online resources, bibliographic instruction, and local library resources for distance students.

BACKGROUND

Nova Southeastern University (NSU) is an independent, nonprofit, co-educational institution located in Fort Lauderdale, Florida. Since its founding as Nova University in 1964, the university has focused on the delivery of non-traditional graduate programs to working adult learners (Manburg, 1983) and on educating students for leadership roles in their professions. In order to further this mission, the university has been a pioneer in distance education (Riggs, 1997) since long before it became fashionable in the 1990s.

At the time that NSU went through its most recent reaccreditation in 1996, the university's enrollment of 16,829 students made it the largest private institution of higher education in the southern United States. NSU was delivering field-based programs at 79 sites in Florida, 66 sites in other states, and 13 international sites. NSU had about one-half of its students in distance programs (Research and Planning, 1997) and 44% attending traditional classes in South Florida. At that time, NSU was already offering a wide selection of distance courses of study for bachelor, master, educational specialist, and doctoral degrees with distance programs in business, education, computer sciences, pharmacology, and the social sciences.

In 1996, the NSU Libraries were comprised of several libraries including the Einstein Library, a law library, a health professions library, an oceanography library, and several school libraries. The

Einstein Library was the university's principal library, serving the undergraduate and graduate programs in business, computer science, and the social sciences. The Einstein Library originally began preparing for reaccreditation in 1992. At that time, it was a small library with a collection of approximately 66,000 volumes, 79,000 microform documents, and 1,100 journal subscriptions. The staff's six and a half FTE (full time equivalent) librarians provided library services to all undergraduate and graduate students on and off campus except for students preparing for professions in the health sciences and law. The collection and staffing of the Einstein Library, however, changed drastically as the library went through the reaccreditation process. In the period between 1992 and 1999, the Einstein Library's professional and clerical staffs more than doubled. In that same seven-year period, the Einstein Library's book collection almost tripled, and half a million dollars was added to the library budget for subscriptions to online resources.

THE REACCREDITATION PROCESS

Before examining the reaccreditation process at NSU, it is important to take a moment to discuss the reaccreditation process in general. In the United States, academic institutions must go through a process known as reaccreditation or reaffirmation if these institutions hope for their degrees to be recognized by other institutions within their own regions and throughout the United States and to receive federal funding for financial aid and student loans. There are five regional accrediting bodies: Middle State Association of Colleges and Schools, New England Association of Schools and Colleges, North Central Association, Northwest Association of Schools and Colleges, Western Association of Schools and Colleges, and Southern Association of Colleges and Schools. Because Nova Southeastern University is located in Florida, it fell under the jurisdiction of the Commission of Colleges for the Southern Association of Colleges and Schools (SACS).

Obtaining regional reaccreditation is a long and painstaking process that usually occurs once every ten years. NSU was originally scheduled to go through its most recent reaccreditation in 1995. The process at NSU, however, took much longer than anticipated. The delays started when the academic institution, then known as Nova University, merged with Southeastern University of the Health Sciences on January 1, 1994. Because NSU's efforts to prepare for the reaccreditation process were complicated by the merger, SACS agreed to postpone NSU's reaffirmation process until March 1996. The Commission of Colleges then requested its own delay for administrative reasons which postponed the visit by SACS to the main campus until October 1996. Once the actual visits to the campus and field-based sites were completed, SACS was extremely slow to provide NSU with its response. In fact, SACS took almost a full year to notify NSU of the agency's decision to fully reaccredit the university. Being fully reaccredited, however, did not finish the process. Even though SACS granted NSU full reaccreditation, it also made a number of follow-up recommendations, several of which related to library issues which had to be addressed. The end result was that the NSU Libraries did not completely finish with the reaccreditation process until mid 1999.

PREPARING FOR REACCREDITATION

NSU started to prepare for reaccreditation by embarking on a self-study in the fall of 1992. The Educational Support Services Subcommittee, one of 12 subcommittees established to participate in NSU's self study, examined a full range of support services for students both on and off campus. As a result, this subcommittee examined library services offered to field-based and online students.

Fortunately, the Einstein Library had been proactive in providing library services to distance students. The Associate Director of the Einstein Library had been attending Off-Campus Library Services Conferences since the 1980s and had already been working to provide library services to distance students at the university. In order to accomplish this, the Associate Director had been instrumental in integrating services for distance students into the fabric of the Einstein Library. The first step in this effort was the incorporation of the services of what later became known as Distance Library Services into the Einstein Library in 1992. Until that time, efforts to provide off-campus students with mediated searches and document delivery had fallen outside the province of the library. Instead, a department known as the Information Resource Services had handled these services.

When NSU started its self-study, the array of services being provided by Distance Library Services seemed impressive. The services included unlimited free document delivery of materials located in the

Einstein Library, mediated computer searches of CD-ROM databases, and dial-in access to two CD-ROM databases. The library also provided students with free copies of ERIC microfiche documents and NSU practicums (applied dissertations). Journal articles were faxed to distance students at no additional charge. In addition, in 1994, the Einstein Library began providing students with free access to over 50 FirstSearch databases and five InfoTrac databases by way of a dial-in access via a toll-free number. As for bibliographic instruction, students were provided with an introductory library video, a training booklet, and optional training if the students came to institutes that programs held once or twice a year or attended classes on campus.

After examining the services offered to distance students, the Education Support Services Subcommittee concluded that the library had laid a solid foundation of library support services for distance students. The subcommittee, however, was also very concerned that regional accreditation standards for distance library services were becoming much more stringent than had been the case in the 1980s (Kania, 1986).

The subcommittee identified a number of areas that needed improvement. The first area of concern was a library-wide problem: the size of the book and journal collections was not adequate to support doctoral level research. In spite of the fact that the university had begun aggressively funding the building of the collection in the 1990s, the collection lacked the kind of retrospective depth necessary to support doctoral-level research. Although this was an issue that related to the NSU Libraries as a whole, the problem also directly affected the quality of the document delivery service that Distance Library Services (DLS) could offer students who were off campus.

In order to remedy the lack of retrospective depth of the collection, the Einstein Library focused on providing students with access to resources outside the library's collection. The Einstein Library set up deposit accounts with commercial document-delivery suppliers to supplement its journal collection. With the help of an outside consultant, NSU negotiated host agreements with two major academic research libraries, Wayne State University and the University of Michigan, to provide access to book and journal collections. For a set fee per year, the host libraries agreed to mail books and photocopies of journal articles directly to NSU's distance students.

The Educational Support Services Subcommittee went on to identify five additional problem areas that directly related to library services offered to distance students:

1. The turn-around time for processing document delivery requests and mediated computer searches was a problem. Document delivery by Distance Library Services was often taking two weeks or longer to get materials into the hands of distance students.

2. The way funding was allocated for distance library services was an issue. Accrediting agencies did not like to see libraries forced to stretch budgets to include new services being offered to distance students without being provided with additional moneys for the new services. As a result, the subcommittee looked at the issue of funding for library services to distance students in the Einstein Library. The subcommittee concluded that NSU was adequately funding services to distance students because the university had added moneys for staffing and materials when Distance Library Services was created. However, because the funding for DLS had simply been added to the Einstein Library's general budget, the subcommittee still worried that the SACS visiting team might perceive this as an area of concern.

3. Bibliographic instruction for distance students was almost nonexistent. It was true that students received a library video and training manual and were offered "one-shot" training if they happened to come to campus or institutes. Nevertheless, it was also true that students in a number of academic programs never came to campus or to institutes and were therefore never offered an opportunity to receive any bibliographic instruction. Even bibliographic sessions offered at institutes and on campus were only scheduled as optional sessions.

4. Staffing issues were a problem. The subcommittee wanted to ensure that there was sufficient library personnel to provide students in all time zones within the United States with help. The subcommittee was concerned about both Distance Library Services and reference desk staffing.

5. The subcommittee realized that local library resources for students were inadequate. This problem applied to international sites in Panama, Jamaica, and the Bahamas as well as library resources available near cluster sites for field-based students in the United States. Much of the problem lay in the fact that the university only

had formal library agreements with two international sites and in two states where state laws mandated such agreements.

The Einstein Library was able to rectify some of the problems identified by the subcommittee relatively easily. A separate budget for Distance Library Services was created so that the funding commitment of the university would be more visible to the SACS team. Funding was found for an additional staff person so that staffing hours for Distance Library Services could be increased. The library also started to promote its one-on-one reference help that was available to students on and off campus via local and toll-free numbers as well as via email.

The problem of providing some form of bibliographic instruction was more difficult to address. The library was able to get the funding to hire an additional librarian in Distance Library Services to help with training and the development of asynchronous training materials. This, however, did not address the problem of providing library training for students who never came to campus or the fact that academic programs were not willing to provide librarians with opportunities to provide training at cluster sites. Even more frustratingly, the various academic programs were unwilling to offer the library opportunities to integrate library instruction into the curricula.

Library services at the international sites provided another challenge. Because there was little that could be done to remedy the lack of local library resources in certain areas, the Einstein Library decided to put a renewed emphasis on the services provided by the main campus. In order to address resources at international sites, part-time staff were hired in the Bahamas and Panama. These staff members provided local students with help accessing the online resources and with requesting materials to be faxed from the main campus while a librarian was hired in Jamaica. Librarians from the main campus went to the sites to train these staff members. In Jamaica and Panama, there were small print collections of textbooks and journals collected by the business program faculty, while students in Nassau had access to the library at the College of the Bahamas.

The issue of local library resources in the United States was not a problem that the NSU Libraries dealt with. These issues were handled by a non-librarian, the Director of Resource Information for External Programs. This director made decisions about what library resources were adequate, and she negotiated library contracts. One solution for providing off-campus students with access to local library resources was that a number of graduate academic programs would reimburse their distance students for the cost of obtaining library cards at libraries in the students' local areas. Other solutions were developed by the Director of Resource Information for External Programs and included a publication, *A Directory of Selected Academic Libraries Near Off-Campus Program Sites,* to identify the accessible libraries for students at every location where NSU offered site-based instruction. The booklet identified libraries available to the public, libraries where the students could purchase cards and be reimbursed by their academic programs, and libraries where the university had formal library agreements. This publication, however, did not help identify resources outside the cluster areas for students who traveled long distances to attend classes at a site or for students who took online classes.

As the date drew closer for the reaccreditation visits to begin, the librarians in the Einstein Library were increasingly concerned about whether the measures the library had implemented would be considered adequate by SACS. The problem was that SACS standards, like those of other regional accreditation agencies, were nonprescriptive in nature (Bostian & Farynk, 1993; Gilmer, 1995). The fact that the standards were nonprescriptive provided NSU with the flexibility to select which strategies the university wanted to implement. However, the nonprescriptive nature of the standards also meant that they did not provide the university with easy-to-apply formulas (Bostian & Farynk, 1993) that could be used as a yardstick for determining the adequacy of the solutions selected.

In spite of any inadequacies of the self-study, NSU's self-study process was important because it was instrumental in bringing about a number of significant improvements in library services for distance students. The process of going through the self study forced the library administration to take the time to take a critical look at its services and provided the Einstein Library with leverage for bringing about needed changes that would never have taken place otherwise. The self-study provided the library with compelling reasons for the administration to fund online resources, deposit accounts with commercial document delivery suppliers, host agreements with Wayne State University and the University of Michigan, and hire additional staff in Distance Library Services. Last but not least, preparing for the self-study also created the first concrete opportunities for providing library training to distance students.

THE REAFFIRMATION PROCESS

Because NSU was more nontraditional than most academic institutions, the visit by SACS was more complicated than usual. The actual reaccreditation process consisted of visits by teams to both the main campus and a number of NSU cluster sites. Because SACS wanted to include NSU's 150 field-based sites in the reaffirmation process, SACS took what was, at that time, the rather unusual step of sending small teams to a sampling of 15 NSU field-based sites. These site visits were conducted during the spring of 1996 while the principal visiting committee came to the main campus for the reaffirmation visit in October 1996.

Field-based site visits played an important role in the reaccreditation process for NSU and the Einstein Library. During site visits, SACS team members asked students their opinions about both class-related issues and support services. Conclusions drawn by the various field-based teams varied substantially and seemed to reflect, at least in part, the personality of the evaluators. For example, conclusions drawn about bibliographic instruction diverged widely. One team stated that students did "not know how to use the [Electronic Library] system" (LaBurtis & McWilliams, 1996, p. 7). Other teams visiting sites where students received similar library instruction were less critical. The Northern Virginia site team reported that students had been offered the opportunity to obtain library training at summer institutes. The team went on to report that some students still felt they needed training on how to access the online library resources. Still other site teams found library training effective. The report by the Melbourne site team, for example, stated that, "Those interviewed are very pleased with the library resources" (Helm, 1996, p. 3.) Not surprisingly, the visits that were most successful from a library perspective were sites where the academic programs had worked closely with Distance Library Services in advance. At sites where the academic programs did not work with Distance Library Services, the local NSU administrators often had problems answering specific library-related questions and demonstrating how to access online resources.

The reports written by visiting teams produced some useful results for the Einstein Library. The SACS teams visiting Caribbean sites found the library resources and services inadequate. First of all, there were few local academic libraries, and those that existed were inadequate by American standards. Secondly, NSU librarians had not been present at the site visits to explain the services provided at the sites or by Distance Library Services. Instead, student assistants at the sites attempted to provide committee members with explanations about the services. Needless to say, this solution proved less than satisfactory. The result was that the site teams visiting in the Caribbean were quite critical of the services offered. Because of criticism of library services targeted in these site reports, the graduate and undergraduate schools of business agreed to fund research rooms at the sites in Panama, the Bahamas, and Jamaica. These research rooms were equipped with small print collections of books and journals, several CD-ROMs, a computer lab with access to the Internet, and part-time ALA-accredited librarians to provide professional help.

Other institutions faced with the possibility of similar site visits should consider doing two things to prepare for these visits. First, and most important, librarians need to be included on every team that goes to field-based sites. Having librarians present can forestall some of the misunderstandings and misinformation, which occurred in the NSU site visits because librarians had not been present. Secondly, if librarians are included in the university team that attends the site visits, they should bring along documentation (e.g., copies of training rosters and evaluation forms for students' library training) so they can document times and dates of training sessions. Having such documentation on hand can forestall the problem of students at the sites who forget that they had been offered training and mistakenly assert to the visiting committee that the library never provided them with the needed training.

FOLLOW-UP RECOMMENDATIONS

Successfully receiving reaccreditation is not always the end of the story for institutions or their libraries. In the case of NSU, SACS made a number of follow-up recommendations for NSU, several of which specifically impacted the NSU Libraries. The SACS follow-up recommendations that related to library issues stated that:

- the university build an adequate new library,
- all NSU students be provided with information technology training,
- the university continue to fund the host agreements with Wayne State University and the University of Michigan, and

- the Director of Resource Information for External Programs, who represented both the library for accreditation and licensure issues and who negotiated local library agreements, should report to the NSU Libraries.

The NSU Libraries greatly benefited from these recommendations. The most important benefit was that it ensured that money for library projects (e.g., the new library and host agreements) would continue to be available even after the reaccreditation process had been completed. The recommendation relating to staff organization improved the NSU Libraries' role in licensing and accreditation issues by getting the libraries into the university's administrative "information loop." As a result of the reorganization, the NSU Libraries finally started to be included in the decision-making process when new programs and sites were being evaluated. The reorganization also resulted in new opportunities for collaboration between academic programs and the library.

Apart from finding the funding for the new library, the recommendation that presented the biggest challenge for the Einstein Library stated that "Nova Southeastern University demonstrate that it is providing adequate and appropriate access to *information technologies* and systems and *training for their use at all locations where educational programs are being provided* [emphasis added]" (Southern Association of Colleges and Schools, 1997, p. 141). Distance Library Services was the only department at NSU in a position to try to provide services to all programs, but the scope of NSU's site-based classes presented real challenges for the library. Students in six different NSU programs never came to campus. These included three masters and three undergraduate programs in business, education, and the social sciences. In addition, four doctoral programs had students who were not receiving library instruction sometimes a year or more into their programs. The problem was that, even though SACS had not prescribed how NSU had to provide the training, the visiting committee's recommendations clearly demonstrated that they deemed past asynchronous efforts such as training manuals, videos, and Web pages for delivering library instruction as inadequate.

Distance Library Services set out to begin offering all distance students with bibliographic instruction by the end of the 1998/1999 academic year. Setting this as a goal meant that the librarians had to develop more effective methods of delivering bibliographic instruction. The NSU Libraries worked on a plan to offer all NSU graduate and undergraduate students in distance programs with library training. At the time, this meant (1) working with programs to find times when the students came to campus and/or to institutes to deliver training or (2) working with programs to find times and places for librarians to go to sites when the students never attended institutes or came to the main campus. Because NSU had so many different models for delivering distance education, the library had to develop a number of approaches. In some programs, librarians started to visit sites when a new cluster started while, in other programs, library instruction was integrated into research or technology classes. Still other programs began requiring that students come to the main campus for their initial course work, in part to ensure that students would receive technology and library training at that time.

The SACS follow-up recommendations resulted in positive changes for the library. First of all, the Einstein Library received funding for two additional positions to conduct library training at distance sites. Just as importantly, the recommendation forced the various academic programs to work with the library to integrate library instruction into their curriculums. This was significant because, up until that time, the library had been in the position of petitioner, asking for opportunities to provide bibliographic instruction. The recommendation provided the library with a metaphorical "club" that the library used to gain more active cooperation from the institution as a whole and the various academic programs. The end result has been that librarians are now much more directly involved in the academic process at NSU than before.

WIDER IMPLICATIONS

SACS' mandate that NSU provide students with training in how to use information technologies has implications for other institutions who may be preparing for reaccreditation. The reality is that, as information technology continues to make technological leaps, accrediting agencies are raising the bar of expectations for services and training offered to distance students. This means that libraries cannot depend on their being able to simply resort to the successful strategies of institutions that have obtained reaccreditation in years past. The SACS mandate that NSU offer information technology training reflects the concern of reaccrediting agencies both in the United States and abroad with the accelerating change in how information is accessed. Many of these agencies are putting ever-increasing importance on libraries providing these services. The result often is that libraries not only need to offer training in how to use online resources but also must handle underlying problems such as coping with students who lack the prerequisite computer and technology skills to benefit from the library training. Libraries need to do more than just tell students how to do their research. They must go a step further and actually teach students how to use the resources so that students both on and off campus actually become information literate.

On a broader note, accrediting teams that look at library services for distance students are increasingly concerned with the "total picture" of library services rather than simply focusing on local library resources and document delivery. Librarians should not be misled by the fact that the section in the SACS standards labeled *Library/Learning Resources for Distance Learning Activities* (see Appendix) focuses on document delivery and local library agreements. Instead, when librarians prepare for reaccreditation in the future, they must look at providing a full array of library services that are equal, or at least equivalent, to those offered to students on campus. Accrediting teams are increasingly likely to consider such issues as whether distance students are becoming information literate, whether research is being integrated into the curriculum, and whether librarians are collaborating with distance faculty. This broadening of the scope of *issues* that accrediting agencies may focus on means that librarians need to be prepared to broaden the scope of their *efforts* as well.

These broadening expectations have pragmatic benefits for libraries interested in offering library services to distance students. NSU's case illustrates how the reaccreditation process can benefit a library at each step in the process. The reaccreditation process can stimulate change and provide librarians with the necessary leverage to promote innovations. Although the process can open doors of opportunity, librarians must take an active role in promoting innovations and working to bring needed improvements to fruition.

Although other libraries can learn some lessons from NSU's experiences, no two libraries' situations are identical. This means that other libraries cannot use NSU's case study as a blueprint for solutions to be applied at their own institutions. It is true that reaccreditation can open up opportunities for libraries, but reaccreditation, taken alone, is not a panacea that will correct all problems. In the case of the NSU Libraries, there were other forces at work that helped bring about change. First of all, during the reaccreditation process, NSU was maturing as an academic institution. As a result, the university was more ready to improve support services for students both on and off campus, which was significant. Just as importantly, the advent of online Web indexes and full-text databases provided distance students with timely access to information. Suddenly, students were eager to learn more about online library resources. This, in turn, resulted in academic programs becoming increasingly supportive of training that helped students become information literate. Last but not least, librarians at the NSU Libraries had the vision necessary to take advantage of the opportunities that reaccreditation, a maturing academic institution, and burgeoning technology offered. Without this vision of what needed to be done, the library would never have been able to bring about the necessary changes.

CONCLUSIONS

Libraries faced with developing new services for distance students can use reaccreditation as a useful tool when their institutions are reluctant to make changes or to fund new services. Reaccreditation can serve as a catalyst by capturing the attention of academic administrators and by serving as a wake-up call for the academic institutions. Librarians with a vision of what should constitute library services for distance students can use the opportunities created by reaccreditation (1) to implement needed changes and (2) to improve the funding needed to support these services.

REFERENCES

Bostian, R., & Farynk, L. (1993). Satisfying accreditation requirements in lean times. In C. J. Jacob (Comp.), *The Sixth Off-Campus Library Services Conference Proceedings, Kansas City, Missouri, October 6-8, 1993* (pp. 35-45). Mount Pleasant, MI: Central Michigan University Press.
Gilmer, L. C. (1995). Accreditation of off-campus services: Comparative study of the

regional accreditation agencies. In C. J. Jacob (Comp.), *The Seventh Off-Campus Library Services Conference Proceedings, San Diego, California, October 25-27, 1995* (pp. 101-110). Mount Pleasant, MI: Central Michigan University Press.

Helm, K. (1996). *Nova Southeastern University Master of Mental Health Counseling, Melbourne, Florida Site.* Unpublished manuscript.

Kania, T. (1986). Regional accreditation standards and off-campus library service. In B. M. Lessin (Ed.), *The Off-Campus Library Services Conference Proceedings, Reno, Nevada* (pp. 140-146). Mount Pleasant, MI: Central Michigan University Press.

LaBurtis, M. A., & McWilliams, A. E. (1996). *Nova Southeastern University Off-Campus Review Committee, Tampa, Florida site, March 1-3, 1996, programs reviewed: Farquhar Center for Undergraduate Studies: Bachelor's in Education, Bachelor's in Professional Management, Fischler Center for the Advancement of Education: Graduate Teacher Education Program–Master of Science, School of Business and Entrepreneurship: Master's in Business Administration.* Unpublished manuscript.

Manburg, A. (1983, June). *Program delivery in distance education–One successful strategy.* Paper presented at the Annual Conference of the University without Walls International Council, Toronto, Ontario, Canada. (ERIC Document Reproduction Service No. ED 235 884)

Manton, E., Fatzer, J., & Sims, O. S. (1996). *Report of the site committee, Nova Southeastern University, Phoenix, Arizona, March 22-24, 1996.* Unpublished manuscript.

Research and Planning. Nova Southeastern University. (1997). *Demographic characteristics of Nova Southeastern University students by academic center: 1992 to 1996* (Report 97-04). Ft. Lauderdale, FL: Nova Southeastern University.

Riggs, D. (1997). Library services for distance education: Rethinking current practices and implementing new approaches [Editorial]. *College & Research Libraries, 55,* 208-209.

Southern Association of Colleges and Schools Commission on Colleges. (1996). *Criteria for accreditation* (10th ed.). Decatur, GA: Author.

Southern Association of Colleges and Schools Commission on Colleges. (1997). *SACS report.* Unpublished manuscript.

APPENDIX

5.1.7, Library/Learning Resources for Distance Learning Activities, pp. 59-60.

For distance learning activities, an institution *must* ensure the provision of and ready access to adequate library/learning resources and services to support the courses, programs, and degrees offered. The institution *must* own the library/learning resources, provide access to electronic information available through existing technologies, or provide them through formal agreements. Such agreements should include the use of books and other materials. The institution *must* assign responsibility for providing library/learning resources and services and for ensuring continued access to them at each site.

When formal agreements are established for the provision of library resources and services, they must ensure access to library resources pertinent to the programs offered by the institution and include provision for services and resources which support the institution's specific programs—in the field of study and at the degree level offered.

From Southern Association of Colleges and Schools. Commission on Colleges. *Criteria for Accreditation* (11th ed). Decatur, GA: The Commission, 1998.

Working in the Asynchronous Environment: Two Case Studies

Justine Wheeler

University of Calgary

Leslie Fournier

The Node Learning Technologies Network

SUMMARY. Those called upon to instruct or moderate within the asynchronous environment must acquire the skills necessary to engage learners from across a distance. This paper will provide two case studies describing the experiences and practice of working in this environment. The first case study will describe the reference and instructional library support provided to the Master of Continuing Education program offered by the University of Calgary. The second case study will describe the services and resources offered by the Node Learning Technologies Network, particularly those aimed at librarians.

KEYWORDS. Distance education, library services, library instruction, asynchronous communication

INTRODUCTION

As Mark Donovan (1999) observed in *Rethinking Faculty Support,* "There is no magic solution for supporting faculty uses of technology in teaching and learning." What post-secondary institutions have come to agree upon is that supporting practitioners–librarians, instruc-

[Haworth co-indexing entry note]: "Working in the Asynchronous Environment: Two Case Studies." Wheeler, Justine, and Leslie Fournier. Co-published simultaneously in *Journal of Library Administration* (The Haworth Information Press, an imprint of The Haworth Press, Inc.) Vol. 32, No. 1/2, 2001, pp. 425-438; and: *Off-Campus Library Services* (ed: Anne Marie Casey) The Haworth Information Press, an imprint of The Haworth Press, Inc., 2001, pp. 425-438.

tors, faculty, staff, and trainers–is crucial in maintaining healthy and productive teaching in an asynchronous environment. One of the ways in which this can be accomplished is through the use of online networking with a community of those facing similar situations. And of course, it is just as important to provide the same type of support to students, for instance, through the use of an online librarian.

Asynchronous learning is becoming an increasingly popular method of offering distance learning opportunities to adult learners. "Asynchronous learning is defined as learning which takes place between teacher and learner independent of place and time" (McMullen, Goldbaum, Wolffe, and Sattler, 1998, p. 3). This allows incredible flexibility for all of those involved in the environment. However, along with the advantages there are also significant challenges. Those called upon to instruct or moderate within the asynchronous environment must acquire the skills necessary to engage learners from across a distance.

This paper will examine the experiences and practice of working in an asynchronous environment, in two very different contexts. The first case study will describe the reference and instructional library support provided to the Master of Continuing Education (MCE) program offered by the University of Calgary in Alberta, Canada. Examples will be given of how reference and instructional library support has successfully been incorporated within an asynchronous environment.

The second case study will describe the Node Learning Technologies Network. [T]he Node supports research and practice in the arena of new technologies. Accordingly, not only are most of the services and resources offered in an asynchronous format, they also support researchers, educators and librarians working in the asynchronous environment. An overview of the Node will be provided with particular attention paid to those services and resources aimed at librarians.

MCE PROGRAM

In the spring of 1995 the MCE program was launched at the University of Calgary. The program focuses on learning in the workplace, and not surprisingly targets adult learners with workplace experience.

Students are admitted from across Canada, and begin the program by attending an on-campus, three-week, face-to-face institute. After the institute, students return to their workplaces and continue their studies via the computer conferencing system, FirstClass. The following year is similar in structure with the students attending another three-week institute and finishing their course work via FirstClass.

Since the program's inception, library support has been a prominent and heavily used service. This is not unexpected. According to Fidishun (1997), adult students are pressed for time and need library resources when they can use them, which is often outside of traditional work hours. They want to access the library from off-campus, including reference and instruction services. As a result of student and faculty feedback, library services to MCE students have evolved to include annual librarian participation in one of the MCE online courses, and a growing library presence on the Web. However, other services such as email reference and instruction remain perennially well received.

FirstClass

FirstClass is an Intranet client-server software package that provides, amongst other things, e-mail capability, conferences, folders, and the ability to link to the Internet. Folders and conferences are two of the primary methods of sharing information. Folders are used to archive and organize messages and documents. Conferences are forums for participant discussion. Each conference is usually either dedicated to a specific constituency (for example, students enrolled in a certain course) or to a specific topic (for example, library support). Both conferences and folders can contain messages and documents, however, unlike a folder, in a conference you can address a message directly to a group of people (SoftArc 1998). Both are accessible via icons that appear within the FirstClass desktop. Thus, when a user logs on he or she is presented with an array of icons. Some icons lead to conferences or folders, while some icons drill down further to sub-conferences or sub-folders. A student will likely access a folder if she or he is searching for archived information, and access a conference if searching for an interactive discussion.

E-MAIL

When the librarian meets the students during their first face-to-face institute she explains and demonstrates the services and resources available to them. However, she also strongly encourages the students to contact her if they experience any difficulties. This message is reinforced at subsequent library sessions and meetings. The reason for this is that the first institute is rich with experience and learning. It is an introduction to graduate culture, online learning and to a new academic discipline. Given this context, and the ensuing amount of information that the students must absorb, student anxiety levels seem to be greatly reduced when they are encouraged to contact the librarian directly. Overwhelmingly, contact takes the form of email communication. One disadvantage of emphasizing emailing the librarian is that students sometimes contact the librarian before they check other sources such as instruction guides. However, one of the benefits of email communication is that it provides the librarian with the opportunity to continue building the relationships that were begun during the institute. During the first semester MCE students quickly build a sense of community within FirstClass. It is vital that the librarian establishes a presence and asserts herself as a member of the MCE community during this period.

LIBRARY CHAT

Library Chat is a conference that allows students to pose questions, suggestions or comments regarding library services, issues or research. The postings are archived indefinitely and accessible to all members of the MCE community. There is usually some trepidation surrounding the use of Library Chat. Often a posting will begin with a comment such as: "This is probably a stupid question, but . . . ." To alleviate anxiety many techniques, which will be described further on in this paper, are used. Nonetheless, students prefer emailing the librarian to using Library Chat. In response, the librarian has often asked students if she may post the question, that they have sent to her email box, to Library Chat. To date, this request has never been refused. All identifying information is removed before posting the question. Furthermore, if the question is a frequently asked question (FAQ) it is copied to the Library FAQ folder.

PARTICIPATION IN AN ONLINE COURSE

As the students move further along in the program, their research needs often become more in-depth, cumulating in a final written project. The final project "integrates research, theory and experience" (Faculty of Continuing Education, 1999). In order to better facilitate these research needs, in the fall of 1998 the librarian approached an MCE professor and requested to participate in his online course. The librarian set up a sub-conference within the course conference. The purpose of the library sub-conference was to engage the students in context-specific, in-depth discussion regarding library research. The conference was entitled "Justine's Gems" (Justine is the first name of the librarian). The professor and librarian felt the informal and friendly title of the sub-conference would encourage students to post questions. Furthermore, it was also agreed that the librarian would follow the weekly discussions, which took place within a separate course icon. The weekly discussions revolved around the course readings. The librarian's role was to offer pro-active library assistance. For instance, if a student mentioned he or she wanted to read further works by an author, the librarian could suggest search strategies. The reality has been that participating in the weekly discussions has not been successful, because the students focus on analysing the readings, and do not usually comment on their research within this conference. Conversely, Justine's Gems has been a well-used and valued service. Students have posted research questions that have allowed the librarian to illustrate various components of a research strategy. This has offered the librarian the opportunity to build on each question asked. For example, an answer to one question may emphasize the importance of choosing the appropriate databases, another may look at keyword searching, and another answer may focus on the concept of subject headings. This is all done within the context of the students' research question, and thus the students find Justine's Gems meaningful in a way that the more generic and less complex Library Chat questions are not. Interestingly, the librarian has noticed that students often ask questions in Justine's Gems more suited for the Library Chat conference: possibly because they find the smaller community less intimidating.

SUCCESSFUL ASYNCHRONOUS INTERACTION

Since the beginning of the program, the librarian has participated extensively in the asynchronous environment. Her experiences have mirrored many of the experiences others have documented. The following are observations and suggestions for those engaging in asynchronous interaction.

I. Without verbal and physical cues the librarian must find other means of conveying that she is approachable. This can be accomplished by:

- Including a salutation and a signature. While often salutations and signatures are not included in workplace communication, it is this librarian's experience that they are appreciated and expected by MCE students.
- Reassuring the student that a question is valid. Often a response from the librarian will begin with an affirmation such as "good question."
- Using an informal communication style.

II. Effective communication is essential. This can be accomplished by:

- Strong writing skills. Clear instructions are essential for online instruction. (Hara and Kling, 1999). This librarian has also seen students and instructors agree on a "three screen rule." This means that no more than three screens of material can be in any one posting.
- Conducting an online reference interview. This includes the librarian asking if she has interpreted the question correctly and asking what sources the student has consulted.
- Explaining how the librarian came to the reference answer. Every interaction should serve as a learning opportunity.
- Avoiding assumptions. Students have varying degrees of technical and research expertise.
- Minimizing the use of jargon.
- Encouraging students to use asynchronous learning materials. For instance, directing the student to an online instruction guide or message in a conference, or providing a link to a relevant Web site.
- Taking advantage of the written format. For instance using "snipping" when appropriate. Snipping is pasting from one message into another in order to maintain sequence in the conversation (Winiecki and Chyung, 1998).

III. Some further challenges facing the librarian are:

- Written communication is time consuming.
- The librarian may be seen as a point of contact for questions outside of the library realm, such as administrative or technical questions.
- Students require timely feedback. (Hara and Kling, 1999). Students take advantage of the twenty-four hour a day, seven days a week access to FirstClass. They expect that the librarian is also closely monitoring the system, and that they will receive prompt replies to their queries.

Another example of asynchronous learning is that provided by the Node Learning Technologies Network. Among other constituencies, this system is geared towards librarians, and provides them with a glimpse of what it is like to be on the student side of an asynchronous learning situation. The fact that the Node is also a well-designed and heavily used site makes it that much more useful to those striving to gain an understanding of what a successful asynchronous system entails.

THE NODE LEARNING TECHNOLOGIES NETWORK

The Node Learning Technologies Network is a not-for-profit organization, headquartered in London, Ontario, Canada. It promotes effective uses of technologies in education and training. The Web sites, <http://thenode.org> and <http://node.on.ca>, have developed into virtual communities where faculty, staff, librarians, instructional designers, students, professional trainers and others with an interest in teaching with technology meet to discuss areas of common concern.

ABOUT THE NODE

Founded in 1996, the Node Learning Technologies Network forges links between research and practice and between the technical development of new technologies and their evaluation in the field. The Node's online resources, electronic forums, publications, workshops, research and consulting services support informed decision-making by individuals and organizations. Its work has been recognized through many professional reviews and awards, including the Impact Award for "changing the way people learn" from Internet World Canada '99 (http://events.internet.com/award_winners.html).

"theNode.org" is the members' service of the Node Learning Technologies Network, launched in October 1999. Services provided at thenode.org support users in developing and sustaining effective education and training practices and in exploring new ways to use technologies to support their learning objectives.

Membership fees collected for thenode.org support the development of our freely accessible resources designed to help practitioners choose, use and evaluate learning technologies. A growing collection of new resources for members provides direct assistance in teaching and training through technology. All of the materials on thenode.org, both freely accessible and restricted, address critical user needs and issues in this rapidly-changing field. One such issue is the difficulty inherent in providing adequate and timely support to students learning off-campus.

BACKGROUND ON LIBRARY SERVICES
FOR DISTANCE LEARNERS

The history of the Node's involvement in this issue is an interesting one. In June 1998 we published a story in our biweekly newsletter *networking* which highlighted the difficulties inherent in providing adequate library access to off-campus students. At the time, we observed that library services have been blindsided by technological developments, which have broadened access to post-secondary education. The technology which has made a growing number of institutions able to offer entire certificates, programmes and degrees entirely at a distance has done little more than improve the speed of access to library materials, leaving the extent of access unchanged. (The entire story is archived at <http://thenode.org/networking/june1998/>.)

As a result of the phenomenal amount of feedback we received on this story, and in an attempt to bring these issues to our wider audience, we hosted an asynchronous, online forum later that year in which librarians, faculty, post-secondary administration and corporate trainers met to discuss:

- Information literacy/library instruction: what works, what doesn't, new innovations
- Document delivery to distance students: current practices, new innovations, the place of interlibrary loans, and so on
- Policies and experiences with using local libraries
- Collaborating with instructors
- Offering services to students internationally
- Designing, writing and implementing policy guides for distance library service
- Inter-institutional collaboration

The supporting resources for this forum, which now form part of the "Student Support" area of thenode.org's *Notable Issues* (http://thenode. org/notable/) included articles on off-campus library services, practical examples of institutional policies and procedures, guidelines for distance librarianship, links to special interest groups on this issue and a selection of mailing lists. The forum itself is still archived and available at <http://thenode.org/nodeforums/library/>.

SPECIFIC SUPPORT RESOURCES FOR THE OFF-CAMPUS LIBRARIAN

As previously mentioned, the virtual community at http://thenode.org is designed to help users develop and sustain effective online instructional practices. One of the ways we do this is by providing what we call networked support, which harnesses the connecting power of the Internet to provide an online peer support structure for those working in this field.

The services we provide were developed keeping in mind that supporting distance students can often be a lower priority for administration–the students themselves are not always in a position to know what kinds of services they are missing out on, and those who are tasked to support them must often do so in addition to other roles or with a bare minimum of outside assistance, funding or acknowledgment. Institutions, which have not completely "taken the plunge" into the online course environment often have no structures in place to adequately support those who deal with off-campus students. *Networked support* allows our members to draw upon the collective intelligence of our community to work through issues they encounter, solve problems, brainstorm and share experiences around this (and other) issues.

The types of support we provide for distance librarians are:

- Links to current, comprehensive and relevant information on the subject of off-campus librarianship (in *Notable Issues* <http://thenode.org/notable/>, described above)
- Electronic equivalents to "pathfinders" on general and specific subjects (at <http://node.on.ca/support> and <http://thenode.org/subject/> respectively)
- Research roundtables
- Online forums
- thenode.org members' database (restricted to thenode.org members only)

ONLINE "PATHFINDERS"

The Node's *Resources for Learners* (http://node.on.ca/support/) are designed to meet the needs of those with limited access to library, information and peer resources, but we have found it is directly relevant to a much broader spectrum of learners. The objective of these pages is to provide a clear, comprehensive and organized set of resources that learners can use with ease, and trust in the accuracy and currency of its contents. Originally constructed over three years ago, we have continued to review, refine, update and expand them as new tools and resources emerge. They currently include five sections:

I. *The Reference Shelf* is a collection of online reference tools (including dictionaries, encyclopaedias and atlases) for basic research. There are also links to selected reference meta-sites for finding more subject-specific information, as well as links to online libraries and library catalogues.

II. *The Virtual Librarian* includes Node-authored help sheets and links to external resources for learning how to find, evaluate, use and cite electronic information.

III. *The Study Buddy* is a collection of tips to plan effectively, write coherently and study productively. Sections include tips on how to be an effective participant in an online discussion, ergonomics and computer use, and pointers toward grammar assistance.

IV *The Technology Toolkit* provides explanations of the tools most likely to be used by students online, such as e-mail, Telnet, Web browsers and links to Internet glossaries.

V. *The Courses Database* page provides links to the Node's database of distance education courses available at Ontario post-secondary institutions as well as to other databases of distance education courses.

Reaction from both librarians and students has been positive, and demonstrates the need for a service of this kind. Feedback we've received includes:

As a library reference assistant and a student of distance education at Athabasca University, I must commend and thank you for the *Resources for Learners* section of the Node site. I use it to help library patrons and when I'm studying my information systems programme!

–Athabasca University

Great site! Really nice design. It is crisp and fresh and very accessible. I like the look and I have already printed out virtually everything in the Virtual Librarian. Nice!

–University of Iowa Library Systems

Although our initial promotional strategy for these pages targeted post-secondary academic libraries, we have noticed that more and more links to *Resources for Learners* are appearing in public libraries, community access sites, and other Internet access points. The feedback we have received indicates that there is a real need for a comprehensive yet concise set of reliable reference tools. To this end, we have established an internal set of guidelines, which we apply to the development of *all* areas of thenode.org:

• The information must be current, reliable, accurate and unbiased
• Sites must be organized in a clear, intuitive fashion
• Sites included must be readily accessible to lower-speed modems, and not require an extensive amount of browser plug-ins, frames or other restrictive formatting

- There must be a clear indication of authorship
- The scope of coverage must be as wide as possible without being overwhelming

A subsection of thenode.org's Support by Subject pages is devoted to teaching the principles behind finding, evaluating and using information on the Internet–skills which have informed the construction of the Node's Web sites.

SUPPORT BY SUBJECT

Support by Subject (http://thenode.org/subject/), gathers materials and expertise to facilitate online teaching and learning in specific disciplines. Acting as online equivalents to print pathfinders, Support by Subject includes:

- Resource collections for subject areas of interest to thenode.org's members, including relevant online journals; vetted discipline-specific Web sites for instructors and learners; outstanding examples of online courses or course components; articles, reports and/or Web resources for online teaching in the field
- A peer support area of discussion forums and interviews on teaching specific subjects online
- A space for members to post relevant draft research proposals, articles, reports and Web sites for peer review

RESEARCH ROUNDTABLES

Research roundtables are closed, moderated forums featuring small panels of experts who will synthesize knowledge and current practice on significant issues affecting online teaching and training. Results of these discussions are made available to members as reports focusing on implications for practice.

thenode.org MEMBERS' DATABASE

This tool provides a networking source for members of thenode.org. Members of thenode.org may choose to be included in this database, which will contain contact information and areas of interest and expertise. Librarians who are working at providing support to distance/online students may wish to use this resource to connect with others in the same position. We have found this to be particularly useful for the solo librarian confronting the issues surrounding supporting off-campus students for the first time.

FUTURE PLANS

A fundamental principle of thenode.org is the ability to reflect and adapt to members' needs, acknowledging that these requirements can and will change as technological advances warrant. We will continue to develop relevant resources to address the requirements of our community.

CONCLUSION

Ensuring a successful online learning experience depends in part upon the ability to provide adequate bibliographic, technical and academic support to students. Librarian participation in the Master of Continuing Education program is an example of the use of computer mediated communication to deliver effective library support. Alternatively, the example of the Node Learning Technologies Network describes an opportunity for librarians to access learning resources and interact with others providing distance library services. While the MCE example discusses successful techniques for providing library/research support in an academic environment, the Node will allow practicing librarians an opportunity to experience asynchronous instruction from both sides of the table. Both case studies illustrate that the asynchronous environment is a rich place for librarian involvement.

REFERENCES

Donovan, M. (1999). Rethinking faculty support. *The Technology Source* (Online Journal), September/October, 1999. Retrieved November 29, 1999: http://horizon. unc.edu/TS/development/1999-09.asp.

Faculty of Continuing Education, University of Calgary. (1999). *Student Handbook*. Retrieved November 20, 1999: http://www.ucalgary.ca/cted/mce/handbook.htm.

Fidishun, D. (1997). *Can we still do business as usual? Adult students and the new paradigm of library service.* ACRL National Conference Papers 1997. Retrieved October 26, 1999: http://www.ala.org/acrl/paperhtm/c25.html.

Hara, N., & Kling, R. (1999). *Students' frustrations with a Web-based distance education course: A taboo topic in the discourse* (WP 99-01-C1). Retrieved November 17, 1999: http://www.slis.indiana.edu/CSI/wp99_01.html.

McMullen, D.W., Goldbaum, H., Wolffe, R. J., & Sattler, Joan L. (1998). *Using asynchronous learning technology to make the connections among faculty, students, and teachers.* Paper presented at the Annual Meeting of the American Association of Colleges for Teacher Education, New Orleans, LA, February 25-28, 1998. (ERIC Document Reproduction Service No. ED 418 069)

SoftArc Inc. (1998). User documentation, FirstClass, Version 5.5.

Wiesenberg, F., & Hutton, S. (1995). *Teaching a graduate program using computer mediated conferencing software.* Paper presented at the Annual Meeting of the American Association for Adult and Continuing Education, Kansas City, MO, November 1995. (ERIC Document Reproduction Service No. ED 391 100).

Winiecki, D.J., & Chyung, Y. (1998). Keeping the thread: Helping distance students and instructors keep track of asynchronous discussions. In *Proceedings of the Annual Conference on Distance Teaching & Learning, Madison, WI, 5-7 August 1998.* (ERIC Document Reproduction Service No. ED 422 886).

Louisiana Academic Libraries: Partnering to Enhance Distance Education Services

Barbara Wittkopf

Louisiana State University

Elizabeth Orgeron
Trish Del Nero

Loyola University, New Orleans

SUMMARY. The state of Louisiana has a long history of consortial activities among academic libraries. Having this infrastructure in place contributed to the ease of creation of a distance library services network that includes both public and private universities. This paper traces the history of academic library consortia in Louisiana, and provides methodologies and results of several surveys of distance education students. The results of a survey currently being conducted are forthcoming.

KEYWORDS. Library consortia, library services, distance education

INTRODUCTION:
A DECADE OF PARTNERSHIPS

Like other states, Louisiana has experienced significant growth in distance education activities in recent years. In many places, this trend has taken academic libraries by surprise, and librarians have had to

[Haworth co-indexing entry note]: "Louisiana Academic Libraries: Partnering to Enhance Distance Education Services." Wittkopf, Barbara, Elizabeth Orgeron, and Trish Del Nero. Co-published simultaneously in *Journal of Library Administration* (The Haworth Information Press, an imprint of The Haworth Press, Inc.) Vol. 32, No. 1/2, 2001, pp. 439-447; and: *Off-Campus Library Services* (ed: Anne Marie Casey) The Haworth Information Press, an imprint of The Haworth Press, Inc., 2001, pp. 439-447.

create networks for providing library services to distance students from scratch. Luckily, academic libraries in Louisiana have been able to rely on LALINC, a consortium that formed a decade ago, to assist in the creation of distance library services.

LALINC has its roots in the budget shortages that resulted from the crash of the Louisiana oil industry in the 1980s. In part to deal with these financial difficulties, the Louisiana Board of Regents created a Task Force on Libraries in 1990. This task force, which consisted of academic librarians and chief academic officers, was charged with exploring the need for greater cooperation and resource sharing among academic libraries in Louisiana. It soon became clear to the members of the task force that these endeavors would be more easily accomplished if the libraries were automated with a common system. Only a few of the state's academic libraries were automated at that time and it proved impossible for the task force to obtain funding for additional library systems. They did produce a master plan that would guide later activities.

In 1992, the task force was reborn as the Louisiana Academic Library Information Network Consortium (LALINC), and every public and private academic library director in the state became a member. The founders of LALINC envisioned the consortium as a way to procure funding for the automation of Louisiana's public institutions of higher education. Louisiana State University held one of the early contracts with NOTIS, which permitted additional libraries to be added to its NOTIS system, as long as the software remained resident on a single mainframe computer. This contractual piece of luck led LSU to apply for a Board of Regents Louisiana Education Quality Support Fund (LEQSF) grant to proceed with this project. This led to the creation of LOUIS, the Louisiana Online University Information System, which has now evolved into a NOTIS-based electronic network connecting the OPACs of twenty-five Louisiana public institutions of higher education.

In 1995, LOUIS expanded its activities beyond library catalogs to the consortial purchase of a wide variety of bibliographic and full-text databases. This incredibly successful program, which was funded by an LEQSF grant, provides students in even the most rural communities with an abundance of information, which would previously have been available only at large university libraries. In order to expand the scope of the consortium, LOUIS databases were made available outside the public higher education system to public libraries and to members of the Louisiana Association of Independent Colleges and Schools (LAICU). This excellent arrangement ensures that all students in Louisiana have access to extensive resources in electronic format (Louisiana Library Network; Cargill, 1995; Nuckles, 1994).

All of LALINC's activities have benefited Louisiana's distance education students by promoting access to standardized electronic resources throughout the state. The creation of the LOUIS catalog system and the financial benefits of consortial purchase of Web-based resources have enabled institutions to provide more than adequate support for their distance students. To further its service to distance education students LALINC established a Resource Sharing Committee in 1995. The charge of this committee reads in part:

> To maintain and oversee a statewide reciprocal borrowing agreement, facilitate the delivery of materials between members . . . and plan library services for distance education. (Louisiana Library Network)

The Resource Sharing Committee (RSC) has proved an important force in providing library services to distance students in Louisiana (Jung, 1998).

LALINC'S RESOURCE SHARING COMMITTEE

The Resource Sharing Committee wrote an *Agreement for Reciprocal Borrowing,* effective October 24, 1997 (with slight revisions in August 1998), which was signed by the LALINC library directors. This agreement created the LALINC Card, which could be issued by the home institution of faculty and graduate students who wished to borrow materials at other LALINC libraries. This reciprocal borrowing network has been adapted for use by distance students, who can now request a LALINC borrower's card from their home institutions, and can use it at any convenient academic library.

As distance education programs became more prevalent in the state system, the Resource Sharing Committee produced a *Distance Education Agreement* that required all academic libraries to designate a Distance Education Librarian. The DE Librarian serves as a liaison with the Resource Sharing Committee and as a contact for students enrolled in distance classes. *The Distance Education Agreement* provides reciprocal borrowing privileges even for undergraduates if they are enrolled as distance education students. The wording of the Louisiana agreement was based on the second edition of the *ACRL Guidelines for Extended Campus Library Services* and is consistent in format with another successful statewide agreement, the Louisiana Interlibrary Loan Code (Association of College & Research Libraries, 1990; Jung, 1998).

In August 1998, the Resource Sharing Committee created a Distance Education Subcommittee that included two public librarians (Louisiana Library Network). The committee, pleased with the arrangement between the academic libraries, wanted to anticipate future cooperation among other library entities serving distance education students. In order to foster this cooperation, the Distance Education Subcommittee conducted two simultaneous surveys in 1998 for academic libraries and public libraries. Through their respective e-mail lists the DE librarians (identified through the agreement) were asked to complete the academic library survey and the public library directors were asked to respond to the public library survey. The purpose was two-fold: (1) to determine if DE students were heavily using area public libraries and (2) to determine the extent to which public libraries were willing to assist DE students. The results indicated that DE students were primarily using academic libraries in their vicinity although public libraries were extremely willing to assist DE students, limited only by the possible lack of relevant resources. The RSC was pleased but noted that courses are currently being offered and received in areas where academic libraries have a presence.

One of the most exciting initiatives of the Resource Sharing Committee is the DEED-Net (Distance Education Electronic Delivery Network) project. In the summer of 1999, a grant from the Board of Regents provided Ariel software and scanning equipment to the interlibrary loan departments of public and private academic libraries throughout the state. Transmitting interlibrary loan material via Ariel (often within twenty-four to forty-eight hours) has greatly decreased the time it takes to get material from one library to another, making cooperative collection development within the state more attractive, and assisting distance education students in obtaining the materials they need to complete their research. In order to make the DEED-Net project more effective, the project organizers took the innovative step of including the libraries of many private institutions in the equipment distribution. In this way several universities that do not participate in the Distance Education Agreement, but that hold large collections and are heavy net lenders, are able to quickly supply material to others in the state.

SURVEYS OF DISTANCE EDUCATION STUDENTS

The activities of the LALINC Louisiana libraries have been geared towards meeting the criteria of the Southern Association of Colleges and Schools (SACS) for library support of distance education. These criteria include:

- ensuring provision of and ready access to adequate library/learning resources and services to support the courses, programs and degrees being offered and
- owning the library/learning resources, providing access to electronic information available through existing technologies or through formal agreements (Southern Association of Colleges and Schools, 1998)

SACS' criteria for library support of distance learning was an incentive for surveying distance education students. Surveys were initially directed at students enrolled in compressed video classes at Louisiana State University (LSU) in Spring and Summer of 1999. In Fall of 1999 students at sixteen other Louisiana academic institutions who were receiving distance instruction in 260 classes (143 offered through compressed video, forty-one via broadcast, twenty-one by cable TV and fifty-five over computer networks) were also surveyed. These students were identified by course listings on the Louisiana Board of Regents Web site (http://regents.state.la.us).

The survey specifically addressed the SACS criteria that ask whether students *know* about the relevant resources available to them (especially those available through technological means); whether they know how to *access* them; and whether they *actually use* the appropriate resources.

The data gathering also supports the recommendations of the ACRL Distance Learning Section Guidelines (Association of College and Research Libraries, 1998) for documentation of services and resources to off-site students. Having a designated Distance Education Librarian identified at each library, and an established statewide e-mail group list, facilitated rapid communication. Because these Louisiana DE librarians had attended two DEED-Net workshops together they knew the authors of the survey and were comfortable communicating with them.

There were seven compressed video classes that participated in the Spring 1999 survey. One class did not have any remote sites but was included. Of the 136 students surveyed, 100 were on-site and thirty-six were off-site. In Summer 1999, there was only one class of forty-eight students. This class was unique because the professor was in another state (with no audience before him) so, in essence, both were off-site. However, there were nineteen students at the host site and twenty-nine students at other remote sites.

Because only LSU was being polled in the Spring and Summer, resources unique to that institution were surveyed, such as the use of the library's remote access account (called PAWS), its toll free number, and electronic reserves. (These specific questions were dropped when the survey was conducted statewide.) The results showed that DE students were aware of the *library's* home page but not as aware of the *distance education* home page, even though the DE Librarian had asked the faculty of the compressed video classes to mention it and to provide the students with the Reference toll free number. The librarian also offered to come to those classes to explain access; subject specialists in the library also offer to meet with the DE classes.

For Spring and Summer, most on-site students had PAWS accounts but only 78% and 66%, respectively, of the off-site students said they had PAWS accounts, which are necessary for remote access. (All students are eligible for these accounts.) Not surprisingly, the highest use was made of the OPAC, followed by indexes and databases. Because of the lower results regarding e-reserves, paper reserves, e-mail, and interlibrary borrowing, an expanded strategy was used for the Fall statewide survey. Additionally, Summer students were asked several open-ended questions that included asking them to list all the libraries they used for their coursework. Paralleling the RSC survey, most students used academic libraries.

There were 260 distance education courses listed on the Board of Regents Web site for Fall 1999. The authors contacted the DE librarians and provided them with the list of courses, instructors, and mode of delivery that were listed as originating at their institutions, explained the survey that was planned, and asked them to verify that these courses were being delivered at these 176 sites. Permission was granted through the Human Services Department at LSU to conduct this survey of human subjects. Sample letters were sent to the DE librarians that they could forward (1) to their faculty explaining the two-fold nature of the project and (2) to the students alerting them to the resources and services offered by their library. The initial letter to the student was meant to fulfill the SACS requirement that students are aware of the services available to them.

Faculty were asked to let the DE Librarian know if they would participate in the survey and to inform them of the class size of both their on-site and off-site students. This information was used by the DE Librarians to deliver adequate copies of the initial letter and subsequently of the survey forms. The authors sent the survey forms to the DE Librarians towards the end of the semester, suggesting that they forward sufficient copies to the DE classes. At press time students are approaching the end of the semester and the surveys are beginning to be returned. Results will be shared at the conference. The authors have encouraged the DE librarians in the state to begin saving and accumulating this data for their own accreditation purposes and annual reports as well.

NURSING PARTNERSHIPS

Due to the evident success of the library consortium, the Board of Regents has continued to encourage partnerships between institutions. The generous funding opportunities offered by the Board have initiated innovative collaboration among the schools of nursing at four public institutions. The Nursing Consortium is comprised of Southeastern Louisiana University, Southern University-Baton Rouge, McNeese University, and the University of Louisiana at Lafayette. It has become a model of effective collaboration with a strategic plan carrying it into the future of distance education. One of the main goals of the consortium is the elimination of duplicated programs within the public system. Using compressed video technology, core courses are offered by one institution to all of the sites. Another facet of the consortium's strategic plan is the inclusion of information literacy in its programs (RN to BSN and graduate). Subsequently, DE Librarians at each institution have collaborated to ensure a standard level of bibliographic instruction and service through innovative uses of traditional library services and technology.

CONCLUSION

Through partnerships and evaluation projects like the ones described in this paper, Louisiana is well on its way to providing excellent library services to its distance students. And Louisiana has more plans for distance library services on the horizon. To ease access to electronic resources, the LALINC Resource Sharing Committee is *strongly* supporting a statewide authentication system. The staff who administer LOUIS are actively pursuing this. The Resource Sharing Committee has also been charged with training. There are potentials for partnering with other groups, such as the Louisiana Library Association's User Education Interest Group and Distance Learning Interest Group for creating online tutorials. Activities of three other LAINC committees–the Database, Collection Development and Preservation committees–will also benefit distance education students.

REFERENCES

Association of College and Research Libraries. (1990). ACRL guidelines for extended campus library services. *College & Research Libraries News, 50*, 353-355.

Association of College and Research Libraries. (1998). *ACRL guidelines for distance learning library services.* Available: http://caspian.switchinc.org/~distlearn/guidelines/ [1999, December 1].

Cargill, J. (1995). A target of opportunity: Creation of the LOUIS network. *Library Hi Tech, 13*(1-3), 87-107.

Cargill, J. & Hay, R. D. (1994) Achieving a vision of a statewide academic library network. *Journal of Academic Librarianship, 19*, 386-387.

Jung, K. (1998). LALINC Resource Sharing Committee. Available: http://www.selu. edu/orgs/LALINC/RSS [1999, December 1].

Louisiana Board of Regents. (1999). *Electronic and distance learning.* Available: http://regents.state.la.us [1999, December 1].

Louisiana Library Network. (No date). Available: http://lsumvs.sncc.lsu.edu/ocs/ louis/ [1999, December 1].

Network funded by U.S. Department of Education: State university and agricultural college received $2.5 million. (1993) *Library Journal, 118*,(18), 18.

Nuckles, N. (1994) Louisiana network links libraries. *College & Research Libraries News, 55*, 414-415.

Schneider, D.W., & Cargill, J. (1993, Fall,). LALINC: a unified agenda for Louisiana's academic libraries." *LLA Bulletin, 56*, 77-85.

Southern Association of Colleges and Schools. (1998). *Library/learning resources for distance learning activities. Criteria for Accreditation. (Section 5.1.7)* Atlanta: Author.

APPENDIX

Library Distance Education Evaluation: Fall, 1999

Course: _____   ☐ On-Site: ☐ Off-Site:

1. Did you use any of the following library resources: Yes   No

   A. Online Catalog   Yes   No

   B. Indexes and Databases   Yes   No

   C. Reserve Materials   Yes   No

   D. Reference Service   Yes   No

   E. Interlibrary Loan   Yes   No

2. Were there any particular library services that were especially useful for you?

3. Do you have any suggestions for how library services for distance education classes can be improved?

4. Did you need research sources for your class?   Yes   No
   (Comments optional)

5. What libraries did you use?

Index

© 2001 by The Haworth Press, Inc. All rights reserved.   *449*

Integrating Total Quality Management in a Library Setting, edited by Susan Jurow, MLS, and Susan B. Barnard, MLS (Vol. 18, No. 1/2, 1993). *"Especially valuable are the librarian experiences that directly relate to real concerns about TQM. Recommended for all professional reading collections." (Library Journal)*

Leadership in Academic Libraries: Proceedings of the W. Porter Kellam Conference, The University of Georgia, May 7, 1991, edited by William Gray Potter (Vol. 17, No. 4, 1993). *"Will be of interest to those concerned with the history of American academic libraries." (Australian Library Review)*

Collection Assessment and Acquisitions Budgets, edited by Sul H. Lee (Vol. 17, No. 2, 1993). Contains timely information about the assessment of academic library collections and the relationship of collection assessment to acquisition budgets.

Developing Library Staff for the 21st Century, edited by Maureen Sullivan (Vol. 17, No. 1, 1992). *"I found myself enthralled with this highly readable publication. It is one of those rare compilations that manages to successfully integrate current general management operational thinking in the context of academic library management." (Bimonthly Review of Law Books)*

Vendor Evaluation and Acquisition Budgets, edited by Sul H. Lee (Vol. 16, No. 3, 1992). *"The title doesn't do justice to the true scope of this excellent collection of papers delivered at the sixth annual conference on library acquisitions sponsored by the University of Oklahoma Libraries." (Kent K. Hendrickson, BS, MALS, Dean of Libraries, University of Nebraska-Lincoln)* Find insightful discussions on the impact of rising costs on library budgets and management in this groundbreaking book.

The Management of Library and Information Studies Education, edited by Herman L. Totten, PhD, MLS (Vol. 16, No. 1/2, 1992). *"Offers something of interest to everyone connected with LIS education–the undergraduate contemplating a master's degree, the doctoral student struggling with courses and career choices, the new faculty member aghast at conflicting responsibilities, the experienced but stressed LIS professor, and directors of LIS Schools." (Education Libraries)*

Library Management in the Information Technology Environment: Issues, Policies, and Practice for Administrators, edited by Brice G. Hobrock, PhD, MLS (Vol. 15, No. 3/4, 1992). *"A road map to identify some of the alternative routes to the electronic library." (Stephen Rollins, Associate Dean for Library Services, General Library, University of New Mexico)*

Managing Technical Services in the 90's, edited by Drew Racine (Vol. 15, No. 1/2, 1991). *"Presents an eclectic overview of the challenges currently facing all library technical services efforts. . . . Recommended to library administrators and interested practitioners." (Library Journal)*

Budgets for Acquisitions: Strategies for Serials, Monographs, and Electronic Formats, edited by Sul H. Lee (Vol. 14, No. 3, 1991). *"Much more than a series of handy tips for the careful shopper. This [book] is a most useful one–well-informed, thought-provoking, and authoritative." (Australian Library Review)*

Creative Planning for Library Administration: Leadership for the Future, edited by Kent Hendrickson, MALS (Vol. 14, No. 2, 1991). *"Provides some essential information on the planning process, and the mix of opinions and methodologies, as well as examples relevant to every library manager, resulting in a very readable foray into a topic too long avoided by many of us." (Canadian Library Journal)*

Strategic Planning in Higher Education: Implementing New Roles for the Academic Library, edited by James F. Williams, II, MLS (Vol. 13, No. 3/4, 1991). *"A welcome addition to the sparse literature on strategic planning in university libraries. Academic librarians considering strategic planning for their libraries will learn a great deal from this work." (Canadian Library Journal)*

Personnel Administration in an Automated Environment, edited by Philip E. Leinbach, MLS (Vol. 13, No. 1/2, 1990). *"An interesting and worthwhile volume, recommended to university library administrators and to others interested in thought-provoking discussion of the personnel implications of automation." (Canadian Library Journal)*

Library Development: A Future Imperative, edited by Dwight F. Burlingame, PhD (Vol. 12, No. 4, 1990). *"This volume provides an excellent overview of fundraising with special application to libraries. . . . A useful book that is highly recommended for all libraries." (Library Journal)*

Library Material Costs and Access to Information, edited by Sul H. Lee (Vol. 12, No. 3, 1991). *"A cohesive treatment of the issue. Although the book's contributors possess a research library perspective, the data and the ideas presented are of interest and benefit to the entire profession, especially academic librarians." (Library Resources and Technical Services)*

Training Issues and Strategies in Libraries, edited by Paul M. Gherman, MALS, and Frances O. Painter, MLS, MBA (Vol. 12, No. 2, 1990). *"There are . . . useful chapters, all by different authors, each with a preliminary summary of the content–a device that saves much time in deciding whether to read the whole chapter or merely skim through it. Many of the chapters are essentially practical without too much emphasis on theory. This book is a good investment." (Library Association Record)*

Library Education and Employer Expectations, edited by E. Dale Cluff, PhD, MLS (Vol. 11, No. 3/4, 1990). *"Useful to library-school students and faculty interested in employment problems and employer perspectives. Librarians concerned with recruitment practices will also be interested." (Information Technology and Libraries)*

Managing Public Libraries in the 21st Century, edited by Pat Woodrum, MLS (Vol. 11, No. 1/2, 1989). *"A broad-based collection of topics that explores the management problems and possibilities public libraries will be facing in the 21st century." (Robert Swisher, PhD, Director, School of Library and Information Studies, University of Oklahoma)*

Human Resources Management in Libraries, edited by Gisela M. Webb, MLS, MPA (Vol. 10, No. 4, 1989). *"Thought provoking and enjoyable reading. . . . Provides valuable insights for the effective information manager." (Special Libraries)*

Creativity, Innovation, and Entrepreneurship in Libraries, edited by Donald E. Riggs, EdD, MLS (Vol. 10, No. 2/3, 1989). *"The volume is well worth reading as a whole. . . . There is very little repetition, and it should stimulate thought." (Australian Library Review)*

The Impact of Rising Costs of Serials and Monographs on Library Services and Programs, edited by Sul H. Lee (Vol. 10, No. 1, 1989). *". . . Sul Lee hit a winner here." (Serials Review)*

Computing, Electronic Publishing, and Information Technology: Their Impact on Academic Libraries, edited by Robin N. Downes (Vol. 9, No. 4, 1989). *"For a relatively short and easily digestible discussion of these issues, this book can be recommended, not only to those in academic libraries, but also to those in similar types of library or information unit, and to academics and educators in the field." (Journal of Documentation)*

Library Management and Technical Services: The Changing Role of Technical Services in Library Organizations, edited by Jennifer Cargill, MSLS, MSed (Vol. 9, No. 1, 1988). *"As a practical and instructive guide to issues such as automation, personnel matters, education, management techniques and liaison with other services, senior library managers with a sincere interest in evaluating the role of their technical services should find this a timely publication." (Library Association Record)*

Management Issues in the Networking Environment, edited by Edward R. Johnson, PhD (Vol. 8, No. 3/4, 1989). *"Particularly useful for librarians/information specialists contemplating establishing a local network." (Australian Library Review)*

Acquisitions, Budgets, and Material Costs: Issues and Approaches, edited by Sul H. Lee (Supp. #2, 1988). *"The advice of these library practitioners is sensible and their insights illuminating for librarians in academic libraries." (American Reference Books Annual)*

Pricing and Costs of Monographs and Serials: National and International Issues, edited by Sul H. Lee (Supp. #1, 1987). *"Eminently readable. There is a good balance of chapters on serials and monographs and the perspective of suppliers, publishers, and library practitioners are presented. A book well worth reading." (Australasian College Libraries)*

Legal Issues for Library and Information Managers, edited by William Z. Nasri, JD, PhD (Vol. 7, No. 4, 1987). *"Useful to any librarian looking for protection or wondering where responsibilities end and liabilities begin. Recommended." (Academic Library Book Review)*

Archives and Library Administration: Divergent Traditions and Common Concerns, edited by Lawrence J. McCrank, PhD, MLS (Vol. 7, No. 2/3, 1986). *"A forward-looking view of archives and libraries. . . . Recommend[ed] to students, teachers, and practitioners alike of archival and library science. It is readable, thought-provoking, and provides a summary of the major areas of divergence and convergence." (Association of Canadian Map Libraries and Archives)*

Excellence in Library Management, edited by Charlotte Georgi, MLS, and Robert Bellanti, MLS, MBA (Vol. 6, No. 3, 1985). *"Most beneficial for library administrators . . . for anyone interested in either library/information science or management." (Special Libraries)*

Marketing and the Library, edited by Gary T. Ford (Vol. 4, No. 4, 1984). *Discover the latest methods for more effective information dissemination and learn to develop successful programs for specific target areas.*

Finance Planning for Libraries, edited by Murray S. Martin (Vol. 3, No. 3/4, 1983). *Stresses the need for libraries to weed out expenditures which do not contribute to their basic role–the collection and organization of information–when planning where and when to spend money.*

Planning for Library Services: A Guide to Utilizing Planning Methods for Library Management, edited by Charles R. McClure, PhD (Vol. 2, No. 3/4, 1982). *"Should be read by anyone who is involved in planning processes of libraries–certainly by every administrator of a library or system." (American Reference Books Annual)*